DR. SUSAN LOVE'S
BREAST BOOK

DR. SUSAN LOVE'S BREAST BOOK

Susan M. Love, M.D.
with Karen Lindsey

Illustrations by Marcia Williams

A Merloyd Lawrence Book

ADDISON-WESLEY PUBLISHING COMPANY, INC.
Reading, Massachusetts   Menlo Park, California   New York
Don Mills, Ontario   Wokingham, England   Amsterdam   Bonn
Sydney   Singapore   Tokyo   Madrid   San Juan
Paris   Seoul   Milan   Mexico City   Taipei

Table 11-1, page 139, is used with the kind permission of Elsevier Science Publishing Company, Inc.

Table 11-2, page 140, is used with the kind permission of the American Cancer Society.

Table 11-3, page 140, is used with the kind permission of J.B. Lippincott/ Harper and Row.

Table 17-1, page 235, is used with the kind permission of McGraw-Hill Publishing Company.

Many of the designations used by manufacturers and sellers to distinguish their products are claimed as trademarks. Where those designations appear in this book and Addison-Wesley was aware of a trademark claim, the designations have been printed in initial capital letters (e.g., Lactaid, Motrin).

Library of Congress Cataloging-in-Publication Data

Love, Susan M.
  [Breast book]
  Doctor Susan Love's breast book / Susan M. Love with Karen Lindsey
; illustrations by Marcia Williams.
      p.   cm.
  "A Merloyd Lawrence book."
  Includes bibliographical references.
  ISBN 0-201-09665-X
  ISBN 0-201-57097-1 (pbk.)
  1. Breast—Diseases—Popular works.   2. Breast—Cancer—Popular
works.   I. Lindsey, Karen, 1944–   . II. Title. III. Title:
Breast book.
RG491.L68   1990   90-32071
618.1'9—dc20   CIP

Jacket design by Hannus Design Associates
Text design by Anna George
Set in 10-point Palatino by DEKR Corporation, Woburn, MA

    4 5 6 7 8 9-MW-95949392
First printing, April 1990
Fourth paperback printing, October 1992

This book is dedicated to Helen and Katie with all my love and to all the patients over the years who have allowed me to care for them and learn from them.

Contents

Acknowledgments

The authors have many people to thank. Without them this book would never have been completed. We would like to thank all the patients who took the time to fill out questionnaires regarding their feelings about their breasts. Particularly we would like to mention Rebecca Cooper, Carolyn Cummings-Saxton, Mary Carmody, Thalia Dulchinos, Ann Marotto, Elizabeth MacDougal, Karen Paine-Gernee, Cathi Ragovin, Susan Shapiro, Rose Thibault, and Joyce Toth.

In addition, we would like to thank those medical professionals who freely gave of their time in interviews on specific subjects: Ted Chapman, M.D., Estelle Disch, Ph.D., Hester Hill, LIC.S.W., Robert Goldwyn, M.D., Jean Hubbuch, M.D., Susan McKenney, R.N., M.S.N., and Leo Stolbach, M.D. Other professionals graciously critiqued chapters: Jay Harris, M.D., I. Craig Henderson, M.D., Stuart Schnitt, M.D., Paul Stomper, M.D., and Walt Willet, M.D. We appreciate all their help.

Many other people contributed in a significant way, including: Jennifer Abod, Enid Y. Burrows, Ann Caspar, Micki Dickoff, Joan F., Dede Herlihy, Carolyn Muller, and Lori Lowenthal Stern. Our thanks to Amy Schiffman from NABCO for her help with the resource list.

We owe a special debt of gratitude to the staff of the Faulkner Breast Centre for putting up with "the book" for the past three years.

Special thanks to Julie Shea as well as Ann Walsh, Rita Lawler, Cynthia Lemack, Diane Connelly, and Barbara Kalinowski, R.N. Thanks also to Beth Siegel, M.D., and Susan Troyan, M.D., for those last-minute reference checks. My partner Kathy Mayzel, M.D., not only put up with my working on the book but read it for me. She gets my appreciation. And gratitude to Cyndi Saint who not only kept the home fires burning but did numerous errands, and read the book cover to cover as a test reader.

Mark Kramer assisted mightily in getting this project off the ground. Sidney B. Kramer was very helpful in getting it going. And Merloyd Lawrence was invaluable in getting it completed. To all of these literary professionals I give my thanks.

Finally, those who suffer most in the writing of a book are those from whom our time is stolen. Special thanks to Helen Cooksey and Katie Love-Cooksey who have lived with this book from its conception through a long and arduous labor and finally to this birth.

Introduction

"I've always felt unattractive because I'm so flat-chested. Would plastic surgery help?"

"My breasts are lumpy—what does that mean?"

"My mother and grandmother had breast cancer. Will I get it too?"

"My doctor says I have breast cancer: does this mean I have to choose between dying and losing my breast?"

In my years as a breast surgeon, I have constantly been asked questions like these. Women worry about their breasts, in a different way than they worry about the rest of their bodies—and for good reason.

For women in many cultures, breasts have had a deep, often mythical significance. They are the external badge of our womanhood. While the uterus is the center of reproduction, it is invisible; it does not identify us to the world outside as female. When we see an androgynous-looking person, we instinctively glance at the chest to determine the person's gender. If there are no obvious breasts we assume the person is male; the presence of breasts assures us we are looking at a woman.

Perhaps because of this, or because of the breast's associations with nurturance and hence survival, most cultures have eroticized

breasts. In America in our century, this eroticization is highly pro-
nounced, yet inconsistent, and a source of confusion and anxiety for
most women. On the one hand, we are constantly asked to compete
with select and unrealistic images of breasts: Playboy bunnies, bill-
board bikinis, newsstand sex symbols with their seductive cleavages.
But these images themselves change from era to era. In the 1930s,
we had to compete with the small, firm, but clearly outlined breasts
of a Jean Harlow; in the '50s it was the large, very cleavaged breasts
of a Marilyn Monroe. In the '20s, breasts were de-emphasized; in the
'60s small breasts were highlighted by the braless look. Now, fashion
magazines alert us, in all seriousness, that breasts are "coming back"
again. Whatever the prevailing social aesthetic, we have never been
able simply to accept our breasts. We are always made conscious of
their centrality to our "womanhood."

At the same time, we're taught to be ashamed of them. Only the
sex symbols are permitted, and only in clearly defined contexts, to
display their breasts. Just as Muslim women hide their faces behind
the veil, we must hide our breasts in public. Women who violate
these rules can suffer legal penalties, or at least social ridicule. A
woman may not breastfeed in public—despite the fact that feeding
babies is precisely what breasts are for. Women posing bare-breasted
for the cover of *Playboy* are accepted. A woman basking bare-breasted
in the sun for her own pleasure is violating a social taboo, and, as
in a celebrated 1985 case, may find herself in jail.[1]

The result of this taboo is that, even in our supposedly liberated,
sophisticated era, most women know little about their breasts. They
seldom see other women's breasts, except in the "idealized" versions
in magazines. In reality, women's breasts come in a rich variety of
sizes and shapes. But many of us go through our lives consciously
or unconsciously assuming our breasts are unusual and unattractive,
and we are embarrassed by them. We also tend to go through our
lives ignorant about the workings of our breasts. What are they made
of? What happens during breastfeeding? How do they change with
the menstrual cycle, and how does menopause affect them?

Familiarity with our breasts is also clouded by the twin fears of
cancer and mastectomy. Many women avoid regular breast examinations because, consciously or unconsciously, they don't want to
know if they have cancer; they don't want to face the possibility of
a treatment they see as mutilating. Ignorance about our breasts thus
leads to emotional pain, confusion, and sometimes serious health
problems. Many of these fears—so common for women today—are
not necessary. Most women who are afraid they have cancer don't—
they have a variety of other, benign conditions that are usually fairly
harmless.

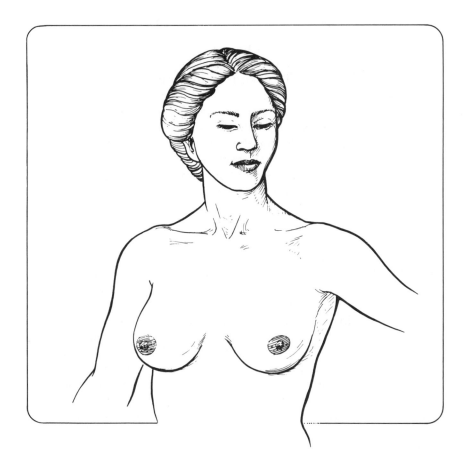

But, of course, some women do get breast cancer—one out of every 11 women in our country, in fact. And these women find themselves dealing with a largely male-dominated medical establishment that is often astoundingly insensitive to the double terror women feel: the terror of death and the terror of mutilation. Ironically, the male culture that emphasizes the importance of beautiful breasts often becomes extremely cavalier about removing those breasts. A frightening number of male surgeons still recommend mastectomies when a less severe operation would be equally helpful—and some even recommend "preventive" mastectomies for women they feel *might* get cancer. (I find it interesting that the ovaries, the uterus, and the breasts are practically the only organs taken out to prevent cancer.) This attitude finds its way into both the privacy of the doctor's office and the medical literature: one promi-nent Boston surgeon wrote in the *Journal of Clinical Surgery* that he believed in "tossing the excess baggage overboard to keep the ship of life afloat."[2] He was speaking only of breasts; it would be inter-esting to learn whether he considered testicles to be "excess bag-gage." A doctor one of my patients had been to—and fled from—made his attitude even more clear: "No ovaries are so good they should be left in," he told her, "and no testicles so bad they should be taken out." (Perhaps it's only ovaries he feels that way about, and breasts are a different matter: my patient didn't wait to find out.)

Early in my surgical career, I realized how widespread such atti-tudes are, and how much harm they do to women. I didn't start out as a breast specialist: I began my practice in 1980 as a general surgeon. I treated a number of patients, female and male, for a variety of conditions, but I soon began to realize that, consistently, women were coming to me with breast problems specifically because I am a woman. For any other form of surgery, they might have chosen, even preferred, a male doctor—but for their breasts, they wanted someone they instinctively felt would understand their bodies and respect the particular meaning their breasts had for them.

I soon realized that I could make a particular contribution in this area: I could combine my experience as a woman with my medical knowledge. I decided to specialize in breast problems. It's not that I believed, then or now, that all male doctors are uniformly insensitive. I have known and worked with many fine, caring male colleagues. But even the most sensitive, sympathetic men can't understand a woman's complex emotional relationship to her breasts. They don't know, in their own bodies, what it means to have breasts: they haven't felt that slight adolescent itching as the small bump on the chest grows into a real breast; they haven't set out self-consciously with their mothers to buy a "training bra"; they haven't fretted over whether a party dress shows too much or too little cleavage. And they haven't faced the nightmare of mastectomy that haunts almost every woman in our culture, and surfaces with even the most harm-less breast problem.

And so I chose my specialty with the hope of combining my medical knowledge with the understanding of breasts built into my own body. In the years since, I have worked with thousands of patients. I have learned much from them, both about the physiology of the breast and about the varied emotional responses women have to their breasts.

I have also geared my research to learning more about the breast and its workings. I've been studying breast pain, duct anatomy, and the various symptoms that doctors have called "fibrocystic disease."

In a paper on fibrocystic disease, challenging the accuracy and the implications of the term, I was able to clarify our understanding of the concept and its relationship to cancer.

Because I want to share this knowledge with as many women as possible, I spend part of my time teaching and lecturing about breasts to medical students, health-care professionals, and women's groups, as well as appearing on radio and television. This book is an extension of that work. I have written it because as a woman and a mother I have experienced the same excitement, joy, fear, and confusion that most women have experienced about their breasts; and because as a breast surgeon I have both the technical knowledge most women are denied and the human knowledge gained from working with thousands of patients.

Unfortunately, much that is published about medical issues is difficult for readers to comprehend. Medical jargon is confusing and intimidating: medical fact is less so. Yet even when the lay reader can understand the jargon, she often finds herself bewildered: without a statistical and medical context, the significance of research findings can be difficult to judge.

My coauthor and I have tried to make this book easily accessible for any woman who wants to know more about her breasts, for whatever reason; and we have broken down the topics in such a way that a reader concerned with only one particular question can find the section of the book relating to it and, if she chooses, read only that section. Most medical terms are explained in the glossary at the back of the book. I have combined my own medical information with the knowledge my patients have shared with me about their subjective experiences of various breast problems and treatments. As a doctor, my expertise is purely objective: I can diagnose a condition with reasonable accuracy, and I can administer a treatment with reasonable competence. But I do not live the experience as the patient does; I do not know, except when she tells me, what it *feels* like to her. And so I have included, in their own words, information given me by my patients.

The women I see in my practice generally fall into one of four categories, and I have so divided the book to include sections dealing with each of those categories.

The first group of women come because they are concerned with some aspect of their breasts' development: they are unsure about whether their breasts are normal, or indeed about what "normal" breasts really are. They are "flat-chested" and want to know if this will affect breastfeeding; their breasts are huge and they worry that it might mean something is wrong with them. Often mothers come in with concerns about their pubescent daughters: one breast is growing more quickly than the other; the girl has hairs around her nipple; she's 14 and her breasts haven't yet begun to develop.

Secondly, I see women with benign breast problems—lumpy breasts, discharge, infections, and so forth. Often they fear these conditions are indicators of cancer, but in any event they are concerned and uncertain about what the symptoms mean.

The third category is composed of women I call the "worried well." These are usually women with a family history of breast cancer—sometimes their mothers or grandmothers, sometimes a favorite aunt—and they are worried that they will inherit the illness. Occasionally it isn't a family member but a friend who has breast cancer: the patient is worried about whether there are behavioral or nutritional causes for cancer. Such patients want to know how likely it is that they'll get cancer themselves, and whether there are preventive measures that will lessen their vulnerability. Sometimes a woman with breast cancer comes to me because she's worried that her daughter will inherit the disease.

Finally, there is the woman who has been diagnosed as having breast cancer. What she needs is information about the various treatments available, and which would be most likely to save her life—as well as which would be the least disfiguring.

There is an understandable, but unfortunate tendency on the part of many patients to want the doctors to offer infallible solutions—and on the part of many doctors to pretend they can offer them. The doctor–patient relationship is all too often that of a paternalistic authority and a blindly obedient child. But doctors are neither infallible nor omniscient: at our best, we are skilled consultants with useful, specialized knowledge. We can tell people what options are open to them in a given situation, and we can give them statistical information about how these options have worked. We cannot tell a particular patient which option she *should* follow: it is her body and her life, and what is right for one patient may be wholly wrong for another.

In this book I have described a variety of alternatives for each situation I've presented: I have not endorsed or dismissed any of them. I've tried to include different women's experiences—and decisions—with each situation I've presented. Many of the decisions are different from each other, and this is important. In dealing with our own lives, there is no objective right or wrong; each of us must make her own decisions, based on the most complete information possible.

The most frightening thing about breast problems really isn't the possibility of cancer. The most frightening thing is not knowing, not understanding what's happening to one's own body. Even the most life-threatening situations are less terrifying when people understand what they're facing. Knowledge is power, and most women have been denied real knowledge about their own breasts. With this book, I hope to give readers some of that power.

PART ONE

THE HEALTHY BREAST

1

The Breast and Its Development

Most women really don't know what a "normal" breast looks like. Most of us haven't seen many other women's breasts and, as I mentioned, we've been exposed since childhood to the "ideal" images of breasts that permeate our society. But few of us fit those images, and there's no reason why we should. The range of size and shape of breasts is so wide that it's hard to say what's "normal." Not only are there very large and very small breasts, but in most women one breast is slightly larger than the other. Breast size is genetically determined—it depends chiefly on the percentage of fat to other tissue in the breasts. Usually about one third of the breast is composed of fat tissue, and the rest of breast tissue. The fat can vary as you gain or lose weight; the breast tissue remains constant. A "flat-chested" woman's breasts will grow as she gains weight, just as her stomach and thighs do; if she loses that weight, she'll also lose her larger breasts.

Breast size has nothing to do with capacity to make milk, or with vulnerability to cancer or other breast disease. Very large breasts, however, can be physically uncomfortable, and, like very small or very uneven breasts, they can be emotionally uncomfortable. We'll discuss this at length in Chapter 4.

Usually the breast itself is tear-shaped. (See Figure 1-1.) There's

3

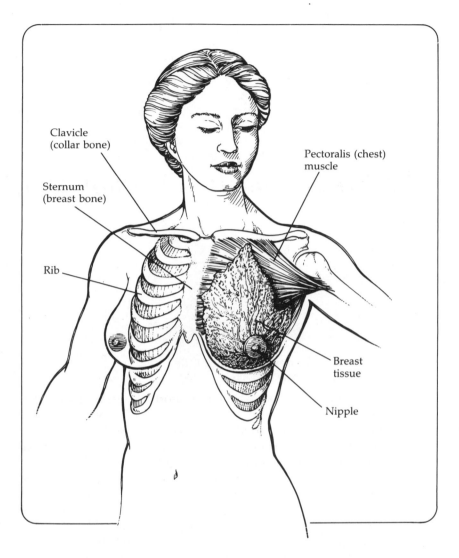

Clavicle (collar bone)

Sternum (breast bone)

Rib

Pectoralis (chest) muscle

Breast tissue

Nipple

FIGURE 1-1

breast tissue from the collarbone all the way down to the last few ribs, and from the breastbone in the middle of the chest to the back of the armpit. Most of the breast tissue is toward the armpit and upper breast, while the fat is in the middle and lower part of the breast. Your ribs lie behind the breast, and sometimes can feel hard and lumpy. When I was in medical school, I embarrassed myself horribly when I found a "lump" in my breast, and frantically ran to one of the older doctors to find out if I had cancer. I found out I had a rib.

Often there's a ridge of fat at the bottom of the breast. This *inframammary ridge* is perfectly normal: it's caused by the fact that, because we walk upright, our breasts fold over themselves.

The *areola* is the darker area of the breast surrounding the nipple. (See Figure 1-2.) Its size and shape vary from woman to woman, and its color varies according to complexion. In blonds it tends to be pink; in brunettes it's browner, and in black-skinned people, it's black. In most women, it gets darker after the first pregnancy. Its color also changes during the various stages of sexual arousal and orgasm.

Many women find that their nipples don't face front; they stick out slightly toward the armpits. There's a reason for this. Picture yourself holding a baby you're about to nurse. The baby's head is held in the crook of your arm—a nipple pointing to the side is comfortably close to the baby's mouth. (See Figure 1-3.)

There are hair follicles around the nipple, so most women have at least some nipple hair. It's perfectly natural, but if you don't like it, don't worry. You can shave it off, pluck it out, use electrolysis, or get rid of it any sensible way you want—it's just like leg or armpit hair. And, as with leg or armpit hair, if it doesn't bother you, you can just ignore it. You may also notice little bumps around the areola that look like goose pimples. They're little glands known as *Montgomery's glands*. The nipple also has *sebaceous glands*, glands that secrete tiny amounts of a lubricating material.

Sometimes nipples are "shy": when they're stimulated, they retreat into themselves and become temporarily inverted. (See Figure

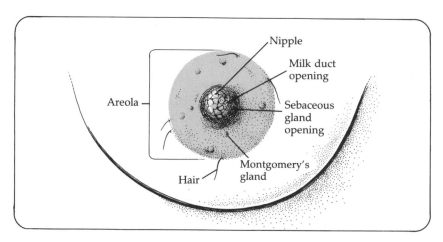

FIGURE 1-2

FIGURE 1-3

1-4.) This is nothing to worry about: it has no effect on milk supply, breastfeeding, sexual pleasure, or anything else. (Permanently inverted nipples are discussed on pages 152 and 371.)

So much for the outside of the breast. Inside, it's made up, as I noted before, of primarily fat and breast tissue. (See Figure 1-5.) The breast tissue is sandwiched between layers of fat, behind which is the chest muscle. The fat has some give to it, which is why we bounce. The breast tissue is firm and rubbery. One of my patients told me while I was operating on her that she thought the breast was constructed like a woman—soft and pliant on the outside, and tough underneath.

Like the rest of the body, the breast has arteries, veins, and nerves. Included in the breast tissue are the all-important *ducts* and *lobules*. The lobules make the milk, and the ducts are the pipes that bring the milk to the nipple. There are between five and nine separate ductile systems. They don't connect with each other, but intertwine, like the roots of a tree. Each has a separate opening at the nipple, so milk comes from more than one opening. There haven't been many studies done on the patterns of the ductal system; it's one of the areas of research I'm involved in now. (Some readers will be interested to know that the breast is actually a modified sweat gland, and the milk it produces is a modification of sweat.)

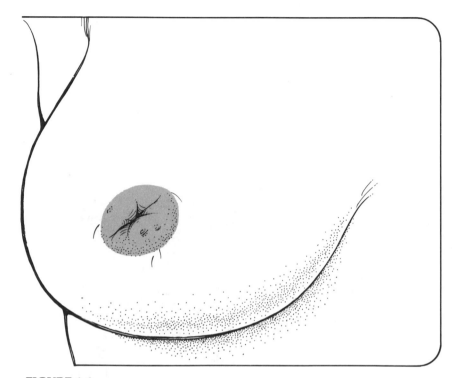

FIGURE 1-4

The breast also has its share of the connective tissue that holds the entire body together. This tissue creates a solid structure—like gelatin—in which the rest of the body parts are loosely set.

There's very little muscle in the breast. There's a bit of muscle in the areola, which is why it contracts and stands out with cold and sexual stimulation and, of course, in breastfeeding. This too makes sense: if the nipple stands out, it's easier for the baby's mouth to get a good grip on it. There are also tiny muscles around the lobules that help deliver milk, as we will discuss on page 34. But the major muscle in the area is behind the breasts—the *pectoralis muscle*. Because of this, the idea that you can grow larger breasts through exercise is false. You can grow stronger pectorals—like bodybuilders do—but all that means is that your breasts will rest on an expanded chest.

Bras

In a society that so fetishizes breasts, it's inevitable that mythologies have arisen around their coverings. The bra is a relatively recent

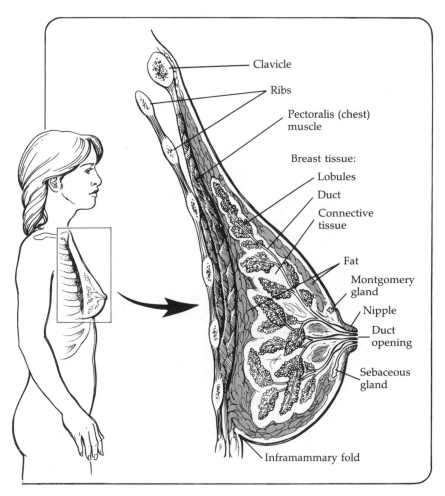

Clavicle

Ribs

Pectoralis (chest) muscle

Breast tissue:

Lobules

Duct

Connective tissue

Fat

Montgomery gland

Nipple

Duct opening

Sebaceous gland

Inframammary fold

FIGURE 1-5

invention—it became popular in the 1920s. As a replacement for the uncomfortable and often mutilating corsets of the 19th century, it was certainly an improvement. However, while wearing a bra is never physically harmful, it has no medical necessity whatsoever. Many of my large-breasted patients find it more comfortable to wear a bra, especially if they run or engage in other athletic activities. As one of them said, "These babies need all the support they can get!"

Many women, however, find bras uncomfortable. Interestingly, I have one patient who gets a rash underneath her breasts when she doesn't wear a bra and her breasts sag, and another who has very sensitive skin and gets a rash when she *does* wear a bra, because of the elastic, the stitching, and the metal hooks (she wears camisoles instead). Except for the women who find bras especially comfortable or uncomfortable, the decision to wear or not wear one is purely aesthetic—or emotional.

For some women, bras are a necessity created by society. One of my patients told me that she enjoyed going without a bra, but that when she did, "men made nasty and degrading comments as I walked down the street." Another patient, who teaches high school, feels obligated to wear a bra, although she describes it as "a ritual object, like a dog collar. . . . I take it off *immediately* after work."

But to other women bras can be enjoyable. Some of my patients like the uplift, and the different contours a bra provides. A woman quoted in *Breasts,* a book of photos and text about women's relationship to their breasts, said that she was "crazy about bras—I think of them as jewelry."[1] She and others find them sexy, and like incorporating them into their lovemaking rituals.

A mistaken popular belief maintains that wearing a bra strengthens your breasts and prevents their eventual sagging. But you sag because of the proportion of fat and tissue in your breasts, and no bra changes that. Furthermore, breastfeeding and lactation increase the breast size (see page 32), and when the breast tissue returns to its normal size the skin is still stretched out and saggy. (This, plus the lack of nutrition, accounts for the extremely saggy breasts one sees in photos of many aged African women.) As I noted earlier, except for the small muscles of the areola and lobules, the only breast muscles are *behind* your breast—muscles that will not be affected by whether or not you wear a bra. If you've been wearing a bra regularly and decide to give it up, you may find that your breasts hurt for a while. Don't be alarmed. The connective tissue in which the ducts and lobules are suspended is suddenly being strained. It's the same tissue that hurts when you jog or run. Once your body adjusts to not wearing a bra, the pain will go away.

No type of bra is better or worse for you in terms of health. Some of my patients wear underwire bras and are told that they can get cancer from them. This is total nonsense. It makes no difference medically whether your bra opens in the front or back, is padded or not padded, is made of nylon, cotton, or anything else, or gives much support or little support. The only time when I would recommend a bra for medical reasons is after any kind of surgery on the breasts. Then the pull from a hanging breast can cause more pain, slow the healing of the wound, and create larger scars. For this purpose, I would recommend a firmer rather than a lighter bra.

Otherwise, if you enjoy a bra for aesthetic, sexual, or comfort reasons, by all means wear one. If you don't enjoy it, and job or social pressures don't force you into it, don't bother. Medically, it's all the same.

Breast Sensitivity

Breasts are usually very sensitive—as you'll notice if you get hit in the breasts. It's very painful, but if you've been told being injured in the breast leads to cancer, ignore it. All a bruised breast causes is temporary pain. Similarly, scar tissue that results from an injury to the breast won't cause cancer. The supposed fragility of women's breasts has been used as an excuse to keep girls from playing contact sports. Interestingly, however, the extreme sensitivity of testicles has rarely been used to keep men from such sports. Your own pain threshold, plus your enthusiasm for the particular game, should determine whether or not you want to avoid risking pain by playing. A bruised breast will hurt, but so will a bruised shin.

The sensitivity of the breast changes within the menstrual cycle. During the first two weeks of the cycle it's less sensitive; it's very sensitive around ovulation, and it's less sensitive again during menstruation itself.[2] There are also changes during the larger development process. There's little sensitivity before puberty, much sensitivity after puberty, and extreme sensitivity during pregnancy. After menopause, the sensitivity decreases slightly, but it never fully vanishes. As in most aspects of the normal breast, sensitivity varies greatly among women. There's no "right" or "healthy" degree of responsiveness.

Breasts also vary greatly in their sensitivity to sexual stimuli. Physiologic changes in the breasts are an integral part of female sexual response. In the excitement phase the nipples harden and become more erect, the breasts plump up, and the areola swells. In the plateau just before orgasm, breasts, nipples, and areola get larger still, peaking with the orgasm and then gradually subsiding. For most women, breast stimulation contributes to sexual pleasure. Many women enjoy having their breasts stroked or sucked by their lovers, but have been told that this too can lead to cancer. It can't. Breasts, after all, are made to be suckled, and your body won't punish you because it's a lover rather than a baby doing it.

Some women's breasts are so erogenous (sexually sensitive) that breast stimulation alone can bring them to orgasm; others find breast stimulation uninteresting or even unpleasant. Neither extreme is more "normal": as we know, different people have different sexual needs and respond to different sexual stimuli. Patients have asked me whether their lack of sexual excitement around their breasts means something is wrong with them. It doesn't. There is an unfortunate tradition in our culture of labeling as "frigid" women whose sexual needs don't correspond to those of their (usually) male partners. Ironically, the converse of this still persists in our supposedly liberated era: a woman who is easily sexually stimulated is seen as a "tramp." All such stereotypes are unfortunate and destructive. If your breasts contribute to your sexual pleasure, enjoy it. If not, enjoy what you *do* like, and don't worry about it.

Lumpiness

Lumpy breasts have inspired some of the most unfortunate misconceptions about our bodies. Women have been told their lumpy breasts are symptoms of so-called fibrocystic disease (see Chapter 6), and have suffered from needless anxiety, fear, and even at times disfiguring surgery.

Lumpy breasts are caused simply by the way the breast tissue forms itself. In some women, the breast tissue is fairly fine and thus not perceived as "lumpy." Others have, very clearly, lumpy breasts, which can feel somewhat like cobblestone roads. Still others are somewhere between the extremes—just a bit nodular. There's nothing at all unusual about this—breasts vary as much as any other part of the body. Some women are tall and some short; some women are fair-skinned and some dark; some women have lumpier breasts and some have smoother breasts. There can also be differences within the same woman's breasts. Your breasts might be a little more nodular near your armpit, or at the top, for example, and the pattern may be the same on both breasts, or may occur only in one. You'll find, if you examine your own breasts, that there's a general pattern that stays fairly consistent. As I will discuss, it's important to do regular breast self-examination and get a sense of what your pattern is.

How the Breast Develops

To understand how the breast typically develops, we need to know what it's for. The breast is an integral part of the woman's reproductive system. It actually defines our biological class: mammals derive their name from the fact that they have mammary glands, and feed their young at their breasts. Different mammals have different numbers and sizes of breasts, but the most interesting, and probably the most significant difference between human females and the other mammals is that we're the only ones to develop full breasts long before they're needed to feed our young. Since humans are also the only animals to be actively sexual when not fertile, this suggests that our breasts have an important secondary function as contributors to our sensual pleasure.

It's also worth noting here that although women have traditionally been thought of as "other" (to use Simone de Beauvoir's term) in our male-dominated culture, biologically we're the norm. The genitalia of all embryos are female. When testosterone is produced at the direction of the Y chromosome, the fetus starts to develop male genitalia. If the testes are destroyed early in fetal development, the male fetus will develop breasts and retain female genitalia. It makes sense to ask whether the basis of "mankind" is, in fact, woman.

EARLY DEVELOPMENT

Human breast tissue begins to develop remarkably early—in the sixth week of fetal life. It develops across a line from the armpit all the way down to the groin, known as the "milk ridge." (See Figure 1-6.) In most cases, the milk ridge soon regresses, and by the ninth week it's just in the chest area. (Other mammals retain the milk ridge, which is why they have multiple nipples.)

So when you're born you already have breast tissue, and it's sensitive to hormones even then—your mother's sex hormones have been circulating through the placenta. When you're born you have little breasts, and infants may even have nipple discharge. This "witch's milk," as it's called, goes away in a couple of weeks, since the infant is no longer getting the mother's hormones. Between 80 and 90 percent of all infants of both genders have this discharge on the second or third day after birth.

PUBERTY

After early infancy, not much happens to the breast until puberty. (See Figure 1-7.) Soon after the pubic hair begins to grow, the breasts start responding to the hormonal changes in the girl's body. (Typically, her period won't start until a year or two after her breasts have begun growing.) They begin with a little bud of breast tissue under the nipple—it can be itchy, and sometimes a bit painful. The rudimentary ducts begin to grow, and the breasts expand more and more until they've reached their full growth—usually by the time menstruation begins. One little girl quoted in *Breasts* described it beauti-

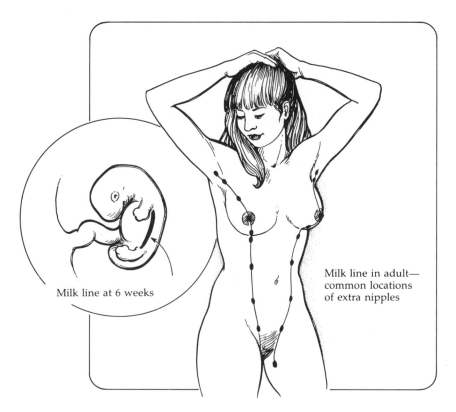

FIGURE 1-6

fully: "At first they were flat, then all of a sudden the nipples came out like mosquito bites. And three or four days ago I noticed that my breasts were coming out from the sides. When I first started they were just little lumps by the nipple."[3]

The first tiny breasts can be confusing to children, and to their parents as well. One of my patients was an 11-year-old girl whose mother had breast cancer, and they found what they were sure was a lump under the girl's nipple. I was certain it was just the beginning of her breast development, but everyone, including the child, was so upset I did a needle aspiration just to reassure them. It's *never* advisable in a situation like that to remove this newly forming breast tissue, since it will never grow back, and the child will never have that breast.

The rate at which breasts grow varies greatly from girl to girl; some start off very flat-chested and end up with large breasts; others have large breasts at an early age. Often one breast grows more quickly than the other. (We'll discuss this more on page 55.)

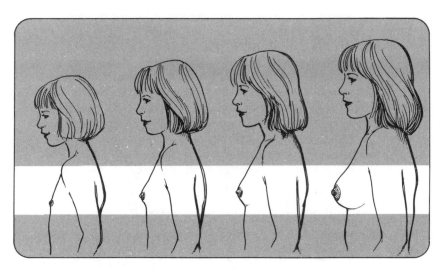

FIGURE 1-7

The emotional confusion around all of puberty can be intensified for the girl growing up in a society that both mystifies and obsesses about breasts. For the adolescent girl, the growth of her breasts can be a source of extreme pleasure or extreme dismay—and often both at once. In a 1980 British survey, researchers learned that 56 percent of the women they questioned had been pleased with their breast development, while 33 percent were shy and 24 percent embarrassed. Ten percent had been "worried" or "unhappy."[4] I did an informal survey among my own patients, with similar results. Of about 200 patients who filled out a questionnaire in my office, 70 recalled having been happy or proud of their budding breasts; 61 had been embarrassed and angry, 20 confused, and 9 ambivalent. One had been "amazed." Not surprisingly, only four were "indifferent."

I've also talked with a number of my patients about their memories of how they felt when their breasts began to develop: again, I found a range of feelings. Two of my youngest patients have had opposite reactions to their breasts' growth. One, 13, says that when her breasts began to grow, "I felt older and I felt mature, that I was becoming a woman." She's proud of her new breasts: "I think that for my age, my boobs are just right," she says. But a 16-year-old patient tells me she was embarrassed when her breasts began to grow, because she "always felt as if people were staring at me and talking about me." She doesn't like her breasts, which she sees as "too hard and lumpy, and triangular, not round."

Similar differences of attitude appear in the recollections of my older patients. One 48-year-old recalls the first day she wore her bra to school: "I was so proud—I was the second girl in the sixth grade to have one. All the other girls gathered around me and I showed them my bra." A 44-year-old remembers "anticipating with joy and awe that my body was changing, and the blossoming of my breasts was such a delightful, exciting period for me. I was becoming a woman!" Others were less delighted. A patient who is now 39 remembers thinking, "Oh, shit, now I'm supposed to be a *girl!*" To her, developing breasts represented confusion and "the world getting much worse." Another, 45, hated her new breasts so much that she would fantasize about ways "to cut them off with my grandmother's long, thin embroidery scissors." She was ashamed of them, and was angry at her mother for making her drink milk, which she was convinced had caused her breasts to grow. A 65-year-old patient said that she hadn't been "ready for this sign of growing up. It was like going down a roller coaster and not being able to stop it." And a middle-aged mother recalls that for many years she wore overlarge sweaters to hide the breasts that embarrassed her. "My teenage daughter does the same thing now," she says, "and it makes me a bit sad to remember that stage of my life." For many women, breasts represented enforced femininity: they could no longer play ball with the boys, and felt they had lost forever a kind of freedom little boys still had.

On the other hand, the *absence* of breasts can be equally upsetting. One of my friends, whose breasts didn't begin developing until her mid-teens, recalls her feelings of inadequacy. "I was so upset," she says. "My grandmother had told me that I'd get breasts if I rubbed cocoa butter on my chest. So for months, every night, before I went to sleep, I rubbed cocoa butter on my flat little chest, hoping I'd wake up with breasts."

Sometimes because of their hormonal development, adolescent boys develop a condition called *gynecomastia*—which translates to "breasts like a woman." For obvious reasons, the boys' reactions don't parallel the ambivalence of the developing girls—for them, breast development is uniformly embarrassing. I remember my seventh-grade boyfriend was so humiliated by it that he paid another boy to push him into the swimming pool: that way, he didn't have to take off his shirt to swim, and didn't have to explain to the other kids why he was swimming with his shirt on. I occasionally have patients suffering from gynecomastia, and their mental anguish, as well as their acute embarrassment at having to show me their chests, is really painful to see. Fortunately the condition usually regresses on its own in about 18 months; if it doesn't, it can easily be helped through surgery.

THE MENSTRUATING YEARS

Initial breast development is soon followed by the establishment of the menstrual cycle, as a young girl's body begins to prepare for reproduction. Hormones play a crucial part in this development, as they do in all aspects of reproductive growth. (See Figure 1-8.) On the ovary are *follicles* (eggs encased in their developmental sacs). These, stimulated by *follicle-stimulating hormone* (FSH), produce the hormone *estrogen*. The resulting high levels of estrogen in the blood tell the pituitary to turn off the FSH and start secreting *luteinizing hormone* (LH). When the estrogen and LH are both at their peak, you ovulate—the follicle bursts and releases its egg into the fallopian tube, where it starts its journey down toward potential fertilization.

The follicle is now an empty sac, but it still has a job to do: it becomes what is known as the *corpus luteum,* and it starts producing *progesterone,* which prepares the lining of the uterus for pregnancy ("progesterone" means "pro-pregnancy"). If the egg gets fertilized, it starts to produce *human choriogonadotropin* (HCG), which maintains the progesterone level until the placenta takes over the production, and you're well on your way to a baby. If it doesn't get fertilized, the progesterone level falls off, the lining of the uterus is shed, and you start all over again.

In addition to maintaining fertility, these cyclical hormones are preparing the breast for a potential pregnancy each month. In a very general sense, estrogen causes the increase of ductal tissue in the breast, and progesterone causes the increase in lobular tissue. This obviously has something to do with the cyclical changes women's breasts go through—swelling, pain, tenderness—but exactly how it does it is still unclear.

Breastfeeding

Breastfeeding, as I've mentioned before, is what the breast is designed for. In a purely technical sense, your breast isn't fully mature until—or unless—you've given birth and your body has begun to produce milk. The breasts of women who do not give birth remain in the earlier stage of development until menopause. Because breast-

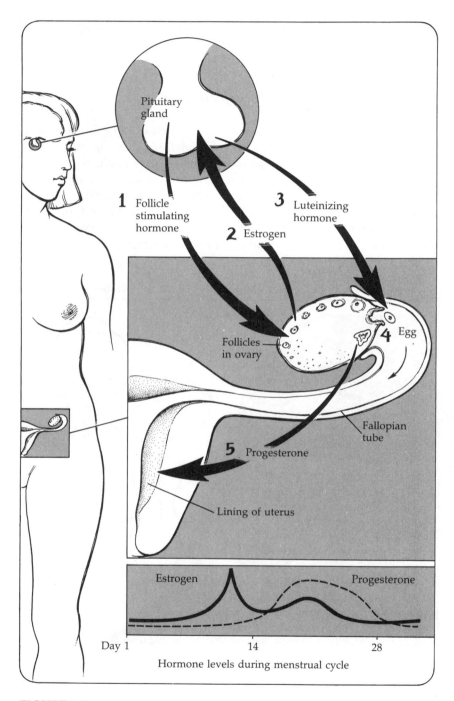

FIGURE 1-8

feeding is so complex, and so central, I've given it a chapter of its own (Chapter 3).

Menopause

By the time you're in your late 40s or 50s, most of your follicles have been used up and you're ready for menopause. (See Figure 1-9.) At this point, your remaining ovarian follicles are unable to produce perfect levels of estrogen and progesterone, and you start having some unusual hormonal symptoms. The cycles start getting shorter because enough estrogen isn't being produced. Because the stimulation is abnormal, your bleeding can start getting heavier. Your breasts may get sore and lumpy, and sometimes form cysts (see

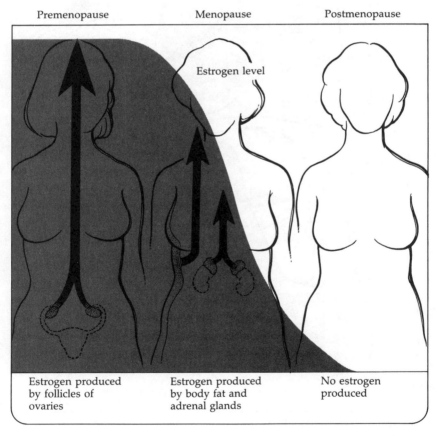

Premenopause   Menopause   Postmenopause

Estrogen level

Estrogen produced by follicles of ovaries

Estrogen produced by body fat and adrenal glands

No estrogen produced

FIGURE 1-9

Chapter 9). Finally you reach a point where there's not enough estrogen, so you miss a cycle. As the estrogen levels in the bloodstream decrease, you start having symptoms of estrogen withdrawal, such as hot flashes. Once the ovary stops producing, then the adrenal gland (see Figure 1-10) produces androgen, which is converted to estrogen—so there's still some estrogen produced, but it's no longer cyclical. (It's interesting to note that, with all the bad press fatness gets and with all the health problems it causes, this is an area where weight is an advantage: heavy women have fewer menopausal symptoms than thinner women, probably because fat makes estrogen and gives them a boost.) After a while, at about age 70, there are no more androgens produced and you have total estrogen withdrawal.

At menopause, the breast tissue decides to retire because of decreased stimulation from ovarian hormones. If you can't make babies anymore, there's no need to make milk. The breast tissue, which has

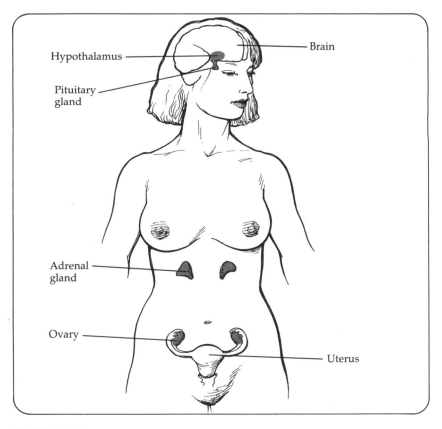

FIGURE 1-10

kept the breast firm and which was ready to make milk, shrinks, and more fat grows in the breast. As a result, the breasts sag. There's nothing wrong with this, except that our society equates beauty and desirability with youth. From a doctor's standpoint, it's actually a plus, since it's easier to examine a breast with less breast tissue, and mammograms are easier to read accurately.

Because osteoporosis is more common in postmenopausal women, many doctors prescribe hormones for their older female patients. These hormones persuade the body that it's still premenstrual, and so, along with renewed menstruation come all its attendant breast symptoms: swelling, breast pain, and so on. They also halt the sagging of the postmenopausal breasts. (Don't, however, expect a fountain-of-youth effect: if your breasts tended to sag before menopause, hormones won't make you look like a *Playboy* centerfold after—nor will they restore your breasts to your premenopausal firmness; they'll simply keep you where you are when you start taking them.) Hormone therapies have implications for cancer and its risks, and I'll discuss them further on page 165.

2

Getting Acquainted with Your
Breasts: Breast Self-Examination

Breast self-examination (BSE) is usually seen only as a form of cancer detection. I think this is unfortunate. Of course, it's used to help detect cancer, but its importance goes far beyond this. BSE is part of the larger process of getting to know your own body, becoming acquainted with who you are, physically. Most women who do BSE will never find a malignant lump; they will, however, have a more intimate awareness of their own bodies.

Unfortunately, women are rarely given the proper information about BSE, and the misinformation often leads to unnecessary anxiety. Health-care professionals tell you how to examine your breasts, but too often aren't clear about what you're looking *for*. Frequently that's because they themselves aren't really sure; even when they are, they don't always communicate it well. They simply tell you to "look for a change." They don't tell you what kind of a change, or what a cancerous lump feels like. So you see the self-exam movie at your doctor's office or on TV, and you go home, stand in front of the mirror, and do the whole routine, and you feel a little nodule, and then you feel the other side and there are some more little nodules, and you get very scared and decide, "Well, if it's cancer it's all over the place and I'm dead anyway, so I'm not going to worry about it anymore." And so you stop doing self-exams, and after a while it's clear that you're *not* dead and all those little nodules weren't cancer, but somehow you remain uneasy, because there are all those little *things* in your breasts. Since those little things are probably normal lumpiness, you're going through unnecessary worry and at the same time giving up a chance to become comfortable with your body. About 90 percent of my patients don't do BSE, and that includes doctors and nurses.

Breast self-exam was invented in an era when women were taught that it was bad to touch themselves "down there"—and "down there" was anyplace below the chin. Sexual prudery in general brought with it massive ignorance about our own bodies, and the concept of breast self-exam was a wonderful breakthrough in helping women begin to understand what their breasts really feel like. It's hard to know when something feels wrong in your body if you have no context for knowing what "right" feels like. And "right" varies from woman to woman. Our breasts are as individual as our faces, and what's normal in your breast might be a danger signal in mine. If you know what your breast feels like at all the points of your cycle, you'll be able to recognize when something's changed in it. This is what BSE is really for. It isn't a search-and-destroy mission, aimed at ferreting out the tiniest lump. Unfortunately, medical professionals often approach it that way, causing their patients needless anxiety.

In general, what you're looking for when you examine your breasts is one lump (or possibly two or three—rarely more) that's at least 1/2 inch in size, stands out, and is persistent and unchanging. (See Figure 2-1.) It doesn't go away or change size after your period, it's there after several cycles, and it stays in the same place. This is a dominant lump, and you should get it checked. You're *not* looking for some tiny beebee-sized thing; as we'll discuss at length in Chapter 9, it's extremely unlikely that a tiny lump is a malignancy. Nor are you looking for a pattern of lumpiness, which is absolutely normal and healthy.

Sometimes doctors will try to reassure patients with lumpy breasts by telling them they have cysts. It may be reassuring, but it's also inaccurate. "Cysts" gets used as a synonym for "nonmalignant," but a cyst is a very specific entity. (See page 111.) If you find "lumpiness" too nonmedical a term, you can call your condition "physiologic nodularity." All that means is that your body has produced perfectly normal nodules.

One final point about breast self-exam: you're usually told to check your breasts once a month and see if there are any changes. But the only change you really need to worry about is that dominant lump suddenly appearing and remaining. Breast patterns are no more static than the patterns of other parts of the body. As you age, your skin

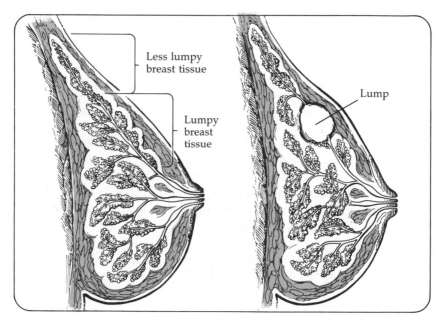

Less lumpy
breast tissue

Lumpy
breast
tissue

Lump

FIGURE 2-1

tone changes, your weight pattern shifts, your hair begins to gray. Similarly, your breasts change. They will be different in your 30s than they were in your teens, different again in your 40s, and, of course, they'll change once more with menopause.

They also change with your regular cycles. In the same way that your period may be heavier or more painful one month than another, your breasts may be lumpier one month than another. So for a change to suggest the possibility of any danger, it must be sudden and distinct, and, if you're premenopausal, it must remain over one or two cycles. If it doesn't meet these criteria, don't worry about it. If it does, there's no reason to panic. It's not necessarily cancer. It could be a cyst, a fibroadenoma, or a pseudolump, none of which are malignant. The important thing is to get it checked out and find out which kind of lump it is.

When to Do BSE

If you're not comfortable doing BSE every month, every two or even three months is okay. If you're premenopausal, it's important to do it at the same time in your cycle: remember, the point is to know what your breasts normally feel like so you can spot any variation from the norm, and to know how your breast looks and feels at different times of your cycle. Most women prefer the time between the end of their period and the beginning of ovulation—usually a week or so after your period is over. This is when your breasts tend to be least lumpy, so there's less stuff in there to confuse or alarm you. If for some reason you prefer a different point in your cycle, that's fine—as long as you remain consistent. (Being on birth control pills will make no difference here; you're still on a regular cycle.)

If you're postmenopausal, and not taking hormones, your breasts won't change cyclically anymore, so the regularity is less crucial. But in order to remember to do it, it's a good idea to choose a particular regular time. Some of my patients like to do it whenever the phone bills come in; others simply pick a date—say, the 10th of every month. If you're taking hormones, you still have cycles, so the best time to do BSE is right after you've finished a cycle of hormones.

It's a little more difficult if you've had a hysterectomy but still have your ovaries. You still have a hormonal cycle, but no period, so you can't be sure where you are in your cycle, though many women actually *do* know exactly when they're ovulating. If you're sure you know, pick a point around that; if not, just pick a time when your breasts are less sore and lumpy; if your breasts don't get sore and lumpy, just pick a regular time, as postmenopausal women do.

How to Do BSE

To begin with, do the visual part of the exam. Look in your mirror for obvious changes. (See Figure 2-2.) You might see a dimpling in your breast that you've never noticed before. One of your nipples might suddenly be inverted. Only rarely can you actually see a lump. You might discover some eczema on your nipple: this can be real eczema, but it can also be a sign of a cancer called *Paget's disease* (see page 272). You might notice some nipple discharge that hasn't resulted from squeezing your breasts (see page 106). Your nipples may have a different color, or the veins may be suddenly prominent. (If you're pregnant, the latter two symptoms are probably related to that.) None of these signs will be subtle: you can't see or feel a breast cancer at an early stage.

It's easiest to see changes in your breasts if you put your arms up

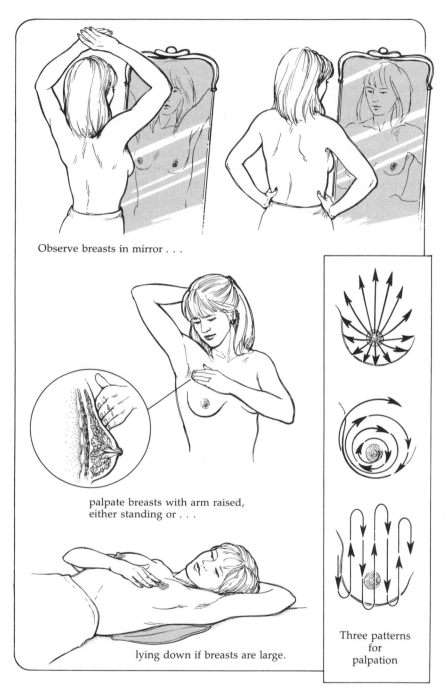

Observe breasts in mirror . . .

palpate breasts with arm raised,
either standing or . . .

lying down if breasts are large.

Three patterns
for
palpation

FIGURE 2-2

25

to stretch the tissue out, and then put your hands on your hips and push in, contracting the pectoral muscles. This allows you to see different areas of the breast undisguised by the overlying skin.

The second part of your self-exam involves *palpation*—feeling your breasts. Some women prefer to do this while they're showering, when they're soaped up—the soap makes the skin slippery and it's easy to feel what's beneath it. If you do it this way, put the hand on the side you want to examine behind your head. This shifts the breast tissue that's beneath your armpit to over your chest wall. Since the tissue is sandwiched between your skin and your chest bone, this gives you good access to the tissue. You want to examine the breast with a firm, but not rough, touch: too soft a touch won't reveal what's in the tissue, while too hard a touch, aside from being uncomfortable, will cause you to feel bone rather than tissue. Then begin exploring your breast in a pattern that assures that you'll feel all the tissue. Use the pads of your fingers—the fingerprint part— rather than your fingertips. (See Figure 2-3.) They are much more sensitive. Don't grab the skin; just press on it.

There are several such patterns you can choose from. One popular way is to see your breast as a clock, with the nipple as its center, and to go through each section of the clock in turn. (This isn't, however, a perfectly round clock: you want to be sure and get the tissue above the breast itself, so be sure and go up to nearly beneath

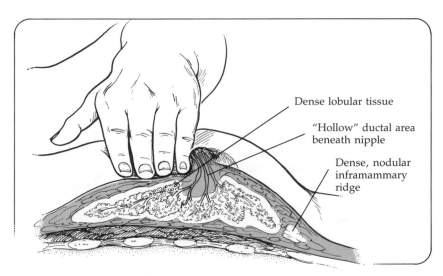

Dense lobular tissue

"Hollow" ductal area beneath nipple

Dense, nodular inframammary ridge

FIGURE 2-3

your collarbone.) Another pattern is to examine in concentric circles, spiraling upward. Yet a third is to examine in strips, beginning from the top of your chest and going all over the breast, strip by strip. It doesn't matter which pattern you use, as long as you pick one and stick with it. You can invent a pattern of your own if you like—all that matters is that you feel the whole breast each time. When you've finished with one breast, reverse the position of your arms and do the other.

Don't squeeze your nipples to see if there's discharge; any discharge that comes only when you squeeze your nipple is fine anyway. Remember that at this stage you're not looking for anything in particular—you're getting to know what your breasts feel like so that, eventually, you'll know them well enough to feel when there's something unusual. Right now, you don't yet know what's usual.

You can check under your armpit if you want, but don't worry unless there's a huge lump—which you'll probably have noticed before this, when you're applying deodorant. Little lumps can be normal lymph nodes that are swelling in response to a mild infection, similar to swollen glands when you have a cold. They can also be ingrown hair or extra breast tissue (see page 51). Often these lumps are sore as well: if the soreness or swelling is persistent and not cyclical, check with your doctor in a few weeks, since you might have a persistent infection. It's very common for the glands in your breast tissue to be tender before your period, and those glands do extend to your armpits.

If your breasts are very large, you might find that examining them standing up doesn't completely work: even with your arm raised, your breasts may still hang down. In this case, it's probably better to do it lying down. Follow the same method: put your arm behind your head, and examine in whatever pattern you find best. If your breasts are so large that even in this position they hang out over the side of your chest, you can put a pillow under one shoulder, shifting your body to the other side, and then shifting the breast tissue toward your chest wall.

Sometimes a patient will tell me that she found a lump she could only feel sitting up and leaning forward. Such lumps are rarely a problem. When you lean forward, glands and lobules in the breasts can feel like lumps. If you prefer to sit up when doing breast self-exam, be sure you lean back, and always keep the arm of the side you're examining behind your head. Remember never to use a grabbing motion. (See Figure 2-4.) Most breasts will seem lumpy when grasped between thumb and fingers.

Although each woman's breasts are different, there are some gen-

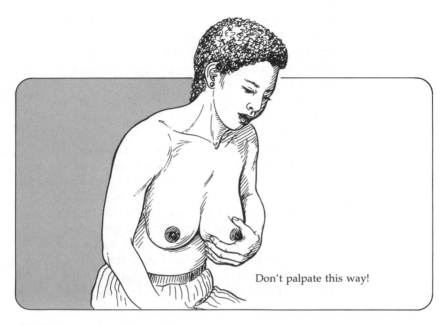

Don't palpate this way!

FIGURE 2-4

eral characteristics that apply to most women's breasts. For example, usually breasts are fuller and there's more tissue in the area between the nipple and the armpit than in other areas of the breast; there's also a lot of tissue right above the nipple. These areas are more likely to swell up before your period and go down afterward. In the middle of the chest, between your breasts, where the breastbone is, there is less tissue, and you can feel your ribs very easily; sometimes a "lump" turns out to be nothing but tissue draped over your rib.

You can also get confused by your inframammary ridge (see Figure 2-3), which can feel thicker and far more nodular than other parts of your breast. There's usually a somewhat hollow spot under the nipple, where the ducts are coming up, with a ridge of tissue around the duct area—somewhat along the lines of a volcano's structure.

If you've had any kind of operation on your breasts, you'll probably have some reminder of it in the breast itself. A biopsy, lumpectomy, or cosmetic surgery can leave scar tissue inside the breast that will feel like a lump. (See Figure 2-5.) A biopsy can also leave a little indent in the breast, if it hasn't been sewn up after the operation. Silicone implants also feel a bit rubbery. Silicone injections can form little silicone lumps inside your breast. It's useful to know what these

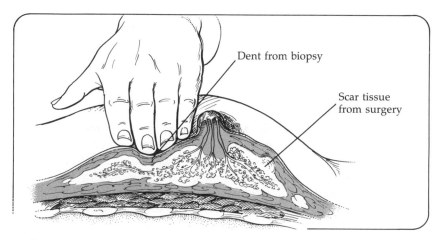

Dent from biopsy

Scar tissue from surgery

FIGURE 2-5

are, and to be able to distinguish them from new lumps that you'll want to check out.

As I've pointed out in this chapter and in Chapter 1, a really dangerous lump or other cancer symptom isn't subtle. You don't want to get panicked over a beebee-sized lump, even if you're sure it *is* new. If you're really nervous, and truly convinced something's wrong, see your doctor. But remember that your breasts will go through gradual changes all your life anyway. Aside from the natural changes of age, you'll find changes in your breasts when you gain or lose a lot of weight—remember, much of the breast is made up of fat tissue. One of my patients who'd recently gone on a very successful diet came in, frantic because she'd found "lots of cysts, everywhere." The "cysts" turned out to be normal lumpiness, which she'd never felt before because the fat tissue in her breasts had covered them up.

I was glad she'd come to me, anyway; I'd much rather examine someone and be able to reassure her than leave her to suffer needless anxiety. Especially when you're just beginning to do self-examination, you might want to go to your health-care provider and discuss your concerns and confusions. This will help you as you discover what your normal breast is like.

What you want to achieve, after you're familiar with your breasts' basic pattern (and this may take a while, as any learning process does), is a balance between learning to listen to your own inner voice when it insists that something is wrong, and recognizing when that "inner voice" is really an irrational fear taking over. Remember, the point of breast self-exam is to make you *more* comfortable with your breasts, not less. Creating a situation where you're constantly going through a cancer panic will be counterproductive in the long run.

BSE and Cancer

Part of the problem for many women is that the importance of breast self-exam in the containment of cancer has been greatly exaggerated. Unfortunately, there's no evidence that breast self-exam affects breast cancer mortality. Breast cancers are slow to grow, and by the time a cancer has formed a palpable lump, you've had it for a long time, and it's probably already in your system. (This does *not* mean you're doomed; as I discuss at length on page 213, most women with breast cancer don't die from it.) For reasons I explained earlier, the lump, when it forms, is never small; you won't feel a very early cancer in your breast. Yet many women are made to feel like they're dooming themselves if they don't do BSE, or if they skip a month or so. They're not. Much more important than breast self-exam for early detection are techniques such as mammograms that can detect breast cancer before it's palpable.

But if BSE won't keep you alive, why bother? There are a number of good reasons to do it, even if it's not a miracle cure. For one thing, there probably is a small subgroup of patients for whom it *does* make a difference in mortality, even if it's so small that it's not reflected in statistics. For another, if you detect a lump and it turns out to be cancer, finding it at a slightly earlier stage than you might otherwise have will allow you to undergo less-disfiguring surgery—there's less to cut out. It may mean the difference between a lumpectomy and a mastectomy, or between a larger or smaller lumpectomy.

Further, BSE can prevent needless biopsies. In our mobile era, you rarely have the same doctor all your life. If you've got a lump from, say, silicone injections or scar tissue from a previous operation, and you go to a new doctor who doesn't know your medical history, the doctor may well feel that a biopsy is necessary. If you can say with conviction, "Yes, I know about that lump: it formed right after my operation 10 years ago, and it's been there ever since," the doctor will know the lump is okay. I've often been through this with pa-tients. If a doctor thinks a lump is okay, but the patient doesn't know whether or not it's been there a long while, the doctor has to assume it might be dangerous, and operate. Remember that you are a per-fectly valid observer of your own body. You don't need to be a medical expert to know that you've had the same lump in the same place and it hasn't grown at all in 10 years. I had one 80-year-old patient who came to me after her doctors insisted that she'd been wrong about a lump in her breast that looked troublesome on her mammogram. Sexism and ageism can be potent forces, and obviously the doctors had decided that the "little old lady" didn't know what she was talking about when she told them her breast had been that way since her last child was born, 50 years earlier. They intimidated her enough so that she decided they must be right and had me do a biopsy. What I found was a congenital condition, perfectly harmless, which she'd probably had all her life. She knew her body, as her doctors couldn't.

It's also possible that BSE will save lives in the future, and it's a good skill to have now, while the research is being done. If we come up with better cures for breast cancer at its comparatively later stages, BSE may well turn into the lifesaver that wishful thinking has already made it now.

So doing breast self-examination is usually a good idea. But for some women, it's highly anxiety provoking. What many of my patients who feel this way do instead is to make more frequent appointments with me than they might otherwise: they come in every three or four months to get their breasts examined. Then they don't have to deal with the anxiety of doing it themselves, but they do get the advantages of relatively early detection of a lump. One of them told me that the extra expense is worth it: it's cheaper than the psychiatrist she'd have to see if she tried to do regular self-examination. Don't feel like you're some kind of nut if BSE freaks you out: we've all got our "crazy" areas, and you're entitled to some irrational feelings.

Finally, breast self-examination—or frequent examination by your health-care provider—is something you should do all your life. It's a good idea to start in adolescence: while breast cancer in young women is rare, it can happen, and in any case it's a good thing for a girl to become accustomed to it early. Its side benefits are marvelous—she learns to be comfortable with her own body, and it can be a pleasing rite of passage, a confirmation of her womanhood. And all women should continue it as long as they live: you can get breast cancer at 80 or 90.

3

===

Breastfeeding

As we've noted before, the purpose of the breast is to make milk, and your breast doesn't reach its full potential development until you've been through a full-term pregnancy.

This stage of the breast's development is evident quite soon after conception. Even before you've missed your period, you may notice that your breasts are unusually tender or your nipples unusually sore. I've had a few patients coming to me complaining of unusual breast pain and I've asked when their last periods were. "Oh, about four weeks ago," they say—and I say, "Well, you could be pregnant." And they either groan or grin, depending on how interested they are in motherhood at that time—and a couple of weeks later they call back to say, "Guess what? I'm pregnant."

Your breasts enlarge very rapidly when you're pregnant, and they become very firm. Your Montgomery's glands—those little glands around your areola (see page 5)—become darker and more prominent, and the areola itself darkens. The nipples become larger and more erect, preparing themselves for future milk production. (See Figure 3-1.)

Two hormones are mainly responsible for milk production work—*prolactin* and *oxytocin*. Both come from the pituitary gland, stimulated by an area of the brain known as the *hypothalamus*. Prolactin is some-

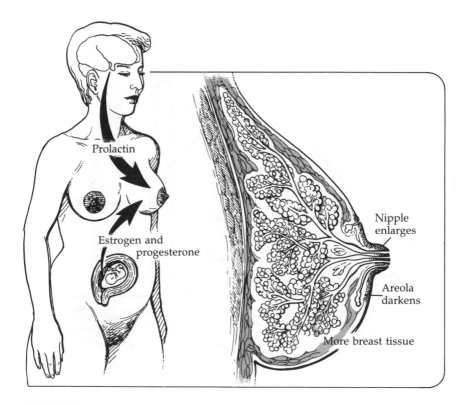

FIGURE 3-1

times known, a bit sentimentally, as the "mothering hormone," because it causes you to make milk and, some theorists believe, has a tranquilizing effect, which presumably makes you feel more maternal. This latter theory, while pretty, is so far unproven.

Prolactin is absolutely crucial to your potential to breastfeed—without it, you'll never have any milk. It begins its work about the eighth week of pregnancy and slowly gets higher for the next seven months, peaking at your baby's birth. With this high level of prolactin coursing though you, you'd begin to spout out milk right away, except that your body is also producing high levels of estrogen and progesterone, which block some of the prolactin receptors and inhibit milk production.

Once your baby is born and the placenta has been delivered, your levels of estrogen and progesterone plummet fast, while the prolactin levels begin a much slower decline, and this is the sign for your breasts to begin producing milk. (See Figure 3-2.) The milk, however,

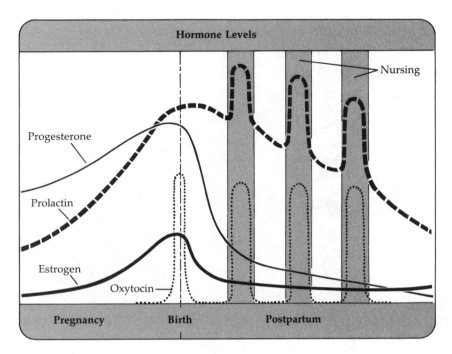

Hormone Levels

Nursing

Progesterone

Prolactin

Estrogen

Oxytocin

Pregnancy | Birth | Postpartum

FIGURE 3-2

doesn't come right away. It takes between three and five days, during which time your breasts are making another liquid, a sort of pre-milk called *colostrum*, which the baby can drink instead of the milk it will soon get. Colostrum is filled with antibodies, which help the infant fight off infections. It's also believed that colostrum decreases the baby's chances of later developing allergies and asthma. Soon the baby's own immune system has begun to develop, and it no longer needs the antibodies supplied by colostrum.

The other major hormone is oxytocin, which delivers the milk that prolactin has produced. (See Figure 3-3.) The baby's suckling at your breast does two things—it brings some of the milk out with its suction, and it sends an important message to the pituitary, via the nipple's nerve endings, the thoracic nerves, and the hypothalamus: send more milk out! The pituitary responds by manufacturing oxytocin, which makes the tiny muscles lining the lobules contract and squirt milk out from the breast. So while some of the milk is actually sucked out by the baby, some simply gushes out into the baby's mouth. The mother experiences this as "letdown"—her milk is literally being let down into her nipples. The milk now exists in two

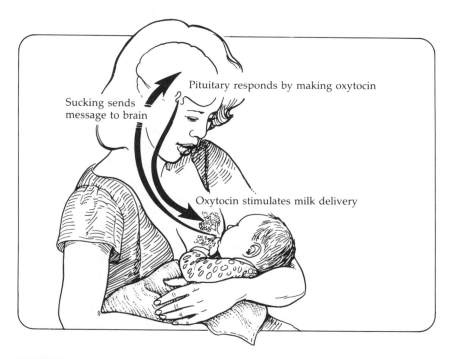

Sucking sends message to brain

Pituitary responds by making oxytocin

Oxytocin stimulates milk delivery

FIGURE 3-3

places inside her breasts: the fore milk is at her nipples, the hind milk up in the lobules. When the hind milk is called forward by the oxytocin, new hind milk is created, ready to be called forward. Unlike prolactin, oxytocin doesn't exist in the body until the suckling process calls it forth.

So suckling does two things: it stimulates prolactin to make milk, and it stimulates oxytocin to deliver milk. It's very much a demand-and-supply process. Your prolactin level, high during pregnancy, slowly drifts down toward its normal level after the baby is born. By the end of the first week after birth, prolactin is down to 50 percent of its normal level, and after three or four months, it's the same as it was before pregnancy. But every time your baby suckles, there's a new burst of prolactin telling your body to make milk and a burst of oxytocin telling it to release the milk into the baby's mouth. The more you nurse the baby, the more milk your body will produce. The baby can't ever use up the milk in your breasts; suckling is the message to your body to make more of it.

Meanwhile, other hormones are at work in the background—

insulin, thyroid, cortisol, and background nutritional hormones. These take part of the food you eat and remanufacture it in a new way, so that it can become part of the baby's milk.

In the 1950s, when breastfeeding was unpopular, doctors typically gave new mothers milk-inhibiting drugs. Often this was done by blocking prolactin with the drug *bromocriptine*. This is rarely used today, partly because social mores have changed: women are much more inclined to breastfeed for a while, and then perhaps switch over to bottle feeding. Though you often hear that having unused milk in your breasts is extremely painful, it's rarely all that bad. When you don't suckle your newborn, the prolactin doesn't signal your breasts to produce more milk and the milk simply stops: you're likely to be uncomfortable for a day or two and then feel fine.

If a new mother is not producing milk within a week of the baby's birth, something is wrong and a doctor should be consulted. Aside from deliberate attempts to inhibit milk, several problems can prevent your breasts from having milk. You may have a problem in your pituitary gland—you might have hemorrhaged into it, or it may be otherwise damaged, and you won't be able to produce the necessary prolactin and oxytocin. Sometimes you'll find that milk has come into your breast, but can't get out. This is caused by damage that's been done to the duct system, usually by surgery around the nipple or perhaps by breast-reduction surgery (see page 65). Sometimes the ducts can be unblocked, but often they can't, and in that case, you will have to bottle feed instead of breastfeed. (The milk will be reabsorbed back into your body.) This happened to a patient of mine in the ob/gyn section of the hospital I work at: I was called in to look at her because her milk had come in, but nothing was coming out. I tried to probe her ducts, but nothing would pass. I discovered that an operation she'd had done on a nipple abscess many years before had scarred over, sealing off her milk ducts.

If you've been breastfeeding and you suddenly stop, your body will stop creating prolactin and oxytocin, so milk isn't being let down and milk production will taper off and stop. For this reason, if you need to stop breastfeeding temporarily—for instance, if you have to travel or are about to be on medication that you don't want the child to consume—you should keep expressing milk manually or with a pump, so that the production continues. Otherwise it may be difficult to resume breastfeeding—the body has to start the whole business over again, and it takes time.

On the other hand, once you've had a baby you can always breastfeed in the future. If, for example, you adopt a child some time after you've breastfed your biological baby, you can have the new baby suck your breast and, with time, that can eventually start the whole process up again.

Breast milk will look different at each stage of its production. According to standard teaching, colostrum is yellow and clear; early breast milk is bluish white, mature milk is white and creamy—what we think of as "milky"—and late milk, as you begin to breastfeed less and less, is thin white. But it may vary. I found my own early milk to be white and the later milk to be blue. It was also interesting to me to find that milk left to stand in the refrigerator layered out with the cream at the top. If I skipped a meal there would be less cream, "skim milk." When I ate regular meals, there was more cream. Interestingly, the milk of a premature baby's mother is different from that of a mother whose baby was delivered at full term: the preemie's nutritional needs are different, and the mother's body knows this and adjusts the milk to her child's needs. Similarly, if you have twins your body will adjust to that, and provide you with twice as much milk. You can even nurse two consecutive children at the same time, tandem nursing. I discovered something else from my own experience: if you freeze early milk and give it to the baby weeks later, it will put the baby to sleep; it has a natural sedative effect.

Another important fact worth noting: you should alternate breasts and not just feed from one. One of my patients found it comfortable to feed on one breast, and ignored the other—which in turn ignored her and stopped making milk. The result is she now has an asymmetry she never had before.

Though having your first baby late in life can have other effects on your body, it won't affect your breast milk at all: you'll be as able to produce good milk for your child at 40 as you were at 20.

After you've stopped breastfeeding, you'll still have some secretions for two or three months, and sometimes as long as a year, afterward.

Usually you can breastfeed for two or three years, though you'll probably want to combine breastfeeding with bottle feeding of breast milk or formula after a while, both for your own convenience and to move your baby on to solid foods. The length of time is up to you. Your child probably won't be traumatized by the change. My sister decided to stop breastfeeding her daughter after three years. She was sure the child would be shattered, and spent a lot of time working out her explanation. When she broached the subject, my niece's response was a cheerful, "It's okay, Mom, I understand."

Breastfeeding has some contraceptive effect, but only in the first three or four months—and even then, it isn't 100 percent effective. Don't assume that because you're breastfeeding you can engage in intercourse without other contraceptives—unless you want to be breastfeeding again in nine months.

If you plan to go back to work while you're still breastfeeding, you can pump your breasts every three or four hours, freeze the milk or just refrigerate it, and use it to feed your baby later. This can be done by manually expressing milk into a sterile container or by using any of the commercially available breast pumps. (See Figures 3-4 and 3-5.) These come in a number of forms—there are hand pumps, electric pumps, and battery-operated pumps. Depending on the type of pump, it will take 10 to 15 minutes on each side—there is even an extra attachment for the electric pump that will allow you to empty both breasts simultaneously. As one of my busy doctor colleagues says, "Why waste a letdown?" Many workplaces (especially hospitals) have pumps available, and many others will rent one for you. It's certainly worth asking your employer, since it is to their advantage to keep you at work. After my daughter was born, I was explaining to a patient how the breast was a milk factory, and in the middle of my session with her I had to interrupt and go pump my breasts—nicely illustrating my metaphor.

FIGURE 3-4

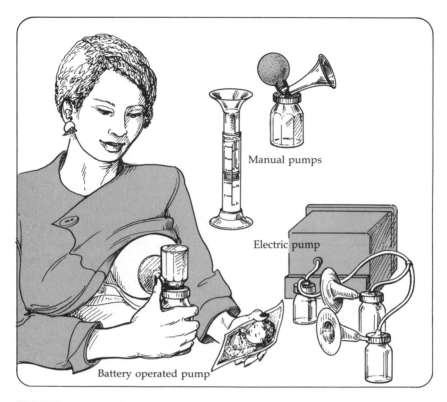

Manual pumps

Electric pump

Battery operated pump

FIGURE 3-5

Sometimes breastfeeding is interfered with by problems in the mother's body. One is sore nipples, created by the infant's suckling. You can often alleviate this by alternating the position in which the child is sucking. You should avoid soaps, which irritate the delicate nipple skin. You can buy a rubber nipple shield to help relieve some of the pain during breastfeeding. Some of the experts actually suggest toughening up your breast ahead of time by sunbathing topless! (Obviously, if you're going to try this method, be aware that the law might not agree with your decision; either find a private place to sunbathe, or be prepared for a court case!)

Women with inverted nipples usually have trouble breastfeeding: I've discussed this on page 71. There's a shell you can buy and put over the nipple, squeezing down and making it more available to the child. (See Figure 3-6.)

Some women suffer from engorgement of the breasts: they fill up too fast and don't empty enough, and then the nipple is so stretched

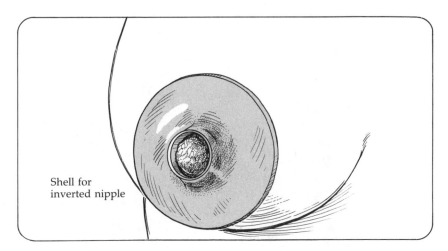

Shell for
inverted nipple

FIGURE 3-6

out the child can't get its mouth around it, and the problem gets worse. This is especially true when the milk first comes in, before the body has figured out the right amount of milk to produce—the first three or four days. It can be *very* uncomfortable, as I learned when my own baby was born. The best thing to do then is to express the milk manually between feedings, or to pump, and to feed the baby as often as possible. Frequent massage, hot tubs, and hot showers will help to express the milk; ice packs and aspirin or Tylenol can help relieve the pain.

Sometimes a duct can become blocked. (See Figure 3-7.) You'll know this has happened if you find a lumpy area in one segment of the breast that doesn't go away after breastfeeding. It's important to treat it right away, because it can lead to infection and, in rare cases, the infection can turn into an abscess. Again, you can treat it with hot soak, hot showers, and massage; if those don't work, call your doctor. There's a detailed description of these problems in Chapter 8.

Some women have too little milk. Occasionally there's no help for this; for some reason, the woman's body simply doesn't make enough milk, no matter what she does. These women usually feel guilty that they have starved their child and failed in their "motherly duties." This is certainly unfounded. Usually, however, a woman could produce more milk by feeding more often—an every-two-hour feeding generally helps. If such a rigorous schedule is impossible for you, it may be time to stop breastfeeding and turn to formula—or at least combine breast- and bottle feeding.

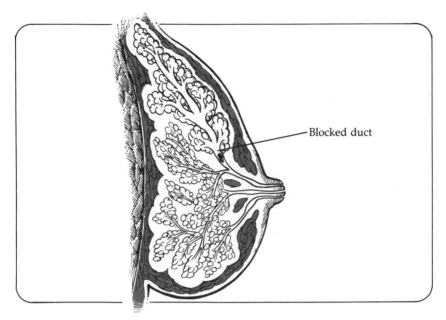

Blocked duct

FIGURE 3-7

At the other extreme is the woman whose body produces too *much* milk, and she finds herself leaking between feedings, or having her milk squirt out into the baby's face when she starts to nurse. This can be dealt with by expressing the milk between feedings, or pumping it and storing it in the refrigerator for future use.

In any case, if you find yourself having any physical or emotional problems with aspects of breastfeeding, or just want moral support, you should contact the La Leche League, or one of the other breastfeeding organizations, which offer counseling, peer support groups, and practical advice. (See Appendix C.)

Breastfeeding and Lumps in the Breast

Pregnancy and lactation don't prevent lumps from occurring: you can get any of the usual fibroadenomas, cysts, or pseudolumps (see page 110). In addition, a nursing mother can get a *galactocele*, a milk cyst that forms when some of the milk closes off in a sac and ultimately gets thick and cheesy. A needle aspiration can determine if the lump is a galactocele. (Figure 3-8.) It's harmless, as is any cyst,

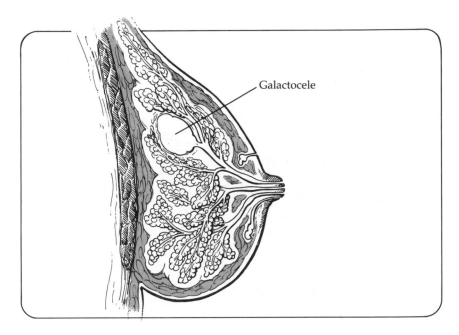

Galactocele

FIGURE 3-8

but you want to be sure that's what it is. I recently had a patient who had two milk cysts, which had been there for at least two years.

And, of course, you can get a cancerous lump, just as you can when you're not breastfeeding. Any dominant lump that doesn't go away with massage should be checked out.

It used to be thought that a woman who gets breast cancer during pregnancy has a worse prognosis than a woman who gets it at another time. This is not true. What *is* true is that for a pregnant woman breast cancer usually gets diagnosed at a later stage,[1] because she and her doctor are focused on the pregnancy and are not thinking about cancer. It's important to be as aware of the possibility of cancer during pregnancy and lactation as at any other time. Continue doing breast self-examination (see page 24). A pregnant breast will feel like a premenstrual breast; it is usually worse in the first trimester and better in the second and third. A lactating breast feels both full and lumpy, as if it had cottage cheese inside, because it's filled with fluid. When you're nursing, the best time to do breast self-examination is right after you've fed the baby, since your breast is emptier and abnormalities will be more obvious.

If a biopsy is called for, neither pregnancy nor breastfeeding need prevent it. When you're pregnant, it's best to do a biopsy under local anesthetic, since a general anesthetic may harm the fetus.

A nursing mother can have either a general or a local anesthetic. I prefer to operate right after a woman has fed her baby, or expressed the milk. I use the lowest percentage of local anesthetic possible, since the child may suck some of it later. It's not terrible for the child to swallow a bit of anesthetic, but I want it to be as little as possible. I also advise the mother not to feed the baby from that breast for 12 hours after the surgery, since a gulp of the lidocaine might be harmful, and you want to give it time to disperse through the breast.

It's messier to perform surgery on a lactating woman than on a nonlactating woman, and it's always possible that the operation can create a milk cyst or leakage, but it's really no great tragedy if it does. It can temporarily make the milk messy, too, since blood from the operation can mix with the milk; but blood won't hurt your baby, so the problem is really mostly aesthetic.

Some surgeons will tell a lactating woman she has to stop breastfeeding if she needs a biopsy. She doesn't. If your surgeon tells you this at a time when you're thinking of stopping breastfeeding anyway, it's probably a good time to stop. Otherwise, find another surgeon who *will* operate while you're lactating.

There are some myths about cancer and breastfeeding that need to be addressed. The first is that if you have breast cancer and your child drinks from the cancerous breast, the child will get your cancer. This theory is based on a study of one species of mouse, which does transmit a cancerous virus to its female offspring through breastfeeding. At this time, it hasn't been found in any other species of mouse, or any other animal, or in humans.

Another myth is that a baby won't drink milk from a cancerous breast. Normally this isn't so. If a breast has a *lot* of cancer, it probably won't produce as much milk, so the baby will, quite sensibly, favor the milkier breast. There's nothing wrong with this: in fact, many babies prefer one breast to another even with a very healthy mother.

A third notion is that breastfeeding helps prevent breast cancer. This statement is often given a slightly moralistic flavor: if the breast is doing what it's supposed to do, it won't get cancer. Research, however, hasn't shown any such effect. Your odds of getting breast cancer appear to be the same whether or not you've ever breastfed a baby. A very recent study of Chinese women indicates that women who breastfed their children for at least nine consecutive years have less breast cancer.[2] This is an interesting finding but not very useful for most women in our culture. (The age at which you first have a baby *does* have an effect on your vulnerability to breast cancer—see page 144.)

Sex and Breastfeeding

There's no reason for breastfeeding to interfere with an active sex life. Breast stimulation may cause some milk to flow out. Sometimes your lover will actually enjoy sucking at your breast and getting some milk. If this is pleasing to the two of you, it's fine—your lover won't be using up your child's milk, only stimulating the breast to produce more. If either of you finds stimulation of the breast unappealing at this time, you can adjust your sexual practices accordingly. On the other hand, you may find that your general libido is markedly reduced while you are breastfeeding, and you're not as interested in sex as you usually are. You and your partner should be aware of this possibility, so your partner doesn't feel rejected and you don't feel like you've suddenly become "frigid."

Many women feel sexual stimulation during breastfeeding, and it's perfectly natural—oxytocin causes the uterus to contract. Don't worry about it: it doesn't mean you're a potential child molester. It's usually a fairly mild form of sexual feeling, and there's no reason not to just enjoy it. (If you *don't* feel it, don't worry about that either; just enjoy the sensations you do feel.)

Breastfeeding When You Haven't Given Birth

If you've never breastfed or been pregnant before, you can still do a form of breastfeeding. This must be done in conjunction with bottle formula (or milk from another woman's breast, as in the case of lesbians raising the biological child of one partner together). Stimulated by suckling, which increases prolactin, the breast will produce a kind of pre-milk fluid, which can provide a small amount of nutrition to the child. Since many women find breastfeeding pleasurable, and since breastfeeding intensifies the bonding of mother and infant, this can be a good idea, as long as the baby is given other forms of nutrition. (Men, by the way, don't have this fluid, since their breasts haven't developed through puberty the way women's have.) This kind of breastfeeding can be enhanced by using an invention called a Lactaid kit. (See Figure 3-9.) It has a bag into which formula (or pumped breast milk) is placed, and a long plastic tube that winds around the breast and ends up at the nipple. The child sucks the milk from a catheter next to the nipple, thus creating the bonding effect of breastfeeding.

The kit might also help a woman who has had a baby (or been

FIGURE 3-9

pregnant for several months) in the past to revive her own milk-producing abilities. In this case she will eventually produce full milk. But the chief virtue of the kit is that it helps you to bond with the child and experience breastfeeding, even if your own milk isn't available.

Hormones have also been used to stimulate breastfeeding, with varying results.

Breastfeeding versus Bottle Feeding

When I was born, breastfeeding was very out of fashion. Bottle feeding was considered less messy, and it gave mothers more mobility than they had with breastfeeding. In the past decade or so, the tendency has reversed itself, and breastfeeding is definitely "in." I think it's unfortunate that there are fashions in baby feeding: they tend to include pressures and guilt trips, or the idea that there's a universally correct way to feed your baby, and that there's something odd and probably immoral about doing it any other way. In reality, there are advantages and disadvantages to both methods of baby feeding, and you need to weigh them all before you decide what you want to do.

What are the advantages of breastfeeding? Probably the most important advantage is the nutritional composition of breast milk. It's tailor-made for the human baby's needs—it's got the perfect combination of water, protein, carbohydrates (mainly lactose), immunoglobin (which helps create immunity against disease), lots of cholesterol (which, though unhealthy for adults, is great for babies), and vitamins and minerals. Cow's milk, on the other hand, is tailor-made for the needs of baby cows, which are obviously somewhat different from those of the human baby.

Formula is our attempt to modify cow's milk to make it as close as possible to human milk. We've done a pretty impressive job, but it's not perfect. For one thing, cow's milk isn't as digestible as human milk: it takes a baby four hours to digest formula, and only two to digest human milk. And no formula has been able to duplicate the immunity-providing properties of colostrum.

Breastfeeding also creates a unique bonding between mother and infant that some psychologists feel is essential to the child's later well-being. While there are plenty of emotionally healthy people who were bottle-fed, and many neurotics who were breastfed, it's clear that the particular bonding created by breastfeeding can't be wholly duplicated in bottle feeding. Many of my patients have talked with me about the importance of this bonding to them emotionally. "The realization of what breasts are meant for was tremendous," says one, who calls it a "generative experience." Another, who had felt self-conscious about her small breasts, changed her attitude when she realized that "my small breasts nursed three sons." I enjoyed breastfeeding my daughter and found that even pumping milk for her was a pleasant interlude in an otherwise hectic day. I think being able to fill her nutritional needs while working made me feel more connected to her.

On the other hand, breastfeeding can create difficulties for the mother that may outweigh the advantages to the child—difficulties that proselytizers for breastfeeding sometimes underrate.

Some women find their breasts aren't producing enough milk. This condition can usually be ameliorated if the woman breastfeeds more often—every two hours is put forth by the La Leche League and others. This may be very difficult for a woman who has a job outside her home, and it's not that easy for the woman at home who has primary responsibility for raising other children and/or doing housework. Bottle feeding allows the mother to get some rest, and to do other work, while her husband or another member of the household does some of the feeding. Sometimes a combination of breastfeeding and bottle feeding (using either formula or breast milk expressed by the mother at an earlier time) can be a useful compromise, but many women still find breastfeeding too demanding of time and energy. Also, lactation can cause problems even for the mother combining breast- and bottle feeding. Oxytocin can be produced by emotional as well as direct physical responses to the baby, and many mothers will find to their embarrassment that, while they're thinking about the baby, milk will suddenly begin to flow. A surgeon colleague of mine stopped breastfeeding when the thought of her baby came to her during an operation and milk suddenly started dripping onto her patient.

Still other women find the idea of breastfeeding unpleasant, even repugnant. This isn't an indication that the woman will be a bad mother; reactions to physical experiences vary greatly among human beings. Forcing oneself to go through with an unpleasant experience will be counterproductive to the bonding experience between mother and child. Some women feel more comfortable with bottle feeding because they know how much nutrition the child is getting, since it's premeasured, and since the exact amount of breast milk the child is getting is not something she can know for certain.

There are also women whose own food habits can make breastfeeding a problem. It's true that the baby will consume, through your milk, everything you consume, and many women really cherish their cups of coffee or their evening martinis. Although small amounts of liquor and caffeine are probably all right, if you want to breastfeed, you should keep them very limited. A recent study from the University of Michigan[3] demonstrated a slight decrease in motor development, but not in mental development, in the year-old offspring of mothers who drank one alcoholic drink per day while nursing. Thus, although some data suggest that a glass of beer a day will actually improve your milk production, it probably isn't worth the potential but slight consequences. And, of course, other recreational drugs are also potentially dangerous. It's probably safest to remain drug- and alcohol-free while breastfeeding. Some women can do this easily, and for them it's worth the sacrifice; for others, it's not, and they may prefer to bottle feed rather than adopt uncomfortable behaviors. It isn't necessarily "selfish" to take care of your own needs as well as your baby's. Similarly, some mothers are on medication for chronic health problems, and some (though certainly not all) medication will harm a breastfeeding baby. Sacrificing your own health or comfort, may not be the best thing for either you or your child.

Yet many women today feel pressured to breastfeed, regardless of their own needs, and often others can play unconsciously into those pressures. A patient of mine recently came to see me in her eighth month of pregnancy. She reminded me that, four months earlier, I'd said to her, "I'll see you again toward the end of your pregnancy, and then again when you've finished breastfeeding." She was concerned because she didn't want to breastfeed, and felt I'd been implying that she should.

At the same time, there are still parts of our culture that have retained the old prejudices *against* breastfeeding, and they can be very damaging to a mother. There's still some feeling that since the breast is a sexual organ, it shouldn't be exposed in public (though the fact that some people view men's breasts as erotic doesn't force men to cover their chests). Thus, a woman who's breastfeeding may find herself pressured to give it up, or to confine it to her own home. I recently went to a wedding and my cousin's wife was sitting off in a corner, very discreetly breastfeeding her baby—to the horror of some of the other guests. Feeding your baby is a perfectly natural and sensible thing to do, and you shouldn't be made to feel like some kind of slut for doing it. Obviously, given social mores, it's usually unwise to bare your whole breast in public, but sensibly chosen clothing can allow for discreet feeding anywhere, and you shouldn't feel guilt tripped by other people's puritanism.

There's another prejudice that can get in the way of breastfeeding. The breastfed baby doesn't gain weight as rapidly as the bottle-fed baby does. That's perfectly fine, except that we've been raised with the image of the chubby, healthy baby. But chubby *isn't* necessarily healthy, and breastfeeding may in fact produce a healthier child.

It's important to realize that antibreastfeeding feelings originated in the early days of formula feeding, and it was very much in the interests of the manufacturers of baby formula. We see this quite tragically in Third World countries, where poor mothers have been told that formula is better for their babies than breast milk, then given formula until their own milk dries up, and then forced to buy more formula at costs they can't afford. Many babies have died as a result, and, shamefully, only the United States refused to sign a United Nations agreement condemning corporate promotion of bottle feeding in Third World countries.   •

Fortunately, most women in the United States are well enough off to be able to choose either breast- or bottle feeding. You should make your choice realistically, taking into consideration your own needs and priorities. If the various social criticisms of one mode or the other make sense to you, take them into consideration. If they don't, ignore them. You want to do what's best for you and your baby, and for the relationship that develops between you. Only you can best determine what that is.

4

Variations in Development

Breasts are found in many different shapes and sizes. Medically speaking, a "normal" breast is one that is capable of producing milk, so there's nothing "abnormal" about large, small, or asymmetrical breasts, or about extra nipples.

There are a number of common variations in breast development. They fall into either one of two categories: those that are obvious from birth, and those that don't show themselves until puberty. The latter are far more common. (There are also variations due to accident or illness, the surgical remedies for which are essentially the same as those used for genetic variations.)

Variations Apparent at Birth

The most common variation to appear at birth is *polymastia*—an extra nipple, or nipples. These can appear anywhere along the milk ridge. (See Figure 1-5.) Usually the milk ridge—a throwback to the days when we were animals with many nipples—regresses before birth, but in some people it remains throughout their lives. Between 1 and 5 percent of extra nipples are on women whose mothers have also had extra nipples. Usually they're below the breast, and often women don't even know they're there, since they look very much like moles. (See Figure 4-1.) Often I've pointed out an extra nipple to a patient, and it's the first time she's known about it.

They cause no problems, and, because of their size and resemblance to moles, usually don't appear cosmetically unattractive. One of my patients is actually very fond of her extra nipple: she told me that her husband has one, too, and that's how they knew they were meant for each other!

Men do sometimes have extra nipples, though as far as we know, less frequently than women do. This may be due to some biological factor we don't yet know about, or it may simply be that men and their doctors don't notice the nipples because they're covered by chest hair.

Extra nipples don't cause any problems, though they may lactate if you breastfeed. There's nothing wrong with this, unless it causes you discomfort. Sometimes a woman will have an entire extra breast, which causes no medical problems.

A variation of the extra nipple is the occurrence of extra breast tissue, without a nipple; this most often appears under the armpit. It may feel like hard, cystlike lumps that swell and hurt the way your breasts do when you menstruate. Like extra nipples, this extra breast tissue is often unnoticed by doctor and patient. One of my patients found that, during her second pregnancy, she had swelling under both armpits: it was probably caused by extra breast tissue and it went down again after she finished lactating. The extra tissue is subject to all the problems of normally situated tissue. I have had patients with cysts, fibroadenomas, or even cancers in this aberrant breast.

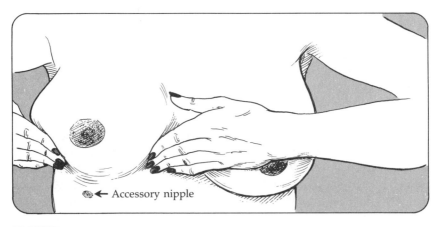

← Accessory nipple

FIGURE 4-1

Unless the extra nipple or breast tissue causes you extreme physical discomfort or psychological distress, there's no need to worry about it. If it does bother you, it's easy to get rid of surgically. The nipple can be removed under local anesthetic in your doctor's office, much the way a mole can, and the breast tissue can be removed under either local or general anesthetic.

A much rarer condition is *amastia*—being born with breast tissue but no nipple. When it occurs, it's usually associated with problems in the development of the chest bone and muscles, like scoliosis (curvature of the spine) and rib deformities. Aside from whatever medical procedures you may need because of the associated problems, you might want to have a fake nipple created by a plastic surgeon, the same way a nipple is created during reconstruction after a mastectomy. A skin graft is taken from tissue on the inner thigh; the skin becomes darker after it's grafted and, if it still doesn't match the color of your other nipple, it can be tattooed to a darker shade. Though this artificial nipple will look real, it won't feel completely like a real nipple: there is no erectile tissue, so it won't vary like your other nipple does; it's usually constructed midway between erect and flat. It will have no sensation because it has no nerves. And, of course, it won't have ducts and so can't produce milk. Its advantages are wholly cosmetic.

Some women have practically no breasts at all. This condition is sometimes called *Poland's syndrome*, and it involves not just the breast but also the pectoralis muscle and the ribs, as well as, in some cases, abnormalities of the arm and side of one side of the body. At times, a woman with Poland's syndrome does have a small but very deformed breast.

Some women have permanently inverted nipples (they grow inside instead of out)—a congenital condition that usually won't manifest till puberty.

Various kinds of injuries can affect breast development. This may happen surgically or with trauma. If the nipple and breast bud are injured before puberty, the potential adult breast is destroyed as well. Sometimes injuring the skin can limit future breast development. Most commonly this occurs as a result of a severe burn. The resulting scars are so tight that they won't allow the breast tissue to develop. In the past, some congenital conditions such as *hemangiomas* ("birthmarks") were treated with radiation, which damaged the nipple and breast bud and prevented later growth. Any serious injury to the breast bud can cause this arrested development.

Variations Appearing at Puberty

Three basic variations appear when the breasts begin to develop: extremely large breasts, extremely small breasts, or asymmetrical breasts.

VERY LARGE BREASTS

Very large breasts can occur early in puberty—a condition known as *virginal hypertrophy*. After the breasts begin to grow, the shutoff mechanism, whatever it is, forgets to do its job and the breasts keep on growing. The breasts become huge and greatly out of proportion to the rest of the body. Sometimes the condition runs in families. In very rare instances, virginal hypertrophy occurs in one breast and not the other. It's worth noting here that "large" is both a subjective and a variable term. A five-foot-tall woman with a C cup is very large-breasted; a five-foot-eight woman with a C cup may not feel especially uncomfortable with her size. A five-foot-eight woman with a DD cup is likely to be very uncomfortable.

Large breasts have been a problem for a number of my patients. "I almost never wear a bathing suit," one patient told me, "because people stare at my breasts." Another, at 71, still "hunches over" when she walks to avoid having her breasts stared at.

Huge breasts can be very distressful to a teenage girl. She faces ridicule from her schoolmates, and—unlike the small-breasted girl—extreme physical discomfort as well. She may be unable to participate in sports, and she may have severe backache all the time. She usually needs a bra to hold the breasts in, but the bra, pulled down by the weight of the breasts, can dig painful ridges into her shoulders.

If the breasts cause this much discomfort, the girl might want to have reduction surgery done while she's still in her teens. There are a number of procedures. Though they're all major surgery, because they're done on the body's surface they're less dangerous than other equally complex operations, and the recovery period is speedier. (We'll discuss plastic surgery at length in the next chapter.)

The procedures vary according to the size of the girl's breasts. If they're really huge, the nipple will have to be moved further up on the newly reduced breast. In this case, the ducts are cut and so breastfeeding will never be possible.

For this reason, some mothers refuse to let their daughters have reduction surgery, urging them to wait until they've had their children. This concern must be weighed against the physical and emotional damage the girl must go through before she has children (if she decides to have children). Pregnancy itself may worsen her problem because when the breasts become engorged with milk, they become even larger, and thus, in a woman with huge breasts, more uncomfortable. Though it's unfortunate that someone so young is faced with a decision that affects her whole life, it's important to realize that *not* having the surgery will also affect her life. Many girls of 15 or 16 are mature enough to make their own decisions if all the facts are carefully explained to them, including the possibility of bottle feeding. In any case, the losses and gains of either choice are the girl's, and she should be given the right to decide for herself what to do. She should be encouraged to talk to doctors, mothers of young children, and very large-breasted women; to read all the material she can find about the pros and cons of the procedure and of breastfeeding; and to make her decision only when she feels she is fully informed.

Not all problems with huge breasts appear right after puberty. Some comfortably large-breasted women find their breasts have expanded considerably after pregnancy; others become uncomfortable after their breast size has increased with an overall weight gain. Many surgeons are reluctant to operate in this latter case, preferring to wait till the woman has lost weight. Sometimes, however, this can backfire psychologically: I've known women who were so depressed by their huge breasts that they compensated by overeating, thus intensifying both problems. In such cases, the pleasing appearance of their breasts created by reduction surgery can be a spur to continue the process of self-improvement.

In all cases, the decision must be made by the individual woman; she's the one who lives with the problem and she's the one who can best judge its impact on her life. Some women with very large breasts don't mind them. One patient who admits that they cause her discomfort says that she nonetheless enjoys their size. "They feel feminine and sexy," she says.

VERY SMALL BREASTS

The opposite problem is extreme flat-chestedness. Like "large-breasted," the notion of "small-breasted" is subjective and relative, and to some extent culturally determined. Some women, however, have breasts so small that their chests look like men's. This causes no physical or medical problems. Yet it can cause psychological ones, making a woman feel unattractive and sexless.

For many women, these problems are solved simply by the use of falsies or padded bras. Others want to have the breasts themselves altered. Until recently, there was nothing that could be done for women who wanted larger breasts. Some surgeons experimented with paraffin injections, with fairly awful results. In the 1960s, the silicone implant and silicone injections were introduced. These implants, their safety and the surgery involved, are discussed on page 66.

The idea of silicone implants has taken on negative connotations— jokes abound about falsely endowed strippers and movie stars. But most women who get silicone implants aren't trying to look like Dolly Parton: they simply want to be what they perceive as normal. The implants have made a difference in many women's lives. One of my patients got her implants in 1980, when she was 40. "For the first time in my life I was proud of my figure," she says. "I felt like a new woman."

Drs. Andrew and Penny Stanway in their book *The Breast* suggest a somewhat surprising alternative to augmentation surgery—hypnosis and visual imagery.[1] Visualization is a form of self-hypnosis in which you put yourself in a state of deep relaxation and then see yourself, as vividly as possible, achieving the state you want to be in. (We'll discuss it at greater length on page 331, which talks about nonmedical components of cancer treatment.)

Andrew and Penny Stanway describe a study in which volunteers were put into a state of deep relaxation and then asked to visualize a wet warm towel over their breasts. When they felt the warmth of the towel, they were told to concentrate on the warmth and the breasts' pulsation. They did this exercise every day for 12 weeks. At the end of that time half the patients reported having to buy bigger bras! The authors suggest that the deep relaxation and visualizing might effect a hormonal change that influences breast size. While the study is hardly conclusive, it's certainly interesting, and you might want to give visualization a try before considering surgery. It's painless, it has no harmful side effects, and it might just produce the results you want in a less expensive and physically invasive way than through surgery. (See Appendix C for books on visualization techniques.)

ASYMMETRICAL BREASTS

There is a third situation that often occurs in puberty: the breasts grow unevenly. In some cases, this is simply a question of the rate of the breasts' growth, and in a year or two the breasts are fairly

symmetrical—for example, one breast will be an A cup size, while
the other is a B-cup size. (Keep in mind that most people's breasts
are slightly uneven, as are their feet and hands.) But sometimes the
breasts remain extremely asymmetrical. Again, asymmetrical breasts
are perfectly "normal" from a medical viewpoint: they can both produce milk. But they can create extreme psychological distress, causing the adolescent girl—and the grown woman—to feel like a sexual
freak. Some girls refuse to date in their teens because they fear their
condition will be discovered and ridiculed. (A friend of mine, now
in her 40s, had her first date at the age of 20—two weeks after her
last silicone injection.) A falsie—or a pile of several falsies—can be
worn on one side, of course, but the girl may still feel like she's
hiding something ugly and somehow shameful.

For a woman who is bothered by extreme asymmetry, cosmetic
surgery can help achieve a reasonable match. Either the larger breast
can be reduced or the smaller one augmented—or a combination of
both can be done. It's important for the surgeon to discuss these
options—often we assume a woman will want her small breast made
larger, and neglect to suggest the possibility of reducing the larger
breast. What a woman decides will depend on the size of both
breasts, the degree of asymmetry, and above all, her own aesthetic
judgment.

It's fortunate that plastic surgery techniques exist for women who
want them. But don't assume that because you have atypical-looking

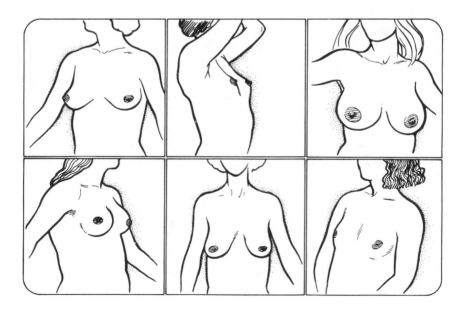

breasts, you *have* to get them altered. Many women are quite pleased with how their breasts look. Some women with large breasts feel, as did the patient I mentioned earlier, that their breasts are "feminine and sexy." Small breasts, too, have their advantages. One of my patients likes her small breasts because "they're unobtrusive, and they worked well during nursing. Occasionally some male person will intimate that they're less than optimal. That's his problem, not mine." Another likes her tiny breasts ("they're really just enlarged nipples") because they don't get in her way when she engages in sports. A patient with very asymmetrical breasts says she used to feel self-conscious about them, but has "come to terms with them" since she nursed her child.

And another patient tells a wonderful story about a friend of hers who had inverted nipples. "When I was 12 and my cousin was 14, we stood before the bathroom mirror and compared breasts. I noticed how different her nipples were; they didn't protrude, the way mine did. We had this big discussion about whose were 'normal.' I was convinced mine were, but she insisted hers were, and since she was older and, I thought, more knowledgeable, I decided she must be right.

"After she graduated from college and was studying in Paris, she became ill and had to be hospitalized. The doctor who was examining her asked if her nipples 'had always been like that.' That's how she learned that she had inverted nipples—and that *mine* were the normal ones!"

Obviously, the woman's inverted nipples hadn't caused her any distress. If you don't object to the way your breasts look, don't think about plastic surgery. You're fine as you are.

5

———

Plastic Surgery

Many women with atypical breasts are perfectly comfortable with them, and never consider having them altered. On the other hand, some women are very unhappy with the way their breasts look. For them, cosmetic surgery is worth thinking about. Women are often made to feel frivolous and "vain" for having cosmetic surgery, while at the same time everything in their culture reprimands them for not meeting an impossible, Hollywood-style standard of beauty. It's no more vain to alter your breasts than to wear contact lenses instead of glasses, or to get a suntan to darken your complexion; it's certainly no more vain than it is for a man to wear a toupee or get a hair transplant to ameliorate his baldness.

Plastic surgery has been done on breasts for a long time. Interestingly, the first recorded breast surgery was done on a man with gynecomastia, in A.D. 625.[1] It was not until more than a thousand years later (1897) that they performed mammoplasty on a woman—but we needn't feel too deprived. With the primitive state of surgery in the past, that poor man in the seventh century can't have had too comfortable a time with it. Good breast-reduction techniques have now been with us for decades. Augmentation, as I mentioned earlier, is a much more recent procedure.

All of the procedures carry the risks that any surgery carries, but all are among the safest surgical procedures that exist. They are often labeled "unnecessary surgery," and, of course, they are unnecessary in the sense that you won't die without them; and some people have questioned the safety of silicone implants (see page 66). But for many women, the risks are worth the chances of improved self-image and, in the case of large breasts, increased physical comfort.

If you're thinking about any of these forms of surgery, you should ask yourself a few questions. The first and probably most important is: who wants the surgery? If you're contented with your breasts, but your mother or boyfriend or anyone else is pressuring you into it, you probably shouldn't do it. It's your body, not theirs.

The second question is: how realistic are your expectations, and how clear an idea do you have about the kind of breasts you want? Dr. John T. Heuston,[2] a noted plastic surgeon, has written some wise words about reduction surgery that can equally well apply to all forms of cosmetic surgery for the breasts. "The concept of an ideal operation," he writes, "carries with it the concept of an ideal breast. The surgeon seeks the best means to construct the breast form—but for whom? For him or her, or for the patient, or both?" As Heuston notes, there is no objectively ideal breast; each of us has her or his own ideal. So you should have a clear sense of what size and shape breast you want, and what your own goals are. The surgeon can't make your breasts absolutely perfect, but if your goals are fairly reasonable, they can come pretty close to being met.

Once you know what you want, don't hesitate to shop around for the right plastic surgeon. You should choose someone you feel absolutely comfortable with and confident in before you entrust this very important task to them. Above all, it should be someone who respects *your* ideal and doesn't seek to impose her or his ideal on you. The surgeon's "beautiful breast" and yours may be very dissimilar. Make sure you find someone who will construct *your* breast. And make sure you find someone who respects who you are, and why you're making your decision. One woman I know went to a plastic surgeon when she was 20, hoping to have her painfully large breasts reduced. The surgeon wanted her to wait until she had children and had breastfed them. She told him that she was a lesbian and didn't plan to have children. "In that case," he told her, "you won't need your breasts—why don't we just cut them both off?" The experience so embittered and intimidated the woman that she still, nearly 20 years later, hasn't had her breasts reduced. Remember that you don't have to submit yourself to the surgeon's prejudices: if the surgeon you've approached acts insulting or condescending, find someone with a more professional and more humane approach.

Of course, there's no guarantee that you'll be happy with your operation after it's done, even if you have taken every precaution possible. But the odds are on your side. I've had very few patients who have regretted having their breasts cosmetically altered, but I've had several who've regretted not having it done. One of my patients is an 80-year-old woman with huge, uncomfortable breasts. When she was younger, she went to a surgeon to try and get her breasts reduced. He told her she shouldn't have the operation. She took his advice—those were the days when doctors were gods, and you didn't question them—and has been uncomfortable and unhappy with her breasts ever since. After we talked about this, she decided to have her surgery done, and is now very happy with her small breasts—and very sad for all the years she could have been this comfortable.

One of my patients is a sophisticated career woman in her early 30s. During our first visit, I noticed that her breasts were extremely asymmetrical, and after a few visits, I asked her if she'd ever thought about plastic surgery. Her face lit up. "Can I really do that?" she asked me. I assured her that she could, and gave her a list of plastic surgeons. She didn't even wait till she got out of the building to call them; she found a phone booth downstairs, made an appointment, and had her implant within the month. She's absolutely delighted with it—but she needed me to suggest it, and "give her permission" to seek help for her asymmetry. The friend I mentioned in the previous chapter had silicone injections for her asymmetry when she was 20. Her breasts are not perfectly matched, and, as she grows older, the augmented breast sags a little more than the natural one. But she is very happy about her decision and says she would make the same choice again today. She keeps in her closet an old V-necked sweater her mother gave her after she finished her injections—a symbol of a freedom she hadn't known before.

The only cases I know of in which patients have been unhappy with cosmetic surgery on their breasts have been when they were pressured into it by other people. When it is their decision, they are usually pleased by the results. Psychiatrist Sanford Gifford writes about a patient feeling she had "gained something lost in early puberty."[3] He observes that the degree of satisfaction is much greater among women who have had plastic surgery for their breasts than among those who have had face-lifts or nose jobs—they don't have the same unrealistic expectations. Often they're happier with their still-imperfect breasts than the surgeon thinks they should be. For some reason, people don't go into this kind of plastic surgery with the same dreams of impossible perfection they bring to facial surgery.

One caution: if you're planning *any* kind of breast surgery after 35, you should have a mammogram first. Since the danger of breast cancer is greater among older women, you want to make sure there's nothing there you don't know about before you go into surgery.

Otherwise, don't let age deter you from the cosmetic surgery you want. My 80-year-old patient is delighted with her belated operation, and I've had many women in their 50s, 60s, and 70s who have had their breasts reduced or augmented. If your health is good enough to sustain surgery, it doesn't matter how old you are.

It's been my experience that, when considering surgery, some patients want to know all the details of the operation, while others just want to know what it will do for them and leave the details up to the doctor. For this reason, I've begun each discussion of cosmetic surgery procedures with a brief mention of what each procedure sets out to accomplish. Those of my readers who are content with that can skip the rest. But for those of you who want the "gory details," read on!

Since I'm not a plastic surgeon myself, I've enlisted the aid of my colleague, Dr. Robert Goldwyn, to whom I've referred many of my patients, in putting together this chapter.

The "Breast-Lift"

Sagging breasts (known medically as *ptosis*) can be made firmer through an operation called a *mastopexy*, which Dr. Goldwyn describes as "a face-lift of the breasts."

A mastopexy can give your breasts uplift, Dr. Goldwyn warns, but it will not make your breasts look like a 20-year-old's. And the operation will leave scars—sometimes bad ones, depending on how your body usually scars. Like a face-lift, it won't last forever: remember, you've got gravity and time working against you.

Your first step is to set up a meeting with your plastic surgeon, who will take a very thorough medical history. Dr. Goldwyn recommends getting a mammogram before proceeding any further, if you haven't had one recently. Be sure to get a full description of both the best and the worst possible results of a mastopexy.

This operation usually involves removing excess skin and fat and elevating the nipple. (See Figure 5-1.) If you're very large-breasted, you may want reduction surgery as well, especially since a mastopexy is less effective on very large breasts: gravity pulls them down. If you're very small breasted, you may want an augmentation. (Both of these procedures are described later in this chapter.)

If your operation doesn't involve reduction or augmentation, it's a simpler procedure, and can be done either in the hospital under

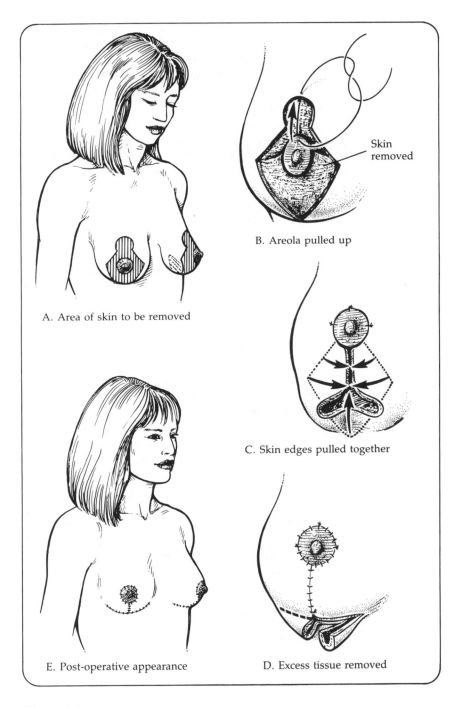

A. Area of skin to be removed

B. Areola pulled up

Skin removed

C. Skin edges pulled together

D. Excess tissue removed

E. Post-operative appearance

Figure 5-1

general anesthetic, or the doctor's office under local. Since insurance won't pay for it, most women prefer the latter. The operation lasts about two and a half hours; the stitches are removed in two weeks. By three weeks, you'll be able to participate in sports. Dr. Goldwyn recommends that you wear a bra constantly for many weeks after surgery. Follow-up is minimal—three or four visits during the year after surgery.

You may experience some very slight loss of sensation in the nipple or areola. Other than that, there are no particular side effects to mastopexy.

If you do decide on a "breast-lift," make sure your expectations are reasonable. Some plastic surgeons like to "sell" their operation— a practice Dr. Goldwyn abhors. "Too often doctors use pictures to seduce patients into surgery," he says. "I think it's a form of huck-sterism." If you're shown pictures of a surgeon's best results, insist upon seeing pictures of the average and worst results as well.

Breast Reduction

Most women come for this operation because they're psychologically embarrassed or because they have discomfort from neck and back pain. As with the other operations described in this chapter, if a woman is over 35, she should have a mammogram to make sure there's no cancer.

On the patient's first visit, says Dr. Goldwyn, "I show them photos of breasts that have had reduction surgery to make sure they know there will be scars." The doctor will explain what sizes are possible; most of Dr. Goldwyn's patients want to be a B, and some want to be a C. It's not always possible to get exactly the size you want, but a good surgeon can approximate it well. Then the operation is scheduled.

There are a number of variations of the breast-reduction operation, but all start with the same basic procedure.

The operation is usually done under general anesthesia, in the hospital, and takes place the day you're admitted to the hospital. It may last up to four hours. Your nipples can be either removed and grafted back, or left on breast tissue and transposed. Most doctors today prefer not to graft the nipples, since it seems to interfere more with sensation.

Most procedures involve some variation of the keyhole technique. The amount of tissue to be removed is determined and a pattern drawn on the breast. (See Figure 5-2.) The nipple is preserved on a *pedicle*, the part of the tissue left attached, while the tissue to be

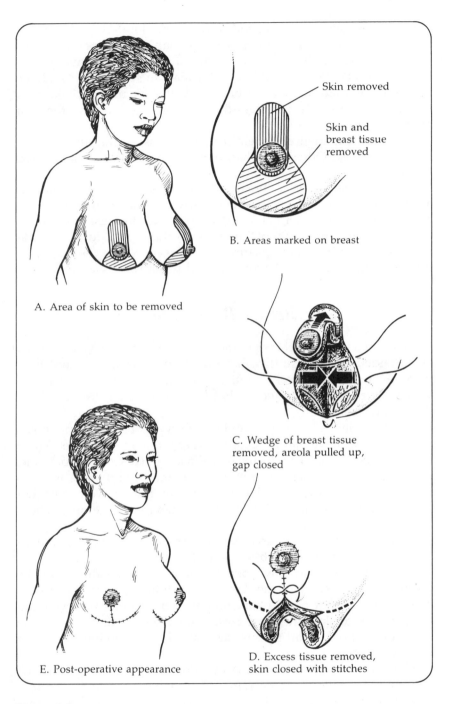

A. Area of skin to be removed

B. Areas marked on breast

Skin removed

Skin and breast tissue removed

C. Wedge of breast tissue removed, areola pulled up, gap closed

D. Excess tissue removed, skin closed with stitches

E. Post-operative appearance

Figure 5-2

removed is taken from below and from the sides. This allows the surgeon to elevate the nipple and bring the flaps of tissue together, giving both uplift and reduction. The resulting scars are below the breast in the inframammary fold and come right up the center to the nipple.

It will be painful for the first day after the operation, but there's not much pain after that, and you can go home two or three days later, wearing a bra or some form of support. The stitches are out in two weeks, and you can go back to work by then; in three to four weeks, you can be playing tennis.

The possible side effects include infection, which can occur with any operation. There's a very slight risk that you'll need blood transfusions, but it's very rare: Dr. Goldwyn has been doing this operation for years and has never had to give transfusions. If you're worried, however, you can give your own blood to the hospital two or three months in advance, and it will be there in case you need it. There's some danger of the operation interfering with the blood supply of the nipple and areola; if this happens the nipple and areola die and need to be artificially reconstructed. It's not a very great danger—it happens in less than 4 percent of operations. The larger your breasts are, the greater the danger. Reduction does not affect a woman's risk of cancer. Your ability to breastfeed will be decreased; studies show that about half of women who have had reductions can still nurse their babies.

Some of the erotic sensation in your nipples and in your breasts themselves may be reduced, though for many women the increased relaxation actually makes sex more pleasurable after reduction surgery. Also, because the nerves in the nipple of the overlarge breast are so stretched out, the nipple is unlikely to have much sensitivity to begin with, and the loss of sensation—both in terms of sexual activity and breastfeeding—will probably be unnoticed. There's also a possibility of some reduction of sensitivity in the breast itself, although again this is minimal. There's no way to know in advance whether or not you'll experience reduced sensation, so you have to decide for yourself how important full sensation is, versus whatever physical or emotional discomfort your large breasts create for you. In any case, you'll still retain most of your breast sensation.

If you do decide to get reduction surgery, be aware that if you later gain weight, your breasts will probably also gain weight, just as they would without the surgery. This has happened to a number of my patients. One woman had her size 36EE breasts reduced to a 36B, but they are now 36D.

According to Dr. Goldwyn, "the more the patient regards the operation as reconstructive, the happier she'll be; the more she sees it as cosmetic, the fussier she'll be about the result. If it's only cosmetic, she's more likely to focus on the scars; if it relieves pain and discomfort, she'll be happier."

Making Small Breasts Larger

One of the first questions for a woman considering breast augmentation will be the safety of silicone implants. In the early days of such surgery, results were mixed. Silicone was injected into the breast in the doctor's office, often without anesthesia (the doctor preferred not to introduce swelling that temporarily, and confusingly, altered the breast's shape). Though some women had excellent long-term results from the injections, many others had problems later. The silicone often traveled through the body, causing unsightly and alarming lumps to form in unexpected spots. The injections are now illegal, but implants have caused fewer problems and are now popular. Implants are pads of silicone encased in a rubber-like shell; they look like nippleless falsies and are surgically implanted, generally under the pectoralis muscle.

There have been some questions raised about the safety of implants since silicone gel has been known to slowly bleed out of the outer covering and implants have been reported to rupture. When injected directly into rats silicone will cause cancer.[4] This has not been reported in women with implants, which have been around for about 20 years and have been used in over two million women. Still, no really good studies have been done. The one retrospective study of 3,111 women had a median follow-up of only 6.2 years. This showed no increase in breast cancer rates but may not have followed patients long enough.[5] In addition, there have been isolated reports of connective tissue disease related to silicone implants.[6] The Food and Drug Administration's General and Plastic Surgical Devices Panel met in the fall of 1989 to review the data regarding silicone implants. The panel, which included consumer representatives, concluded that "a carcinogenic effect in humans could not be completely ruled out, but if such an effect did exist, the risk would be very low." They recognized that there were still questions about the short- and long-term effects of these implants and have required more studies. Until that data is in they have decided to develop educational materials for potential consumers. Any woman contemplating this surgery should make herself aware of the controversies and should ask to see a copy of the package insert. (See Appendix C for further information.)

There has also been some concern that implants may interfere with what can be seen on a mammogram and therefore delay the diagnosis of breast cancer.[7] No good controlled studies have been done. Dr. Goldwyn thinks it does interfere, and advises against augmentation for premenopausal women with a strong family history of breast cancer (see page 146). I don't think we know the answer yet: if it's important enough for you, it may be worth doing. In addition, the most recent data indicate that there are ways to get good mammograms in women with silicone implants.[8] But if you do decide to have implants make sure you have regular follow-ups with a breast specialist, and regular mammograms at an institution that knows how to deal with them.

Before augmentation surgery, in addition to the mammogram (which should precede surgery, as we said, for women over 35), the surgeon should check for cysts that will require needle aspirations (see page 123). As Dr. Goldwyn says, "you don't want to be sticking needles into the patient's breast when there's a silicone gel bag inside it." The plastic surgeon will also take a careful history.

The surgeon should show you pictures of breasts that have been augmented, including those that have left very visible scars, so you know both the best and the worst possible results of your operation. You and the surgeons should also discuss what size you want your new breasts to be, and you need to be realistic about that—you won't have enough breast tissue to turn tiny breasts into huge ones. Dr. Goldwyn tells of a petite woman who wanted to go from a size 34A to a size 34D. "Not only did she lack sufficient soft tissue to harbor such implants," he says, "but the results would have been poor, even bizarre." Most of Dr. Goldwyn's patients want to be a B size.

If you're married, some surgeons will want to make sure your husband feels okay about your having augmentation, since an angry husband might later try to sue the doctor. If you feel that it is your decision alone, let the surgeon know, and try to work it out, or find a surgeon willing to do what you want.

The operation can be done under either local or general anesthetic. Some patients, says Dr. Goldwyn, prefer to use general anesthetic because they fear pain, and some surgeons also prefer it. Another factor in your decision might be insurance: you'll need to check with your insurance company about what forms of plastic surgery they will or won't pay for.

The incision is made either through the armpit, underneath the breast, or around the areola. (See Figure 5-3.) All of these have their proponents. The implant can be placed under the breast tissue between the breast and the muscles or under the muscle itself. (See Figure 5-4.) Putting the implant under the muscles, says Dr. Goldwyn, is more complicated and more expensive, and often, but not

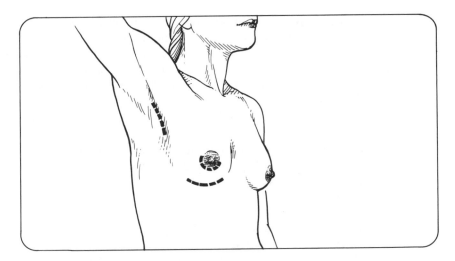

Figure 5-3

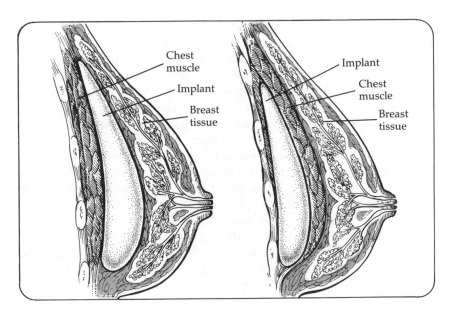

Figure 5-4

always, needs to be done under general anesthetic. But it has two advantages: it seems to carry less risk of contracture, which means the formation of a thick, spherical scar tissue that causes the breast to be firm (see Figure 5-5), and, even more important, it's less likely to hide a cancer if one develops in the future.

Contracture is also lessened if you use saline-filled implants instead of silicone, but the saline implants have a history of leaking, so many plastic surgeons prefer to stay with silicone.

The operation is usually done on an outpatient basis; it takes about two hours or more, depending on whether the surgeon puts the implant under the muscle or not (it will take longer if the implant is under the muscle). You go home after the operation. The stitches will be removed about 10 days later. You'll be out of work for about a week or 10 days, and shouldn't drive a car for a week. In three weeks you'll be able to jog or play tennis.

Side effects can include infection, which occurs in less than 1 percent of cases, and bleeding, which is equally rare. There may be permanent altering of sensation in the nipple or areola, which occurs in less than 2 percent of cases, and there is also a slight possibility of reduced sensation in the breast itself.

There's also the possibility of visible scarring, which we mentioned earlier. And there is some possibility that lactation will be interfered with if the surgeon makes the scar next to the areola.

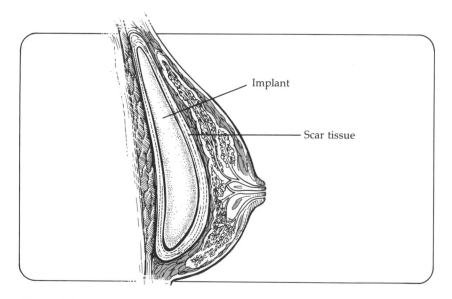

Figure 5-5

The biggest problem is the contracture we discussed above, which occurs in 1–18 percent of cases in which the implant is under the muscle, and between 18 and 50 percent of cases in which it's between the muscle and breast. This firmness can be so minimal that it's unnoticeable, or it can feel like solid wood—or anything in between.

A woman can massage the breasts to try and reduce the firmness, and this sometimes helps. If it's extremely severe, it can be operated on. This is done in one of several ways. The surgeon can squeeze the breast and pop the scar tissue around it, making it softer; this only works in 25–30 percent of cases. Or the surgeon can go back into the breast and cut a wider space around the implant, which works in about 65 percent of cases. Or, if the implant is above the muscle, it can be removed and a new implant inserted below the muscle; however, if it's done on one side, asymmetry may result. Giving steroids can reduce contracture, but can also cause the breasts to weaken and sag. If you decide on augmentation surgery, you should be prepared for the possibility of contracture.

Implant rupture is the second complication. This can occur through strenuous physical force or just spontaneously. It is not common but is a serious complication when it occurs. The patient will need immediate surgery to remove the implant and to try to remove all the silicone.

One thing you should keep in mind: if you've had silicone implants for either small or asymmetrical breasts, and problems occur later, the implant may have to be removed and a new one put in sometime after the operation. It's important to know the size of your implant to be sure the replacement is the right size.

Asymmetry

To correct asymmetry, the doctor can use one of three procedures, and it's important for you as the patient to know which of the three you want. You can have an implant put in one, or you can make the other smaller, or you can have a combination of both. Your doctor may assume you want the smaller breast augmented; if you don't, make that clear.

If your asymmetry results from Poland's syndrome or an injury, such as we discussed on page 52, an artificial breast can be constructed using flaps of skin, muscle, and fat from your back or abdomen. This procedure, usually used to reconstruct a breast lost through mastectomy, is discussed in detail on page 349.

If you're thinking of surgery for asymmetry, you should keep in mind that *exact* matching is unlikely. If there's a difference in nipple and areola size, the implant operation will stretch the nipple and areola on the smaller breast, but it may be a little less elastic as a result. And, since silicone has now been added to the distribution of fat and tissue in the breast, the breasts will probably sag at different rates as you grow older. Still, these differences are minor compared to the original asymmetry, and it's likely that you yourself will be the only one to notice.

Inverted Nipples

There are operations that can reverse inversion of nipples, but they don't always work, and the inversion may recur. It's a very simple procedure, usually done under local anesthetic with no intravenous medication, and you can go back to work two or three days later. The stitches will come out in about two weeks.

The nipples are usually inverted because they are tethered down by scar tissue or other tissue from birth. To reverse it, the surgeon will reach down, pull the nipple, stretch it, and make an incision, releasing the constricting tissue. (See Figure 5-6.) There are a number of procedures, and each one has its advocates. If the inversion recurs, the operation can be redone.

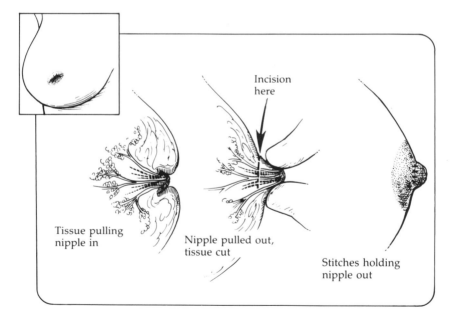

Incision
here

Tissue pulling
nipple in

Nipple pulled out,
tissue cut

Stitches holding
nipple out

Figure 5-6

71

Dr. Goldwyn finds that this operation can make a psychological difference for teenagers, who often feel extremely self-conscious about their inverted nipples. The operation will definitely interfere with breastfeeding, but women with inverted nipples usually have difficulty breastfeeding in the first place.

While none of these operations are medically necessary, we're lucky to live in an age when they're available. For a woman deeply unhappy with the way her breasts look, plastic surgery offers a solution that can make a major psychological difference in her life. No operation will make you look "perfect" (whatever that is), but all of these procedures can help you feel more comfortable in your own body.

PART TWO

COMMON PROBLEMS OF THE BREAST

6

The Myth of Fibrocystic Disease

You're concerned about your breasts: they get swollen and hard just before your period. Or they're painful, so painful you can't get any work done. Or there's discharge when you squeeze your nipple.

So you go to the doctor, who examines you carefully and gravely announces, "Well, I've got good news for you. It isn't cancer. It's only fibrocystic disease."

The doctor seems to think this will cheer you up, and in a way, it does—you *are* relieved to know you don't have cancer.

But you're also a bit disturbed—you do have another disease, and that's scary, even if it won't kill you. So you decide you'd better find out a little more about this illness you've got, and you check around. You find an article in one of the women's magazines, and you learn about fibrocystic disease. And now, you're *really* scared. Fibrocystic disease, you read, can increase your risk of cancer.

So, very sensibly, you go back to your doctor and demand a treatment for your disease. And the doctor prescribes vitamin E, or tells you to eliminate caffeine from your diet.

By now, whatever your physical discomfort is, your mental anguish is far worse. Every little breast pain seems like cancer. You stare at your breasts in the mirror: surely they look different than they used to? You start seeing signs of malignancy everywhere.

75

And it's all unnecessary. Because in reality, there is no such thing as fibrocystic disease.

Your symptoms—and I can't stress this enough—are very real. It is the diagnosis that is unreal. "Fibrocystic disease" is a meaningless umbrella term—a wastebasket into which doctors throw every breast problem that isn't cancerous. The symptoms that it encompasses are so varied and so unrelated to each other that the term is wholly without meaning. Some doctors recognize this and have stopped using the term. Others, unfortunately, have not. Still others will use equally bad terms such as "chronic cystic mastitis" or just "cystic mastitis."

What are doctors talking about when they use the term "fibrocystic disease"? Well, to begin with, it depends on what kind of a doctor is using the term. First, there's the doctor who examines you. This doctor can be addressing one or more symptoms. His (or her) "fibrocystic disease" can be swelling, pain, tenderness, lumpy breasts (a condition that should not be confused with breast lumps—see Chapter 9), nipple discharge—any noncancerous thing that can happen in or on the breast. That's the clinical version of our mythical disease.

If the doctor is concerned that your problem might be a symptom of cancer, your breast will be biopsied, and the tissue examined under a microscope by another doctor called a pathologist. And what does the pathologist find? You've got "fibrocystic disease." But the trick is, it's not the same fibrocystic disease the examining doctor discov-

ered. The pathologist's report has to do not with your original symptom, but with any one of about 15 microscopic findings that exist in virtually every woman's breasts, and which never reveal themselves except through a microscope. They cause no trouble, and they have no relation to cancer—or to anything else, except the body's natural aging process. They are the result of natural wear and tear, no more a disease than gray hair or age lines. And the only reason they showed up in the particular breast tissue that was biopsied was because it *was* biopsied: if you'd had another area of your breast biopsied, they'd find them there, too: those harmless little changes that take place throughout your breasts. (Only one of these—a fairly rare one—is a danger sign: it's called *atypical hyperplasia*, and, combined with a family history of breast cancer, it *can* suggest an increased breast cancer risk. I'll discuss atypical hyperplasia on page 193.) But your doctor won't make this distinction. The doctor will just tell you what you already know: you've got "fibrocystic disease." Again, you're grateful not to have cancer, but upset that you're diseased.

If this isn't confusing enough, there's a third kind of fibrocystic disease, discovered by the radiologists who read your mammogram. Mammography is the new kid on the block—it's only been around 10 or 15 years—and the radiologists want to get in on the game. So when the radiologists began reading mammograms, they discovered that younger women tended to have very dense breast tissue, while older women tended to have less dense breast tissue. "Why?" they asked the surgeons. And the surgeons answered—what else?—"fibrocystic disease." And now the radiologists have their very own fibrocystic disease to diagnose—completely different from the clinical or pathological versions.

What really causes the radiologists' fibrocystic disease? Interestingly enough, it's exactly the opposite of what causes the pathologists' version: it's simply youth. You know those firm, unsagging breasts that women in their teens and early 20s so often have—the breasts the rest of us are supposed to envy? Well, they're firm because they've got comparatively little fat and comparatively more breast tissue, and the more breast tissue you've got, the denser the tissue is. If you've read Chapter 1 of this book, you'll know that dense breast tissue is in fact very normal, especially in young women. There's nothing diseased about it, except in the imaginations of some doctors.

If you're beginning to feel a little like Alice after she fell through the looking glass, you should. "Fibrocystic disease" is as fanciful as anything Lewis Carroll ever invented. It's not only fanciful, however;

it's dangerous. It causes a number of problems for those women who, as we say in the medical world, "carry the diagnosis." The dangers fall into three categories.

The first danger isn't a medical one; it's economic. Many insurance companies won't insure a woman who's been diagnosed as having fibrocystic disease—as they won't insure people diagnosed as having any chronic disease. If they'll insure you at all, they may exclude breast problems—with the result that you won't have insurance coverage should you ever get a real breast disease.

At the same time, if you're already insured when you're diagnosed as having fibrocystic disease, your company may pay for your mammograms. Because of this, a well-meaning doctor is often tempted to diagnose fibrocystic disease so your mammogram will be paid for. But your advantage then lasts only as long as you remain with the same insurance company: should you ever want to sign up with another company, your "disease" will work against you, and you'll be stuck with the label for the rest of your life.

Medically, the dangers range from minor to very serious indeed. First of all, your mental health isn't going to be improved by your conviction that you're especially prone to breast cancer. Second, the medical "treatments" can be anything from ineffective (like eliminating caffeine from your diet) to devastating: some doctors even recommend a form of mastectomy to prevent the cancer you're supposedly likely to get.

Finally, the existence of the diagnosis "fibrocystic disease" has negatively affected the research done on the specific clinical symptoms women experience—symptoms that, as I said earlier, are as real as the disease is unreal. The research done in the United States on nonmalignant breast symptoms isn't very good—and you can see why. Since a large number of completely different symptoms have been thrown together, they're not studied individually, as they need to be if we're going to learn anything useful about them. We aren't sure, for example, why some women have extreme breast pain before or during their periods, or why some women have especially lumpy breasts—and we're certainly not sure that there's any relation between the various symptoms so conveniently thrown together in the same useless term. If we're to help alleviate these symptoms, we need to research each one on its own terms.

Origins of the Term

If fibrocystic disease is a useless and inaccurate diagnosis, how did it gain such widespread acceptance? It's not only the popular press that's responsible for the misinformation—the medical literature also talks about fibrocystic disease and its supposed associations with breast cancer.

The problem is that medical literature tends to be a bit incestuous—doctors read a study, are impressed with it, and use its information in their own articles. Their work, in turn, is rewritten, often without attribution, by other doctors. Hence, it can appear that impressive numbers of medical authorities have independently come to the same conclusion.

With the help of some associates, I investigated the literature on fibrocystic disease and found that almost all of the articles were based on the same data. I researched this data and learned that the evidence linking so-called fibrocystic disease with breast cancer was, at best, extremely shaky.[1]

To do our research, my colleagues and I first had to sort out papers referring to clinical symptoms from those talking about people who'd had biopsies. Most of the early work—done in the '30s and '40s—was done on people who'd had biopsies, not on people who'd simply had symptoms. This in itself made its universal applications highly suspect, because most people with symptoms don't ever have biopsies.

We found that the studies broke down into three types. In the first, breasts that had been removed because of cancer were studied to see what else was there. "Fibrocystic disease" was found in most of these breasts, and so the researchers brightly concluded that fibrocystic disease was linked to cancer. Their findings were ludicrous: a kind of medical guilt-by-association. They might as well have decided that, since all the cancerous breasts had nipples, nipples cause cancer. When these studies were compared with other studies done from autopsies on women who had died from a variety of noncancerous causes, it was discovered that the women without cancer actually had a higher incidence of "fibrocystic disease." (This makes sense when you remember that what the pathologists call fibrocystic disease is simply the wear and tear that happens over the course of time and that many of the women autopsied had died in old age, while many of the cancer victims biopsied were still comparatively young.) So the first category of studies could be dismissed.

Another, different type of study also suggested that women with fibrocystic disease were more likely than others to get cancer. These studies looked at women who had cancer and asked them if they had had previous biopsies. The researchers compared these women with others who didn't have cancer, but who went to the breast clinic for one reason or another. They were also asked if they had had biopsies. The studies were fairly specious, since they equated having a biopsy with having fibrocystic disease. All they showed was that a woman who has had one biopsy is likely to have others, probably because she is now aware of her breast problems and more likely to keep checking to make sure her breasts are all right. This is interesting, but it says nothing at all about the relation of the entities that have been dubbed fibrocystic disease, to cancer.

There was, however, one category of study that seemed to have some validity. This was studies on women who'd had biopsies that showed fibrocystic disease and who were followed over a period of years to see if they developed cancer. They were compared to a group of women who had never been diagnosed as having fibrocystic disease. This kind of study might show that women with microscopic fibrocystic disease got cancer more often than those without it.

Indeed, as we examined some of these studies, we discovered that they appeared to show that the women diagnosed as having fibrocystic disease after being biopsied appeared to have twice the incidence of breast cancer that women in the general population had. But it didn't seem to matter what the biopsy showed. Even more perplexing, it didn't seem to matter which breast the biopsy was done on: a woman who'd had a biopsy done on something found in her left breast might later develop cancer in her right breast.

The studies, we realized, hadn't taken into account the subjective nature of the decision to do a biopsy. A surgeon doesn't do a biopsy on every woman with a breast problem. It depends on how worrisome the particular situation seems to be. If, for example, a 20-year-old woman comes into my office with a questionable area in her breast and has no risk factors that would make cancer likely, I probably won't do a biopsy. If, however, I've got a 40-year-old patient with the same kind of area, and her mother and two sisters both had breast cancer, then I'll probably do a biopsy. So the decision is influenced somewhat by the patient's cancer risk.

One study did take cancer risk into consideration. Dr. David Page,[2] of Vanderbilt University, had corrected for risk factors, making sure that both the women who'd been biopsied and the control group of women who hadn't been biopsied had the same number of risk factors. And he found there was a smaller increased rise in breast cancer risk among the biopsied women—1.3 instead of 2.

Since then, Dr. Page has done another study, looking at 10,542 biopsies to see if any of the microscopic entities led to breast cancer. He distinguished the various forms of "fibrocystic disease" from one another, and it was in this study that the relationship between breast cancer and the rare entity atypical hyperplasia was discovered. (See page 193.) None of the other, far more common, entities were found to have any connection at all to cancer. This explains most of the increased risk of breast cancer associated with biopsies that have revealed "fibrocystic disease."[3]

I wrote about my findings in the *New England Journal of Medicine* in 1982. Interestingly, no doctors wrote to the *Journal* to argue against my findings. But it took four years for the College of American Pathologists to come out with a statement that fibrocystic disease doesn't increase the risk of cancer.[4]

Caffeine, Vitamin E, and "Fibrocystic Disease"

As doctors have foisted on women the concept of fibrocystic disease, they've also come up with a number of fairly useless "treatments"— which, like the idea itself, have gained a lot of publicity and generated a lot of anxiety. For some of the specific symptoms that really *do* exist, there are some more or less effective treatments, and I'll go into them in the next three chapters. Meanwhile, here I'll discuss some of the popularly accepted "fibrocystic disease" treatments.

Probably the most popular of these treatments is the removal from the woman's diet of caffeine, which supposedly causes fibrocystic disease in all its alleged manifestations. The idea originated with an Ohio surgeon named Dr. Minton,[5] who in 1980 decided to test his theory on 40 women with "clinical symptoms"—pain, lumpiness, swelling, and so on—and told them to stop all caffeine intake. Twenty of them ignored his advice; of the remaining 20, 13 said their breasts felt better as a result. He accepted their reports on face value and did no objective testing—mammograms, for example. While it's true that we need to respect women's definitions of their own sensations, it's also true that a study without objective components is never sufficient. For this type of study to be valid, it needs to be randomized, controlled, and double-blinded—that is to say, a given number of randomly chosen subjects must be taking the substance under study while an equal number of subjects, also randomly chosen, must not be taking it; and neither the researcher nor the subject must know which subjects are getting the treatment and which are being given a placebo—an ineffective, "sugar pill" substitute. The latter is very important; it prevents the unconscious expectations of both the subject and the researcher from clouding the perceived results.

In spite of its glaring inadequacy, Minton's research got a lot of press, and it wasn't long before it was extended in the popular imagination to include cancer prevention. Since fibrocystic disease led to cancer and caffeine consumption led to fibrocystic disease, people reasoned, then obviously cutting caffeine from the diet re-

THE BIRTH OF A MYTH

duced the risk of breast cancer. So we now have a double fallacy to contend with: the symptoms associated with "fibrocystic disease" don't lead to cancer, and caffeine doesn't cause the symptoms in the first place. So giving up caffeine, however beneficial this may be in other health areas, won't keep you from getting breast cancer.

Other studies, slightly better designed than Minton's but still far from conclusive, followed in the wake of the newly popular caffeine theory. One 1984–85 San Francisco study,[6] limiting itself to the effects of caffeine on lumpy breasts, did have a randomly chosen control group, and both groups were studied by a nurse practitioner who examined their breasts every month for several months. She divided each breast into quadrants, and graded each quadrant on a scale of 1 to 4, repeating the procedure with each examination. A score of 16 indicated that the breasts were very lumpy, while a score of 2 indicated that the breasts had little lumpiness. One of the problems was that, since she checked each quadrant, a small change—say, 1/2 point—in each quadrant could create a 4-point difference in the total, giving the impression of greater overall change than really existed.

But there were worse problems than this. In the study the nurse was not "blinded": that is, she knew whether the woman she was examining was in the caffeine-consuming group or the noncaffeine group. So her own prejudices may well have affected the fact that she did find significant improvement among the women who had given up caffeine. Two circumstances strongly suggest that this was the case. The first is that there were other components to the study:

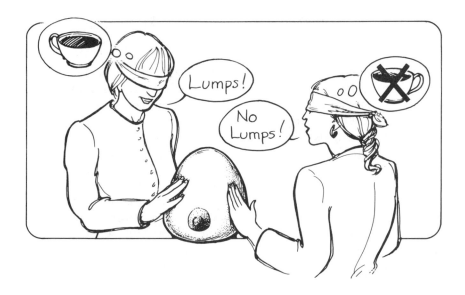

they had also done mammograms on all the subjects, as well as needle biopsies (see page 124), to determine if there was caffeine in the breast tissue. Neither of these tests showed any differences between caffeine consumers and nonconsumers.

The other circumstance clearly illustrates the extent to which even a trained medical professional can be misled by preconceptions. Unknown to the nurse or the researchers, several of the women in the caffeine-consuming group (who had not been told what it was they were testing) had heard that caffeine was linked to breast problems and had independently given it up. The nurse, who, of course, believed they were still taking caffeine, found that their lumpiness had gotten worse.

Another, more recent study shows both the lack of substantiation for the anticaffeine theories and the power that the belief that caffeine decreases breast symptoms can have on people. Dr. Sharon Allen,[7] in Minnesota, conducted a randomized and blinded study of caffeine and its possible connection to breast pain and lumpiness. She divided 56 women into three groups. One, the control group, was given no dietary advice, and the second, the experimental group, was put on a caffeine-free diet. A third group was asked to eliminate cholesterol from their diet: this group was added to see if a major change in the diet could, in and of itself, improve breast symptoms. At the beginning of the study patients were examined and their breasts were graded for lumpiness by one of three "blinded" examiners. In addition, they were asked to describe the amount and severity of their breast pain in a 5-item questionnaire, which was then scored. The women in all three groups were followed two months later and again four months later.

The study showed that decreasing caffeine had no effect on either the pain experienced by the patients or the lumpiness found by the examiners. The patients on the cholesterol-free diet likewise experienced no change in their breast symptoms.

Aside from suggesting that diet has no effect on breast pain or lumpiness, this study has another intriguing component. In the months following the study, the participants were telephoned and interviewed. They were asked if they had previously heard of a connection between caffeine and fibrocystic disease and whether they had decreased their caffeine intake on their own before the study. In addition, they were asked whether their pain had worsened after the study when they had resumed caffeine. Finally, the women in the study group were questioned about their recollection of the effect that decreasing caffeine had had on their symptoms. Seventy percent of the participants were reached, and, of these, 82 percent said they'd heard about the supposed link between caffeine and breast disease before the study. Fifty-three percent of those who had previously (average one and a half years before) decreased caffeine on their own reported a decrease in pain, tenderness, or lumpiness as a result. Of the 10 patients who had increased their caffeine intake after the study, three reported an increase in pain and tenderness. Most interestingly, of the 36 percent who did decrease their caffeine as part of the study, 25 percent reported they had experienced less pain, and 27 percent reported less lumpiness. This is in contrast to the objective data, which showed no change in patients' accounts of pain or examiners' accounts of lumpiness. In other words, retrospective self-reporting appears different in many respects from actual data. This may explain some of the discrepancies in other studies: those using patient recall may be less accurate and more prone to selective memory than those with objective measurements.

Other studies of the effect of caffeine have been done on women who had been biopsied and diagnosed as having fibrocystic disease. Their caffeine consumption was determined and compared to that of women in a control group with no breast complaints. If women who consumed caffeine were more likely to have biopsies, presumably this would mean they had more lumpiness. The study found that caffeine consumers were no more likely to need biopsies than non–coffee drinkers.

A study[8] done with rats—pretreated with caffeine and then injected with a carcinogen that usually gives rats cancer—showed that they actually got *less* breast cancer than those not given caffeine! The caffeine seemed to stabilize the cells, and kept them from responding to the carcinogens. (See page 147 for a description of how carcinogens work.) Rats, of course, aren't people, and we can't conclude from this that drinking coffee will keep you from getting breast cancer—but it doesn't help the caffeine-leads-to-fibrocystic-disease-leads-to-breast-cancer theories.

Neither does an epidemiological—number-based—study done in Israel.[9] There they looked at 854 women who had been diagnosed with histological (as seen under microscope) fibrocystic disease, and compared them to 755 women who had had surgery for some other reason and to 723 women who were living in the same neighborhood. Their intake of caffeine and all methylxanthines (a substance found in tea, chocolate, and other foods) was examined. No association between coffee or methylxanthine intake and benign breast disease was found. In a second study[10] of 818 newly diagnosed breast cancer patients, their intake of methylxanthines was compared to that of others in the same neighborhood and with the same surgical controls. They found, interestingly, that the coffee drinkers had a slightly lower incidence of breast cancer.

This study, too, has major limitations, since they didn't look into other aspects of the women's lives that might or might not affect cancer risk. But again, it offers no support to the idea that caffeine causes breast problems.

Vitamin E has also been put forth as a preventive for "fibrocystic disease," and thus, by extension, of breast cancer. Unfortunately, studies have shown this effect also to be chimerical. Dr. Abrams[11] in Boston first articulated the theory back in 1965. It was later popularized in 1978 by Dr. London[12] of Baltimore, but he abandoned it when his own tests—a double-blinded, randomized, controlled study[13]—showed vitamin E had no effect on breast symptoms. Though some studies have suggested that a low-fat diet may prevent breast cancer (see page 152), no evidence has in any way linked such a diet to the easing of benign breast symptoms.

Having said all this, let me add that individual women report that specific dietary changes have indeed lessened some of their breast symptoms—lumpy breasts, painful breasts, swelling, or all of these. I see no reason to doubt these women: they know what they're feeling. One of three possibilities—or a combination of them—are likely to cause the changes.

It also may be that the diet actually has caused the change. While our bodies are essentially similar, there is also large variation from person to person—and medicine doesn't always know what the variations are, or what causes them. Thus, it is quite possible that giving up coffee, for example, or taking vitamin E, or drinking herb tea, or any of an infinite number of dietary additions or subtractions, will ease your breast pain or lessen your lumpiness while the same thing is having no effect, or even a reverse effect, on your sister or your next-door neighbor.

Secondly, 54 percent of all benign breast conditions go away on their own after a while. If the condition vanishes after the woman has changed her diet, she may very reasonably attribute this to cause-and-effect.

Finally, there is the "placebo effect," which researchers have noted and named but rarely given the study it deserves. The placebo effect is what occurs when a person's belief that something will work actually makes it work. In other words, your belief that a particular substance, or withdrawal from a particular substance, will relieve your lumpiness or pain or swelling may, in itself, cause it to do so. (This is probably what happened in the follow-up in Dr. Allen's study.) This doesn't mean you're gullible or stupid or imagining things; it means that the mind affects the body in ways we don't yet fully understand, and that fortunately the body–mind interaction is working in your favor.

Fair-minded doctors will acknowledge the individual variations in patients' bodies and the placebo effect. It's very important that we all do take these things into consideration. Unfortunately, however, the placebo effect can also be used in a manipulative manner. Some doctors present patients with unproven data and tell them, or imply, that it *is* proven, in order to trigger a placebo effect. An honest statement about the effects of caffeine might be as follows: "Some women have found that reducing caffeine in their diets has helped alleviate their breast symptoms. We have no medical evidence to back it up, but it works for them and you might want to try it for a while and see if it helps you." Unfortunately, too often that's not what doctors say; instead, they tell you that you have fibrocystic disease and that it's caused by caffeine, so you have to give it up.

When they're challenged on this, many doctors will admit there's no evidence, but still defend their actions. Coffee, they reason, isn't good for you anyway, and it's easy to give up, and it makes you feel better to be given a diagnosis and a "cure." This is extremely insulting to an adult woman, who is entitled to honesty from her doctor, and it also ignores the social importance of caffeine in our culture. For many people, giving up caffeine is a hardship: they give up not only coffee but tea, cola, and chocolate. These may or may not be socially or emotionally important to them. To give them up because you've thought about it and decided, based on accurate information, that it's worth it for you is fine. But you shouldn't give them up because of your doctor's prejudices, presented as medical fact. Giving a patient a nonexistent cure for a nonexistent disease is hardly in her best interest.

When the College of American Pathologists issued their statement admitting that "fibrocystic disease" didn't cause cancer, they suggested altering their terminology by substituting "fibrocystic condition" or "fibrocystic change." Neither term helps much: a "condition" still sounds like a disease, while a "change" suggests it was something else before. And we still end up with a catch-all term. I have similar objections to other terms that have been used over the years: chronic mastitis, chronic cystic mastitis, cystic disease. They're all useless at best, misleading and frightening at worst.

If we throw away these terms, how can we classify the various symptoms? It might be useful, for a start, to look to European medicine. In Europe, they've kept the term "fibrocystic disease," but only to define one specific symptom—lumpy breasts. They call breast pain *mastalgia*, a sensible enough term, since "mast" is Latin for breast and "algia" for pain. By separating out the different symptoms, they allow each symptom to be studied on its own—a vast improvement.

We can also look to our own history. In the late 19th and early 20th centuries, there was no "fibrocystic disease"; there were simply symptoms: you had breast pain, or lumpiness, or nipple discharge. It was only later that the silly term came into existence and became the wastebasket into which everything that wasn't cancer got thrown. I suggest dropping the term "fibrocystic disease" altogether, and replacing it with the following six categories:

1. Normal physiological changes, such as the minor tenderness and swelling and lumpiness most women experience during or before their periods
2. Mastalgia, which is severe breast pain, cyclical or noncyclical, that interferes with the patient's normal life
3. Infections and inflammations
4. Discharge and other nipple problems
5. Lumpiness or nodularity, which is a general lumpiness beyond the amount most women have
6. Dominant lumps, such as cysts and fibroadenomas

The next few chapters will discuss these symptoms, and their treatments, in detail.

7

<hr>
<hr>
<hr>

Breast Pain

If you don't have fibrocystic disease, what do you have? This and the next two chapters will discuss the various kinds of benign breast conditions.

One common breast symptom is pain—frequently called mastalgia, or *mastodynia* (one's Latin, the other's Greek, and they both translate to "breast pain"). The medical approach to breast pain has been somewhat contradictory. On the one hand, its reality is acknowledged as part of the conglomeration of "fibrocystic disease" symptoms. On the other hand, its reality is denied, as menstrual pain was denied 10 years ago. It's "psychosomatic"; it's all in our heads.

So prevalent has this belief been that in 1979, Dr. Preece,[1] in Cardiff, Wales, as part of a larger study of breast pain, did a study measuring the degree of neurosis in female patients in three of the hospital's clinics: the breast pain clinic, the psychiatric clinic, and the varicose vein clinic. To the surprise of the doctors, who expected to find the breast pain sufferers highly neurotic, the breast pain and varicose vein patients showed the same degree of neurosis, which was significantly lower than that of the psychiatric patients. It seems like an awful lot of time, energy, and expense to find out what any woman could readily have told them, but the study did give validation to what we've known all along—many women experience breast pain that's as real as a bellyache or a broken arm. And it runs the gamut of discomfort—from a minor irritation a couple of days a month through permanent, nearly disabling agony, and everything in between.

Unfortunately, studies of breast pain itself have been few and far between—chiefly because of the dual misconceptions about it. The people who call it fibrocystic disease think it's already been covered, so what need is there to do more research? And the people who think it doesn't exist aren't about to explore its causes, except in psychiatric terms—which won't say much about a physical reality. So we know very little about what creates breast pain and thus how to treat it.

The failure to acknowledge breast pain is a relatively recent phenomenon. Literature from the 1850s[2] describes "pain syndrome" as something distinct from "cystic disease," their term for lumpiness (see page 110). But by the 1940s,[3] the literature that mentions breast pain treats it as interconnected with lumpiness. In the United States it has been believed that lumpiness causes breast pain,[4] while in Europe, it's believed that breast pain eventually *leads* to lumpiness.[5]

Actually, there is no evidence of relationship at all. Some women have breast pain and never have lumpiness; some have lumpiness and never have breast pain, and some experience both. Dr. J.W. Ayres of Chicago took 15 fertile women who complained of mastalgia and 15 fertile women with no breast pain complaints and studied their breasts and their hormonal levels.[6] First he did ultrasound examinations of their breasts to try and quantify the degree of lumpiness. To his surprise, he found that the degree of lumpiness shown on the ultrasound had no connection to the amount of pain the woman was experiencing. About half of the women with mastalgia showed lumpiness on ultrasound and half did not, while half of the asymptomatic women had lumpiness on ultrasound and half did not. He concluded that lumpiness and pain were two distinct problems.

The Welsh clinic in Cardiff that conducted the study mentioned earlier in this chapter has documented three main categories of breast pain: cyclical (pain related to the menstrual cycle), noncyclical ("target-zone" pain), and pain that is nonbreast in origin. Of these, the most common by far is cyclical.[7]

Cyclical Pain

We know that cyclical mastalgia is related to hormonal variations. The breasts are sensitive right before menstruation, then less sensitive once the period begins. For some women tenderness begins at the time of ovulation and continues until their period, leaving only a couple of pain-free weeks during their cycles. Sometimes it's barely noticeable, but some women are in such pain they can't wear a T-shirt, lie on their stomachs, or tolerate hugs. Sometimes it's only in one breast, and other times it radiates into the armpit, and even down to the elbows, causing its poor victim to think she's got cancer spreading to her lymph nodes.

Understanding precisely the part hormones play in cyclical mastalgia is clouded by the fact that women's hormonal cycles haven't themselves been all that well researched. Although we know roughly how the levels of estrogen and progesterone go up and down during each cycle and that FSH and LH are the main pituitary hormones, we don't yet understand the "fine tuning" of these hormones, and how the hormones regulate and affect the different parts of the body. Just as we don't understand menstrual cramps and bloating and PMS, we don't understand breast pain.

Some studies in Europe have given us preliminary clues to the role of hormones in breast pain. Dr. Mauvais-Jarvis[8] in France has shown that the amount of progesterone put out by the ovary in the second half of the menstrual cycle seems to vary in patients with breast pain: he found a decreased ratio of progesterone to estrogen in patients with mastalgia. Other investigators (Watt-Boolsen[9] and Kumar[10]) have found that an abnormality in the regulation of prolactin seems to affect breast pain. Although prolactin blood levels in the subjects of these studies appear to be normal, these women are much more sensitive to stimulation with thyroid-stimulating hormone: they are "hyperreactive." Dr. Ayres's study, mentioned earlier, confirmed both of these hormonal abnormalities. He found that the patients with mastalgia had a lower progesterone to estrogen ratio, as well as a hyperreactiveness in the regulation of prolactin, while the women in the control group did not. Predictably, the lumpiness demonstrated on ultrasound did not relate to the hormonal aberrations—only pain did.

Hormones may also affect cyclical breast pain in a more subtle way, as a result of stress, for example. We know that stress can affect the menstrual cycle: you can miss your period, or have a particularly heavy period, or an early or late period, when you're under a great deal of stress, positive or negative. Similarly, your breast pain can increase or change in its pattern with the hormone changes of stress. We also know that hormones vary at different points in your life and that the incidence of breast pain often follows these shifts. It's usually most intense in the teens and then again in the 40s—at both ends of the fertile years. It almost always ends with menopause, though, in some rare cases, it lasts beyond menopause—perhaps because of the continuing estrogen production of the adrenals (see page 19). And, of course, if a postmenopausal woman is taking hormones, her body thinks she's still premenopausal and she's as likely to get breast pain as she was before. We also know it's common in pregnant women; indeed, unusual breast pain can be an early sign of pregnancy.

The relation to hormones doesn't appear to be absolute—there must be other factors, since most often the pain is more severe in one breast than in the other, and a purely hormonal symptom would have to affect both equally. It appears to be caused by a combination of the hormonal activity and something in the breast tissue that responds to that activity. More research clearly needs to be done; I hope my own current work will contribute to our understanding of cyclical mastalgia.

Breast pain is annoying, but it usually isn't unbearable—what *can* be unbearable is the fear that it's cancer. The best "treatment," therefore, is reassurance. The study in Cardiff suggests that 85 percent of women with breast pain are worried much more about the possibility of cancer than about the pain itself. Most of them, when reassured that their problem has no relation to cancer, are relieved, and feel they can live with their pain. Only 15 percent of the women have pain that's incapacitating and needs treatment.

The treatments of cyclical breast pain that have been proposed are many and varied, but unfortunately none of them works very well. In the last chapter, I discussed the specious "fibrocystic disease" remedies, such as eliminating caffeine or taking vitamin E. Since some physicians believe that the pain comes from water retention, they have recommended diuretics ("water pills"). These also have given little relief. Others have tried everything from ginseng tea, vitamin A, vitamin B complex, iodine, to just a firm support bra. A group of doctors in Wales[11] have recommended Evening Primrose Oil (a naturally occurring triglyceride), which, taken on a regular schedule, will relieve cyclical mastalgia in 20 percent of women.

All these therapies are interesting, but if cyclical mastalgia is a hormonal problem it makes more sense that the treatment be hormonal. Various hormones or hormone blockers have been tried and several have had some good results. All have side effects, however, and as usual you have to weigh carefully the risks and benefits of any treatment you are about to undergo. (See Figure 7-1 for an explanation of where the treatments described have their effects.)

One hormonal treatment that has been helpful to some women is birth control pills. They stabilize the amount of hormone each month, unlike the ovaries, which vary the hormone amount. I recommend it for patients in their early 20s who are planning to use a contracep-

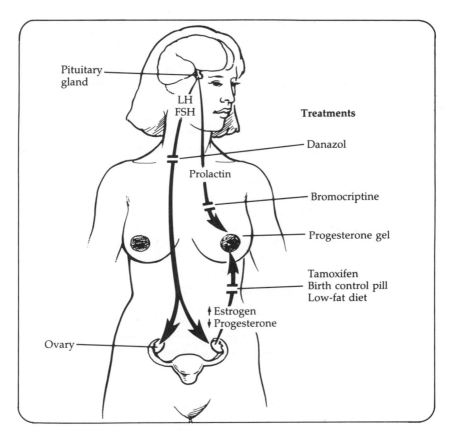

FIGURE 7-1

tive measure anyway, since the pill is actually the safest form of contraception for that age group, especially among nonsmokers. This holds true in spite of recent reports that it may slightly increase your risk of cancer.[12] (See page 163 for a discussion of this risk.)

Other hormones have been tried. In England, bromocriptine has been used, which blocks prolactin in the hypothalamus.[13] This helps around 30 to 40 percent of women who've tried it, but it has some bad side effects, and shouldn't be used for any length of time. Right now it's more useful as a research tool to help us understand the causes of breast pain. Danazol[14] has the greatest effect on breast pain, but it's a male hormone; you may get hair on your chin, your voice may get lower, and you will probably stop getting your period. It also costs $200 a month. So unless you're seriously incapacitated by pain (and well-insured or rich), it's not very appropriate.

Some investigators feel thyroid hormones[15] can help, since they're related to prolactin. But there are no good controlled studies at this time. Tamoxifen is an estrogen blocker (see page 324). According to an English study,[16] it's very good at relieving mastalgia. We don't know its long-term effects on premenopausal women. However, it brings on a chemical menopause and therefore may affect osteoporosis and heart disease. All four of the above treatments have serious enough side effects or potential side effects to suggest caution and to make them inappropriate for all but severe breast pain.

There are two treatments that are the most promising, and both relate to progesterone. Dr. Mauvais-Jarvis and his group, in line with their theory that mastalgia results from a decrease in progesterone compared to estrogen in the second half of the cycle, have been working on ways to increase progesterone.[17] Taking progesterone by mouth doesn't work because it's broken down in the liver before it gets to the bloodstream and thus the breast tissue. What's needed is a way of increasing the level of progesterone in the breast without also increasing it in the rest of the body and causing side effects. This French group has been working with a progesterone gel that can be rubbed onto the breast so that it's absorbed into the breast tissue, thus evening out the imbalance of estrogen and progesterone and easing the pain that results from it. They claim the gel works 95 percent of the time but they haven't published any good randomized controlled studies to document this. (The gel is an over-the-counter item in France, but it's not available in this country except on an experimental basis. I'm in the process of trying to study the gel here to see if it indeed has any merit.)

The second, an even more benign remedy, is a low-fat diet, which has been studied and shown to have some effect on cyclical mastalgia and hormone levels.[18, 19]

By now you're probably confused: all these experiments sound interesting, but you're in pain now, and possible future treatments don't do much good. What *can* you do in the present for your cyclical breast pain? First, get a good examination from a breast specialist, or someone knowledgeable in the field who will take your symptoms and concerns seriously (this may take some searching). If you are over 35, have a mammogram. Once you know you don't have cancer you can decide if you are able to live with your discomfort or if you want to explore treatment further. The studies on low-fat diet seem promising, and such a treatment won't have undesirable side effects, so you might want to try that; it gives you the possible additional benefit of decreasing your breast cancer risk (see page 152). In Appendix B I've listed some recommendations for a low-fat diet.

Another possibility is the use of meditation and visualization techniques, such as those discussed on page 332. A number of studies have shown that these techniques can be effective in reducing pain, and they may well help relieve both cyclical and noncyclical breast pain.

If you are in your 20s you may want to try the pill. You may also want to try Evening Primrose Oil (found in health-food stores), but keep in mind that it isn't safe to take if you're trying to get pregnant, or are pregnant, since it causes miscarriages. Analgesics like aspirin, Tylenol, and ibuprofen can offer some relief, and wearing a firm bra will at least prevent bouncing breasts from increasing your discomfort. If none of these helps you might ask to try Danazol.

Eventually, we will be able to invent something as specific for breast pain as some of the anti-inflammatory drugs are for menstrual cramps, and women will no longer have to suffer from it.

Noncyclical Pain

Noncyclical pain is far less common than cyclical pain. It also feels a lot different. To begin with, it doesn't vary with your menstrual cycle—it's there, and it stays there. It's also known as "target-zone breast pain," because it's almost always in one specific area: you can point exactly to where it hurts. It's anatomical rather than hormonal—something in the breast tissue is causing it (although we usually don't know what). Very rarely, it can be a sign of cancer, so it's always worth checking out with your doctor.

One cause of noncyclical breast pain is trauma—a blow to the breast will obviously cause it to hurt, and any breast biopsy is likely to leave some pain (see page 132). Many women get slight shooting or stabbing pains up to two years or more after a biopsy. And you're never quite perfect after any surgery—just as after breaking a leg you can always tell when it will rain. This kind of pain is usually pretty obvious: it's on the spot where your scar is. It's unpleasant, but it's nothing to worry about.

Often, we simply don't know what causes noncyclical breast pain: we'll operate and remove the area, have the tissue studied, and find nothing abnormal.

The treatment for this kind of breast pain is more difficult than that for cyclical breast pain. Again, you must start with a good exam, and, if you're over 35, a mammogram. If there's any obvious abnormality, it can then be taken care of. For example, sometimes a gross cyst (see page 111) will cause localized breast pain or tenderness and can be cured with aspiration.

Hormonal treatments are less likely to work in these patients, since noncyclical pain is rarely caused by hormones. Some women, however, will find relief with the other kinds of treatments mentioned under cyclical mastalgia,[20] and you may want to try them. Sometimes (though not invariably) having a biopsy of the area done will relieve the pain—though, of course, it will add the pain of the biopsy itself. A good test is for your doctor to inject some local anesthesia into the spot: if it gives relief, then surgery may well work; if not, then it probably isn't worth it.

The best treatment is probably a good exam and a negative mammogram with the reassurance that goes with it. This, of course, does nothing to relieve your pain, but it *does* relieve what's usually much worse than the pain—the fear that you have cancer.

Non-Breast-Origin Pain

This third category isn't really a form of breast pain, though that's what it feels like to the patient. It's usually in the middle of the chest, and doesn't change with your period. Most frequently, it's arthritic pain, in the place where the ribs and breastbone connect—an arthritis called *costochondritis*.[21] (See Figure 7-2.) When men get costochondritis, they think it's a heart attack; when women get it, they think it's breast cancer. You can tell it's arthritis by pushing down on your breastbone where your ribs are—if it hurts a lot more, that's probably what you've got. Similarly, if you take a deep breath and the middle

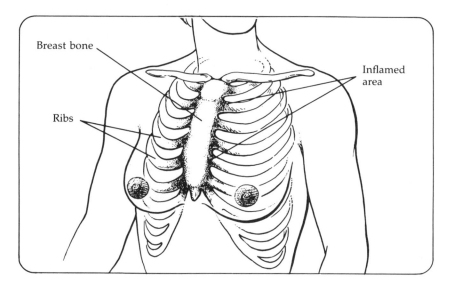

FIGURE 7-2

part of your breast hurts, it's probably arthritis. If you take aspirin or an anti-inflammatory agent and it relieves the pain, it's probably arthritis, since they work especially effectively on conditions like arthritis.

You can also get non-breast-origin pain from arthritis in the neck (a pinched nerve),[22] which can radiate down into the breast the way lower-back arthritis goes into the legs. There's also a special kind of phlebitis (inflamed vein) that can occur in the breast, called *Mondor's syndrome*. It gives you a drawing sensation around the outer edge of your breast that extends down into your abdomen. Sometimes you can even feel a kind of cord where it is most tender. None of these problems are serious. When a non-breast condition appears in the breast area, it's treated as it would be in any other part of the body. That usually means, for the conditions just mentioned, aspirin or another anti-inflammatory agent. These pains are usually self-limited and will go away in time.

Cancer Concerns

How likely are any of these forms of breast pain to be cancer? Cyclical pain never has any relation to cancer at all, so don't worry. Non-cyclical pain is rarely a sign of cancer, but it can be, so it's worth checking out. One of my patients discovered while she was traveling in Europe that her breast hurt when she lay on her stomach; though she couldn't feel any lump, she had it checked when she came home and discovered she did indeed have a very tiny cancer on the spot. About 10 percent of all target-zone breast pain is cancer. Non-breast-origin pain, as I said before, is probably arthritis, and you can confirm this by the methods I suggested. If you're still in doubt, have it checked by your doctor.

8

Breast Infections and Nipple Problems

Breast infections and nipple discharge are other symptoms often misdiagnosed as fibrocystic disease or its equally invalid synonym, cystic mastitis (see Chapter 6). They're fairly uncommon, and usually not much more than a nuisance, but can cause much anxiety to the woman who experiences them.

Breast Infections

There are two major categories of breast infection: intrinsic and extrinsic. Intrinsic breast infections—those occurring only to the breast itself—break down into three categories: lactational mastitis, nonlactational mastitis, and chronic subareolar abscess.

LACTATIONAL MASTITIS

Lactational mastitis is the most common of these infections.[1] It occurs, as its name suggests, when the woman is breastfeeding. The breast is filled with milk, a medium that encourages the growth of bacteria. You've got a baby biting and sucking on your breast on a

regular basis, causing cracks in the skin and introducing bacteria—
it's really amazing that more nursing mothers *don't* get infections.
Probably it happens as seldom as it does because the milk is always
flowing through and flushing the bacteria out. However, sometimes
when you're breastfeeding, a duct will get blocked up with thick
milk that doesn't flow very well. Then it's a setup for infection: the
bacteria is trapped in the breast, the milk helps it grow, and suddenly
you've got a reddened, hot, and very painful breast. (See Figure
8-1.)

Your doctor will probably initially suggest that you try to unblock
the duct with massage and warm soaks; sometimes they'll suggest
heat (which liquifies the milk for better flow, but unfortunately increases metabolic rate of breast tissue and thus accelerates the bacteria's growth) or ice packs (which slow the bacteria's growth rate
but unfortunately hardens the milk). If the infection persists, antibiotics are the next step. Usually that will take care of it. Don't worry
about the antibiotics affecting your nursing child: your obstetrician
will know which antibiotics are safe for children to ingest, and will
be careful about which are given to you. Nor will the bacteria hurt
the child; since it's going into the gastrointestinal system, the bacteria
will be killed by the baby's stomach acid. And it's actually good for

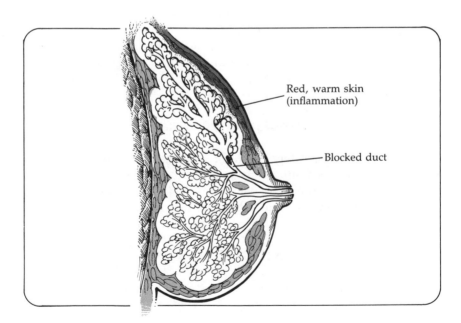

Red, warm skin
(inflammation)

Blocked duct

FIGURE 8-1

you if the child goes on nursing: the sucking helps keep the duct unblocked.

Antibiotics will almost always get rid of the infection, but in about 10 percent of cases, an abscess forms, and antibiotics are useless in eliminating abscesses. An abscess, like a boil, is basically a collection of pus, and the doctor has to drain the pus. If it's an extremely small abscess, the pus can be aspirated with a needle. If it's bigger, the doctor will have to make an incision large enough to allow the pus to drain. (See Figure 8-2.) This can be done under local anesthetic, but it's difficult, because the inflamed tissue is highly sensitive and it's hard to inject an anesthetic that will really numb the area well. If it's an extremely small infected area, I'll tell my patient to bite the bullet, the pain will soon be over—and go with the local. But if it's a large area, I find it far more effective to put the patient to sleep. (See page 279 for a discussion of general anesthetic.)

Once the cut is made, the pus drains out and the pain abates quickly. The surgeon will never sew up a drained abscess; that would lock the bacteria into the abscess, and almost insure the infection's return. I tell my patients to go home and rest, then, after 24 hours, begin taking daily showers; let the water run over the breast and

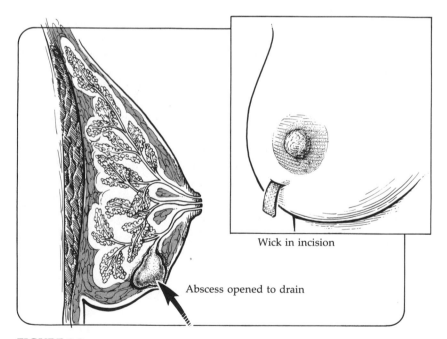

Wick in incision

Abscess opened to drain

FIGURE 8-2

wash away the bacteria, and then put a dressing over it to absorb oozing fluids from the incision. Some surgeons will put a wick, or a drain, in the corner of the incision in order to keep it open; that way, it heals from the inside out, and closes within a week or two.

Some surgeons will tell you that if you need an operation, you have to stop breastfeeding. Many women really want to breastfeed, and there's no reason they should give it up. It *is* messy, since not only are you oozing fluids, you're also oozing milk. But if you're willing to put up with the mess, there's no reason not to breastfeed. It's usually just one breast, and just a segment of the breast at that; there's plenty of room for your baby to suckle.

NONLACTATIONAL MASTITIS

Though the kind of mastitis described above is usually only found in lactating women, it can sometimes occur in nonlactating women, especially in particular circumstances. For example, it may occur in women who've had lumpectomies followed by radiation, in diabetics, or in women whose immune system is otherwise depressed: such women are prone to infections, either because some of the lymph nodes, which help fight infection, have been removed, or because their immune systems are generally less strong than those of most people. This type of infection will usually be *cellulitis*—an infection of the skin—red, hot, and swollen all over rather than just on one spot. It's generally accompanied by high fever and headache: both characteristics of a strep infection (staph infections, by contrast, are usually local). It will be treated by your doctor with antibiotics, usually penicillin, and you may be briefly hospitalized.

Skin boils (or staph infections) can form on the breast, as they can on other parts of the body. If you're a carrier of staph and prone to infection as well—as in the case of diabetics—this is more likely to occur than in noncarriers or people less infection-prone. It's also possible to get an abscess in the breast when you're not lactating and don't have any of the other risk factors, although this is unusual. Both cellulitis and these abscesses can mask cancer (as we'll discuss below), so, though such cancer is rare, if you've got one of these conditions, it's important to have it checked out by a doctor.

CHRONIC SUBAREOLAR ABSCESS

The second most common breast infection—and it's pretty infrequent—is the chronic subareolar abscess. We really don't understand it well, but we're getting some insights from Dr. Bruce Derrick,[2] at Temple University in Philadelphia, and Dr. Otto Sartorius[3] in Santa Barbara.

Until recently, this infection was believed to be a blocked duct. The nipple has about 15 to 20 little holes around it, and we've always believed these holes were all ducts. But Dr. Sartorius has shown that they're *not* all ducts; only about half of them are. The others are little glands that make a sebaceous material; it's a white, oily, cheesy substance, like that you find in a whitehead pimple. These little glands are found all over the body. We don't know what they're for, or why there are so many around the nipple. My own theory is that the body produces them to provide a coating and protection for the skin—sort of your own little skin-care system. The nipple, designed to be sucked on, is especially vulnerable to getting chapped and sore, so it makes sense that it would have a lot of these glands.

Whatever their function, these little, dead-ended glands can get infections, whether you're nursing or not. Bacteria from the skin or mouth of your child or lover gets into the gland; thickened secretions block it so it can't drain well, and it gets infected. This kind of infection is most common in women with inverted nipples, because their glands have narrower openings.

When this infection occurs, an abscess can form, which can't drain through the usual exit, and therefore tries to drain through the weakest part of the skin in the area—the border of the areola and the regular skin. (See Figure 8-3.) The abscess is a red, hot, and sore area on part of the border of the nipple—like a boil. It looks and feels fairly awful, and the frightened woman often thinks she's got breast cancer. She doesn't, and the infection doesn't affect her vulnerability to breast cancer.

If the infection is caught very early, before an abscess forms, it can be helped by antibiotics, but often it can't be; it needs an incision and draining. Like the lactational abscess described above, it can be drained under local anesthetic or general anesthesia. I prefer to do the incision on the border of the areola, so that it doesn't show later. Once the pus is drained, it's okay—for the time being. The trouble is that this type of infection tends to recur. The gland is a little blind tract, with no internal opening, so it tends to reinfect itself and drain again at the same point. Eventually this leaves a permanent open tract.

We've had some luck reducing these recurrences by removing the entire gland or tract, but it hasn't been as successful as we'd like. And it's a surgical procedure—you have to remove a tiny wedge of nipple to get the tract out.

Since the gland is small and the surgery is relatively minor, I used

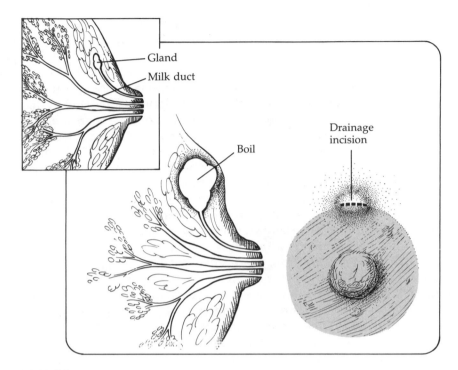

Gland
Milk duct
Boil
Drainage incision

FIGURE 8-3

to do it under local anesthetic. But it's hard to get a chronically infected area thoroughly numb, especially as sensitive an area as the nipple—the same problem we faced above in lactational mastitis, only more severe. So I found that in my anxiousness to end my patient's discomfort, I sometimes didn't get the whole gland out, and the infection would often recur.

Now I tend to put people under general anesthetic and give them antibiotics before the operation. I pass a probe through the tract and then take it out, including both openings. This requires removing a wedge of nipple. (See Figure 8-4.) The nipple is then closed and sewn up. There's some controversy about whether or not to close the incision: some doctors are afraid that if there's lots of bacteria to begin with there's a greater chance that the gland will reinfect itself if it's closed off; others are more concerned with the cosmetic loss if the nipple is left with a hole in it. I prefer to close it, but I always tell my patient the pros and cons of both, and then do what she wants.

Unfortunately, even in the best-done operations, the problem often recurs.[4] Perhaps the infection spreads from one gland to an-

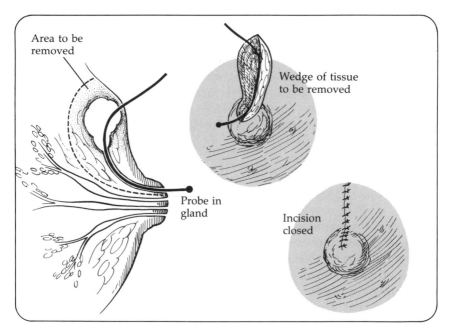

Area to be removed

Wedge of tissue to be removed

Probe in gland

Incision closed

FIGURE 8-4

other, or perhaps there's still lining left from the old gland that the surgeon isn't aware of.

So if you have a chronic subareolar abscess, it's well worth trying to have it taken care of. But you have to understand that you might have to keep dealing with it. About 40 percent of these infections do recur, sometimes as often as every few months.

As so often happens with women's bodies, there are many doctors who think disfiguring surgery is called for. One patient came to me after her doctor said he was fed up with these recurrences and wanted to remove both breasts. Fortunately, she had the sense not to listen to him. A well-planned, nonmutilating operation solved her problem—but even if it hadn't, the most drastic procedure that would have made any sense at all would have been to remove the nipple and leave the breast—then at least a plastic surgeon could reconstruct a new nipple, leaving the breast intact. (See page 52.)

But if you have this condition, it's really unlikely that you'd want even that done. The condition is unpleasant and a nuisance, but it's not life-threatening. It doesn't interfere with breastfeeding, nor should it restrict your sexual life, except insofar as you're obviously not likely to want your nipple touched while it's hurting from the infection.

Extrinsic Infections

Extrinsic breast infections are those that involve the whole body and show first on the breast. These are extremely rare, especially in this country, so I'll mention them only briefly. Tuberculosis and syphilis have both been known to emerge first on the breast; such an infection would be treated the same way the disease would be treated if it showed anywhere else.

Infection and Cancer

As I said earlier, breast infections never lead to breast cancer. However, some breast cancers lead to infections, or can look like infections (see page 269): as the cancer grows, some cancer cells die off for lack of blood supply, and the necrotic (dead) tissue can get infected. So it's possible for a breast cancer to show up first as a breast abscess. It's extremely unusual; I haven't seen it in my years as a breast specialist.

If you get an infection, don't worry about it—but do see your doctor right away. The infection won't give you cancer, but it should be treated and gotten rid of, and you do want to make sure it *is* an infection.

Nipple Problems

DISCHARGE

The nipple is an especially sensitive area, and it's subject to a number of problems, such as the subareolar abscess just discussed. The most common nipple problem—or rather concern, since it's not always a problem—is discharge. Its significance has been exaggerated by the public and by the medical profession as well. The American Cancer Society, for example, says that if you have any nipple discharge you should go to your doctor immediately. Those movies that show you how to do breast self-exam (see page 24) always show the woman squeezing her nipple to find out if there's any discharge. And a lot of internists and gynecologists will squeeze your nipple to see if there's discharge.

It's a pointless and self-defeating exercise. Most women *do* have some amount of discharge when their breasts are squeezed, and it's perfectly normal. A study at Boston Lying-In Hospital breast clinic was conducted,[5] in which women had little suction cups, like breast pumps, put on their nipples and gentle suction applied. Eighty-three percent of these women—old, young, mothers, non-mothers, previously pregnant, and never pregnant—had some amount of discharge. Yet women are continually encouraged to be frightened by breast discharge.

The typical scenario is this: a woman is bathing and washing her breasts, or her lover is squeezing her breast, and she discovers a little bit of discharge, produced by the pressure on her breasts. Alarmed, she squeezes the nipple to see if there's something in there—and more discharge comes out. What she doesn't realize is that the very act of squeezing the nipples *creates* more discharge, because it increases prolactin. Prolactin, as we discussed on page 32, is the hormone in the brain that stimulates the breast of a lactating woman to produce milk; the sucking of the infant is what usually announces to the brain that it's time to send in the prolactin; we need more milk here. So when you squeeze your breasts you're telling your brain to please produce some liquid for the breasts, and the brain obliges. (See Figure 8-5.) So the discharge increases, and the poor woman is convinced she's not only got cancer, but a terrible, advanced cancer at that. She runs to her doctor in a state of terror. I've had women come in with breasts they've bruised and battered, after wringing them out in a desperate attempt to find out how bad their "cancer" really is. Often by this point the discharge is bloody, and no wonder—they've beaten their poor nipples to a pulp.

It's a pity, because most discharge is nothing to be alarmed about. The kinds that are have very specific characteristics, which I'll discuss below. The ducts of the nipple are pipelines; they're made to carry milk to the nipple. The fact that there's a little fluid in the pipes shouldn't be surprising. (This fluid may come in a number of colors—gray, green, or brown, as well as white.)

Sometimes people can confuse nipple discharge with other problems—weepy sores, infections, abscesses (see above). Inverted nipples (see page 52) can sometimes get dirt and dried-up sweat trapped in them, and this can be confused with discharge.

Some women are more prone to lots of discharge than others: women on birth control pills, on antihypertensives such as Aldomet, or on major tranquilizers such as Thorazine, tend to notice more discharge, because these medications increase prolactin levels. It may seem aesthetically displeasing, but beyond that there's nothing to worry about.

There are also different life periods when you're more likely to get discharge. There's more discharge at puberty and at menopause than between them. Newborn babies often have a little discharge, called

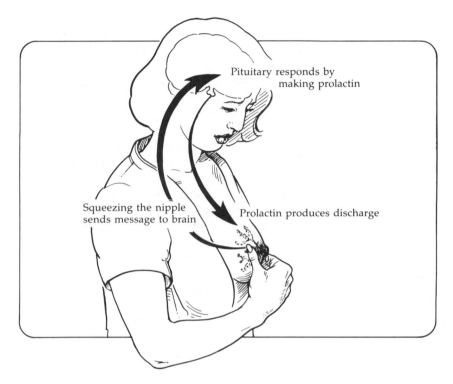

Pituitary responds by making prolactin

Squeezing the nipple sends message to brain

Prolactin produces discharge

FIGURE 8-5

"witches' milk." This makes sense, since the discharge is a result of hormonal processes.

WHEN SHOULD YOU WORRY?

The time to worry about nipple discharge is when it's spontaneous, persistent, and unilateral (only on one side). It comes out by itself without squeezing; it keeps on happening; and it's only from one nipple and usually one duct. It's either clear and sticky, like an egg white, or bloody. You should go to the doctor right away. There are several possible causes:

1. *Intraductal papilloma.* This is a little wartlike growth on the lining of the duct. It gets eroded and bleeds, creating a bloody discharge. It's benign; we remove it to make sure that's what it is.
2. *Intraductal papillomatosis.* Instead of one wart, you've got a lot of little warts.

3. *Intraductal carcinoma in situ.* This is a precancer that clogs up the duct like rust: it's discussed in detail on page 198.
4. *Cancer.* Cancers are rarely the cause of discharge. Only about 4 percent of all spontaneous unilateral bloody discharges are cancerous.

The doctor will first test for blood by taking a sample, putting it on a card, and adding a chemical called guaiac. If it turns blue, there's blood (which may not be visible to the eye alone, because of the color of the discharge itself). He or she may then do a Pap smear, very like the Pap smear you get to test for cervical cancer. Discharge is put on a glass slide and sent to the lab for the cells to be examined. Though this is far from 100 percent accurate, it may help to determine if there are abnormal cells.

Next, the doctor will try and figure out the "target zone," by going around the breast to find out which duct the discharge is coming from, though often the woman herself can give the doctor this information. If you're over 30 you'll be sent for a mammogram to see if there's a tumor underneath the duct.

You can then be given a ductogram—a tool I find increasingly useful. The radiologist takes a very fine plastic catheter and, with a magnifying glass, threads it into the duct, squirts dye into it, and takes a picture. (See Figure 8-6.) The procedure sounds uncomfortable, but it really isn't that bad—the duct is an open tube already, and the discharge has dilated it. The ductogram provides a "map" for the surgeon who will do the biopsy, and may also show the

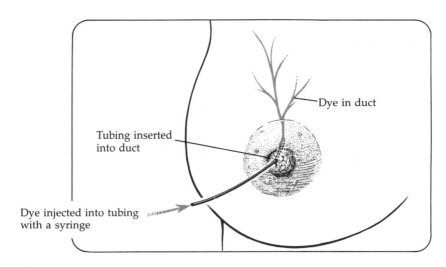

FIGURE 8-6

source of the discharge. Not all surgeons order a ductogram, but I find it extremely useful.

The biopsy itself is fairly simple; it's a specialized form of the regular breast biopsy (see page 125). It can be done under local anesthetic, and on an outpatient basis. A tiny incision is made at the edge of the areola; the areola is flipped up, and the blood-filled duct located and removed. (See Figure 8-7.) Sometimes we will have the radiologist cut a fine suture and pass it into the duct to the point to be removed, or blue dye can be injected into the duct to help identify it. Both of these techniques will help the surgeon to pinpoint the right area.

If you're past your childbearing years, or if you're certain you won't want to breastfeed, the surgeon may remove all the ducts instead of just the one, to make sure the involved one isn't missed. Even if they're not all removed, the ducts are so close to each other that the removal of one can cause scarring that will interfere with future breastfeeding, though you may still be able to nurse from your other breast.

Another form of problematic discharge is one that is spontaneous, bilateral (on both sides), and milky. If you're not breastfeeding, and haven't been in the past year, this is probably a condition called *galactorrhea*. It occurs because something is increasing the prolactin levels—sometimes a small tumor in the brain. This may not be as

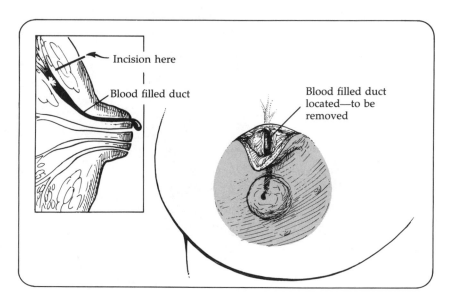

FIGURE 8-7

alarming as it sounds: often it's a tiny tumor which may not require surgery. A neurosurgeon and an endocrinologist together need to check this out. Sometimes you can be given bromocriptine to block the prolactin. Galactorrhea is often associated with *amenorrhea*—failure to get your period. It can also be caused by major tranquilizers, marijuana consumption, or high estrogen doses.

Galactorrhea is only diagnosed when the discharge is bilateral. Many doctors don't understand this, and send patients with *any* discharge for prolactin level tests. They shouldn't; the unilateral discharges are not associated with hormonal problems. Unilateral spontaneous discharge is anatomical, not hormonal, and the money spent on prolactin tests is wasted.

OTHER NIPPLE PROBLEMS

Discharge is the most common nipple problem women experience, but there are a few others as well. Some patients complain of itchy nipples. Usually itchy nipples don't indicate severe problems, especially if both nipples itch. You can get dry skin on your nipples, as elsewhere. You may be allergic to your bra, or to the detergent it's washed in. And, of course, pubescent girls with growing breasts often experience itching as the skin stretches itself. Otherwise, we don't know what causes itchy nipples—but they're not usually a problem. If they bother you, you can use calamine lotion or other anti-itch medication.

There is a form of cancer known as Paget's disease which doctors and patients often confuse with eczema of the nipple. It looks like an open sore area, and it itches. If it's only on one nipple, and it doesn't go away with standard eczema treatments, check it out. A biopsy can be performed on a small section of the nipple. (Paget's disease is discussed at length on page 272.)

If the rash is on both nipples and you tend to get eczema anyway, don't worry. Anything that can happen to other parts of the skin can happen to the nipple.

Most of these various infections and irritations are benign—they're more of a nuisance than anything else. If they appear, get them checked out, just to make sure they're what they appear to be, and to get the relief available.

9

Lumps and
Lumpiness

To begin with, you need to remember that lumpiness, as I discussed on page 11, isn't the same as having one dominant lump. It's a general pattern of many little lumps, in both breasts, and it's perfectly normal. The distinction between "lumps" and "lumpiness" is an important one; the confusion of the two can cause a woman days and weeks of needless mental anguish. Lumpiness is not a disease— "fibrocystic" or otherwise. It's simply normal breast tissue.

Patients aren't the only ones who get lumpiness and lumps confused: doctors who don't usually work with breast cancer—family practitioners and gynecologists—often get nervous about lumpy breasts and are afraid they're malignant. So your doctor may send you to a specialist—a surgeon or a breast specialist—to make sure you don't have a cancerous lump. If your doctor or you are uncertain about whether you've got a lump or just lumpy breasts, it's probably not a bad idea to check it out further. But understanding more about what a lump really is might make the trip to the specialist unnecessary.

The most important thing to know about dominant lumps—benign or malignant—is that they're almost never subtle. They're not like little beebee gun pellets: they're at least a centimeter or two, almost an inch, or the size of a grape. The lump will stick out prominently in the midst of the smaller lumps that constitute normal lumpiness. You'll *know* it's something different. In fact, that's why most breast cancers are found by the woman herself—the lumps are so clearly distinct from the rest of her breast tissue.

The obvious question here is, how do I know the beebee-sized thing isn't an early cancer? The answer is that you usually don't feel a malignant lump when it's small. The cancer has to grow to a large enough size for the body to begin to create a reaction to it—a fibrous, scarlike tissue forms around the cancer, and this, combined with the cancer itself, makes up the palpable lump. The body won't create that reaction when the cancer is tiny, and you won't feel the cancerous lump until the reaction is formed.

At the same time, if it's much bigger than a walnut—if it feels like a section of the breast itself—you're probably still okay. You'll know by checking it through a couple of menstrual cycles, when you'll see that it changes through different parts of your cycle. A cancer lump that large would probably have been noticed earlier, by even the most absentminded person. But if it *doesn't* go away or change significantly after two menstrual cycles, have it checked out; it's not likely that it's a cancer, but it could be, and you don't want to take the chance. This will be easier for you to realize if you've been doing regular breast self-examination, which we discussed in Chapter 2.

There are four types of dominant lumps, three of which are virtually harmless. It's the fourth type, of course, the malignant lump, that you're worrying about when you have your lump examined by a doctor. I'll discuss cancer at length in Parts 4 and 5. It's worth noting here, however, that only one in 12 dominant lumps is malignant. We don't know the cause of any of the noncancerous lumps, though we do know they're somehow related to hormonal variations. (See page 16.) Two kinds of lumps—cysts and fibroadenomas—are formed only during a woman's menstruating years, but can show up years later, when breast tissue has shifted. Pseudolumps can occur in women of any age. It's interesting that two of the three kinds occur most often at opposite ends of a woman's fertile years: fibroadenomas occur when the woman is just starting to menstruate, and cysts when she's heading toward menopause.

Cysts

Usually when you think of nonmalignant lumps, you think of cysts, because doctors have a tendency to describe all nonmalignant lumps as cysts. They're not. A cyst is a particular, distinct kind of lump. Typically it occurs in women in their 30s, 40s, and early 50s, and is most common in women approaching menopause. It will rarely occur in a younger woman, or in a woman who's past menopause. However, I've had patients in both categories—including a teenager and a woman who'd finished with her menopause long ago and wasn't on artificial hormones. (If a woman is taking estrogen to combat menopausal symptoms, she'll have fooled her body into thinking it's still premenopausal.)

A gross cyst—gross meaning "large," not, as in popular usage, "disgusting"—is a fluid-filled sac, very much like a large blister, that grows in the midst of the breast tissue. It's smooth on the outside and "ballottable"—squishy—on the inside, so that if you push on it, you can feel that it's got fluid inside.

This, however, can be deceptive. Cysts only feel like cysts when they're close to the surface. (See Figure 9-1.) Cysts that are deeply imbedded in breast tissue tend to distend that tissue and push it forward, so that what you're feeling is the hard breast tissue, not the soft cyst. In these cases, the cyst tends to feel like a hard lump.

The classical cyst story goes something like this: A woman in her 40s will come to me and say, "I went to the gynecologist six weeks ago and everything was fine. I had a mammogram, and that was fine, too. Then all of a sudden, in the shower last night, I found this

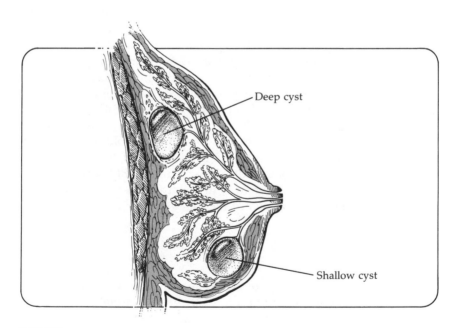

FIGURE 9-1

112

lump in my breast, and I know it wasn't there before." So I examine her and sure enough, there's a hard lump in her breast.

Because of its overnight appearance, I'm pretty sure it's a harmless cyst, but, of course, it's something the doctor—not to mention the patient—wants to be absolutely certain about. So I try to aspirate it.

To aspirate a cyst, the doctor takes a tiny needle, like the needle used for insulin injections, and anesthetizes the sensitive skin over the breast lump. Then a larger needle—like the kind used to draw blood—is attached to a syringe and stuck into the breast, where it draws out the fluid. The cyst collapses like a punctured blister, and that's that. (See Figure 9-2.)

Aspirating cysts is one of the medical procedures I most enjoy doing. It's very easy, and as soon as it's done my patient and I both know she's okay. We're both delighted that she doesn't have cancer, and she thinks I'm the greatest doctor in the world, having simultaneously diagnosed and cured her condition. It does wonders for my ego.

An added pleasure is that it's usually almost painless for the patient. It sounds scary and grim—a little like descriptions of acupuncture—but in reality, most of the nerves in the breast are in the skin, and that's been anesthetized. Some women with greater sensitivity to pain or especially sensitive breasts do find it painful, but

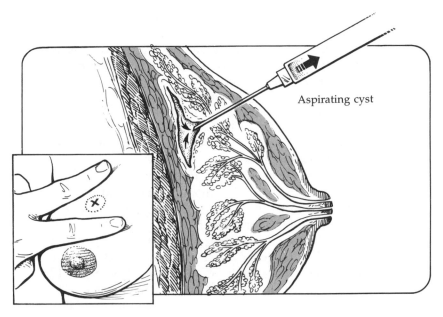

Aspirating cyst

FIGURE 9-2

most don't. The only possible complications from aspirating a cyst are bruising or bleeding into the cyst, neither of which is more than slightly uncomfortable.

The fluid itself is pretty disgusting-looking, but it's harmless. It can be almost any color—usually it's green or brown or yellow. Sometimes the fluid can even be milk—a breastfeeding woman can form a milk-filled cyst called a galactocele, which is treated the way any other cyst is. There can be any amount of it—from a few drops to as much as a cup. One patient came to me with asymmetrical breasts; after I aspirated her cyst, her breasts were the same size.

Some doctors have the fluid analyzed in the lab, but frankly I think it's a waste of the patient's money. The chances of getting a correct diagnosis from cyst fluid are very low, and false positives are common. The fluid's usually been around a while and it's old, and its cells, which are harmless, often seem weird when they're checked. The tests are virtually useless, and they're costly. Most specialists just throw the stuff down the sink.

In Sweden, they think injecting air into the cyst after you've aspirated it prevents the cyst from recurring.[1] It's an interesting theory, but it hasn't been proven. Still, it's worth a try if the cyst has recurred many times.

Usually a woman will get only one or two cysts in her entire life. But some get many, and they get them often. If a patient has recurring multiple cysts, I like to see her every three months, and aspirate as many as I can to keep the multiplication of cysts under control. If a malignant lump is forming, the cysts, harmless in themselves, can obscure it, and that, of course, is dangerous. If a woman has multiple cysts, the chances are she'll go on getting them until menopause—only rarely are they a one-time occurrence.

If cysts are harmless, why do we bother to aspirate them? There are a number of reasons, but the most important is that we need to be sure it really *is* a cyst. You can't be sure a lump in the breast isn't cancer until you find out what it really is. Once we know it's a cyst, doctor and patient can both rest easy.

There are other ways of finding out it's a cyst—it may show up as an area of density on a routine mammogram, and then you can have an ultrasound test done to see whether it's a cyst or a solid lump. The ultrasound test works like radar. If you have a solid lump, the waves from the ultrasound will bounce back and there'll be a shadow behind it. If, however, it's a cyst, the sound waves will go right through it and there won't be a shadow. (See pages 176 and 178 for a discussion of mammograms and ultrasound techniques.)

If you've discovered a cyst through a mammogram and ultrasound and it doesn't bother you, you don't have to bother having it aspirated as well—you already know it isn't cancer.

The other reason we sometimes aspirate cysts is when they are painful. This occurs especially if they've developed very quickly. Aspirating the cyst will relieve the pain.

Cysts themselves are almost never malignant. There's a 1 percent incidence of cancer in cysts, and it's a seldom-dangerous cancer called *intracystic papillary carcinoma*. (See Figure 9-3.) It usually doesn't spread beyond the lining of the cyst, and unless there are specific signs that it might be present, it's not worth the risk of a biopsy. A biopsy is surgery, though minor surgery, and it's better to avoid it when you can.

If there are signs that cancer might be present in the cyst, I do operate on it—never otherwise, and only after I've aspirated it. I'll operate if the cyst has recurred after I've aspirated it three times. I'll also operate if the fluid comes out bloody—that usually means something else is going on, and I want to find out what it is. Finally, I'll do a biopsy if the lump doesn't go away after I've aspirated the cyst.

Sometimes a doctor will aspirate a cyst and won't get any fluid. This isn't a cause for panic. It can happen for a number of reasons. The lump may not be a cyst after all, but a nonmalignant solid lump like those discussed on the following pages. Or the doctor may have missed the middle of the cyst. The doctor tries to get the cyst between her or his fingers and then puncture it, but it's easy to miss the middle, especially in a fairly small cyst.

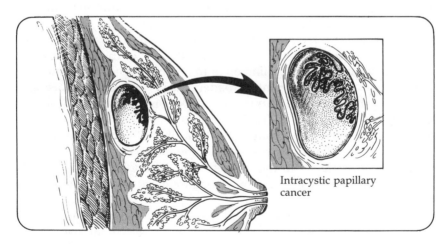

Intracystic papillary
cancer

FIGURE 9-3

When this happens to me, I'll decide how sure I am it's a cyst and, if I have doubts, I'll send the patient for an ultrasound test rather than operate. Operating on a cyst should only be a last resort— it simply isn't necessary in any but the most unusual situation.

It used to be believed that aspirating a cyst was dangerous if someone unknowingly had breast cancer—that the process of aspiration would spread the cancer over the needle's track. We now know that's completely untrue.[2] *Any* dominant lump should be aspirated before it's biopsied. It might be a cyst, and surgery can be avoided.

Cysts don't increase the risk of cancer. Only one study—Dr. Cushman Haagensen[3] of Columbia University—suggests it does, and his evidence is sketchy. Dr. David Page's[4] research is a little better; he's found that there is a slight risk increase in women who have gross cysts and who have a first-degree relative with breast cancer—that is, a mother or a sister. Most other research shows no relation between cysts and cancer.

The real risk is mental rather than physical. A woman with frequent cysts is likely to feel a lump and shrug it off as just another cyst—only to learn later that it was a malignant growth. Every lump should be checked out, to be sure it isn't dangerous.

Fibroadenomas

Another very common nonmalignant lump is the *fibroadenoma*. This is a smooth, round lump that feels the way most people think a cyst should feel—it's smooth and hard, like a marble dropped into the breast tissue. (See Figure 9-4.) It moves around easily within the breast tissue. It's often found near the nipple, but can grow anywhere in the breast. And it's very distinct from the rest of the breast tissue. It can vary from a tiny 5 millimeters to a lemon-sized 5 centimeters. The largest are called "giant fibroadenomas." A doctor can usually tell simply by feeling the lump that it's a fibroadenoma; if a needle aspiration is done and no fluid comes out, the doctor knows it isn't a cyst and is even more convinced it's a fibroadenoma. We can get a few cells by doing a fine-needle aspiration (see page 124) and sending the tissue off to the lab just to make doubly sure. Fibroadenomas will usually be clear on a mammogram or ultrasound test. (See page 180.)

Fibroadenomas are harmless in themselves, and they don't have to be removed, as long as we're *sure* they're fibroadenomas. Teenagers are both more prone to fibroadenomas and less likely to get breast cancer than are older women, so we might consider not re-

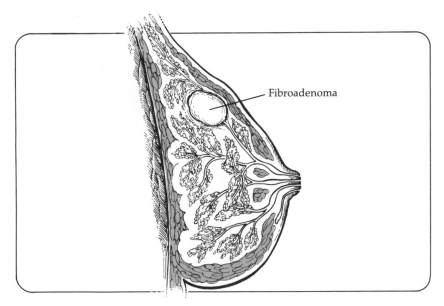

FIGURE 9-4

moving fibroadenomas in them. In women middle-aged or older, we tend to remove all fibroadenomas to be sure they're not cancer. It's usually a good idea, though, for any woman to get them removed, because sometimes they grow, especially with pregnancy and lactation. At that stage they can alarm the patient, and then it's especially messy to remove them, so we prefer to do it early on.

They're easy to remove—it can be done under local anesthetic, and the surgeon can simply make a small incision, find the lump, and take it right out. (See Figure 9-5.) (Some surgeons prefer to make a small incision around the nipple and then tunnel their way to the lump, since an incision at the nipple scars less noticeably. I don't think this is a great idea, however: it's harder to find the lesion that way. If you cut over the fibroadenoma, you're bound to get it, and the scarring doesn't usually remain all that noticeable in most patients.) If you feel nervous about your fibroadenomas, it's probably a good idea to get them removed for your own peace of mind; if there's no reason to get them removed and you don't want to, don't worry about it.

Most women have one fibroadenoma; it's removed, and they never get any more. But some women do get several over their lives—and a few women get many of them. One of my patients had a fibroadenoma in her left breast, and I removed it; she returned a couple

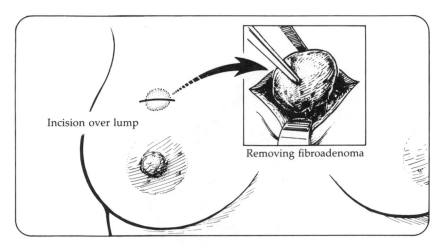

Incision over lump

Removing fibroadenoma

FIGURE 9-5

of years later with another one on the exact same spot in her other breast—a kind of mirror image.

Patients often call their fibroadenomas "fibroids"—and, while it's inaccurate, it makes sense in a way. Fibroids by definition exist only in the uterus, but there are similarities between the two conditions. In both cases, one section of glandular tissue becomes autonomous, growing as a ball in the midst of the rest of the tissue. But there's no correlation except for that—having one doesn't mean you're likely to get the other. In fact, they usually occur at different times in a woman's life: fibroids when you're heading toward menopause, fibroadenomas in your teens or early 20s.

They *can*, however, occur at any age, although not after menopause, unless, as in the case with cysts, you're taking hormones that trick your body into thinking it's premenopausal. It's true that, as we do more mammograms on "normal" women, we find more and more fibroadenomas in women in their 60s and 70s. Probably they've had them since their teens and simply, in those premammography days, didn't know about them. There are some very rare cancers that can look like fibroadenomas on a mammogram, so we usually do either a fine-needle aspiration or, if that doesn't give us the information, an excisional biopsy (removal of the whole lump), just to make sure it *is* a fibroadenoma, in these older women.

There's also a rare cancer called *cystosarcoma phylloides* that can occur *in* a fibroadenoma. (See page 272 for a discussion of this cancer.) It only occurs in about 1 percent of fibroadenomas, and those are usually giant fibroadenomas—lemon-sized or larger. It's usually a relatively harmless cancer, in that it doesn't tend to spread to other parts of the body. Some doctors will insist on removing all fibroadenomas on the theory that this cancer might be present. It's not a very sensible attitude, because of both the rarity and the lack of danger. Unless the lump is large, it's almost never going to contain this cancer—and even if the cancer is present for a long time, it probably isn't going to kill you. When it's discovered, the surgeon simply has to remove the lump and it's gone.

Finally, fibroadenomas in no way predispose you to cancer. They're a nuisance, and they can scare you into thinking you might have cancer—but that's the only bad thing about them.

Pseudolumps

Studies have shown that pseudolumps are the lumps that most confuse surgeons. If you line up patients with fibroadenomas, with cysts, and with breast cancers, and have surgeons who haven't been told which patient has which kind of lump examine them, usually the surgeons will agree in their diagnoses. Give them patients with pseudolumps, however, and you'll get all kinds of different diagnoses. These innocent lumps of breast tissue cause no physical problems, but all kinds of confusion.

"Pseudolump" is a descriptive term for an area of breast tissue that feels more prominent and persistent than usual. The surgeon checks it out and just can't be sure that it isn't another kind of lump.

If I think a patient has a pseudolump, I'll usually see her at least twice, several months apart and at different parts of her cycle, just to make sure it isn't normal lumpiness. Deciding what is or isn't a lump in these cases can be very subjective. If I've recently done a lot of biopsies and they've all turned out to be pseudolumps, I'll tend not to operate; but if I've missed a cancer, I'll operate on a lot of them. Unfortunately, diagnosis is not an exact science. That's the other reason I like to see the patient a few months after my first diagnosis—to balance out whatever effect my mood has had on my decision.

A pseudolump, then, is usually just exaggerated lumpiness. It's distinct and persistent enough, however, that we have to check to be certain that's all it is. It's usually what's meant when doctors say you have fibrocystic disease. (See page 75.) Or a pseudolump can be caused by a rib pushing against breast tissue and causing it to feel hard and lumpy. (See Figure 9-6.) Sometimes women who have had silicone injections to enlarge one or both breasts (see page 66) will get lumps that turn out to be hardened chunks of the silicone. If

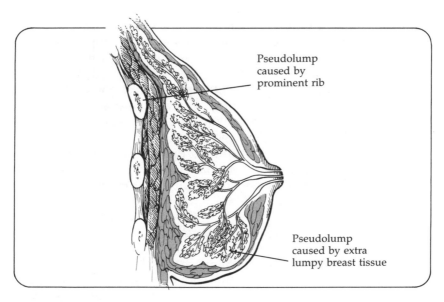

Pseudolump
caused by
prominent rib

Pseudolump
caused by extra
lumpy breast tissue

FIGURE 9-6

you've had injections and get a lump, check with either a breast surgeon or a plastic surgeon (preferably one who's old enough to have worked with silicone injections when they were legal). Surgery on the breast can cause pseudolumps through hardened scar tissue. A pseudolump can also be caused by "fat necrosis"—dead fat—resulting from trauma due to a previous biopsy, a lumpectomy and radiation in the removal of an earlier, cancerous lump (see page 284), or to breast reconstruction surgery (see page 349). But in all these cases, the best judge will be a breast surgeon who's done all the procedures.

Lumps and Cancer

The fear of cancer is, of course, the main reason we worry about any of these lumps: you get a cyst aspirated, or a fibroadenoma or pseudolump biopsied, chiefly to make sure they *aren't* cancer.

It's reasonable to be afraid of getting breast cancer, and to check out any suspicious lump. But remember that a dominant lump doesn't mean you have cancer. In premenopausal women, there are 12 benign lumps for every malignant one. The statistics change dramatically in postmenopausal women who aren't taking hormones, not because they get that much more cancer but because they no longer get the lumps that come with hormonal changes, cysts and fibroadenomas. And even for postmenopausal women, it's only a 50–50 chance that a lump is cancer. We'll discuss malignant lumps in Chapter 16. The main thing to remember is to be cautious, but not paranoid. If you've got a lump, it may be cancer, but it probably isn't. Get it checked out right away. Then, if it's cancer, you can start working on it; if it isn't, you can stop worrying.

What to Do If You Think You Have a Lump

If you have something that feels like it might be a lump, the first thing to do, obviously, is to go to your doctor. The chances are that the doctor will check it out, tell you it's not a lump, and send you home. But a doctor who's a general practitioner or a gynecologist and hasn't spent years working on breasts might not be sure, and may send you to a breast surgeon for further examination. Often when you hear the word "surgeon" you get scared—sure the doctor knows you've got something awful and will have to undergo major surgery.

Probably you won't. The doctor is simply, and sensibly, taking no chances, and sending the patient on to someone who has more experience with breast lumps and is thus more able to determine whether or not it's a true dominant lump. But sometimes even the surgeon can't be sure. In this case, depending on your age, the surgeon will probably send you for a mammogram for additional information. The mammogram might show evidence of a real lump, or a pseudolump. If it doesn't—if even the combination of an examination and a mammogram doesn't give the surgeon the necessary clarification—it's wise to do a biopsy to find out what it is. In the past, we were afraid of unnecessary surgery, and didn't want to biopsy these "gray area" lumps. The problem is, you don't know until you have done the biopsy that it *is* a pseudolump, so the operation isn't unnecessary at all. It's far wiser to risk a fairly safe operation than to take a chance on letting a cancer go.

One thing is important to stress, and I'm becoming more and more aware of its importance. If you're sure something is wrong with your breast, get it biopsied, whatever the doctor's diagnosis. Often a woman is sure she has a lump, the doctor is sure she doesn't, and a year or two later a lump shows up on her mammogram. She's sure the doctor was careless. She's not usually right: a cancer that shows on a mammogram probably wasn't a lump two years earlier, or it would be a huge lump at that point. But I think it's very likely that the patient—who, after all, experiences her breast from both inside and outside, while the doctor can only experience the patient's

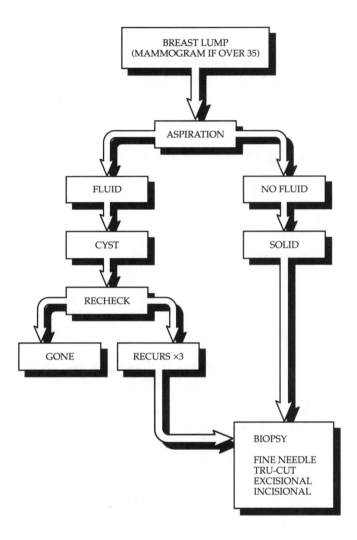

breast from outside—has *sensed* that something is wrong, and interpreted that in terms of the concept most familiar to her, a lump. I'm
convinced that this is the basis of many of the malpractice suits that
arise when a doctor has "failed" to detect what later proves to be
cancer. If you really feel something is wrong in your breast, insist on
a biopsy. If you're wrong, you'll put your mind at rest—and if you're
right, you may just save your own life. It's minor surgery with low
risks and potentially high gains.

10

Biopsy

When the doctor tells you you'll need a biopsy, you'll want to find out what kind. There are four different kinds of biopsy—two done with needles, and two "open" biopsies that require surgical cutting. A *fine-needle* (like the kind used to draw blood) biopsy takes only a few cells out of the lump; a *larger-needle* biopsy, called a "tru-cut," cuts a small piece out of the lump. An *incisional* biopsy takes a much larger piece of the lump out, while in an *excisional* biopsy the entire lump is removed. (See Figure 10-1.)

If you aren't clear what kind of biopsy the surgeon is planning, you may discover that you assume only a little piece will be removed, while the surgeon really means to remove the whole thing. Then you'll end up angry because you've had an operation, and the surgeon will end up defensive, because you were *told* you were getting a biopsy done.

Usually with fibroadenomas or pseudolumps we take the whole lump out. It's just as easy as removing a piece of the lump, and it has a couple of important advantages. For one thing, there's always a chance that a piece of the lump won't accurately represent the whole thing, and that we'll miss something. The other is that the presence of the lump can cause future confusion. As your breasts change, you might find yourself wondering if this is the same lump,

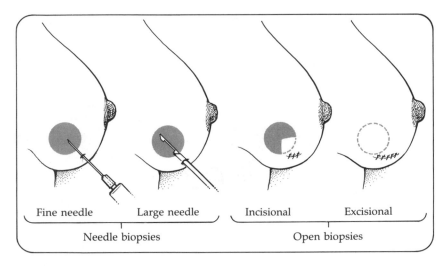

Fine needle | Large needle | Incisional | Excisional
Needle biopsies | Open biopsies

FIGURE 10-1

or if the old lump has disappeared and this is a new one, because now, with your breast feeling different, the lump feels different. Or you may be seeing a new doctor who's worried about this lump and wants to make sure it's okay. These are minor hassles that are easily prevented by getting rid of the lump when we do the biopsy. Even though the lump is harmless, it doesn't serve any function, and you may as well be rid of it.

If the lump is very large, however, the surgeon might want to do an incisional biopsy, because an excisional one would require general anesthetic and be a more serious operation; in that case, we'd decide whether or not further surgery was necessary after we got in the lab results.

I prefer to do fine-needle biopsies only if I think the lump is likely to be malignant. That way, if my patient needs surgery to remove the cancer, she won't have to face two operations. Unfortunately, needle biopsies are more accurate when they're positive than when they're negative: if the results show you *do* have cancer, they're probably right, but if they show you don't, they may well be wrong. So if my needle biopsy results are negative, I'll hope they're right, but I'll schedule my patient for an excisional biopsy just to be sure.

The term "biopsy," by the way, refers to the operation itself, not to the process of studying the lump in the laboratory, which the pathologist does later. Anything that we cut out of the body is always sent to the pathologist for analysis, and the connection of the two procedures has caused people to confuse them with each other. But if you're having a biopsy performed, it's useful for you to know the precise meaning of the term.

SURGICAL BIOPSY

What is the process of an incisional or excisional biopsy like? Well, to begin with, there's the setting. You may have your biopsy performed in your doctor's office, or, more frequently, in the hospital's "minor" operating room. If you had a biopsy several years ago, you might find this confusing—especially the minor operating room. In the past, most surgery was performed in what we now call the main operating room, and the surgical rituals may be very different from those you recall.

Most hospitals have two or three kinds of operating rooms. I like to think of them as similar to restaurant types, in which the food is basically the same, but there are different varieties served in different places and the rituals accompanying them are different.

In the hospital where I work, there are three kinds of rooms. The minor operating room is like the snack bar—you can go in barefoot and wearing your bathing suit, and order your hamburger, and it's cheap and it tastes good. The ambulatory surgery room is more like the coffee shop; you have to wear shoes and be fully dressed, but

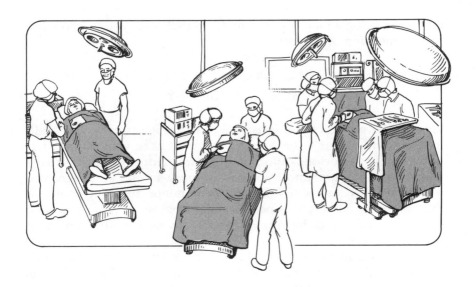

it's okay to wear jeans, and you sit at a table and are waited on. There's a larger menu, which still includes your hamburger. And finally there's the main operating room, which is like the formal dining room—you've got to be a bit dressed up, and there's a fancier menu, and the waiter grinds pepper onto your salad. Again, you can still get your hamburger, though it will cost you more. In each place, the hamburger's the same, but the rituals around it are different.

Similarly, you can have your biopsy in any of the three operating rooms, though the ambulatory and main rooms are equipped with a larger "menu" that includes more complex operations as well. The difference is in the ritual. And the rituals are always defined by the room they're performed in, *not* by the particular operation.

There's nothing wrong with the rituals—every profession has its rituals, and they're very useful to us. But if you don't know what the rituals are, or even that they *are* rituals, they can be intimidating.

Most of the surgical rituals are holdovers from the turn of the century, when they served a very practical purpose. Earlier, little was known about germs and the danger of spreading them through unsanitary practices. So doctors would go straight from the morgues, where they were doing autopsies, into the operating rooms where, without washing their hands or changing their clothing, they performed surgery—and then wondered why so many of their patients were dying on them. Then a Hungarian physician named Semmelweis figured out that washing hands between autopsies and operations would save patients' lives—it was quite a revolutionary discovery.

So the majority of the rituals began then—the frequent hand washing, the surgical gowns and masks, and so forth—but nowadays, when people shower every day and wash their hands a lot, and we have antibiotics to combat infections, the extreme degree of attention to totally sterile cleanliness is less necessary and, as I said, partially ritualistic. Predictably, the fancier the operating room, the fancier its attendant ritual.

Much of the diagnostic breast surgery done today is done in either outpatient, free-standing ambulatory clinics or in the minor operating room. It's much cheaper than the same surgery performed in the main operating room: in the latter, you're paying for all that specialized equipment used for complicated procedures like open-heart surgery. Neither patients nor their insurance companies want that, so more and more, the "snack bar" facilities are being used. (The ambulatory room is a bit more sophisticated than the minor operating room, but far less so than the main.) Often the ambulatory and minor operating rooms are used interchangeably. Keep in mind, however, that all this varies from hospital to hospital, and from region to region.

So, if you had a biopsy 10 years ago in the "formal dining room," you may be expecting all the formal ritual, and be disturbed by its absence. Don't be. The operation and the care you're receiving are the same, and they're what matter.

If a patient has other medical problems—a heart or a respiratory condition, for example—then it's probably wiser to perform the operation in the main operating room, in case any complications arise that need more sophisticated equipment. If you're concerned about possible complications and how they'll be handled, talk with your doctor beforehand about which room will be used and what you're likely to need.

So much for the setting—now let's get to the procedure itself. It can be done under either local or general anesthetic, but most doctors and patients prefer local. Some doctors like to give their patients a tranquilizer, but I prefer to help them stay calm through reassuring conversation. Tranquilizers require that the doctor monitor the patient's pulse and blood pressure during the operation, and I want to be able to focus my attention on the operation itself. (In some hospitals, pulse and blood pressure are routinely monitored, but it's only essential if a general anesthetic is used or if the patient is on other drugs.) In some cases local/standby is used. This means the operation is done under a local anesthetic but an anesthesiologist or nurse-anesthetist is standing by to give some mild drugs which will make you indifferent to the procedure. The anesthesiologist can also put you to sleep if general anesthesia becomes necessary.

In the minor operating room or the doctor's office, the patient usually just has to change from the waist up; in the main operating room, where the dress code is more formal, the patient has to change into a hospital johnny and the surgeon wears a scrub suit.

Often in a biopsy, the surgeon will use a machine, called an *electrocautery*, to seal off the small blood vessels and prevent bleeding. Since there's a small risk of a short circuit, which would give the patient an electric shock, a grounding pad will be put on your leg, back, or abdomen to ground the current. It's a plastic pad with a cool gel inside which initially will feel freezing cold but will prevent electric shock. (See Figure 10-2.)

Next, the surgeon will wash her or his hands and put on surgical gloves, and then paint you with an antiseptic solution. Usually this is done two or three times—no particular reason, but three is a nice ritualistic number, so why not? Then sterilized towels (paper or cloth, depending on which room you're in) are framed around the area that's going to be operated on.

Then, with a sterile felt-tipped pen, the surgeon marks the spot over the lump, and then injects, through a small needle, the local anesthetic. (We usually use lidocaine, not novocaine, these days, but "novocaine" is still the popular term—like calling any facial tissues "Kleenex.") When the needle first goes in, there's a little pain and a little burning. The slower the anesthetic goes in, the less pain there is, so it's worth taking the time to do it slowly.

But don't be misled by the "novocaine"—it's not like the anesthetic you get at the dentist's. For one thing, it hurts a lot less. The dentist has to poke around your mouth looking for a nerve, and then deaden it, and you have to wait till the novocaine takes effect, and then your whole mouth goes out and you end up chewing the inside of your cheek. It's not the dentist's fault: dental work requires a nerve block, since drilling into a tooth is felt all through the jaw.

But the process in the biopsy is different. Since we're cutting only into soft tissue, we can use "local infiltration," which numbs only the area where it's put, not the whole breast. And it works immediately. (This confuses some patients, who get scared when the surgeon starts to work right after injecting the anesthetic.)

I usually test the anesthetic right after I inject it, by pinching the skin with small tweezers. This assures both the patient and me that the area is really numb. Then I point out that it's only the area we're operating on that's numb, so she'll feel me touching her in other parts of the breast.

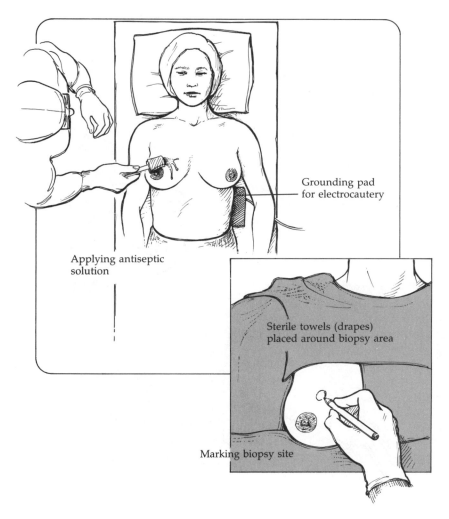

Grounding pad
for electrocautery

Applying antiseptic
solution

Sterile towels (drapes)
placed around biopsy area

Marking biopsy site

FIGURE 10-2

I also point out that *I* won't feel any pain, so she has to tell me if something hurts. Occasionally the surgeon will unknowingly wander outside the anesthetized area. Never feel embarrassed to yell if it hurts—there's plenty of anesthetic, and we can always give you more, at any time during the operation. Don't try to be "polite," or a "good girl": there's no reason for you to suffer.

Now the surgeon makes the incision, going through skin, fat, and tissue to get to the lump. (See Figure 10-3.) Most of the process isn't actually cutting; it's just spreading tissue apart till the lump is

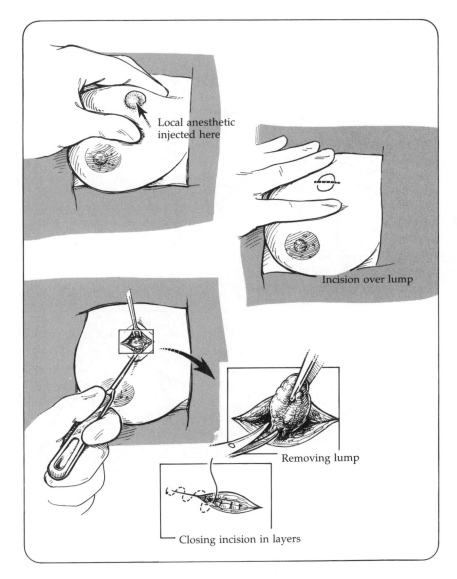

Local anesthetic injected here

Incision over lump

Removing lump

Closing incision in layers

FIGURE 10-3

reached. There's little bleeding, because there aren't many blood vessels here, and the cautery takes care of the few there are. The lump is cut away from the surrounding tissue and removed.

The incision is then sewn up, usually in layers—tissue, then fat, then skin. This prevents a dent from forming in the breast when it heals. Most surgeons use dissolvable stitches that tend to leave less scarring.

Sometimes you'll feel some pulling when the surgeon is pulling the lump out and clamping it before cutting it out. This is painless, but unpleasant-feeling. Occasionally a patient might feel a sharp, stinging pain when the surgeon is tying off the blood vessels—there are nerves in the lining of the blood vessels, and sometimes the surgeon can't avoid them. If this happens, tell the surgeon, who can immediately anesthetize the spot.

By the way, you *don't* have to keep perfectly still—it's not that kind of operation. Obviously you can't be jiggling around all over the place, but you can wiggle your toe or bend your knees or your fingers, and it's a good idea to let your body move a bit. Sometimes a patient is so nervous she lies there perfectly rigid through the whole thing, and afterward her breast feels fine but her muscles are killing her.

I like to play music while I operate, to entertain both the patient and myself. If we like different kinds of music, I'll just give the patient my Walkman, so I can play what I like and give her what she likes. It's a good idea to pick something soft and soothing, something that isn't your favorite music—you don't want to ruin your future enjoyment of it by associating your favorite songs with surgery. One of my patients had Vivaldi on during her surgery, and now says that every time she hears Vivaldi her breast hurts!

Some surgeons get distracted if their patients talk to them while they're operating, but I don't mind it at all—a pleasant chat can make it a more comfortable experience for both of us.

While many surgeons drape their patients in such a way that the patient can't see the surgeon, I find that to be alienating and im-practical. Often, when patients are in pain that they don't consider intense enough to bother the doctor with, they won't complain, but will wince or grimace; and if I see that I can ask if they'd like more anesthetic.

After the surgery, what happens? Well, the surgeon, who has bandaged the incision, will probably tell you when you can take the bandage off and when you can shower. I usually have the patient remove the bandage the next day and shower as soon as she wants to. We used to think that you shouldn't shower until the stitches came out, but we have found that water doesn't hurt stitches at all. The more you bounce, the sorer you'll be, so whether or not you usually wear a bra, it's a good idea to wear one for a couple of days after the surgery—a good, firm, sensible bra, not a pretty, lacy, flimsy one. You'll probably want to keep it on all night as well. On the other hand, some women find the bra so uncomfortable in bed that they prefer the soreness. If the incision is near the bra line, the bra may cause more discomfort than it's worth. Use your own judgment; the point is to make you as comfortable as possible.

The anesthetic wears off much more quickly than the dentist's does: just as it goes to work right away, it wears off right away, usually within an hour after the biopsy is finished. You're usually not in much pain after the operation—many patients find that Tylenol is all they need. By the next day, you can usually go back to work and resume your normal activities. (Be sensible, of course: if your normal activities include weight lifting, give it another couple of days.)

Usually there won't be a lot of scarring, but this is something you should talk with your surgeon about before you have the procedure done. Most surgeons are sensitive to their patients' concerns and will try to give you the most cosmetic incision possible. If you feel the surgeon is being flippant, or not taking your concerns seriously, find another surgeon. At the same time, be aware that some people have bodies that make big keloid (thick) scars, and the best surgeon in the world can't prevent that. If you're one of these people, you probably know it from previous experience, although there's always that chance that, if you've never had a major cut before, you won't know till after the surgery. All you can do is measure your unhappiness at the aesthetic loss against the peace of mind that comes from knowing you don't have cancer, or the possibility of saving your life through early treatment if you do have it.

While you're resting up from the operation and getting on with your life, the lump is being analyzed by the pathologist, to whom the surgeon has immediately sent it. Sometimes the pathologist will do a "frozen section," which is a quick but crude method of testing the lump. The lump is cut in half; a piece is quick-frozen to make it solid, then thinly sliced, placed on a slide, and stained right away. Sometimes this will give you the answer, but it's not 100 percent accurate. In the old days, when we were doing immediate mastectomies if the lump was found to be malignant, this method was always used to allow the surgeon to proceed with the operation immediately. Nowadays, however, we usually do it in two steps— the biopsy is performed, the results discussed with the patient, and, if further surgery is called for, it's done later. (See page 221.) So we don't often do a frozen section any more.

Far more reliable is the regular procedure, the "permanent section." Here the tissue is removed and cut into small pieces. It goes through several stages. First, it's dehydrated by putting it in different strengths of alcohol, then fixed in paraffin wax, so the piece of tissue is imbedded in a block of paraffin. This is then put on a microtome, a knife that slices it into very thin slices. Each slice is then put on a slide, the wax melted away, and the tissue stained with different colors. This whole process takes about 24 to 36 hours.

When the slides are ready, the pathologist looks at them and makes a diagnosis; this probably takes another day. The pathologist then dictates a report, which is sent to the doctor, who will probably have it in a week. Some doctors wait till the report comes in, but others prefer to call the pathologist the day after the operation. This is what I do, because I like to let my patient know what's happening as soon as possible, and because, for all patients, the waiting and uncertainty can be terrifying. But whatever your doctor's practice, you'll know in a week or so what the biopsy has shown.

As with any surgical procedure, there are sometimes complications in a breast biopsy. The two most common are infection and *hematoma*. If a hematoma occurs, it will be within a day or two of the procedure. It's caused by bleeding inside the area where the surgery was done, causing a blood blister to form. (See Figure 10-4.) It turns blue and forms a lump right under the skin. The body usually simply absorbs the blood and recycles it, as it does with any bruise. But sometimes before the body can do that you'll bump into something or someone will bump into you, and it will burst open, causing black blood to come out. It looks gross and disgusting and you'll think you're dying, but don't worry—you're not. It's old blood; you're not bleeding now. What you need to do is go home, clean up the mess, and take a shower. If you're worried about it, call your doctor. If an infection occurs, it will show up a week or two after surgery—there'll be redness and swelling and fever, and the doctor will treat it as infec-

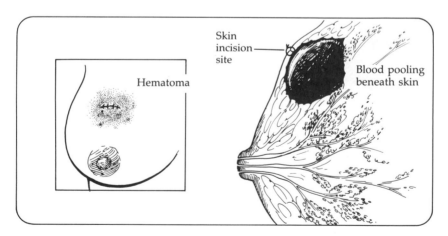

Skin incision site

Blood pooling beneath skin

Hematoma

FIGURE 10-4

tions are usually treated, with antibiotics. Again, it's more of a nuisance than anything else.

Sometimes, you'll get a combination of infection and hematoma—the blood mixes with pus, like an abscess or a boil, and needs to be drained by the doctor. Sometimes when stitches are removed after breast surgery—either biopsies or cosmetic procedures—a small nondissolvable stitch is overlooked and remains in the breast, which will then get infected, as was the case with one of my patients. (No, I wasn't the surgeon who removed the stitches!) It's easy to treat with antibiotics and removal of the stitch and the skin around it.

And, yes, the worst patient nightmares do occasionally occur—I had one patient who had a persistent infection following a biopsy, and when they finally operated on her they discovered that her surgeon had left a sponge inside her. I'm not quite sure how a surgeon could manage to do that, but this one did. Fortunately, it's very, very rare—and my patient is fine now.

These complications are pretty infrequent—they only occur in about 10 percent of breast biopsies, and, while they're unpleasant and inconvenient, they're not life-threatening and they don't have any long-term effects.

Remember, when your surgeon decides to do a biopsy, it doesn't mean you have cancer—just that you *might* have cancer, and it's important to find out as soon as possible. Most likely, the pathology report will show a nonmalignant lump, and you'll have a large weight off your mind. And if it should be cancerous, you'll know that you've got a problem, and can begin to deal with it in the most effective way possible.

PART THREE

RISK, PREVENTION, AND DETECTION OF BREAST CANCER

11

Risk Factors:
Hormonal
and Genetic

Every woman would like to know what her risk of getting breast cancer is and what she can do about it. Before discussing figures and risk factors, however, it is important to be clear about the derivation of any numbers used, since they're often used in confusing and misleading ways. For example, an advertisement calling milk "99 percent fat-free" suggests that it has 1 percent as much fat as whole milk. Actually, however, what it means is that 1 percent of the milk is made up of fat. Since only 3.6 percent of whole milk is made up of fat, whole milk could be called "96.4 percent fat-free." While this is still a substantial difference, it means that whole milk has three and one half times as much fat as 1 percent fat milk—not 99 times as much. Likewise, when media headlines say that three alcoholic drinks a week increase breast cancer risk by 50 percent, they don't mean one has a 50–50 chance of getting breast cancer, but rather that these drinks increase the relative risk by 50 percent, and that one's lifetime risk is now about 5 percent rather than 3.3 percent (see below). Thus, it is important that we examine the common statistics used in breast cancer research and review exactly what they mean.

There are three kinds of risk commonly referred to in discussing breast cancer: absolute risk, relative risk, and attributable risk. (See Figure 11-1.)

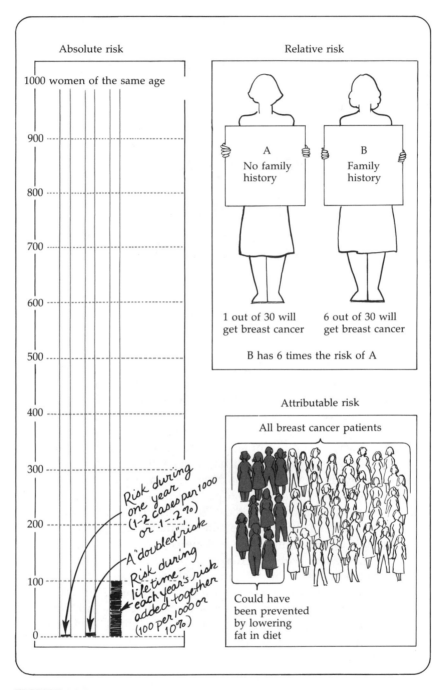

FIGURE 11-1

Absolute risk is the rate cancer or mortality from cancer occurs in a general population. It can be expressed either as the number of cases per a specified population in a particular time period (e.g., 50 cases per 100,000 annually), or as a cumulative risk up to a particular age. This cumulative risk is the source of the familiar 1 in 10 lifetime figure for white women. It is important to recognize that this number can't be applied to any one individual woman. It describes the "average" risk of breast cancer in white American women and is calculated to take into consideration other causes of death over the life span. This figure will overestimate the risk for the woman with no risk factors and underestimate for the one with risk factors.

Your risk at any one time depends to a great extent on your age. For the average white woman, it is something like 1/1000/year at age 40, or 0.1 percent. This number increases with age, since breast cancer becomes more common as women get older: for example, at age 50 the average white woman has a 1/500/year (0.2%) risk of getting breast cancer. (See Tables 11-1 and 11-2.) For women of color, the risk is actually less (see Table 11-3.)

The second method is determining *relative risk*. This is the comparison of the incidence of breast cancer or deaths from breast cancer among people with a particular risk factor to that of people without that factor, or to a reference population. This type of measurement is more useful to an individual woman because she can determine her risk factors and thus calculate how they will affect her chances of getting the disease. Even here you have to be very careful. For comparison, you can't use the 1 in 10, or 10 percent, generated in the absolute risk equation (see above) because that is based on all women regardless of their risk. Rather, you need a number that will

Table 11-1. **The Average Risk of Developing Breast Cancer in a Given Year in White Women[a]**

Age	Risk Per Year
30	1 in 5,900
35	1 in 2,300
40	1 in 1,200
50	1 in 590
60	1 in 420
70	1 in 330
80	1 in 290

[a] Adapted from P.C. Stomper, R.S. Gelman, J.E. Meyer, and G.S. Gross, "New England Mammography Survey 1988: Public Misconceptions of Breast Cancer Incidence," *Breast Disease*, May 1990.

Table 11-2. Probability of Developing Breast Cancer for the Population of White Women[a]

Age Interval	Risk of Developing Breast Cancer	Risk of Dying of Breast Cancer
Birth to 110	10.2%	3.60%
20–30	0.04	0.00
35–45	0.88	0.14
50–60	1.95	0.33
65–75	3.17	0.43

[a] H. Seidman et al., *CA: A Cancer Journal for Clinicians* 35(1985): 36–56. Reprinted with permission.

Table 11-3. Probability of a Woman Developing Breast Cancer by Age 75[a]

Ethnic/Racial Group	%	No.
White	8.2	1 in 12
Black	7.0	1 in 14
New-Mexican Hispanic	4.8	1 in 21
New-Mexican American Indian	2.5	1 in 40
Japanese-American	5.4	1 in 19
Chinese-American	6.1	1 in 16

[a] J.W. Berg, "Clinical Implications of Risk Factors for Breast Cancer," *Cancer* 53(1984): 589. Reprinted with permission.

reflect the risk of a woman without the factor being considered. For a woman with no clear risk factors at all (no previous cancers, no family history, menarche after 10, menopause before 55, first pregnancy prior to 30), this is 1 in 30, or 3.3 percent, significantly lower than the average of 10 percent.[3]

If you call the risk of the woman with no risk factors 1.0, you can report the risk of those with risk factors in relation to this. This is how relative risk is derived. A woman with a mother who had breast cancer in both breasts before the age of 40, for example, has a relative risk of 6 over her lifetime—that is, six times that of the woman with no risk or 1 in 5 women with this risk factor (20%), not, as it might appear, six times the 10 percent we mentioned above. (See Figure 11-1.)

How any increase in relative risk will affect your absolute risk is also, of course, dependent on your age at the time. For example, a threefold relative risk (compared to the general population) at a young age will increase your absolute risk by about 20 percent, while by age 50 the woman with the threefold increased relative risk has a lifetime risk of about 14 percent. One third of the breast cancers occur before age 50 and so her risk is only 2/3. She has about a 4.5 percent chance of developing breast cancer over the next 10 years and about 10.5 percent in the next 20 years, compared with the average risks of 1.5 and 3.5 percent, respectively.[4]

When reading any study or hearing one reported in the media, it is important to check the basis for the relative risk numbers. Most authors will compare those women with a specific risk factor to women without it. This, of course, is somewhere in between, using the average population mentioned above or using the woman with no risk factors at all. It's like the fat in the milk: the numbers can be extremely misleading if you don't take the time to put them in context.

Finally, we must consider the *attributable risk*. This concept relates more to public policy. It looks at the amount of disease in the population that could be prevented by alteration of risk factors. For example, a risk factor could convey a very large relative risk but be restricted to a few individuals, so changing it would only benefit a few individuals. Dr. Anthony B. Miller[5] has concluded that if every woman in the world were to have a baby before 25, 17 percent of the world's breast cancer would be eliminated. If you were looking at this from a public health policy perspective, you'd have to weigh the possible advantages of pushing early pregnancy against the problems of young and possibly immature parents, and of possible increased population growth. Miller also came up with other attributable risk formulas. He thought postmenopausal estrogen caused 8 percent of breast cancer, and total fat in diet 26–27 percent (see page 152). This is interesting, because the largest factor here is fat intake, and that's changeable. Nevertheless, 75 percent of breast cancers would not be affected by decreasing dietary fat. (See Figure 11-1.)

But what do we mean by risk factors, and how are they determined? "Risk factors" is a term referring to identifiable factors that make some people more susceptible than others to a particular disease: that is, smoking is a "risk factor" in lung cancer, and high cholesterol is a risk factor in heart disease. Medical researchers attempt to define risk factors in order to discover who is most likely to get a particular disease, and also to get clues as to the disease's cause and thus to the possible prevention and/or cure. (See Tables 11-4 and 11-5 for risk factors for breast cancer.)

A risk factor is usually determined by taking a large population of people—say, two to three thousand or more—and identifying a variety of features about them, determining who gets the disease under study, and then seeing what the relationship is between the disease and the features that commonly occur.

You have to be careful how you use your findings. If you determine that out of 20,000 people under study, 5,000 got the disease and all 5,000 drank milk as infants, you can't decide from this that milk drinking causes cancer. If none of the other 15,000 (your control group) drank milk as infants, you might be on the right track; if, as is more likely, all 15,000 did drink milk, you've learned nothing except that most people drink milk as children. (This is the kind of flaw that led researchers to decide that "fibrocystic disease" causes cancer. See page 79.)

Sometimes, as in the case of lung cancer and smoking, risk factors are dramatic, and can make a clear difference in the individual's

Table 11-4. Family History and Risk of Breast Cancer[a]

	Relative Risk
First-degree relative with breast cancer (mother, sister, daughter)	2.3
premenopausal	2.7
postmenopausal	2.5
mother	2.1
sister	2.1
mother and sister	13.6
Second-degree relative (aunt, grandmother)	1.5
First- and second-degree relative	2.2

[a] Adapted from R.W. Sattin, G.L. Rubin, L.A. Webster, et al., "Family History and the Risk of Breast Cancer," *Journal of the American Medical Association* 253(1985): 1908.

Table 11-5. Reproductive Factors and the Risk of Breast Cancer

	Relative Risk
Menstrual History	
Age at first period < 12	1.3
Age at menopause > 55 with > 40 menstruating years	2.0
Pregnancy[a]	
First child before age 20	0.8
First child between ages 21 and 29	1.3
First child after age 30	1.4
Nulliparous (no pregnancies)	1.6

[a] Adapted from W.D. Dupont and D.L. Page, "Breast Cancer Risk Associated with Proliferative Disease, Age at First Birth, and a Family History of Breast Cancer," *American Journal of Epidemiology* 125(1987): 769.

likelihood of getting the disease. Unfortunately, it usually doesn't work this way. In breast cancer, we have come up with some risk factors—such as family history—which we'll look at in this chapter. But so far, there is nothing comparable to the connections found between cholesterol and heart disease or between smoking and lung cancer.

Although we have determined some of the risk factors in breast cancer, the sad reality is that we can't say, as with lung cancer, "You're fairly safe because you're not in this particular population." In fact, 70 percent of breast cancer victims have none of the classical risk factors in their background.[6] It's important to understand this for two reasons. If you overestimate the importance of risk factors, you may suffer needless mental anguish if you have one of the risk factors in your background. On the other hand, you may create a false sense of security if you *don't* have them. I can't count the number of times patients have come in to me with a suspicious lump that turns out to be malignant and, stunned, say, "I don't know how this happened! No one in my family ever had breast cancer!" I tell them they're in good company—most breast cancer patients don't have a family history of breast cancer. By virtue of being women, we are at risk for breast cancer.

Another thing to note is that risk factors don't necessarily increase in a simple arithmetical fashion: if one risk factor gives you a 20 percent risk of getting breast cancer, and another gives you a 10 percent chance, it doesn't always mean that now you're up to 30 percent. The interaction of risk factors is a tricky and complicated process. One interesting example is that the recent studies on alcohol and breast cancer (see page 159) show that women with other risk factors who also drank liquor don't increase their risk at all, while women with no other risk factors who drank tend to increase toward the risk level of women who already had risk factors.

It would be much more convenient if we could say "this causes breast cancer so don't do it." But breast cancer is what is known as a "multifactorial disease"—that is, it has many causes which interact with each other in ways we don't understand yet.

Hormonal Risk Factors

The first and most obvious risk factor is hormonal. We know that hormones play a large part in breast cancer because it's a form of cancer common in women and rare in men, and, as we discussed on page 12, women's breasts undergo a complex hormonal evolution that men's don't. We don't yet understand what the hormonal risk factors are but we have some interesting clues. We know that it has something to do with age and menstrual cycling: the younger a woman is at her first period, and the older she is when she goes into menopause, the more likely she is to get breast cancer. It seems that the more periods a woman has over her lifetime, the more prone she is to breast cancer: if she menstruates for more than 40 years, she seems to have a particularly high risk. If your ovaries are removed early, and no hormone replacements are given, your risk of breast cancer is greatly reduced.[7] It's not exactly a cure-all, however, since it would also greatly increase your danger of osteoporosis and coronary heart disease. If you've had a hysterectomy, it may or may not influence your vulnerability to breast cancer, depending upon whether your ovaries, as well as your uterus, are removed. If you still have ovaries, your body is still going through hormonal cycles, even though you have no periods.

Pregnancy also appears to affect breast cancer risk. Women who have never been pregnant seem to be more at risk than women who have had a child. Women who have a child before 30 are less at risk than women who have their first child after their early 30s. However, this doesn't appear to apply to pregnancies that have been terminated through miscarriage or abortion.[8] The key time seems to be the amount of time between the first period and the first pregnancy. There are a few theories about why this is so. (See Figure 11-2.)

One explanation is that between menarche and the first pregnancy, the breast tissue is especially sensitive to carcinogens. This seems to be true. As we'll discuss a little later, such factors as diet, alcohol consumption, and radiation exposure all seem to have a greater effect on a woman's breasts between her first period and her first pregnancy than they do later. So it may indeed be that the "developing breast" is more susceptible to carcinogens than the breast that has gone through its complete hormonal development. This increased sensitivity may relate to the breast cells' capability of mutating up until the first pregnancy. There may be something about the first pregnancy that stops them from being able to mutate; thus, the more time cells have to mutate, the greater the chance that they'll mutate in response to a carcinogen and in a way that develops into cancer. ("Mutation" is one of those words that science fiction has made sound very sinister, but many mutations are in reality perfectly harmless.)

This may be explained by the "estrogen window theory" of Dr. S.G. Korenman,[9] which suggests that there are two periods of particular susceptibility to carcinogens, when the hormone balance is imperfect—at puberty, when the hormones are gearing up, and at

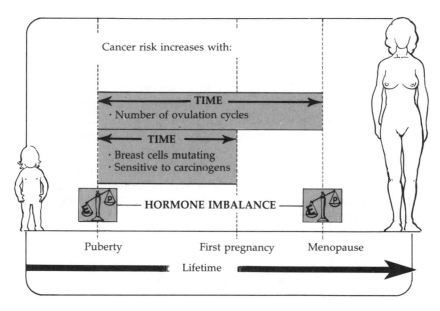

FIGURE 11-2

menopause, when they're gearing down—and that estrogen that isn't balanced by progesterone is carcinogenic. This is a pattern often seen in anovulatory cycles—cycles when you don't ovulate. (See page 16 for discussion of hormones and their relation to pregnancy and fertility.)

Dr. Malcolm Pike,[10] however, offers a somewhat different theory. If hormone balance were the issue, Pike says, then we could assume that infertile women would get more breast cancer—but they don't.[11] Pike thinks the total number of ovulatory cycles a woman has gone through is a factor in her vulnerability to breast cancer, since it's the length of time between menarche and menopause that seems to count. So it could be the number of ovulatory, not anovulatory, cycles that matters. In fact, a recent Swedish study[12] found that the total number of regular menstrual cycles prior to the first full pregnancy was a better predictor of risk than age at first period or age at first pregnancy. As you see, we're still very much in the theorizing stage: we still don't know why there is this vulnerable time in a woman's life and why or how internal hormones affect breast cancer.

Is there any way we can use this information to help prevent breast cancer? One method would be to encourage earlier first pregnancies, although, as mentioned, this would only prevent 17 percent of all breast cancers. A second approach may be to increase adolescent athletics. Rose Firsch,[13] of Harvard Medical School and Harvard School of Public Health, has shown that women who were involved in athletics during high school and college have a decreased risk of breast cancer. The mechanism for this protection is yet to be determined. This may just be secondary to a lean physique (see page 156 for a link between breast cancer and obesity), or it may be that reduction of body fat can make menstrual cycles irregular or cease altogether. This will reduce the total number of ovulatory cycles.

As a result, a theory[14] has been very seriously put forth that I find delightful: put increased funding into high school athletics for girls, and less into chemotherapy—not a bad use of our resources. (I do *not*, of course, advocate anorexia—whatever it may save in possible breast cancer is more than lost by the other health hazards it entails.)

Genetic Risk Factors

The second major category of risk factors is genetic. This factor is often exaggerated: women come to me convinced that since their mother and aunt had breast cancer, they have a 50 percent chance of getting it. While it's true that breast cancer in the family increases a woman's chance of getting breast cancer, the increased risk for most women may not be that great.

Genetically, we divide breast cancer occurrences into three groupings. The first, and most common, is sporadic—that's the 70 percent of breast cancer victims who have no known family history of the disease. The second is genetic—there's one dominant cancer gene, and it's passed on to every generation. Most people assume that these are the only two kinds of breast cancer: the kind that is inherited and the kind that isn't. In fact, it is the third group that is much more common than the genetic group. It's what we call "polygenic," and it occurs when there is a family history of breast cancer that isn't directly passed on through each generation in one dominant gene— some members of the family will get it and others won't.

Dr. Henry Lynch,[15] of Creighton Medical School's oncology clinic in Omaha, Nebraska, did a study looking for percentages of these genetic groupings of breast cancer within a particular population. He looked at 225 patients with breast cancer and found that 82 percent had sporadic breast cancer (or no family history), while 13 percent had polygenic and only 5 percent had true genetic breast cancer.

So pure hereditary breast cancer is rare, but it does occur—between 5 and 7 percent of all breast cancers fall into this category. In this case, the mother (or father) has a breast cancer gene, and there's a 50–50 chance it will be passed on to the daughters. If a daughter, or son, has inherited the gene, that gene again has a 50–50 chance of passing on to the next generation. I've had one family with a dramatic instance of genetic cancer. The grandmother had it, and the mother had it. She's fine now, but two of her five daughters died of breast cancer, and two others have had breast cancer. The fifth has decided to have her breasts preventively removed—an operation I'm normally hesitant to perform, but which in her case really does make sense. (This is a very different situation from the more common one, when the family members with breast cancer are aunts or cousins rather than mother and sisters.) Interestingly, we have found some evidence that people with breast cancers transmitted through a dominant gene have a better overall survival rate than other breast cancer patients. This may have to do with the ways in which that particular form of cancer works, or it may simply reflect the tendency of women with breast cancer in their immediate family to have frequent exams.

Dr. A.G. Knudson[16] has proposed a theory about hereditary breast cancer. He theorizes that two mutations in sequence are needed to get breast cancer. (See Figure 11-3.) For example, initially you'd be susceptible to a mutation caused by hormones, then to a mutation caused by diet. The person with genetic breast cancer has passed the gene on to her daughter, so the girl is born with her first mutation and only needs the second to get breast cancer. If the second mutation were something that could be altered (for example, diet), it is possible that changing her diet really *could* prevent her from getting breast cancer. Unfortunately, at this stage we have no way of determining what the sequence is likely to be, or who is vulnerable to which risk factors. But it's an interesting theory to think about, and, if it turns out to be true, would tell us a lot about the link between environment and genetics.

There are some rare syndromes in which people tend to have a run of combinations of cancers in their family, and several of these include breast cancer. One is called SBLA—sarcomas, breast cancers, lung cancers, leukemias, and adrenal cancers.[17] Another combines skin cancers and breast cancers;[18] another ovarian and breast cancers.[19] Researchers are studying these clusters, but as of now, we know little about what causes them.

Right now, two major kinds of research are being done around genetic breast cancer. The first involves trying to find a biomarker—a blood test or some other test that would make it possible to tell a woman, "Yes, you have a positive gene," or "No, you don't." The second involves trying to find a way of looking at DNA and identifying where the cancer-carrying gene is. In late 1990 scientists in Boston reported they had discovered the gene for Li-Fraumeni syn-

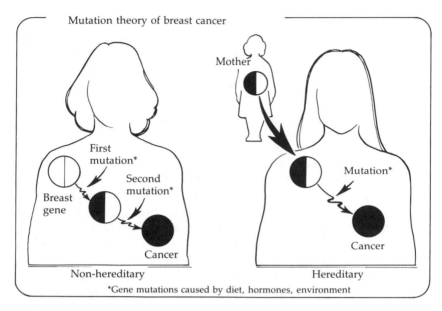

Mutation theory of breast cancer

Mother

First mutation*

Second mutation*

Breast gene

Cancer

Non-hereditary

Mutation*

Cancer

Hereditary

*Gene mutations caused by diet, hormones, environment

FIGURE 11-3

drome (a familial cancer cluster). This may be the first step in decoding genetic breast cancer. If it is true we might be able at some time in the future to do genetic engineering, taking out the faulty gene and replacing it with a harmless gene. It could also be used in prenatal testing, though that will, of course, bring into play all the ethical questions already existing around how to use information about the fetus's susceptibility to particular illnesses and disabilities. In any case, only 5 percent of breast cancers are genetic, so genetic testing may be of little direct use to most women.

More important, because it is more common, is the polygenic breast cancer. Here, there is a familial tendency but not a dominant gene. There can be a number of explanations for polygenic breast cancer. It's possible that there's one gene that, while not a cancer gene itself, makes a woman particularly vulnerable to environmental causes of cancer. If, for example, you are particularly vulnerable to the carcinogenic effects of a high-fat diet, and you've always eaten a high-fat diet, and so have your sisters and cousins, you may find that a number of family members have breast cancer. Or you may be genetically inclined to begin menstruating early and/or going into menopause late, and that increases your risk and that of other family members. Or you may come from a family of women whose lifestyle and values tend to cause them to postpone childbearing until their

30s. Some support for this possibility comes from immigrant studies. Some families may not be at high risk in their native country (say, Japan), but on moving to an environmentally more dangerous country they will have more breast cancer. Thus, genetic and nongenetic factors mix to increase breast cancer risks slightly in the same family. Most family history cases of breast cancer fall into this category.

The critical question for any particular woman is whether her family has the genetic or the polygenic type of breast cancer and what *her* risk is. There are two major studies which help to shed light on this question.

Dr. David Anderson,[20] of M.D. Anderson Hospital in Houston, looked at all the patients at the hospital from 1944 to 1969 and found 6,550 who'd had breast cancer. Of those, he picked out the ones who had relatives with breast cancer—there were 500 of these, or 7.6 percent of the total. He studied these to try and determine whose cancer was caused by dominant genes and whose was polygenic. He concluded from his study that it was important to know whether the relative had breast cancer in only one breast, or in both, or whether the relative was first- or second-degree—that is, a mother or sister versus a cousin. Though his earlier studies suggested that the risk was affected by whether the affected first-degree relative was pre- or postmenopausal, his later work found this to be insignificant. On the basis of his findings, he described what he felt were criteria for the dominant gene type (hereditary) of breast cancer. He concluded from his study that a 30-year-old woman who had two first-degree relatives (mother and sister, or two sisters), one of whom had cancer in both breasts, had a 25–28 percent risk of getting breast cancer by age 70. But if she had a sister and a second-degree relative, her risk was actually only slightly different from that of the general population.

These characterizations were studied in Sweden by Dr. H.O. Adami,[21] who studied a general population. Since Sweden is a small country and has socialized medicine, he was able to get records of all the women in the country who'd been treated for breast cancer over 14 months (1,423 women altogether), and to examine how many of them had a family history of breast cancer and what its pattern was. He looked at all the factors in that family history—was the cancer pre- or postmenopausal? Uni- or bilateral? Unlike Anderson, he found no relationship to age or to whether the cancer was in one breast or both. This might have been because he had in his population only 149 patients who had an additional relative with breast cancer. This small number would make it harder to demonstrate an association with clinical findings. In addition, he found that, overall, when a mother or sister had breast cancer, an individual's chances of getting the disease were only 1.7—a small increase in relative risk (instead of 1/1,000/year at age 40, 1.7/1,000/year). Since Adami studied all the women with breast cancer rather than just those with risk factors, his work is probably more representative of most women with the disease than Anderson's.[22]

All these studies make it clear that family history does affect your risk of getting breast cancer. But so far we don't really know for certain how great the effect is, and, more importantly, how it relates to other risk factors.

Preventative Mastectomy

We can't really change the factors we just discussed. In the next chapter we will discuss the factors relating to breast cancer that we may have some control over.

What if you do indeed have a significant increased risk—is there anything you can do to reduce it? First of all, you can look carefully at the environmental and lifestyle factors that may relate to breast cancer risk (discussed in the next chapter) and decide what to do about them. Second, some women will be encouraged by surgeons to consider prophylactic mastectomies. This is a very controversial idea: in very few other parts of the body do we suggest removing an organ to prevent a disease from occurring. In addition, the indications have been nebulous. Many surgeons will suggest "increased risk" or "cancer phobia" as reasonable indications for breast removal. But their definition of increased risk is very shaky, and includes women who have polygenic breast cancer in a second-degree relative, or women who have never had children. In addition, cancer phobia is often induced by the surgeon. If a surgeon tells you that you are at very high risk for getting breast cancer and your breasts are so lumpy that it will be impossible to find a cancer when it does occur, you will rightly react with fear. Whether this fear is warranted, and whether it justifies removing a normal breast, is another matter. To put these recommendations into perspective, I suggested (on ABC's *Nightline*) that we take out men's testicles and replace them with Ping-Pong balls to prevent testicular cancer. Somehow the men in the audience didn't think this was as good an idea as preventively removing breasts.

If, however, you really do have a serious risk and you are considering preventive surgery, what operation should you have and who should do it? There is an operation that plastic surgeons around the country are offering called a *subcutaneous mastectomy*,[23] which I have to warn against. They make a small incision and remove most (80–

90%) of the breast tissue keeping the nipple and areola intact. They then put in a silicone implant either behind or in front of the pectoralis muscle (see page 351) to reconstruct the breast mound. They say you will be as good as new with no, or reduced, cancer risk. There are a few fallacies in this argument. For one, removing 90 percent of the breast tissue doesn't remove 90 percent of the risk of breast cancer. It leaves 10 percent of your tissue at full risk. In a study done with rats, which have 12 breasts normally, prophylactic mastectomies were done to remove one quarter, one half, or three quarters of the breast tissue.[24] The rats were then given a carcinogen. All the rats developed the same number of tumors regardless of the amount of tissue that had been removed. Although we always have to be careful about applying rat studies to humans, the fact that women have developed breast cancer after prophylactic subcutaneous mastectomies gives some credence to the theory that a subcutaneous mastectomy doesn't alter your vulnerability to breast cancer.[25] In addition, this particular operation has a high level of complications.

If a woman really wanted to have a preventive operation, I would suggest that she have bilateral total mastectomies with immediate reconstruction. A total mastectomy removes virtually all the breast tissue and the nipple. (See page 292.) If you are going to have a preventive operation you want as close to a guarantee as you can get.

Again, I don't want to appear to be advocating this operation. I have only done it once—on a physician who was convinced it was what she wanted. She does not regret her decision. More often than not, when I see women in consultation who are considering this drastic step, I find that a good explanation of the risks and benefits will usually convince them that it is not for them. I suggest that anyone who is considering this procedure get several opinions about what her risk of breast cancer really is and see several surgeons before she decides on such a drastic step.

12

<u> </u>

Risk Factors: External

Unlike the hormonal and genetic influences just discussed, diet, alcohol, and certain medications carry risks over which we have some control. The amount of fat and liquor we consume may play a role in increasing our susceptibility to breast cancer. Hormones taken by postmenopausal women, as well as birth control pills, are also a matter of choice and are being studied in relation to breast cancer. Radiation has always been known to increase cancer risk, and may or may not be something over which we have control.

Diet

Though different theories have connected breast cancer to all kinds of foods, the most compelling studies are those involving fat in the diet. These studies are by no means definitive so far, and are frequently at odds with each other. They are also unclear as to whether the danger that seems to exist comes from all fats, animal fats alone, some combination of animal and vegetable fats, or even just calories. Finally, it's important to remember that even the most convincing studies suggest that only about 27 percent of breast cancers are attributable to dietary fat.[1] While this is impressive, it also suggests that 73 percent of breast cancers aren't connected to fat intake at all.

While of great interest to researchers, the studies provide only hints as to the kind of diet that might help lessen the odds of breast cancer or the disease's severity once it has already occurred. They're well worth looking at, and considering as a basis for a different diet, but they don't provide any of us with a magic amulet against breast cancer.

ANIMAL STUDIES

In the 1940s, Albert Tannenbaum discovered that giving rats a high-fat diet increased their rate of breast cancer. Rat studies done since then have confirmed that the percentage of fat in their diet affects their vulnerability to breast cancer—as does the total intake of calories. Ernst Wydner[2] has established an apparent threshold level: rats with 20 percent or less fat in their diet have a lower breast cancer rate, and once above 20 percent, it doesn't seem to matter what percentage of fat they consume; the rats with 30 percent fat in their diet do as badly as those with 40 percent or more.

Most of this animal research indicates that the fat consumption doesn't actually cause breast cancer, but simply promotes it. Something else probably initiates the process, or causes the first mutation (see page 147)—possibly a virus, or a gene.

DESCRIPTIVE EPIDEMIOLOGY

A direct study is the most useful, but obviously can't be done on human subjects. For a study to have any value, we'd have to put the subjects on a high-fat diet at about the age of five and follow them through a lifetime, making sure their diets were unchanged—clearly an impossible task. So we have to rely on less direct means of studying the effects of diet on breast cancer in humans. One technique is called "descriptive epidemiology." In this, we take a particular group of people—possibly a specific geographical population—and compare it to another group. Since diet varies in different cultures, it can be useful to compare the rate of breast cancer and the dietary habits of one culture with those of another culture. However, if women in country X get more breast cancer than women in country Y, and they also eat more fat, that doesn't necessarily prove that fat causes the increased cancer. These women may also chew more bubblegum, marry younger, do more outdoor exercise, wear different fabrics, and do a hundred other things differently than women in country Y, any of which may or may not relate to their cancer rate.

Nevertheless, this type of epidemiological study has produced interesting data. A chart of breast cancer incidence plotted against dietary fat intake (see Figure 12-1) shows a correlation.[3] For instance, women in Japan have had a lower rate of breast cancer than women in the United States, and their fat intake has also been much lower— 12–15 percent of their calories is fat, as opposed to 40 percent of American women's calories. But as Japanese women have become more westernized, their average fat intake has increased to about 25 percent, and their breast cancer rate has increased somewhat.[4]

In Iceland, the typical diet used to be low in fat, and the breast cancer rate was also low. Again, as the fat in their diet increased, so did their incidence of breast cancer.[5] But there's an important difference: their breast cancer is rising at a much faster rate than that of the Japanese women. This suggests the likelihood that fat alone isn't the issue. Perhaps the Icelandic women have more genetic or hormonal susceptibility to breast cancer—or perhaps there are other changes involved in the westernization process: different stress levels, for example.

Studies of Japanese women who have migrated to California, and who have gradually switched to a more westernized diet, found that the breast cancer rates increased—slightly for the women themselves, but *more* for their daughters.[6] This might indicate that dietary factors make more difference when the body is young and still growing, and less in older people.

Often within the same culture there are subgroups whose diets are significantly different from those of the general population. One revealing study was done with a group of Seventh-Day Adventists in California.[7] Since some Adventists are strict vegetarians and others aren't, they provided a useful study and control group. The study

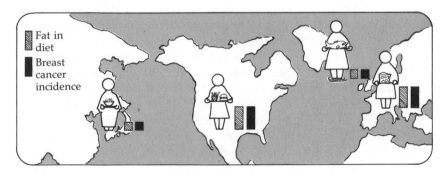

Fat in diet

Breast cancer incidence

FIGURE 12-1

showed that there wasn't much difference in the rate of breast cancer between the vegetarian and nonvegetarian members. A similar study[8] of an order of vegetarian nuns in England had similar results: their breast cancer rates didn't vary significantly from the rates of other never-pregnant women who ate meat. A study of cancer rates in 65 rural counties in China where fat intake ranged from 5 to 47 percent of energy showed no correlation with breast cancer rates, which were about one tenth of those of the United States.[9]

These studies don't necessarily negate the fat-and-breast-cancer findings, however. Both the vegetarian Adventists and the nuns ate a lot of dairy products, which may have kept the total amount of animal fat constant. A study of women on a strict macrobiotic diet, who eat no meat or dairy products, might shed some light on this question. The Chinese data, however, strongly suggest that some of the international comparisons may be related to industrialization rather than to fat in the diet.

The timing of the fat consumption might also be important. Both the nuns and the Adventists had adopted their lifestyles in adulthood (as had the Japanese immigrants), by which time the damage may well have already been done. The time between the first period and the first pregnancy may be the time in which women are most vulnerable to breast cancer promoters, as we mentioned in the last chapter.

CASE-CONTROL AND COHORT STUDIES

Other types of studies are designed to look more accurately at this problem. In *case-control studies*, X number of women with breast cancer are studied, along with the same number of women picked at random. The diets of all these women are then studied to see if there's any difference. Most of these studies have shown either a weak association or no association between dietary fat and breast cancer. It is exceedingly difficult to get an accurate evaluation of diet, however, and small differences might well be missed.

Cohort studies, on the other hand, involve identifying a defined population of individuals who have been exposed to a particular factor and another population not exposed, following both groups over time for the development of cancer. A recent cohort study,[10] which got a lot of publicity when it was released, did not demonstrate a breast cancer–dietary fat link. This 1987 Harvard School of Public Health study followed a group of nurses for a long period of time, looking for a number of different things. They found no relation between fat intake and breast cancer. However, *all* the women in the study ate a lot of fat: the lowest had a fat intake of 32 percent. In rats, remember, the reduction of fats didn't seem to make much difference until it got down to 20 percent or below. That may or may not suggest a similar pattern in human females. (The Harvard study, by the way, did find a correlation between breast cancer and alcohol consumption, which we'll discuss later in this chapter.) What the nurses ate as teenagers might also have been significant, rather than what they were eating as adults.

An additional part of the problem may be the fact that fats are not all the same. Fats from milk-producing animals (butter fat), other land animals, fish and shellfish, vegetables, and hydrogenated vegetable oils all differ substantially in their chemical properties.

There are some studies that suggest that the amount of fat we eat may be a more indirect cause of breast cancer. Being high in calories, fat creates greater weight. Some data show that the taller and fatter a postmenopausal woman is, the more susceptible she is to breast cancer. It's worth noting that one of the countries with the highest breast cancer rate is Holland, whose people have high-fat diets and are typically much taller and heavier than the Japanese, who eat less fat and have less breast cancer. Other studies indicate that it may not be either height or weight, but the interaction of both—the lean body mass. This holds true in studies of rats as well: if you give rats a lower-calorie diet that stunts their growth, they have a lower rate of breast cancer.

The risks related to diet may also differ in pre- and postmenopausal breast cancer. F. de Waard suggested that premenopausal breast cancer has no relation to food but is purely hormonal.[11] But postmenopausal breast cancer, he says, may result from a hormone imbalance caused by "overnutrition." He studied 7,259 postmenopausal women and found an increased risk of breast cancer among those who were taller and heavier.[12] Women who were over 154 pounds and over five-foot-five had 3.6 times the risk that women under 132 pounds and below five-foot-three had. Women whose height and weight fell in between those measurements had a risk that was also between that of the larger and smaller women. (Remember those second-generation Japanese-American women we talked about earlier? As a result of their changed diet, they were taller and heavier than their mothers.) If height is really partly responsible for increased risk of breast cancer, it also supports the early period of vulnerability: you can adjust your weight as an adult, but height is determined early in life, and though part of it is genetic, part is also nutritional.

So it's quite possible that the problem isn't fat itself, but overall nutrition: people who eat more may be more vulnerable to breast cancer. Overnutrition might have some connection with some of the other risk factors: girls with lower food consumption stay thinner and often begin menstruating later than more heavily nourished girls. People who eat more also tend to be those who can afford to—those with an overall higher standard of living, who appear to be at greater risk for breast cancer.

Vitamins and minerals may also be included here. Selenium and vitamins A, C, and E may help protect against breast cancer. It's possible that a combination of low-serum selenium and high fat are bad, but that if the selenium content is high a high-fat intake won't hurt you. Selenium is an essential trace element, found in the soil in varying amounts, which plays a key role in an enzyme in your body, and it seems to have a protective effect against cancer. It's an antioxidant, which blocks the division and growth of cells—including, it appears, cancer cells. If you supplement it in animals, you can reduce their incidence of breast cancer—even if they've been given a carcinogen. It may block the promoting of cancer, just as fat may cause the promotion.[13] However, not only do we need to be careful about applying this kind of data from rats to women, but the data are again inconsistent. High regional selenium intake, when estimated by soil content, is correlated with less breast cancer in women.[14] The risk of cancer, in all sites, was two times greater in patients who had low selenium than in those with high.[15] There were only 17 cases of breast cancer in this study, however. Two recent studies have failed to support the hypothesis that low dietary selenium increases breast cancer risk.[16, 17] Trying to supplement your selenium intake with pills is clearly premature: in large doses, selenium is highly toxic.

Vitamins A and E also affect the metabolism, and seem to compound the effects of selenium: low vitamin A and E, combined with low selenium, may increase susceptibility to cancers more than lack of one of the elements alone.

Vitamin A, particularly the vegetable form, betacarotene, seems to decrease the incidence of several cancers: people with lower betacarotene levels have been shown to get more lung cancer, for example. But it's not clear that massive doses of vitamin A or betacarotene supplements will change anyone's risk of breast cancer.

Zinc may also have an effect on the growth of breast cancer, but the studies so far are extremely contradictory. Some even suggest that large amounts of zinc may increase the risk of breast cancer.

I'm currently involved in a study at the Harvard School of Public Health, with Dr. Walt Willet, looking at the relation between fat and breast cancer. Part of the study has involved looking at selenium, vitamins, and fatty acids. We're asking a group of women who developed breast cancer after menopause to fill out extensive dietary questionnaires. We then take samples of their body fat to analyze different fatty acids, analyze their toenail clippings for selenium, and do blood tests for vitamins. We compare them to a control group of women without breast cancer. As of this writing, it's too early in the study to draw any conclusions.

If fat intake does indeed increase the risk of breast cancer, what makes it happen? There are a number of theories. Some researchers think it changes the metabolism of estrogen. According to one study[18] people with a high-fat diet tend to have more estrogen in their blood and low urinary excretion of estrogen; vegetarians who eat dairy foods excrete more estrogen, leaving less in the blood, and people on macrobiotic diets, which include a very low amount of fat, have even lower levels of estrogen in their blood and secrete less in their urine. As we noted in Chapter 1, your fat cells can make estrogen, so it is also possible that if you're obese, you have an oversupply of estrogen, which could increase your vulnerability to cancer. Studies attempting to confirm this hypothesis have been inconsistent.

It's also possible that cancer cells grow better in an environment with a lot of overnourished cells, and the fatter you are the more such cells there are for the cancer cells to grow with. There's also some evidence that among victims of breast cancer, those with a low-fat diet have a better prognosis than those with a high-fat diet. The studies, however, are not extensive, and we can't be at all certain of them.

The medical profession hasn't embraced the theory of a high-fat diet contributing to breast cancer, for a number of reasons, good and bad. As we've seen, the evidence is far from conclusive, and many doctors are rightly unwilling to present unproven theories as fact. Many will argue that they don't want to push women into trying to change eating habits that are difficult and uncomfortable to change.

Many of them mean what they say. But given the alacrity with which so many doctors accepted the evils of caffeine and its effects on the nonexistent "fibrocystic disease," I'm puzzled and suspicious. The evidence linking fat to breast cancer is much better than any of the evidence against caffeine, and surely it's as hard to give up coffee as it is to reduce fat in one's diet.

For one thing, the dairy and meat lobbies are very strong: medicine is usually reluctant to go up against powerful lobbies, unless (as is the case with tobacco and lung cancer) the evidence against the lobbyists' products is unusually good. It's unfortunate that big business can have such a great effect on the medical profession, but it does, all too often. No doubt there are other nonscientific reasons to account for the resistance of the medical profession to this theory.

It is extremely difficult to do a good prospective study. Not only is it hard for large numbers of women to change their diets permanently, but accurate results mean studying huge numbers of women for a long time. A large prospective study was planned by the National Institutes of Health (NIH) and later canceled because of scientific and monetary difficulties. Political pressure has caused the National Cancer Institute (NCI) to reinstate this Women's Health Trial in late 1990. It will study 24,000 women ages 50–69 over 15 years. Forty per cent of the women will be taught to follow a low fat diet (20% calories from fat) and the incidence of breast cancer, colorectal cancer and heart disease will be compared. We desperately need this kind of research to tell us not only exactly what the culprits are in our westernized "fat" diet, but also when these culprits do their dirty work. If it is during adolescence, then it is fruitless for us to encourage 50-year-old women to change their diets as a method of lessening breast cancer risk.

Overall, it seems likely, from the material in the various studies, that fat consumption and calorie intake do have some effect on your vulnerability to breast cancer. While there isn't nearly as solid proof as there is with smoking and lung cancer, the data are strong enough to make it worthwhile to seriously consider cutting back your animal fat consumption—especially when you consider that animal fat *has* been proven to be a factor in many other illnesses, and nothing good has ever been shown about high animal fat consumption, except perhaps that it tastes good. And if you're the parent of a teenage daughter, it may be wise to consider encouraging her to eat a low-fat diet, since the evidence suggests that much of the fat-related damage may be done early in life. Without expecting miracles, you may do well to encourage your kids to spend a little less time at McDonald's, and to eat more low-fat, nutritional food. (See Appendix B.)

Don't, however, expect miracles. Even if lowering fat in the diet does have an effect, it is likely to be a small one. Women on low-fat diets should not neglect screening. (See page 175.)

Alcohol Consumption

Related to the question of diet is that of alcohol consumption. A number of recent studies suggest that drinking alcoholic beverages, even in moderate amounts, may increase your risk of breast cancer. Walt Willet of the Harvard School of Public Health conducted the study of dietary habits of a group of nurses that we cited earlier in this chapter.[19] He followed a group of 89,538 nurses between 34 and 59 years of age for four years after studying their nutritional habits. He found that consuming hard liquor, beer, and wine appeared to increase women's risk of breast cancer. Women who usually had between three and nine drinks a week had a 1.3 increase in relative risk of breast cancer (1 being the norm: see page 139 for a description of relative risk). Those who had more than nine drinks a week had a 1.6 increase. It was interesting to note that in this study drinking had little effect on those women who were already at high risk but rather mainly on those women with no risk factors.

Interestingly, women under 55 with no other risk factors who had more than nine drinks a week had a more dramatic increase than those over 55: they had a 2.5 increase—two and a half times the susceptibility to breast cancer of nondrinkers with no risk factors. (In all these cases, Dr. Willet looked to see if there were dietary differences as well: there weren't.)

Studies in France and Italy, where wine is consumed regularly by virtually everyone, have supported this connection. Women there do have a higher incidence of breast cancer than do women in the United States, though it's a slight increase—only 1.2 to 1.9 times.

In the same issue of the *New England Journal of Medicine* that Dr. Willet's study appeared in, there was a similar study from the NCI, which looked at 7,188 women between 25 and 77 over a 10-year period.[20] Among the group of regular drinkers a woman's risk of breast cancer was increased by 1.5. The NCI also published another study in 1987 comparing 1,524 women with breast cancer against a control group of 1,896 women without the disease.[21] Again, they found that alcohol consumption increased the risk of breast cancer— but only in those who had drunk liquor before age 30. Consumption of alcohol after 30 didn't seem to matter. Again, the authors looked for other possible compounding factors—differences in diet, socioeconomic position, age of first childbirth—and didn't find them.

As with fat consumption, it may well be that the main effect of alcohol in increasing breast cancer risk is during the vulnerable period of youth. More precise information as to when and how the effect manifests itself is needed before we can make concrete recommendations. Whether to stop drinking or not is unfortunately one of the many decisions we all must make on inadequate information. The risk increase isn't great, but it definitely exists. You alone know how much pleasure you get from your glass of wine or beer, and how alarmed you are at the thought of breast cancer. If it's not all that

important to you to drink, you might want to reduce your alcohol consumption to a glass of champagne on New Year's Eve and major celebrations. Although it may be wise for any number of reasons to discourage your daughters from drinking, this is an area, like many in parenting, where you may not have a lot of control.

Radiation

One of the known risk factors for breast cancer, as well as a variety of other cancers, is radiation. At least three major studies have confirmed that there is indeed a link between radiation and increased risk of breast cancer.

The first study came out of one of the major tragedies of the 20th century—the bombings of Hiroshima and Nagasaki at the end of World War II. The people in the immediate area of the bombings died instantly, or shortly after the bombs were dropped. But it soon became evident that those within a 10-kilometer radius of the bomb sites developed far more cancer than others in comparable populations, and scientists began studying these survivors to learn more about the dangers of radiation. They measured the amount of radiation these people had been exposed to, and then followed them over the years to see what cancers they developed.[22]

Among their other discoveries, the researchers found that while breast cancer rates rose among the general female population exposed to the radiation, the increase was far more dramatic among women who were younger at the time of the bombing than among those who were older—thus strengthening other findings about the particular vulnerability of the developing breast to carcinogenic agents. The effects were greatest among women in their teens and early 20s, and nearly nonexistent in women in their 50s and 60s. Recent reports have indicated an increased risk in the women who were less than 10 years old at the time of the exposure. This effect took longer to be revealed because it didn't appear until the women had reached the age at which breast cancer normally occurs.

Two other studies back up the atom bomb studies. The first is a Canadian study that looked at women who had been treated for tuberculosis with fluoroscopy.[23] This was a common treatment in the 1930s and 1940s, before we knew of the dangers of radiation and saw it as something of a magic cure-all. The typical treatment for TB was to collapse the infected lung to rest it, and then check it with X rays every day to see how it was doing. When the women were studied in the 1970s, they were found to have an increased incidence of breast cancer. I've come across a similar case in my own practice. A patient I just diagnosed with breast cancer, now 58, had had TB in her early 20s. She lived in France and was treated with intensive radiation in the sanitarium. Her two best friends at the sanitarium, treated with the same radiation therapy she was given, have also developed breast cancer.

The third study has examined a group of 606 women in Rochester, New York, who had suffered postpartum mastitis—painfully in-flamed breasts (see page 97)—and had been given radiation averaging between 50 to 450 rads for both breasts to alleviate their pain.[24] They too had a rate of breast cancer higher than that of the general pop-ulation. And the risk was dose-related. This study is interesting for a second reason. The radiation was given after the first pregnancy. Yet it was during lactation, a time of high activity in the breast.

All three studies show that the danger is from exposure to mod-erate doses of radiation (10–500 rads), and the last two show that the danger is only to the area of the body at which the radiation has been aimed. Thus, people exposed to radiation for cancer of the cervix did not show an increased rate of breast cancer.[25] Obviously the survivors of Nagasaki and Hiroshima had their whole bodies exposed to the radiation, and, in fact, they have suffered increased vulnerability to virtually all kinds of cancer. Another interesting find-ing in all these studies is the long latency period. The excess risk of cancer does not appear until the age at which breast cancer commonly occurs. This fact helps to explain why we are only now noting it in those women who had received radiation when young. Both women who received radiation to their thymus (a gland in the chest) as infants[26] and adolescents who received multiple diagnostic X rays for scoliosis[27] have recently been shown to have a subsequent increased breast cancer risk when they reach their 30s and 40s.

This would suggest that radiation is only part of the early picture and that there are other moderating influences that come later and affect the development of breast cancer. The duration of the increased risk from radiation is also not known, but in all these series of patients (atomic bomb survivors, fluoroscopy patients, and mastitis patients) it appears to have lasted at least 35 years from the time of exposure.

This kind of exposure is very different from the kind of exposure that you get with occasional diagnostic X rays such as chest X rays or mammograms. Many people are legitimately concerned about getting such X rays, but it's a mistake to throw out a highly useful diagnostic tool. Remember that the danger comes with a total cumulative dose of radiation. If you had a chest X ray every week for two years, you probably would risk increasing your risk of getting breast cancer. But the danger of leaving pneumonia undetected, if you have reason to believe it may exist, is far greater than any danger from infrequent chest X rays. Similarly, the level of radiation in up-to-date mammograms (1/4 of a rad) won't increase your risk of breast cancer. (See page 177.)

Radiation to treat cancer puts us at the other end of the spectrum: very high levels of radiation are used, on the order of 8,000 rads. In these cases, however, the risk of radiation is far outweighed by the risk of cancer. For example, radiation is used in the treatment of *Hodgkin's disease* (cancer of the lymph nodes). By itself and in conjunction with chemotherapy it has been responsible for many cures. However, some women who had this treatment many years ago are now showing up with breast cancer. We suspect that the radiation to their chests that they received (which in fact saved their lives) is responsible now for these second cancers.[28] It won't be surprising if some of the children treated for cancer with radiation in the chest region will also eventually have an increase in breast cancers.[29] This is unfortunate, but since radiation was responsible for their being around long enough to get a second cancer, most of these patients may have no regrets.

Hormone Medications

BIRTH CONTROL PILLS

We discussed earlier the effects of your body's hormonal system on breast cancer. Since your own hormones can affect breast cancer, it stands to reason that hormones taken externally as drugs will also have an effect—and studies have shown this to be the case.

The birth control pill, which was originally seen as the magic solution to unwanted pregnancy, quickly became vilified as its negative side effects became apparent. As is often the case, the reality of the pill falls somewhere between its panacea/demon images. The pill did indeed, especially in its early forms, seem to contribute to a number of illnesses, including stroke (especially in combination with cigarette smoking in women over 30). Recent studies, however, have suggested that it may also be useful in protecting against certain diseases, such as ovarian cancer. [30, 31]

Part of the problem in discussing "the pill" as though it were a single entity is that, like many other inventions, it has gone through many permutations. The earlier pills used much more estrogen and progesterone than current pills do: we've changed both the amounts and the proportions of those hormones. So early findings aren't necessarily applicable to the pill used today. A study that says it's looking at women who have been on the pill for 10 or 20 years is actually likely to be looking at women who have been on a number of different pills at different times—which explains in part why we seem to get so many contradictory results with studies on the relationship between breast cancer and the pill. The timing of pill use may also be relevant. A long duration of pill use prior to the first pregnancy may be more relevant than the same amount after pregnancy.

Since the pill has been around for only about 20 years, we're now coming into the time period when its relation to breast cancer, if in fact there is any, might surface. In early 1989 some preliminary data came out supporting the fact that long-time pill use prior to the first pregnancy may well increase cancer risk, somewhere between two (if use was less than 10 years) and four times (if use was greater than 10 years). [32] (This means the risk of a 40-year-old goes to 2/1,000/year, or at worst 4/1,000/year, 0.2% or 0.4%.) These data need to be confirmed before we can accept them as true. But even if they do prove correct, the risk may be worth it for the benefit of a convenient, sure method of birth control. This is a decision only you can make, weighing any evidence of increased breast cancer against the risks of other contraceptives, of unwanted births, or of abortion.

DES

Another external hormone women have taken is the estrogen diethylstilbestrol, or DES. It was used in the 1940s through the 1960s to increase fertility and to prevent miscarriage.

Recent studies show a slight increase—1.4—in breast cancer among women who took DES while pregnant.[33] Since there's a lot of estrogen going through your body anyway when you're pregnant, it's not clear why an increased external dosage would be harmful, but it appears to have been, at least for some women. One theory is that exposure to estrogen during the period of rapid growth of breast tissue during pregnancy may increase risk.[34] We don't know yet what effects DES had on the breast cancer rate among daughters of women who'd taken it, since the daughters are only now approaching the age when breast cancer is most common. There *has* been an increase in vaginal cancer among this population, but it's not as aggressive as we once thought it was.

Hormone Replacement Therapy

The question I'm asked more often than any other in my practice is, "What effects will taking postmenopausal hormones have on my risk of breast cancer?" It's a question I hate getting, because I simply don't know what to answer.

During the '40s and '50s, it was popular to give women going through menopause estrogen—gynecologists would routinely prescribe it whether the woman had any complaints or not. And since in those days most women did what their doctors told them to do, they took it. Then studies appeared linking long use of estrogen with uterine cancer: there was a big scandal, and everyone stopped taking it.

But like birth control pills, estrogen therapy pills have been changed over the years. Progesterone has been added to balance the estrogen, and it seems to help protect against uterine cancer.

But there's a problem. Some studies show that taking estrogen for a long time (over 15 years) or at high doses may slightly increase breast cancer (though other studies show no effect at all on breast cancer).[35] And there is no evidence that progesterone acts the same way on the breast as it does on the endometrium.

The only study in favor of progesterone in addition to estrogen (Premarin and Provera) decreasing breast cancer risk is a prospective survey at Wilford Air Force Base in Georgia.[36] At the time of their routine visit, all postmenopausal women were registered according to epidemiological information as well as use of postmenopausal hormones. These women were then followed and their subsequent incidence of cancer was noted. Although the women on Premarin and Provera had a decreased incidence of breast cancer, this study hardly proves the safety of adding progesterone. For one thing, the study was not randomized or controlled. This means that there were probably biases as to which women were given which therapy. It may well be that the women who were high risk for breast cancer were not given the hormones. The best way to answer the question would be a randomized controlled trial, but we may get a good idea about the risk of breast cancer with additional follow-up of those women who have taken or are taking the combination.

In August of 1989 a Swedish study attempted this.[37] Dr. Leif Bergkvist and his colleagues in Uppsala, Sweden, studied 23,244 women aged 35 and older who had been prescribed postmenopausal hormones. After an average of 5.7 years of follow-up they found 253 women with breast cancer, indicating both an increased incidence of breast cancer in women who took estrogen for more than nine years (relative risk of 1.7) and an even higher increase in women who took both estrogen and progesterone for more than six years (relative risk of 4.4). It is important to note that the Swedish women took a different form of estrogen than is used here in the United States, so the findings are not necessarily applicable; however, they are worrisome.

Gynecologic experts in the United States have reacted cautiously to this data, stating that it is inadequate to warrant a change in the current practice.[38] They have argued that these hormones are similar to the pill and the pill hasn't been shown to increase breast cancer risk (see above). Not only has this fact been recently questioned, but the logic is flawed. The pill is being given to women at a different age, and that may make a large difference. The fact is that we need more studies to make even a reasonable guess about postmenopausal hormones and breast cancer.

I do have some problems with the idea that we're supposed to keep taking these hormones indefinitely—there must be some reason that menopause exists in the first place, and maybe our bodies really need to stop having these hormones at some point. I'm concerned because once again gynecologists are casually giving out hormones without sufficient research, and we may well end up with another DES-type situation on our hands.

Those who favor hormone therapy argue, with some validity, that we're not "supposed" to live long enough to go into menopause in the first place: in the old days people died in their 30s and 40s. We live as long as we do because human intelligence has created artificial environments that prolong life. They are convinced that hormone replacement is needed to prevent osteoporosis and cardiovascular disease.

I think it's important to look at the data. Not every woman is at risk for osteoporosis. Recent data indicate that daughters of women with osteoporosis have a lower bone density to start with rather than a higher rate of loss.[39] This means it is possible to test women for bone density and predict who may need preventive treatment with estrogen. Two new devices have become available to look at bone density: dual photon absorptiometry and quantitative digital radiography. Dr. Meryl LeBoff,[40] of the skeletal health and osteoporosis clinic at Brigham and Women's Hospital in Boston, recommends that all perimenopausal women have a bone density test done. She recommends treating with estrogen only the women who are found to have bone density at the lowest third of age-matched controls. Prophylactic estrogen therapy is not recommended initially for women whose bone densities are in the middle and upper thirds unless there are additional risk factors for osteoporosis. Dr. LeBoff goes on to suggest that a repeat test be done in several years to monitor the rate of bone loss. Estrogen is usually started within 10 to 15 years of menopause and only continued for 10 years. Other recommendations for avoiding osteoporosis include calcium supplements (1 gram in premenopausal women and 1.5 grams in postmenopausal women), exercise (walking three times per week for 30–60 minutes), and decreasing alcohol, caffeine, carbonated beverages, and excessive intake of protein.

If not every woman needs postmenopausal estrogen to prevent osteoporosis, the same may be true regarding cardiovascular disease. Although there are definite data showing that the estrogens will favorably affect cholesterol and cardiovascular disease, there are no data showing just which women are likely to benefit. If there is no history of heart disease in your family and your cholesterol and blood pressure are low, then estrogen may well not add anything. In addition, there is evidence that adding progesterone to the estrogen (Provera) counteracts all the good effects of the estrogen on cholesterol.[41] More studies are desperately needed before we recommend hormone replacement to all women.

What do *I* recommend? I think that all postmenopausal women need to be informed that postmenopausal hormone replacement is still experimental. We don't have enough information to properly inform women about the potential risks and benefits. If a woman is high risk for heart disease or osteoporosis, it may well be reasonable for her to consider taking estrogen. The further addition of progesterone is less clear. If the woman has had a hysterectomy there is no reason for her to add progesterone. If not, she has to weigh the unknown risks of progesterone, especially as regards future breast cancer, against the possibility of uterine cancer. Any woman taking postmenopausal hormones needs to be very vigilant about mammography and breast exams as well as gynecological checkups.

Many women take hormones not to prevent possible future illnesses, but to alleviate current discomfort. You may experience incapacitating hot flashes, or extreme vaginal dryness, which ruins your enjoyment of sex. In this case, you may well decide it's worth the risk of taking hormones. If your symptoms are mild and don't disrupt your life particularly, you may not want to bother. You may well want to look into some of the nonhormonal ways to alleviate your symptoms, described in current books on menopause. (See Appendix C.)

What if you've had breast cancer, or a strong family history, and you have horrible menopausal symptoms or a high risk of osteoporosis—should you take hormones? I wish I had an answer, but I don't. There is some circumstantial evidence that it may not be so bad. There is one study of atypical hyperplasia (see page 193) and other benign breast problems showing no increased risk of breast cancer in those women who took estrogen.[42] And we think that women who get pregnant (increasing their levels of hormones tremendously) don't have a higher rate of recurrence. (See page 365.) And we sometimes treat hormone-sensitive cancer with estrogens. (See page 327.) It's something that simply hasn't been studied enough. Until there are more studies done, I can only suggest that you do what seems best to you. If you're in agony from your symptoms, maybe it's worth the risk; if you fear breast cancer more than osteoporosis, it may not be worth the risk.

Prevention of Breast Cancer

Taking into consideration all the factors we have reviewed, the real question is: how far can we now go in preventing breast cancer? Age-standardized rates of breast cancer[43] show that the lowest in the western world is in rural Poland, at 16.2, while the highest is in Hawaiian whites, at 87.5. This would suggest a *potential* for prevention in the Hawaiians of 82 percent. Similarly, among Japanese in Los Angeles the rate is 57.3, while in rural Japan it is 8.9, indicating a prevention potential of 84 percent. Unfortunately, our knowledge about the specific ways to prevent breast cancer is still meager. According to Anthony Miller,[44] the major factors that seem amenable for prevention are diet, reduction in obesity, reduction in the use of estrogens at menopause, and possibly a shift back to earlier ages at first birth.

In Table 12-1, I list the attributable risks for some of these environmental and lifestyle risk factors. Remember, attributable risk is the amount of breast cancer that can be attributed to a certain risk factor (or eliminated if that factor is changed). The degree of certainty

Table 12-1. **Attributable Risks for Breast Cancer**[a]
(percent of breast cancer cases that can be attributed to each factor)

	Attributable Risk
Age 25 or greater with first birth	17%
Estrogen replacement therapy	8
High-fat diet	26
Obesity	12

[a] A.B. Miller, "Epidemiology and Prevention," in J.R. Harris, S. Hellman, I.C. Henderson, and D.W. Kinne, eds., *Breast Diseases* (Philadelphia: J.B. Lippincott, 1987).

varies for each risk factor. These are all very interesting from a public health standpoint, but may or may not be applicable to any one individual woman, and I don't advise using them as the sole influence in decision making. For example, I had my first child at 40 and do not regret it. The advantages to me far outweighed the slight potential increased risk for breast cancer that this may entail. On the other hand, I do eat a low-fat diet, often accompanied by a glass of wine.

Finally, it is important to realize that all of these factors have a long latent time. A proposal for reducing breast cancer by 25 percent in the United States by the year 2000 includes reducing the amount of fat in the diet to, at most, 100 grams per day, and the amount of obesity to 5 percent of the population. Miller has pointed out that the dietary modification would probably have to start at age five, with a 20-year lag until an effect would be seen, and 80 years until the maximum effect would be realized.[45]

13

Detection: Mammography and Other Techniques

Since there is as yet no foolproof way to prevent breast cancer, many researchers have put their efforts into detecting it at the earliest stage possible. This has included techniques for screening as well as diagnosis.

Screening

Screening is the process of looking at healthy people with no symptoms, in order to pick up early signs of disease. The Pap smear is the most successful screening technique to date—it has changed the incidence of cervical cancer by picking up precancers and allowing them to be treated before they grow into cancer, and it has affected the cure rate of that cancer. Cervical cancer is now diagnosed and treated at an early stage, and significant numbers of lives are saved. We're still looking for a Pap smear equivalent for breast cancer.

What we need is a test that's easy to do, widely acceptable to patients (i.e., cheap and painless), sensitive enough to pick up the disease (avoid false negatives), and specific enough not to give false positives. To date we have three good, but imperfect, screening devices—breast self-exam, breast exam by a doctor, and mammography.

Before we go into them, it's useful to look at a few common biases that complicate the issue of early detection. (See Figure 13-1.)

The first is *lead-time* bias—the assumption that catching a disease early in its existence will necessarily affect its rate of progress. This is sometimes true and sometimes not. Let's assume you have a disease that usually kills you eight years after it starts. If we diagnose the disease in the fifth year, you'll live three years after the diagnosis. If we diagnose it in the third year, you'll live another five years—and we gleefully proclaim that our early diagnosis has given you a longer survival span. Actually, it hasn't—it's just given you a longer

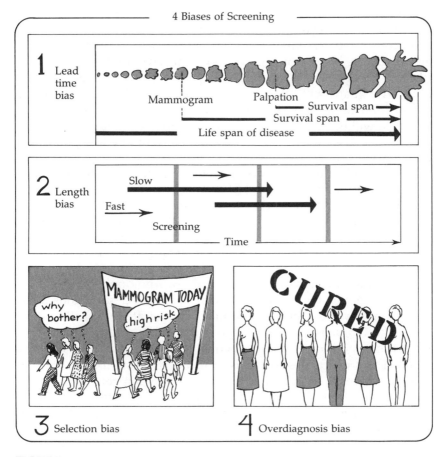

FIGURE 13-1

171

time to know you've got the disease, which may or may not be a benefit. So just looking at years of survival after diagnosis isn't enough—we need to know how many people actually die of the disease with and without early detection. Most breast cancers, it appears, have been around six to eight years by the time they appear on mammogram, and most women with breast cancer survive many years, so this bias can be very misleading.

The second bias is *length* bias. For instance, take a test done every two years on a large number of people. Fast-growing tumors aren't around as long, so there's less time in which they can be detected. Slow-growing tumors are around longer, so you have time to find them. If, for example, one tumor takes six years to become 2 centimeters, and you do a test every two years, you're likely to find it before the six years are up. Another very aggressive tumor grows to 2 centimeters in nine months. You won't find it in your first test, and before you do your second, it's become a palpable lump and has been found. So screening tests select against fast-growing tumors, and catch the slow-growing ones—which have a better prognosis. It's like a nighttime security guard going around the bank every hour. The guard will catch a slow robber who takes three hours to get the job done, but the fast robber, who can do the job in 20 minutes, will be in and out before the guard shows up. The chances are that the fast robber is also the most efficient one; the guard will only get the slower, less dangerous criminal.

Then there's the *selection* bias. If you make mammograms available in, say, Boston, and you don't offer any extra incentives to take the test, who's likely to take you up on your offer? For the most part, it'll be the people who perceive themselves as high-risk: they've already had a breast cancer, or their mother has had breast cancer. The women who don't worry as much about getting the disease are less likely to bother getting the test. So usually the women who go for screening have a higher risk than those who don't.

Finally there's the *overdiagnosis* bias. You detect suspicious areas on a mammogram—they may or may not indicate cancer. Precancer (see page 198) falls into this category: if it were never diagnosed, in many cases nothing would happen and you'd never know you had it. But if it's overtreated—that is, preventive mastectomies are performed wherever it's found—the cure statistics can get very inflated. If, as we currently believe, only 30 percent of precancers will ever become cancers, and mastectomies are performed on all women found to have precancer, huge numbers of women will appear to have been cured, whereas the majority—70 percent—would never have gotten cancer in the first place.

What's needed for a truly accurate study is a randomized controlled study with mortality as its endpoint, to take care of the lead-time bias. If you take a group of women and pick randomly who'll get the test and who won't—that takes care of self-selection and overtreatment. If you have the same numbers of fast- and slow-growing tumors, this counters the length bias, and ensures that both the study group and the control group have the same risks of, and the same kinds of, cancer.

Until recently, breast self-exam—the obvious first step in screening for breast cancer—has never been tested in this careful way to see if it can change the mortality rate of breast cancer. The Russians, British, and Canadians are all now studying it, and the results will be forthcoming in the next decade. Not only has BSE escaped rigorous study up until now, but physical examination by a doctor has also never been studied as the sole method of screening.

There is, however, at least one good randomized controlled study where both physical exam and mammography were combined, and it forms the basis for much of our understanding of the advantages of screening. In New York in 1962, the HIP, a health maintenance organization, chose 62,000 of its female members between the ages of 40 and 64 and divided them into two matched groups of 31,000 each. They then offered the women in one group breast cancer screening, including mammography and physical examinations, with follow-up exams and mammograms once a year for three years. The women in the control group received their usual care. (This was before the days of routine mammography, so it is unlikely that many women in the control group received any mammograms.) The 31,000 women in the study group were invited to get mammograms, and two-thirds of them accepted and had at least one mammogram. (To avoid selection bias here—since the women who were most likely to attend were those at higher risk—all the women who were invited were included in the statistics, rather than just those who actually came. If anything, this would underestimate the benefit of mammography.) One third of the cancers detected were on mammogram only, while two fifths were on physical exam only and one fifth on both. After seven years of follow-up, there was a one-third reduction in mortality in the members of the screened group who were over 50. After 14 years of follow-up,[1] this difference has been maintained, and there is now also a significant difference in the mortality of the women under 50 as well. In fact, at 18 years' follow-up the decrease in deaths from breast cancer was equal in the older and younger group.[2] This was the first study to show the advantage of screening for breast cancer, and it was done with the rather crude mammography being employed in the early '60s. It's important to remember, however, the HIP study included a physician's exam in the screening, and it is interesting to note that physical examination seemed to be more effective in the younger women (40–50), while mammography was more effective in the older group.

On the basis of this study, the National Cancer Institute and the American Cancer Society funded several centers around the country to do annual mammography and physical examinations as a demonstration of the feasibility of national screening. This project has been termed the BCDDP (Breast Cancer Detection Demonstration Project).[3] Although the BCDDP has produced a lot of data, it was not randomized or controlled and so is subject to all the biases. Nonetheless it does seem to confirm the HIP study, and it continues to show increased survival of the women screened in both age groups. In addition, it shows that 80 percent of cancers were detected by mammography alone.[4]

It would be hard to do a study to confirm the HIP data in the United States now that mammography has become so ubiquitous, but they've managed to do it in Sweden,[5] which has socialized medicine. They've taken 134,867 women over 40 living in two different counties. All the women in one county were being offered mammography screening every two to three years, while those in the other county were not. After six years' follow-up (1977–1984) they have found a 31 percent reduction in mortality in the screened group of women over 50 who had single-view mammograms done every three years. This study not only confirms the HIP data in the older population, it also shows that the physical exam included in the HIP study may not have added much to the effectiveness of screening in older women. Although some have concluded that it also shows that mammograms every three years are just as good as when they're done every year, we have to remember that what we are comparing is modern mammograms every three years to poor mammograms (those used in the HIP study) every year. The optimal frequency of mammograms in the older population has yet to be determined. Most specialists recommend once every year or two.

Thus far in the Swedish study the younger age group (40–50) has shown no difference in mortality between the screened women and the control group, but it is still early. The HIP study took over seven years to show this difference, and, as we have noted, the HIP study included physical exam in their screening. There are other nonrandomized studies from the Netherlands, which have confirmed the results in the older patient but not in the younger.[6] These are also studies of just mammography and not physical exam. All of this inconclusive data have led to a raging controversy about the optimal frequency of mammograms in women between 40 and 50.

On the one hand, one camp argues cancers that occur between 40 and 50 seem to be the faster-growing cancers. They feel the reason many studies are not showing the value of mammography in this group is the fact that the mammograms are not being done frequently enough. They think we should close up the intervals in those years—especially since those are the years when you've still got a lot of dense breast tissue that can mask a cancer. Cancers that occur after 50 seem to be slower growing, and the breasts are easier to see on X ray because they have less dense tissue. So it may make sense to have a mammogram every year between 40 and 50, and every two years after 50. Others point out that the only well-established benefit of mammograms has been shown in women over 50, and that we should stop doing them in women between 40 and 50 entirely because it is not cost-effective. It should be pointed out that these arguments refer to the value of recommending frequent mammography as a public policy: the benefit to the individual woman may be very different.

Is there any harm in doing screening mammograms? The risk-to-benefit ratio in women over 50 has been shown consistently and few would argue against encouraging it in this group. In the 40-to-50-year-old group, however, the data aren't so clear. These days, mammography offers very little cancer risk, since we've reduced the amount of radiation significantly. However, as David Eddy,[7] of Duke University, has pointed out, the side effects of mammography have not always been taken into consideration. First of all there is the anxiety provoked by having a screening test for cancer. Then there are the unnecessary biopsies that are performed because of false positive readings. The biopsies cause mental anguish as well as the risks of surgery and the potential for scarring, which decreases the future ability to detect cancer. On the other end, a false negative mammogram (one that is read as normal when the patient actually has cancer) will give a woman a false sense of security and may even delay the diagnosis of her lesion. Finally, there is the cost of mammography, which is often not covered by insurance. In Eddy's analysis, the additional benefit of mammography over and above physical exam was not worth it in women under 50. He recommended that each woman decide for herself whether to have a screening mammogram and that no blanket recommendations be made for women in the 40–50 age group.

Screening Recommendations

So, you want to do everything possible to protect yourself from dying of breast cancer, and from facing disfiguring surgery: what should you do? At the current time I would recommend the following: if you're very young, don't worry: breast cancer is unusual in women under 40, and rare in women under 25. At 25 or so, you should begin doing breast self-exam every month or two—and continue doing it for the rest of your life. Have your doctor examine your breasts during your regular checkups: after 40, make sure to get this done at least once a year. Consider getting a mammogram every year between 40 and 50. After 50 make sure you have a mammogram every one or two years. All three screening devices are important. None of them offers guarantees, but together they provide a useful means of detecting the cancer as early as possible, and doing the best that can be done for it.

Mammograms

A mammogram is, simply, an X ray of the breast—"mammo" means breast and "gram" means picture. It isn't the same as a chest X ray, which looks through the breast and photographs the lungs. Mammograms look at the breast itself, and take pictures of the soft tissue within the breast, allowing the radiologist to notice the presence of anything unusual or suspicious. Mammography can pick up very small lesions—about 1/2 centimeter (or 1/5 inch), whereas you usually can't feel a lump till it's at least a centimeter (2/5 inch). Sometimes mammograms can pick up precancers (see page 198), which are even smaller.

It has its limits, though. The mammogram can only take a picture of the part of the breast that sticks out—the plates are put underneath the breast, or on the sides of the breast—so it's easier to get an accurate picture of a large breast than of a small one. The periphery of the breast will not get into the picture at all. (See Figure 13-2.) In addition, if your breasts are dense, the lump may not have shown through the tissue. So a mammogram isn't 100 percent accurate. Physical exams and mammograms are complementary, not substitutions for each other: you can see some lumps on a mammogram that you can't feel, and you can feel some lumps through palpation that you can't see on an X ray. And, of course, there are some cancers that are "hidden" to both techniques. These cancers are either very fast growing and come up between exams (interval cancers) or are very subtle and don't show up as a lump or shadow until they are fairly far along. Women sometimes feel that their cancer was "missed" if it is diagnosed when it is large or has spread to the lymph nodes (see page 210). In fact, not all cancers can be detected early, even with the most sophisticated technique.

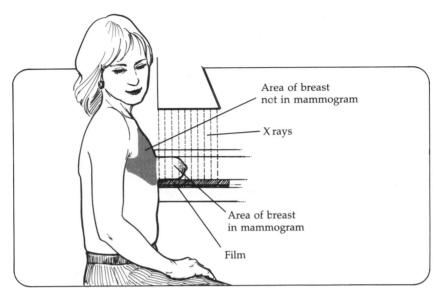

Area of breast
not in mammogram

X rays

Area of breast
in mammogram

Film

FIGURE 13-2

RADIATION RISKS

When mammography first started, it was seen as the Great New Hope: in typical American fashion, it was hyped as the answer to breast cancer. All any woman had to do was get a mammogram every six months, and she had nothing to worry about. Then, in 1976, Dr. John C. Bailar, III[8] calculated that if young women in their 20s started having mammograms every six months, we'd cause more cancer than we'd cure. There were scary news stories, and mammograms were viewed as a major health hazard.

Predictably, the truth is somewhere in between. Mammography, as we have seen, is a helpful tool in controlling breast cancer. It can give you better survival odds and more options for treatment. These days, mammography offers very little radiation risk, since we've reduced the amount of radiation significantly in recent years. As we noted on page 163, the risk of getting cancer from exposure to radiation is greater when you're young, and decreases as you grow older. In terms of mammography, this works very well, since mammography is virtually useless in a young woman with dense breast tissue, and increasingly useful as she ages and breast tissue gives way to fat. By the time you've reached the age where you're most vulnerable to breast cancer, you've also reached the age where you're least vulnerable to cancer from radiation. Most specialists now feel that the radiation risk of mammography after age 35 is negligible or nonexistent.

DIAGNOSTIC MAMMOGRAMS

Mammograms are done for two reasons—screening, as we have discussed, and diagnosis. The procedure is the same in both cases. You get a diagnostic mammogram when you find a lump or have another breast complaint and your doctor sends you to get a mammogram to get a better sense of what the problem is. If, for example, you have lumpy breasts and there's one area that may be a dominant lump, your doctor may send you for a mammogram. If a lump looks jagged, not smooth, on the mammogram, it's a sign to your doctor that further investigation may be called for. If you've got a lump your doctor thinks may be cancerous, a mammogram can help determine if there are other lumps that should be biopsied at the same time; it can also document the location of the lump.

TYPES OF MAMMOGRAMS

Mammography has changed over the years. In the beginning, in the 1950s, radiologists used big X-ray machines—the same ones they used for chest or bone X rays. These produced a fair amount of radiation, and the pictures weren't as clear. So they began refining the process, and designed an X-ray machine specifically geared to do mammograms, one that could be aimed more precisely at the breast, and could rotate to get most of the breast tissue. Over the years they've also refined the X-ray techniques used, so that now very little radiation is actually used. In fact, one radiologist I work with has said that the amount of radiation of one mammogram is equal to the amount of radiation you would get by walking on the beach nude for 10 minutes or until you got caught.[9]

Several years ago, they developed a mammographic technique called the xerogram. It was a form of X ray very different from the earlier mammogram, whose X-ray pictures came out looking like a negative of a photo. The xerogram's picture came out on blue and white paper, giving a very clear picture that was easier for the radiologist to read. It also used less radiation.

Now there's an even better technique—film-screen mammography. It goes back to negative-type pictures, but these pictures give much more precise definition of what the tissue looks like, and it uses even less radiation. Although there have been advances in the xerography technique, most radiologists agree that film screen is the best technique we have, with xerography second.

Film-screen mammography is a bit more uncomfortable than xerography: the breasts have to be squeezed more between the plates to get an accurate picture. Sometimes patients will complain that the technician isn't as good as the one who did their last mammogram, because this one is more uncomfortable. It may not be the technician's fault—she's just using a different method. And the slight discomfort is well worth the gain in accuracy and in lower radiation.

WHAT MAMMOGRAMS SHOW

A mammogram, like any other X ray, presents a two-dimensional view of a three-dimensional structure. Denser areas appear as shadows. Breast tissue, for example, is very dense, and shows up white on the mammogram. Fat, which is not very dense at all, shows up gray.

As you'll recall from our discussion in Chapter 1, when you're young, in your teens and early 20s, your breasts are made up mostly of breast tissue, and are very dense. As you grow older, the breast ages, much as your skin does, and as it ages, there's less breast tissue and more fat. When you're in your 30s and 40s, it's about half and half. (This varies with your weight; if you're very heavy there'll be a lot more fat; if you're thinner, there'll be more breast tissue.) Once you're in menopause, the breast tissue goes away, and there are usually only a few strands of it left. Of course, women vary in the proportion of breast tissue remaining after menopause.

How does this affect the reading of a mammogram? Cancer and benign lumps are the same density as breast tissue. So if you've got a little hard white cancer in the middle of an area of dense tissue, it won't show up on the mammogram—the tissue will hide it. But if the same cancer is sitting in the middle of fat, it'll be very obvious— a white spot in the midst of gray. So mammography is more useful in older women, who have more fat, than in younger women, who have more breast tissue. Sometimes I'll get a patient who's been for a mammogram and has been told that her breasts are so dense that mammography isn't useful to her. That's ridiculous—what it means is that mammography isn't as useful to her now as it would be if she had fatty breasts. Often the woman is around 30, when her breasts should be dense. What it really means is that there's a higher chance that something could be missed (9–20%), and yet also an 80–90 percent chance of picking up something early. This is not to say we are recommending screening mammograms for women at 30, but that a diagnostic mammogram may have some value.

When mammograms show something round and smooth, it's likely to be a cyst or a fibroadenoma (see pages 111 and 116)—cancers are rarely smooth-looking. The mammogram can't distinguish between cysts and fibroadenomas; you'd follow up with an ultrasound to see if it's a cyst (see later in this chapter). If there are jagged, distinct, radiating strands, pulling inward, it's more likely to be cancer. But until it is taken out, you can't tell whether or not it's cancer. In fact, several benign conditions can mimic cancer on a mammogram. Actual scarring or fat necrosis (dead fat) will look very suspicious; as will a noncancerous entity called a radial scar. This lesion can even be confusing under the microscope and often requires a breast pathologist to be sure it is not cancer.

A mammogram may also show intramammary (in the breast) lymph nodes. In fact, until the invention of the mammogram, we didn't know there were lymph nodes in the breast. We now know that about 5.4 percent of women will have them. It can also show calcifications—little specks of calcium. These can sometimes be an early sign of cancer, but they're usually not—80 percent of calcifications are completely harmless (see later in this chapter).

INTERPRETING THE MAMMOGRAM

Sometimes you'll hear about a "normal" mammogram. But there's really no one pattern you can call normal, since there's no real "normal" breast.

I also have trouble with the concept of a "baseline mammogram"— a mammogram taken when a woman is 35 or 40, which is used as a basis for comparison with all her future mammograms. The breast changes with age, and your breast at 50 won't look like it did at 35; nor will it look the same at 60 as it did at 50. The idea seems to have come from the use of baseline chest X rays for TB, which were done years ago. These made more sense: your lungs don't change much over the years, and probably will look pretty much the same at 50 as they did at 30. Actually any time you have your first mammogram could be called your baseline. What's more important is that you have serial mammograms: several a year or two apart so that comparisons can be made. This is what makes mammography the most accurate.

In mammography reports, some radiologists will use words loosely—as if they can see what the pathology is when they're looking at the shadows on the mammogram. So they'll tell you you've got "cystic changes," which is a variation of our old nemesis, fibro-cystic disease. All that means is that you've got dense breast tissue. Or they'll tell you you've got "mammary dysplasia," which sounds very serious and means you've got abnormal cells—cells en route to cancer. But you can't see the cells on the mammogram—only a biopsy can show cells. What they really mean is, once again, you've got dense tissue in your breasts. All they can really tell you is how much breast tissue there is and how much fat tissue, and whether there are any abnormal areas of density.

Twenty percent of women have some degree of variation in the size of their breasts, and that variation is reflected on the inside as well. It will appear on the report as "asymmetry," and it probably doesn't mean anything at all—though sometimes, rarely, an asymmetry can be caused by cancer, so you might want to get a second mammogram several months later, just to make sure: if it's cancer, it's likely to have changed somewhat during that time. One of the most absurd cases I've come across is one in which a patient came to me who'd had a mastectomy on one side, and had a reconstruction done. The report on the mammogram said it showed "marked asymmetry." Of course it did! The breasts were completely different in their composition; they were meant to look the same on the outside, not the inside, and there is absolutely no reason to do a mammogram on a reconstructed breast, since it isn't really a breast at all. (See page 349 for a discussion of breast reconstruction.)

As soon as we started using mammograms, we started studying them to get more information about the breast and what's in it. This is, of course, a good and useful way to pursue knowledge, but it can go a bit overboard. In 1976, John Wolfe came up with a system that's since been called "Wolfe's classification,"[10] which tried to predict the risk of breast cancer by looking at a mammogram. According to his system, if you have a P-1 mammogram, you have no risk, but if you have a D-Y mammogram, you have a high risk, or you can fall into a number of in-between categories. It was based on the density of breast tissue, and has never completely worked. The more we've worked with mammograms, the more we've realized that nothing on the X ray can predict the risk of breast cancer. But since many radiologists were trained with Wolfe's classification, you'll sometimes see on a mammogram report that you've got a P-1 or D-Y breast pattern. Ignore it.

One of the more important discoveries from the study of mam-mograms is that very often cancer is associated with some very fine specks of calcium that appear on the picture—they look a bit like tiny pieces of dust on a film. We discovered that these microcalcifi-cations, as we called them, were sometimes an indication of cancer, or of precancer (see page 198). So the radiologist will always mention in a report any microcalcifications that show up. But it's nothing to panic about—80 percent of microcalcifications have nothing to do with cancer: they're probably just the result of normal wear and tear on your breast. You can even have harmless calcifications in the skin, which may look like they are in the breast if the radiologist doesn't look very carefully. It's interesting that when you age, calcium leaves your bones, where it's needed, and shows up in other places, where it's not. It can show up in arteries, causing them to harden, and in joints, causing arthritis. The microcalcifications in your breast won't cause any problems if they're not indications of cancer or precancer. (The appearance of this calcium in your body has no relation to how much calcium you eat or drink, by the way.)

If there are a lot of microcalcifications in both breasts, there's probably no problem. If the microcalcifications are new, but there are only one or two of them, the radiologist might not call in the surgeon, but will instead tell you to come back in six months to determine whether there are any changes and whether a biopsy is really needed. What concerns doctors is the appearance of a cluster of microcalcifications in one breast—especially if it's new. This calls for a biopsy.

Of course, if it's your first mammogram, you have no way of knowing if a density or calcifications are new: don't worry. If they don't look worrisome for cancer, there's no need for an instant biopsy—you can wait six months or so to see if the calcifications have changed. Sometimes patients will ask why we don't repeat the X ray sooner, say, in three months. Three months is really too soon to show any changes—six months makes more sense. At that point, if there has been an increase or change, you should probably get a biopsy; if not, you're probably fine. As with breast self-examination, which we described in Chapter 2, screening mammography is a way to learn what *your* breasts are normally like, so you can be alert to possibly dangerous changes.

Some problems arise because many radiologists don't have much experience reading mammograms—the technique is too recent. The older radiologists weren't trained in it at all. How familiar your radiologist is with the procedure may well reflect how well the X ray is read. A more experienced mammographer may be willing to state his or her opinion that something is almost certainly benign. A radiologist anxious about missing something will be more likely to say, "I don't think it's cancer, but it could be, and a biopsy is recommended to be absolutely sure." As a result of these kinds of readings, we're doing more operating than ever on benign lumps. In the next decade or so, as mammograms become more common and routine, we may be able to avoid some of this unnecessary surgery.

A typical story these days is a patient in her early 60s who comes to my office after her first mammogram and tells me they found something strange. I look at the X rays and it's small and smooth, like a fibroadenoma, and she's probably had it for 40 years and never knew about it. The radiologist has written, "possible fibroadenoma; cancer can't be ruled out." I can do one of two things. I can have her wait six months and check it out again: if it's cancer, it probably will have grown. Or if she's really anxious, I can do a biopsy (see page 123), which is invasive surgery, but it will put her mind at ease. In these cases, I leave it up to the patient to decide. It's not very likely that she has cancer, but it *is* possible, and she has the right to decide how to deal with the situation.

If you've gotten your mammogram report and the radiologist or your doctor tell you it means you need a biopsy, you don't have to take their word for it. If the thought of a biopsy makes you nervous, get a second opinion. Call the radiologist at a hospital that does a lot of breast work, get your X rays from your original hospital, and bring them in to the second radiologist, or to a breast surgeon.

WIRE LOCALIZATION

As you might imagine, it's difficult to biopsy something you can see only on an X ray. But never fear—we've developed a technique to get around the problem: a wire localization biopsy. In this procedure we use a thin wire to show the surgeon where the lesion is. It's usually done in the X-ray department. The radiologist will give you a local anesthetic, put a small needle into the breast, pointing toward the lesion. He or she will then pass a wire with a hook on the end through the needle, and then position the wire so that it rests where the calcifications or density is (see Figure 13-3). The wire is left in the breast and you're taken to the operating room. The surgeon gives you more anesthetic (usually local but sometimes general) and makes an incision. He or she follows the wire and takes out the area of tissue that's around the wire, hoping it's the right place. The tissue is then sent to the radiology department. There they X-ray it to make sure it *is* the area with the calcifications or lesion, and then it is sent to the pathology department. (See page 132.)

With this procedure, you can't be sure whether the surgeon got *all* the calcifications. If the area is benign this won't matter, but you

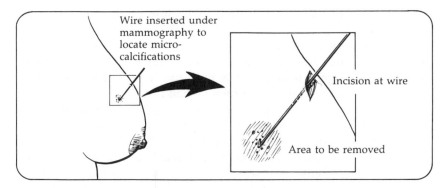

Wire inserted under mammography to locate micro-calcifications

Incision at wire

Area to be removed

FIGURE 13-3

will want to know that there are still some benign calcifications inside. So it's important that you get another mammogram three to six months later to show how you look after the surgery. Since the surgeon can't see or feel calcifications, it is also possible to miss them with the surgery. In this case the specimen mammogram will not show calcifications and you may need to get another biopsy.

It's unfortunate that an incision is necessary, and we're now working on a method of fine-needle aspiration—needle biopsy (see Chapter 10)—that could be done under X-ray guidance. The procedure so far hasn't been perfected. But if it *is* perfected, it will make these open biopsies obsolete.

WHERE TO GET A MAMMOGRAM

As we pointed out, the quality of mammograms, and of the radiologists reading them, varies greatly. It's worth your while to investigate and find the best place in your area to get a mammogram. Since the newest equipment uses the least radiation, you want to be sure the place you go to uses dedicated (used only for mammography) modern equipment purchased within the last few years. Since taking and interpreting mammograms takes skill, you want to find the place that has a designated mammography technician: the technician who does an occasional mammogram, along with foot and lung and kidney X rays, is less likely to do an excellent mammogram than the technician who does mammograms all day; the same applies to the radiologist reading the mammogram. You should ask if there is a mammographer who has had special training and experience and has been singled out as the local expert. Some parts of the country have breast centers, which are specialized and do no X rays but mammograms. There are even mobile vans now that go to workplaces to do mammograms—they're usually very good; generally they send the mammograms they've taken to a mammographer who does nothing but read mammograms.

There are two different setups used for screening. One is the hospital or free-standing clinic which has a radiologist present who will check the quality of the films as they are taken and order extra films as necessary. The other is what is called a low-cost, high-volume clinic. These have been set up in an effort to reduce the cost of mammography. They do a large number of X rays in a day. At the end of the day the radiologist will review all the films at once. If there is any question the woman will be sent a call-back card and told to return for more views. Again, this doesn't mean that there is cancer, only that a conscientious effort is being made to do the best studies possible. Both types of centers have their advantages and disadvantages.

Depending on where you live, it will be more or less simple to find a good mammogram. You can start off by calling the American Cancer Society and asking for a recommendation (see Appendix C). Once you have a few names, you can begin calling the places on your list and asking them if they are accredited by the American College of Radiology (ACR) to do mammograms. The ACR has a voluntary program to evaluate mammography units for equipment quality, staff qualifications, quality of the image, and the amount of patient exposure to radiation. Since accreditation is voluntary, its absense doesn't necessarily mean a center is bad, but on the other hand, its presence suggests that the center is good, and can give you confidence in that facility.[11]

If a hospital or center is *not* accredited, you can ask a number of questions. When did they buy their machine, and is it used only for mammography? Is the person who takes their mammograms a dedicated technician, and is the person who reads them a dedicated radiologist? The answer to all these questions should be "yes." And there's one final question—what is the amount of radiation used per projection? The answer to that should be about 300 millirads.

Don't necessarily go to the place that does the highest number. Some clinics are just set up to make money with high volume at the expense of poor quality. And don't just go to a place because your doctor is friends with the radiologist, or because it's nearby. I see an enormous number of patients with bad mammograms—bad mammograms are blurry, like bad photos, and they can't be read accurately. It may be inconvenient to drive an hour to the best center, but it's worth it. Remember that you're getting radiation to your body, even if it's a minimal amount, and radiation is cumulative; it won't fade away. It's well worth the risk for a good mammogram, but it's not worth it for a bad one, which will simply put extra radiation into your body and give you nothing in return. And once you find a good place go back to it so that all your X rays will be taken at the same place and will be comparable.

It is important to note that insurance coverage for screening mammography varies. As of July 1989, 24 states had passed legislation requiring third-party insurers to pay for the procedure.[12] Federal legislation has also been recently passed regarding Medicare coverage for screening mammography.

PROCEDURE

Don't wear any talcum powder or deodorant the day you're scheduled for a mammogram—flecks of talcum can show up as calcifications on the mammogram. You should also avoid lotions, which can make the breast slippery. Some places will tell you not to take in any caffeine for two weeks before the X ray; unless you yourself have experienced some problem with caffeine, ignore them. (See page 81 for a discussion of the myths about caffeine and the breast.)

The atmosphere you face when you get there will vary from hospital to hospital—some are cold and clinical, others provide a warm ambience and reassuring, friendly personnel. But the actual procedure is pretty standard. You have to undress from the waist up, and you're usually given some kind of hospital gown. You'll probably be X-rayed standing up. The technician—usually, but not always, a woman—will have you lean over a metal plate, and help you place your breast on the plate. Another plate is then pressed toward the first one. It can be cold and a bit uncomfortable. Two pictures of each breast are usually taken, one from the side, the other vertical. Twenty percent of the time it will be necessary to take additional views, or do special magnification or spot pictures. This should not be interpreted as a sign of cancer, but rather of the painstaking care mammography technicians and radiologists are taking to get accurate film. In addition, the way the technologist takes the X rays is important. The flatter they can squeeze your breasts, the more accurate a picture they can get.

The process really isn't all that painful. Paul Stomper did a multi-center study[13] interviewing people right after their mammograms, asking how painful the process was, and what point they were at in their menstrual cycle. He was pleased that 88 percent of the women reported no pain or discomfort at all, and were surprised to learn that their cycle didn't seem to have any effect on their comfort level.

Sometimes women are surprised that a mammogram doesn't hurt. A patient of mine, an older woman, asked her gynecologist if she should have a mammogram—he told her not to because it would be too painful. Recently she decided to do it anyway. "It didn't hurt at all," she told me indignantly. "I shouldn't have listened to my doctor in the first place."

There's a small percentage of women whose breasts are unusually sensitive, and for them a mammogram *can* be painful. In Stomper's study none of the women who reported that the procedure was painful felt that it would stop them from having a second study.

The process lasts only a few minutes; when it's done, you have to wait for a while till the pictures are developed, so you might want to bring a good book or a Walkman along. The radiologist (an M.D., and not the technologist) who looks at the pictures will sometimes see something on the periphery that isn't completely clear, and will want to take another picture, focusing on that area. Or she or he will want a magnification view, which can magnify the breast in a certain area to show it more clearly. This latter is often done when there are little spots of calcium—microcalcifications.

In some places, the radiologist will come out and tell you what the mammogram shows. This is nice, since, even if you're just there for a screening mammography, it's a reminder of the possibility of cancer and you tend to be nervous. But some radiologists are uncomfortable talking to the patients, and some doctors feel a bit territorial about other doctors giving their patients information. So often you'll just be told to go home and wait for your doctor to call you in a couple of days. I find this unfortunate: if there are no problems, you're stuck with a few days of needless worry, and if there are problems, you're stuck with frustrating uncertainty. If you have had your X ray at a high-volume, low-cost center, you have to go home and wait until the X rays are sent to the radiologist to be read and the report filed.

Technologists aren't supposed to say anything: they're not M.D.'s, and their job is taking the pictures, not reading them. Most of them are highly trained and dedicated to their job. So it's not fair to put a technologist on the spot and ask her or him what the mammogram shows.

To date, mammography is by far the best way to look inside the breast, since it can pick up very small lesions, but there are a few other methods in existence.

Thermography

Thermography is a recent invention, based on the concept that cancer gives off more heat than normal tissue. It was originally a much-heralded technique, since it doesn't involve radiation, or putting anything else into the body. A sensor is put on the breast and heat coming from different parts of the breast is measured. From this a map is made, a beautiful colored picture in which blue shows cold areas and red shows hot areas. The hot areas are supposed to be the cancerous ones. Unfortunately, this technique hasn't proved accurate—there are too many false positives and false negatives. Not all cancers give off heat, and of those that do, some are too deep, or located under wedges of fat, and the heat doesn't register on the device.

Though thermography doesn't detect cancer, some European physicians believe it can define the aggressiveness of a cancer known to exist: the more aggressive a cancer is, the more heat it gives off. This hasn't been substantiated, and thermograms have not been used for this purpose in the United States.

Transillumination

Another technique, transillumination, is based on the idea that light will shine through most breast tissue but will be blocked by a lump. A light source is placed by the breast, shone through, and scanned from the other side. Like thermography, its advantage is that it doesn't use radiation; also like thermography, its disadvantage is that it doesn't work. It can't pick up small lesions, which is what you really want for early detection. At this point it is of use only in a research setting.

Ultrasound

In the ultrasound method, high-frequency sound waves are sent off in little pulses, like radar, toward the breast. Jelly is put on the breast to make it slippery, and a small instrument called a transducer is slid along the skin, sending waves through it. If something gets in the way of the waves, they bounce back again, and if nothing gets in the way, they pass through the breast.

Part of the problem is that in the process, the breast is compressed, changing the sound waves. Initially, practitioners had patients lie on their bellies with their breasts hanging in a tub of water and the waves were transmitted through the water. But it still wasn't an accurate screening process, because it didn't detect lumps under 2 centimeters.

So ultrasound isn't really good for screening. But it *can* be useful in looking at a specific area; if you know a lump is there, you can use ultrasound to get more information about it. It can help determine whether a lump is fluid-filled or solid—if it's fluid-filled, like a cyst, the sound waves go through it, and if it's solid, like a fibroadenoma, pseudolump, or cancerous lump, the sound waves will bounce back. So if a lump shows up on a mammogram that you can't feel in a physical examination, and you want to determine whether it's a cyst or a solid lump, ultrasound can give you the answer. Sometimes if I have a very young patient with a lump I can feel, but I don't want to do a mammogram because at her age the radiation can be dangerous, I'll send her for an ultrasound test instead, to see what the lump is. If it's a cyst it can be aspirated; if not, it will be biopsied.

Neither ultrasound nor transillumination uses radiation. However, we've never studied the long-term effects of high-frequency sound waves, or of light waves.

CAT Scanning

Another type of test, CAT scanning, does use radiation—far more than mammography does. It works by visually cutting a part of the body into cross-sectional slices. It's very good for detecting cancer in the belly and the lungs, and brain tumors, because of the composition of those organs. But the amount of radiation needed to make slices close enough to pick up a 5-millimeter lump in the breast is simply too high for safety, and you're wiser to stick with mammograms.

MRI

Magnetic resonance imaging (MRI), a method also known as nuclear magnetic resonance, takes advantage of the electromagnetic qualities of the hydrogen nucleus. Hydrogen is part of water, and water is part of our bodies. MRI is a huge magnet; you get put in the middle of the magnet, and the magnetic field is turned on and then off again. The way the magnetized cells return to normal gives a picture. Like CT scanning, this test has proven useful in the brain, but not in the breast. It may also have long-term effects we don't yet know about. For now, mammography remains the best way of detecting signs of breast cancer.

14

Precancerous Conditions

As we discussed in Chapter 6, virtually none of the symptoms mis-named "fibrocystic disease" are related to breast cancer. There are, however, certain microscopic findings in breast tissue that may well lead to cancer.

You'll recall that I've described the breast as a milk factory, with two parts—lobules that make the milk, and ducts, like hollow tubes, that carry it to the nipples. (See Figure 14-1.) Over the years, you

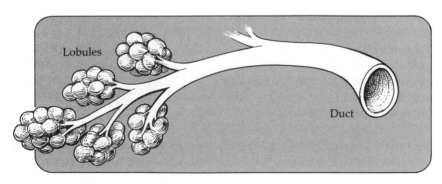

Lobules

Duct

FIGURE 14-1

can get a few extra cells in the ducts—sort of like rust in a metal pipe. This is called *intraductal hyperplasia*, which simply translates to "too many cells in the duct." In itself, this "rust" is no problem. Sometimes the cells can begin to get a bit strange-looking, and this condition is called *intraductal hyperplasia with atypia*. If they keep on getting odd-looking, and multiply within the duct, clogging it up, they're known as *ductal carcinoma in situ* (meaning "in place") or *intraductal carcinoma*. (See Figure 14-2.) These three steps are all reversible. We don't yet know how but suspect it has something to do with hormones.

Finally, if cells break out of the ducts and into the surrounding fat, they are called *invasive ductal cancer*.

The first two conditions do not cause lumps (the third rarely does). They take place inside the duct, so you can't feel them by examining your breast. Though they're found during a biopsy, they aren't in the lump itself—they're next to the lump in the rim of "normal" tissue and the pathologist comes across them by accident. If you look at autopsy studies of women who've died of causes other than breast cancer, you'll see that 30 percent or so have some degree of either hyperplasia or atypical hyperplasia.[1] So probably a lot of us are walking around with these conditions, and we don't know it because we're fine, we have no reason to have biopsies, and they don't show on mammograms.

David Page,[2] of Vanderbilt University, studied 10,000 biopsies and found, not surprisingly, that there is a progression of increased risk with each of these entities. The women with hyperplasia and no atypia had a slightly increased relative risk (barely significant), which was worse when compounded with family history (1.5 and 2.1, respectively). Interestingly, and not easily explained, he also found that women with gross cysts and family history had an increased

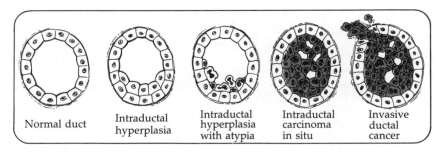

| Normal duct | Intraductal hyperplasia | Intraductal hyperplasia with atypia | Intraductal carcinoma in situ | Invasive ductal cancer |

FIGURE 14-2

relative risk of about 3. Finally, and most significant, the women with atypical hyperplasia had an increased relative risk of 3.5, and if they had a family history in a first-degree relative this rose to 8.9 over 15 years. Although this certainly sounds high, it must be pointed out that there were only 39 women who fulfilled these criteria. In fact, of the 10,000 benign biopsies Page reviewed, only 3 percent had atypical hyperplasia. (See Table 14-1.)

We're not quite sure whether atypical intraductal hyperplasia increases the risk of cancer because it's dangerous in itself, or because it's a response to something else that's dangerous and that we don't yet know about—the way, for example, a bruise that doesn't heal isn't harmful itself but may be failing to heal because it's over a cancer site. It is interesting to note that the risk of invasive cancer in these patients was equal in either breast, and some of the patients even had bilateral cancers. This makes it more likely that we are picking up women at high risk in this specific group, rather than a condition that is dangerous in itself.

There are obviously still many questions. The most vital, however, to the woman diagnosed with atypical hyperplasia is the question of what to do. At this time most surgeons would agree that the best program is close follow-up. This will not detect *more* atypical hyperplasia, but may detect an intraductal carcinoma (by mammogram) or invasive cancer in its early stages. This would include BSE, physical

Table 14-1. Benign Breast Disease and Risk of Breast Cancer[a]

	Relative Risk
Previous biopsy[b]	1.8
Gross cysts	1.3
with first-degree family history	2.7
Atypical hyperplasia	4.4
with first-degree family history	8.9
with calcifications on mammogram	6.5
with first birth after 20	4.5
Lobular carcinoma in situ	7.2
Ductal carcinoma in situ	11.0

[a] Adapted from W.D. Dupont and D.L. Page, "Breast Cancer Risk Associated with Proliferative Disease, Age at First Birth, and a Family History of Breast Cancer," *American Journal of Epidemiology* 125(1987): 769.

[b] S.M. Love, R.S. Gelman, and W.S. Silen, "'Fibrocystic Disease': A Non-disease?," *New England Journal of Medicine* 307(1982): 1010.

exam by a doctor every four to six months, and yearly mammograms. Some women may even consider a more drastic approach and have preventive mastectomies (see page 150). Although I don't usually recommend it, there are some women who feel it is worth it if they have a first-degree family history and atypical hyperplasia.

If we consider atypical hyperplasia as "pre-precancer" in situ cancer, the next step along the path can be considered precancer. Some doctors prefer to call it "noninvasive cancer"—a term I find misleading, since in most people's minds, cancer is by definition an invasive disease. I prefer the term "precancer" because the lack of invasion means that these lesions don't metastasize; they therefore can't kill you.

Precancers in the breast, like atypical hyperplasia, rarely cause lumps, pain, or any other symptoms. They are also usually found incidentally. As opposed to atypical hyperplasia, however, they can sometimes show up on mammograms, and the increased use of mammography for screening has shown us that they're actually far more common than we'd thought. The process of learning about and treating breast precancers is similar to that for cervical precancers, which were rarely seen until the routine use of Pap smears showed them to be fairly frequent.

There are two kinds of precancer of the breast: ductal carcinoma in situ (DCIS), which we have described and will discuss more below, and lobular carcinoma in situ (LCIS). As its name suggests, lobular carcinoma in situ occurs in the lobules. The difference is not only in the lesions' locale: the two behave very differently.

Lobular Cancer in Situ

Under the microscope, LCIS is seen as very small, round cells stuffing the lobules, which normally don't have any cells inside them. (See Figure 14-3.) If there are only a few cells and they're not too odd-looking, you have lobular hyperplasia, while if they fill the whole lobule and do look very atypical (odd), you have LCIS. Such collections of cells are usually what we call "multicentric"—you can find them scattered through both breasts.

The natural history of LCIS became better known when Cushman Haagensen,[3] a leading breast specialist, did a study in which, rather than perform mastectomies on patients in his breast clinic who had LCIS, he carefully monitored them. He saw them periodically for about 30 years, examining them every four months. (This was in the early days of mammography, and Haagensen, who didn't much trust

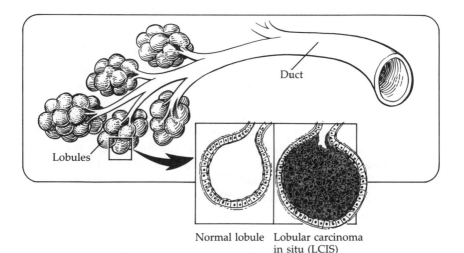

Normal lobule   Lobular carcinoma
in situ (LCIS)

FIGURE 14-3

mammography, used only physical examination.) Out of 211 patients, only 36 (about 17%) developed invasive cancer over 30 years. This made their risk 7.2 times the normal risk: that is, if one patient per thousand per year, age 40–50, normally got breast cancer, then about seven per thousand per year, age 40–50 with LCIS, got breast cancer. These cancers occurred in either breast, and anyplace within the breast: they weren't confined to the spot where the original LCIS was found, or even to the lobular system itself. This strongly suggests that LCIS doesn't grow into cancer, but simply is a sign that cancer is a possible danger—the way, for example, an overcast day warns you it might rain. Because of this, some experts believe that lobular carcinoma in situ, in fact, isn't a true precancer.

Having LCIS indicates a degree of risk similar to that faced by a woman whose mother and sister have breast cancer. It is cumulative risk, spread out over your entire life (see page 139).

It's also important to note that of the women in Haagensen's study who did develop breast cancer, only six died of it. And none of the six had come back for regular examinations. In Haagensen's opinion, they died because they ignored the warning sign of LCIS, and didn't monitor the condition of their breasts after the LCIS diagnosis.

Haagensen's was the benchmark study, but others that have followed have had similar results, showing that people with LCIS have a range of 16–27 percent risk of breast cancer in either breast over 30 years.[4,5,6] This risk can be compounded by other risk factors for breast cancer.

What can you do if you have lobular carcinoma in situ? Removing the LCIS isn't enough, since the LCIS isn't what grows into cancer. Basically there are two options: bilateral mastectomy or no treatment and close follow-up. The more drastic, and the more foolproof, is bilateral mastectomy. If you have no breasts, you won't get breast cancer.

Some of my patients have made that choice, and are quite happy with it, feeling that they are relieved of the constant fear of breast cancer and are going about their lives in comfort. One patient told me, "I knew instantly what my decision should be. I was astounded to see how greedy for life I was." This patient was already in a high-risk group because of her family history; she had seen members of her family go through breast cancer, and was determined not to have to suffer with it herself. She was uncomfortable with the studies about monitoring, which she felt were too recent: mastectomy, she reasoned, had been around a long time. (This patient also had breast reconstruction, a plastic surgery option discussed on page 349.)

There's a variant of the bilateral mastectomy that's very popular with some doctors—the subcutaneous mastectomy, which leaves the nipple and outer breast skin intact. It's a little better cosmetically, but self-defeating, since it still leaves some breast tissue, which is as vulnerable to cancer as the tissue that's been taken away. So it has much of the disfigurement of a whole mastectomy, without the guarantee that you won't get breast cancer, which is the sole justification for the operation.

Another surgical option that I find just as foolish as the subcutaneous mastectomy is a one-sided mastectomy with a quadrantectomy on the other breast—that is, the removal of one breast and the upper outer quadrant, where most of the breast tissue is, of the other.[7] It, too, combines the worst aspects of both options. Since cancers that follow the appearance of LCIS can appear in either breast and in any section of the breast, all this procedure will do is subject you to major surgery and disfigurement, without assuring you that you won't get breast cancer. There is no evidence that reducing the amount of breast tissue by a certain percentage reduces the risk of breast cancer proportionately. If you're going to subject yourself to the disfigurement of surgery, you may as well get the protection that goes with it; if you're going to subject yourself to the risk increase, you may as well keep your body intact.

The alternative to surgery is to take the appearance of LCIS as a warning that you need to be closely watched. This means follow-up exams every three or four months, with a yearly mammogram. That way, if a cancer does develop you're likely to catch it at an early stage and can decide then if you want to have a mastectomy, or a lumpectomy and radiation (see page 258). If a cancer doesn't develop, you've been spared the ordeal of major and disfiguring surgery. This was Haagensen's recommendation, and for the most part I agree with him. Most of my patients have opted for this course.

What's important is that you give yourself the time to figure out what you want to do. LCIS doesn't call for an immediate decision. When a patient of mine is undecided, I usually suggest that she take the follow-up route, and see how she feels about it after six months or a year. If she's comfortable living with it, then she can continue the follow-up course for the rest of her life, or until a cancer occurs. If she finds herself living in a constant state of anxiety, waking up every morning thinking, "this is it—this is the day I'll find the lump," then maybe a bilateral mastectomy is what she needs. If you're uncertain, it makes more sense to try out the follow-up course. You can always decide on mastectomy later, but you can't undo a double mastectomy.

What you really want to know, in order to help you make your decision, is not so much what your risk is of developing breast cancer at all, since most breast cancers if caught early enough can be treated and cured; but what your risk is of developing a cancer so aggressive that by the time it's diagnosed it will have spread through the rest of your body and it's too far gone for any treatment to work. Although there is no exact figure, this risk is probably quite low—about 5 percent.

Radiation and chemotherapy haven't any effect on LCIS, because it's not really cancer. One thing we're in the early stages of considering is the possibility of treating patients who have LCIS with hormones—probably anti-estrogen hormones like tamoxifen (see Chapter 23). It's still too early to be sure if this works, however; studies are now being carried out in Europe.

Sometimes when a patient has a lump that turns out to be cancer, the pathologist will find LCIS in the adjacent tissue. What does this mean? Well, it may just mean that the patient was at a higher risk for breast cancer, and sure enough she got it. But it may also mean that the other breast is also at a higher risk for breast cancer, so some surgeons like to do what we call a "blind biopsy" on that breast. It's called a blind biopsy because they really have no way of knowing what they're looking for: sometimes they'll take out the upper outer quadrant because that's where most of the breast tissue is; or sometimes they'll take out the mirror image of the section they've removed from the breast with LCIS. It's pretty chancy, since there's no evidence that the cancer is more likely to show up in either the upper

197

outer quadrant or the mirror image, and you might find something that looks worrisome pathologically but is biologically insignificant. Most doctors prefer to simply follow the woman closely, with breast examinations every three to four months and yearly mammograms.

The National Surgical, Breast and Bowel Project (NSABP), a nationwide cooperative group that does large studies of breast and bowel problems, is doing a large, countrywide study on LCIS, which will hopefully help us to better understand the condition. Meanwhile, careful monitoring is the wisest course.

Ductal Carcinoma in Situ

DCIS is more complex than lobular—and unlike lobular, it's more than a marker that cancer may appear in the breast: it's a lesion that can in itself grow into a cancer. It rarely forms lumps, but may sometimes form a soft thickening (caused by the pliable ducts becoming less pliable because they're filled with cells). (See Figure 14-4.)

DCIS is now found far more frequently because of mammograms, where it appears with microcalcifications. In fact, it's probably very common. Autopsies done on women who died from all kinds of causes show that between 6 and 16 percent had DCIS.[8,9] This would

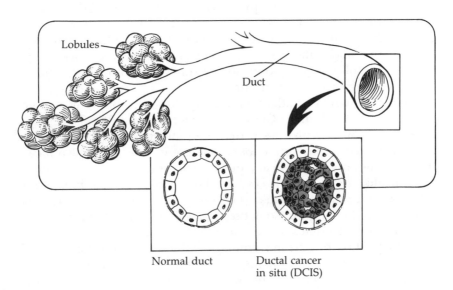

Normal duct   Ductal cancer
                   in situ (DCIS)

FIGURE 14-4

suggest that many of us have it and never know it—it is probably not, as we used to believe, a rare condition.

In the past, standard treatment was a mastectomy of the breast with the lesion. That worked—you can't get breast cancer in a breast that isn't there. But it might not have been necessary—and since the breasts had all been removed, we had no way of studying what happened when a breast that had DCIS wasn't removed.

There have been a few small studies, however, that have given us a clue. Three studies followed people who were biopsied and thought to have something benign. W.L. Betsill,[10] at Sloan Kettering Institute in New York, reviewed all the pathology the hospital had done on 10,000 breasts between 1940 and 1950 and, on reexamining the pathology reports, found 25 cases of people who had been misdiagnosed: the biopsied tissue had been described as benign but actually had had early intraductal lesions. (These lesions are often small, and very easy to miss.) Obviously, no further treatment had been done. Of these 25, only 10 had been regularly followed for 22 years. They contacted these women and found out what their breast history had been since the biopsies had been performed. They found that seven had developed invasive cancer in the 22 years after the original diagnosis.

Other similar studies have led us to believe that about 20–25 percent of women with untreated DCIS will go on to get invasive cancer within about 10 years.[11]

Since all the studies together add up to only 78 patients, this is not enough to be sure they're representative. Furthermore, their lesions were on the border between atypical hyperplasia and DCIS, or they would have been diagnosed initially: the studies don't address the situation of women with obvious DCIS. What is clear from these studies is that untreated DCIS can go on to invasive breast cancer, and also that in the majority of women it does not seem to do so.

A further complexity is that some of the lesions don't stay in the precancerous stage, but revert to either intraductal hyperplasia with atypia or just plain intraductal hyperplasia. Unfortunately, at the moment we don't know how to make this happen, nor do we know how to tell which ones will become cancer and which won't. There's a lot of research going on right now on the molecular biology level to try and determine whether there's some kind of a marker that would clearly show which lesions are on their way to cancer, and which won't ever become cancer. If we found a clue, it might help predict what treatment would be best for those that we knew would become cancer. In a few years, we'll probably have that knowledge.

Without a thorough understanding of the natural history of DCIS, it's hard to devise a logical treatment. However, there is increasing interest in treatments for DCIS that are less drastic than mastectomy—chiefly, wide excision. This is the same principle as the lumpectomy in breast cancer (see page 284), except that there's usually no lump involved, so the surgeon tries to remove the entire area that has the DCIS, along with a rim of normal breast tissue.

Some experts argue against this, claiming that DCIS, like LCIS, is multicentric, but I've seen no evidence to support this idea. Whenever DCIS treated by wide excision recurs, it recurs in the same area of the same breast. If it were truly multicentric, it would most likely occur in different parts of the breast and in either breast, but it does not appear to.

The problem is that no one has ever mapped out the anatomy of the ductal system—something I'm working on in my own research now. If we had such a "map," the surgeon could remove the particular ductal system that's affected, while leaving the rest of the breast alone. Then we'd be sure of getting out the entire dangerous area. Now we just remove the area around the lesion, with no way of knowing whether or not we've gotten out the whole ductal system—which may account for the recurrences that happen.

Another worry is that the lesion may have become invasive in the immediately surrounding area, and is no longer a precancer but an invasive cancer, which needs to be treated as such.

The best data we have on the results of limited surgery for DCIS come from Michael Lagios[12] in San Francisco—a pathologist who's done some fine and careful work. He first looked at mastectomies done on women with DCIS to see if he could correlate the sizes of the lesions with the chance of having a tiny spot of invasion that can only be seen under a microscope. He found that if the lesion was less than 25 millimeters (one inch), there was almost no chance of hidden invasion, and if the lesion was more than 50 millimeters (two inches), microinvasion was highly probable. Once he felt that invasion in the smaller lesion was highly unlikely, he and his group tried treating them with surgery less severe than mastectomy. They took 79 patients with lesions of 25 millimeters or less and did wide excisions, including a rim of normal tissue around the lesion. They followed them up for an average of eight years and found eight recurrences: four invasive cancers and four precancers—10.1 percent of the women he'd operated on. That's about one third of what the untreated patients had shown in previous studies.[13] Unfortunately, his wide excisions were "blind"—he couldn't see or feel the lesions—and so his recurrences probably represent leftover cancer cells he was unable to detect. Mastectomies done on the same women, although more drastic, would probably have resulted in no recurrences.

Is radiation useful for treating DCIS? There have been three small studies on radiation and DCIS—one looking at 40 women,[14] one 14,[15] and one 34.[16] They suggest a risk of between 5 and 10 percent of subsequent invasive cancer within about five years—a bit better than just wide excision, but not a lot better. The only randomized data were on the more advanced lesions reported by the NSABP. In a nationwide study they called B6,[17] which compared, for *invasive* cancer, mastectomy, lumpectomy alone, and lumpectomy plus radiation, the pathologist Edwin Fisher reviewed all the slides. He reclassified 78 of the patients who he believed had DCIS rather than invasive cancer. The confusion was caused by the fact that the lesions were right on the border of being invasive—lesions that were perceived as invasive by the earlier pathologists. This study showed that patients who'd had wide excisions plus radiation for their DCIS had a 7 percent recurrence rate within four or five years, as opposed to 23 percent recurrence among those who'd had only wide excisions. It's worth noting that most of these women had lumps or DCIS of 2.5 centimeters or larger. This suggests that lumpectomy and radiation is more effective in treating *advanced* DCIS than lumpectomy alone, probably because the radiation kills the cells that were inadvertently left behind. It may also be that radiation is more important the closer the lesion is to invasion.

But this study is still too small and too limited to draw generalizations from, so the NSABP is now doing a bigger study, B17, throughout the country, randomly dividing women with DCIS into one group that gets wide excisions alone and one that gets wide excisions plus radiation. I think that any woman with DCIS who lives in an area that's cooperating in this study—and they're all around the country, in large and small cities—should try to get involved in it, unless she's already clear about what kind of treatment she wants. If enough participants are signed up, it can give us some of the answers we so vitally need. Ask your surgeon for more information about getting into this study.

TREATMENT OPTIONS FOR DCIS

You've gotten your routine mammogram; it's shown a cluster of microcalcifications, and your doctor has done a wire localization biopsy, described earlier, after which you're told you've got DCIS.

The first step is usually to do another mammogram—to see if the biopsy has gotten rid of all the microcalcifications. Then you've got three choices:

You can have that breast removed, which is close to 99 percent foolproof—it's as close to a guarantee as we get in medicine.

You can have a wide excision biopsy, hoping that the surgeon can remove the dangerous area completely. The pathologist will look at the edge of the tissue around the area removed: if there's no sign of DCIS there, we assume the breast will be okay—it's fairly accurate, but not 100 percent. You still have between a 10- and 20-percent chance of a subsequent cancer.

Finally, you can have a wide excision biopsy followed by radiation, which reduces your chances of subsequent cancer to between 5 and 10 percent.

Usually you don't have to have the lymph nodes removed, since this is precancer and isn't, at this stage, capable of spreading. But if the lesions are big (greater than 5 centimeters), some experts think they may hide microinvasion, and recommend removing the lymph nodes as well.

I try to encourage every woman to participate in the NSABP study, unless she has a definite preference or unless there are reasons to pick a particular treatment. Apart from the study, we currently use the size of the lesion seen on mammogram to determine our treatment recommendation, in view of Lagios's work discussed earlier. If the lesion is less than 2.5 centimeters, we offer the patient any of the following three options: wide excision alone, wide excision with radiation, or mastectomy. Generally we favor wide excision alone, since the results in this situation seem to be the same with or without radiation (about 10%). If the lesion is 2.5 to 5 centimeters, we feel it is closer to those in the NSABP study and recommend either excision followed by radiation or mastectomy. Finally, if the lesion is 5 centimeters or larger, we would recommend a mastectomy, since a wide enough excision would probably be the equivalent of a mastectomy in most women.

As new studies and information come in, we will be able to refine this and have a better basis for determining treatment. Every patient should have the final say in what treatment she gets: some women don't want a mastectomy no matter how big the lesions are, while, at the other extreme, some patients don't want to gamble even on a tiny lesion. When Nancy Reagan had precancer in the fall of 1987, she chose to have a mastectomy even though the lesion was tiny— 7 millimeters.

Remember, there's not one single treatment for precancer; there are a number of possible treatments. The only treatment for which we have clear data is mastectomy; the others must still be considered experimental. You don't have to rush into any one treatment because your doctor or your friend or anyone else says you should. It's your breast, and your life. Take the time to decide what's best for you.

PART FOUR

MAKING THE DIAGNOSIS
OF BREAST CANCER

15

Breast Cancer: An Overview

One of the reasons there's been a major shift in the treatment of breast cancer is that there's been a shift in the whole way we think about breast cancer. In the mid-19th century, when breast cancer first began to be seen as a treatable disease, it was thought that the cancer started in the breast and then grew out from it in a continuous way—it would go directly into the lymph nodes, directly into the lungs, or directly through the liver. (See Figure 15-1.) Nobody realized that it spread through the lymphatics (the vessels that carry lymph through the body) or the bloodstream. In those days, by the time a woman with breast cancer came to a doctor, she probably had a large tumor that took up most of the breast: it had already metastasized to the liver and other organs, and the doctors didn't think to question how it had gotten there. Women didn't find lumps until they were large: there was no concept of breast self-examination, and respectable women weren't supposed to touch their breasts any more than was essential for washing and dressing.

The theory of the continuous spread of cancer held sway until the late 19th century when doctors first began to realize the importance of the lymphatic system. At that point, the German surgeon von Volkmann demonstrated that extension wasn't the only way breast cancer spread—it also spread through the lymphatics. Cancer

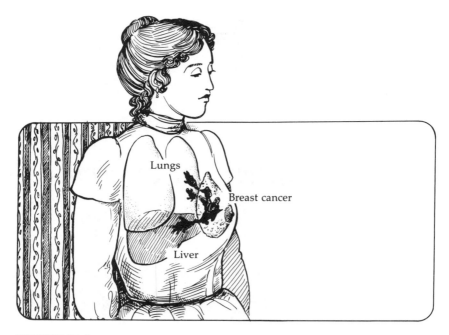

FIGURE 15-1

was then thought to start in the breast, get slowly bigger and then go cell by cell into the lymph nodes. When it got to the last lymph node, it went quickly into the rest of the body. Thus, the reasoning went, it was necessary to remove the lymph nodes as well as the breast and chest-wall muscles—to get out the tumor and all the lymph nodes in the vicinity of the breast. Based on this reasoning, William Stuart Halsted developed the operaton known as a radical mastectomy (it was first done in England in 1857 by Charles Moore) during the 1890s at Johns Hopkins. When this radical surgery didn't always work it was thought to be not extensive enough. Halsted tried removing the supraclavicular nodes (above the collarbone) and Sampson Handley, a London surgeon, included removing part of the breastbone and ribs to get the internal mammary nodes. Neither of these radical operations was shown to add to survival, but both became popular, and both are sometimes still done today.

The fact that extending the surgery didn't improve survival led to the thought that timing was the key element. If you don't operate immediately, they reasoned, the cancer might jump from the lymph nodes into the rest of the body, and the patient would be lost. This is the basis of the belief that held sway for many years—that as soon as the biopsy was performed a frozen section should be performed (see Chapter 10) and, if cancer was found, an immediate radical mastectomy should follow.

As early as the 1930s, critics started complaining that the radical mastectomy was of no use in patients whose cancer had spread and was too extensive for early lesions. Geoffrey Keynes in England and R. McWhirter in Scotland were both exploring combining radiation therapy and lesser forms of surgery. In the 1940s, D.H. Patey and W.H. Dyson, also in England, responding to an anatomical study of breast lymphatics by J.H. Gray, argued for a less extensive operation that removed the breast and axillary lymph nodes while leaving the chest muscles intact. This was termed a modified radical mastectomy.

In spite of the good reports from England, American surgeons were slow to try this lesser surgery. But when educated women got wind of these new developments, they demanded that their doctors try the less mutilating form of surgery. Over time, studies comparing patients who had radical and modified mastectomies found no difference in survival rate or local recurrence. By the mid-1970s the modified radical mastectomy had replaced the radical mastectomy in most hospitals. While it was an improvement in terms of less disfigurement and impaired mobility, it still didn't increase the survival rate.[1]

By this time, pioneers such as Oliver Cope in Boston and George Crile, Jr., in Cleveland were pushing for even less disfiguring surgery and trying partial mastectomies, with and without radiation. However, the real shift came about 15 years ago, when Bernard Fisher of Pittsburgh began to develop an alternative theory.[2] He looked at current research, including a study by J. Gershon-Cohen that followed breast cancer metastasis—areas where the cancer had spread—over time to see how fast they grew.[3] He was able to calculate that the average doubling time for a cancer cell was about 100 days. It took 100 days for the first cell to become two cells, those two to become four, those four to become eight, and so on. Since it takes 100 billion cells to have about a centimeter's worth of cancer, that means that most cancers have been around nine years before they can be seen on a mammogram and 10 years before they can be felt as a lump. (See Figure 15-2.) This isn't a hard-and-fast rule: some cancers grow faster, and some slower, and it's possible that cancers grow in spurts, growing and then resting and then growing some more. But it is true that cancer has had the opportunity to spread microscopically many years before we can detect it. If this is true, Fisher reasoned, then taking out the lymph nodes at the time of diagnosis shouldn't have much to do with survival. Rather, survival would be determined by how well the immune system handled whatever cancer cells had already spread from the breast. In 1971

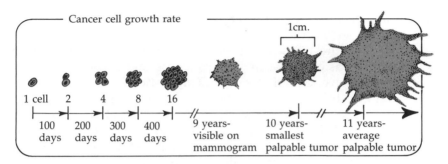

FIGURE 15-2

Fisher set up a protocol to study this, randomizing women into three treatment groups.[4] In one, women had a radical mastectomy, in one a simple mastectomy and radiation, and in the third only a simple mastectomy, leaving the lymph nodes intact. After 15 years the survival rates for the three groups were exactly the same.

There has been some concern that Fisher's study was not large enough to detect a small difference in survival with lymph node removal, but even the critics can only hypothesize that at most 7 percent of women would be likely to benefit if there is indeed an advantage to lymph node removal at the time of surgery.[5]

In one way, this notion of very early cancer spread is a depressing thought, but it's helpful in that it shows the folly of assuming that a mastectomy must be performed the instant a cancer is discovered: you won't stop the cancer from spreading because it probably already has, and if somehow it hasn't spread in 10 years there's no reason to assume it's going to suddenly begin in the next half hour. This research also opened up the way to exploring treatment for breast cancer that involved less surgery than mastectomy, as well as pointing out the importance of some type of systemic treatment in addition to the local one.

When we first diagnose breast cancer, the question we have to ask is not whether the cancer cells have gotten out, but how well we think the patient's body has taken care of whatever cells might have gotten out. We determine this in a number of ways. One of these is to look at the places where the cancer is likely to have gone. Different cancers seem to have an affinity for different parts of the body, and breast cancer cells, although they can go anywhere, seem especially drawn to the lungs, liver, and bones. We do tests called staging tests (see page 229) on these three areas and then examine the lymph nodes to decide if there is microscopic spread.

What do we do with that information once we have it? The answer

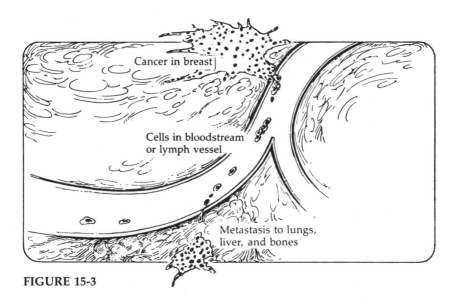

Cancer in breast

Cells in bloodstream
or lymph vessel

Metastasis to lungs,
liver, and bones

FIGURE 15-3

to this is what has really revolutionized the approach to breast cancer. If we think, for whatever reason, you might have microscopic cells elsewhere that the body hasn't successfully destroyed, we give you systemic treatments—either chemotherapy or hormone therapy. These involve the use of drugs, given either intravenously or orally, that go into your bloodstream and circulate through it, getting to all the places the cells might be and trying to destroy them. Surgery can only take care of the large cancer in the breast itself—if only one cell has left the breast and is sitting, alone, somewhere else in your body, untouched by the immune system, the most extensive mastectomy in the world won't keep the cancer from returning. That cell will multiply and the cancer will grow. Radiation, too, is a local treatment; it will clean up the cells around the area that's been operated on, but it doesn't get any cells that have left that area. So a systemic treatment is needed, and we choose one that works well on breast cancer cells such as chemotherapy or hormone therapy. Having decided on that, we then decide on a local treatment determining what combination of surgery and radiation will be most effective. Both are important.

Are there some women in whom we can find the cancers at an early stage, before there's been any metastasis at all? There's still some debate about this. The screening data (see page 174) say that doing mammography will pick up breast cancers earlier (maybe at six years instead of eight) and that this improves survival, at least in older women. This could mean that a cancer must reach a certain threshold before starting to metastasize, or that once there are a certain number of cells in the bloodstream the immune system can no longer handle them effectively. We don't have any scientific evidence about this, but I personally favor the latter theory. I think that any breast cancer large enough to be detected has already spread. But a smaller cancer has obviously sent fewer cancer cells into the bloodstream than a bigger one, and an aggressive cancer has sent off more cells than a slower-growing cancer. (See Figure 15-4.) So I think that in the early stages, if a cancer is small or nonaggressive, the body has probably been able to kill off whatever cells the cancer has thrown into it. After a while, when the cancer has had time to grow and send off more and more cells, the body is less and less able to fight off those cells. Whichever theory is correct, it remains true that early diagnosis can make a difference in some women—it potentially can catch a cancer at a point when local treatment alone will be able to cure it.

The danger of cancer depends on the balance between the cancer and the ability of your body's immune system to fight it. It's similar to infection and bacteria. In the old days, before antibiotics, pneumonia was often, but not always, fatal. Many of its victims died, but many others went through the crisis, their fever broke, and they survived. The survivors were those whose bodies were able to fight off the bacteria. Even after the invention of antibiotics, the body's immune system played a part: antibiotics don't kill every last bacteria, but they reduce the bacteria to a level the body can fight off.

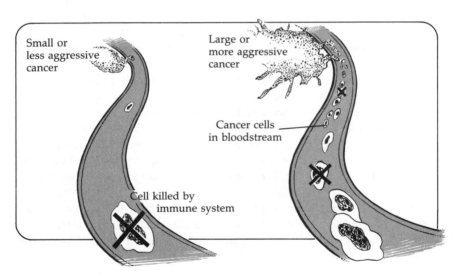

FIGURE 15-4

Surgery and radiation reduce the bulk of cancer cells but not all of the microscopic ones. Chemotherapy or hormone therapy helps to wipe out the microscopic cells, but it probably doesn't kill them all. We hope that it kills off enough so the body's immune system can take over and get the rest.

The next logical step would be to find some way to try and stimulate the immune system. Much research is being done on this matter (see page 383), but so far we don't have a reliable method that can be used in all patients. Most of the complementary treatments (see Chapter 24)—whether meditation, diet, "positive thinking" techniques, or visualization—are methods that practitioners hope will strengthen the immune system to help it fight off the cancer. Theoretically, they can work well in conjunction with chemotherapy—the chemicals kill the cancer while the complementary method bolsters the body's own fighting resources. Although we have no scientific proof, I feel from my own experience that, if nothing else, their ability to empower the woman and give her a role in her own care can't help but be strengthening. The possibility that stress may damage the immune system, lessening the body's ability to fight off cancer cells, also needs further research.

With breast cancer, unlike some other cancers, five years without recurrence doesn't mean you're cured. Because it's usually a slow-growing cancer, it can spread to another part of your body and go undetected for 10 or even 20 years. The longer you go without a recurrence, however, the less likely a recurrence is, and the more treatable it will be if it does happen. Many women will live out their normal lifespans, though you will only know if this is true for you in retrospect, when you're dying of something else at a ripe old age. Therefore, you're wise to think of breast cancer as a chronic disease, like high blood pressure or diabetes or asthma, that you'll always have in your life. You're also wise to remember that it's very likely that, as with other chronic diseases, it's something you can *live* with.

It might be useful here to clarify some cancer terminology that often confuses people (these and other words will be found in the glossary). First of all, there's *metastasis,* which means the spread of the cancer to another organ. Sometimes we also call spread to the lymph nodes metastasis, acknowledging that the cells had to come through the bloodstream. But a cancer that has "metastasized" to the lymph nodes, as we have said, is considered differently than one that has spread to other organs. When these cells are microscopic in other organs, and in fact undetectable by modern techniques, we call them *micrometastasis.* If it is detectable it is a metastasis.

If this metastasis occurs after the original treatment and is large enough to be detected we call it a *recurrence.* A cancer that's recurred elsewhere in the body can rarely be cured—but it can be put into *remission*. A remission is essentially a slowing down of the cancer's progress for a period of time, so that you live longer—and, depending on a number of factors, that "longer" can be a few months or 20 years.

Treatments for a primary cancer given in addition to the local therapy are called *adjuvant treatments*, which differ from metastatic treatments.

And finally, there's the research *protocol* (sometimes called a clinical trial)—a concept I'll discuss at length here, because it's so important in our efforts to understand and eventually eliminate cancer. Although the term "protocol" sounds like we're talking about who goes into the operating room first, a medical protocol is actually a program designed to answer some specific questions about the effectiveness of a particular approach. The questions can be about methods of diagnosis, types of treatment, dosage of drugs, timing of administration of drugs, or type of drugs used. So one protocol, for example, will study node-negative breast cancers in women between 30 and 60 to see whether they would benefit from chemotherapy. A large-enough group of patients who fit the criteria is recruited, and they're *randomized* (picked at random either to receive the treatment or not). Those selected to receive the drugs will be given them on a very strict regimen: for instance, they will be given X amount, on day 1 and 3, and a particular blood test will be given on day 5. This precision is important for the question to be answered—no variation is permitted, or our understanding of how well the treatment works will be impaired. The other women, or *control group*, will not receive the drugs but will be followed just as rigorously. What makes it a protocol is the fact that it is asking a question: will the women receiving the chemotherapy do better than the women who are not? By participating in this study these women will get reasonable treatments and at the same time help us to figure out the answer.

Often a doctor will tell you they are using the same "protocol" as the one used at a cancer center, when what they mean is that they are using the same drugs in the same dosages. But unless it's part of a study designed to answer a fundamental question, it isn't really a protocol.

New treatments used in protocols are tried out in three phases. *Phase one* treatments are used on people who have advanced disease and are willing to be guinea pigs, on the long shot that this may be the miracle that saves them. These studies are to determine the toxicity of the drugs and what dosages are safe to use. In addition to looking at toxicity, they're trying to give patients the drugs in the doses that will work if the drug does work. These are usually new drugs and there is always the chance that one of them will be effective. In *phase two* (done if phase one has been successful) we are testing the efficacy of the drug against different cancers. These studies are often done on women whose cancer has recurred but are not in a life-threatening situation. Once we've determined the effectiveness of the drugs and the best dosages, we're at *phase three*. Phase three studies are comparison studies done on new drugs which seem to show some effectiveness without undue toxicity. They compare the new treatment to the standard treatment. Phase three studies use patients with all degrees of cancer.

This is an ethical way to experiment with drugs, but it does create some limitations. Since in the early stages we use only those patients who have not responded well to other drugs, we can't be sure that, when our new treatment fails also, it would not have worked with a patient with less widespread disease. In fact, there are now efforts to try some new drugs earlier, at the first sign of recurrence, which may indeed be a fairer way to test them. Even with this limitation, however, we've made amazing advances in chemotherapy in the past decade.

It's important to understand that a phase three protocol is never an early stage of experimentation. By the time we have a large-scale protocol, we're using drugs or treatments that are already used. What we're changing is dosages, timing, and combinations of drugs or their indications. Often what's being studied is the dosage of a particular drug we know to be effective, or timing of treatments. In these studies patients are randomly divided into two groups, one given the higher dosage and one the lower. If one group does better than the other, we'll know which dose is best; if both do the same, we know the low dose is all that's needed.

Although it may seem a little scary to participate in research, it is important to remember that no doctor should put you on a protocol or clinical trial unless she or he is convinced that the treatment being investigated will be at least as helpful to you as the standard treatment. As in the example cited earlier, your treatment will be chosen by an unbiased computer. You could be part of a control group that gets only standard treatment. If the experimental treatment proves not to work, you will be better off; if it proves better, you will often be offered it at a later date. In addition, there is a Human Experimentation Committee in every hospital which reviews every protocol to make sure it is safe and well-designed. They oversee all clinical trials and are responsible for making sure that the informed consent is readable and the potential benefits of the study outweigh its risks for the subjects being studied. Of course, you'll always be given the choice. It's both unethical and illegal for a doctor to put you on a protocol treatment or clinical trial without your full and informed consent, and you have every right to refuse.

There are very good reasons for participating in a protocol, and many women are eager to do so. Susan McKenney, a nurse practitioner and oncology nurse who works extensively with breast cancer patients, has talked with many patients at the Dana Farber Institute in Boston. She finds that, once the women understand that they're not just guinea pigs and that the treatments can be helpful both to them and to other women, they are often anxious to participate. "Breast cancer treatment has changed over the last 20 years because women have participated in protocols," she says.

Only about 3 percent of breast cancer patients in the United States participate in protocols. This is much lower than in Europe, and not something for us to be proud of. Many hospitals or doctors here simply don't offer them. If you're being treated at a research hospital such as Dana Farber in Boston, the Mayo Clinic in Minnesota, or the M.D. Anderson in Texas, you'll usually be offered protocols if you qualify, and large numbers of patients there do participate. As McKenney observes, women who choose such hospitals for treatment tend to be those who seek out the most advanced, sophisticated treatments; that's why they go to a big research hospital. They feel safer in an environment where the major purpose is to study and fight cancer.

And some doctors don't offer protocols. There are several reasons for this. Some aren't convinced that protocols—or a particular protocol—offer as good a treatment as the standard treatment. Others don't want to bother: they have to fill out a lot of forms, or do blood tests on very specific days—a protocol is more work for the doctor. Still others are willing enough to offer protocols, but haven't the interest or the ability to explain them well. If a doctor simply says, "You can have the standard treatment or be part of an experiment," you're probably going to take the former. If you're not offered a protocol, it is important for you to ask your doctor why he or she is suggesting a particular treatment. Sometimes it's because there is scientific evidence that supports it, but more often than not, it is because they feel, based on their experience, that it is the right treatment. Both of these may be valid reasons, but you deserve to know which is being used. At the same time, if you are not being offered a protocol or clinical trial you deserve to know why. In that case, I think you should seriously consider asking the doctor about what protocols are available, and then decide whether or not to be part of them, and how. They are tremendously important; they're the only way we can learn anything and they may well insure that you are getting the best treatment available. And there are protocols available, even to doctors who aren't affiliated with research hospitals. The NSABP (see Appendix C for the number to call for information) runs many protocols, working with doctors all over the country. The National Cancer Institute (see Appendix C) also has many protocols and will pay the expenses of any woman who participates. The drawback is that you must be treated at the National Cancer Institute in Washington, D.C. In addition, there is the Community Cancer Outreach Program, which includes 52 community programs in 31 states. These have been selected by the National Cancer Institute to participate in the introduction of the newest clinical protocols and to bring patients to clinical trials. Finally, all doctors have access to a computer program from the National Cancer Institute that lists all the available protocols for breast cancer, and the latest treatments. You may or may not decide that you want to be part of a protocol, but you owe it to yourself, and to other women, to find out what the protocols that you are eligible for are and what they involve, before you decide.

16

Diagnosis and Types of Cancer

Once you've discovered a symptom that alerts you to the possibility of breast cancer (see page 12), what should you do? The first step, obviously, is to see a doctor. Start with your own primary-care physician or gynecologist. If you're over 35, your doctor should send you for a mammogram. Even if the mammogram shows no abnormalities, if the symptom persists, ask to be referred to a surgeon or a breast specialist. In some areas of the country, there are surgeons like myself who specialize in breast disease; in other areas you may be referred to a general surgeon. Don't be scared by the word "surgeon"—the fact that you're going to see a surgeon doesn't automatically mean an operation. Surgeons are the doctors best trained to diagnose breast problems. And if you're unsatisfied with the answers you're getting from one surgeon, find another one.

Types of Biopsy

What might the surgeon suggest? Very possibly, some form of biopsy. As we discussed on page 124, this covers four distinct procedures, so it's important that you understand which kind your doctor is talking about. Often the patient thinks it means taking out a small piece of tissue, while the surgeon really means removing the whole lump.

In the first, and mildest, form of biopsy, the *fine-needle aspiration*, the surgeon holds the lump between her or his fingers, anesthetizes the surrounding skin, and then passes the small needle in and out of the lump a few times, and gets out cells that can be analyzed. (See Figure 16-1.)

There are two ways these cells can be analyzed. In the first method, the pathologist will squirt them out onto a slide, the way one would for a Pap smear, and the slide is stained. In the second, they're squirted out into alcohol in a test tube which is then centrifuged (spun around) so the cells are separated out, and then the slides are made from those cells. The method used depends on the preference of the doctor and the hospital you're using. Neither is better than the other.

The advantage of the fine-needle aspiration biopsy is that you can find out the answer relatively quickly, it doesn't require surgery, and

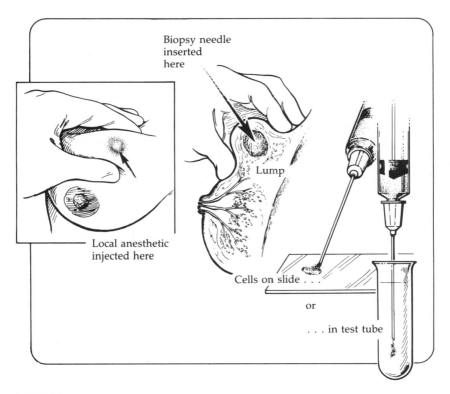

Biopsy needle
inserted
here

Lump

Local anesthetic
injected here

Cells on slide . . .

or

. . . in test tube

FIGURE 16-1

you can then begin to discuss what the possibilities are. The problem is that it's most accurate when it's positive. If you have a lump that's very suspicious and you have a fine-needle biopsy done that comes out positive, you probably have cancer. If it comes out negative, however, you still may have cancer. So with a negative finding, you'd still want to follow up with a surgical biopsy.[1]

In the past, there was another problem with fine-needle aspiration—you couldn't use it to test for hormone receptors (see later in this chapter). Now, however, there's a new technique which enables cells to be analyzed for hormone receptors using just a very few cells, so we should be able to do hormone-receptor tests with cells we get from fine-needle aspirations. Other tests can be done on these cells to determine the aggressiveness of the cancer and are discussed later.

Fine-needle aspirations require a really good cytopathologist (cell specialist) who is used to looking at isolated, individual cells under the microscope, which is different from looking at a piece of tissue and seeing the cells in the larger context.

The second form of biopsy, the *tru-cut needle biopsy*, removes a core from the center of the suspicious tissue, instead of just a few cells. This core, like any tissue removed in a biopsy, can be made into a slide. The problem is that the lump has to be fairly large and hard for a core to be taken out of the middle. It's a bit more uncomfortable than the fine-needle aspiration, since the surgeon has to push harder to get the core out. But it can still be done easily in the office, and can give a diagnosis without surgery. It doesn't provide enough tissue for a standard hormone-receptor test, but the new technique just mentioned can be used. In addition, it gives enough tissue to make an accurate diagnosis. Fine-needle aspirations are supplanting tru-cuts in most places now, since they're less hassle. But the tru-cut is a good alternative if there's no cytopathologist available.

In the third kind of biopsy, the *incisional biopsy*, a wedge is taken out of the lump. It's usually done under a local anesthetic. The surgeon makes a small incision, goes down into the lump and takes a piece out of it, which is sent to the pathologist. Usually this is done only in cases where the lump is so large that taking it all out would be a big operation. We used to need to do an incisional biopsy to get enough tissue for hormone-receptor tests, but now that we can do them with fine-needle biopsies, it's not as necessary.

Finally there's the *excisional biopsy*—taking the whole lump out. That's what most surgeons mean when they say they're going to do a biopsy. It's usually done under a local anesthetic, but sometimes a general is used (see page 279). As we mentioned, if the lump isn't palpable but is seen on a mammogram, the excisional biopsy needs to be done with the guidance of wire localization (see page 183).

What I do first when someone comes to me with a lump is try to decide whether it seems likely to be malignant. If it seems so to me, then I'll do a fine-needle aspiration to confirm the diagnosis. In that way, if I'm right and the findings come back positive, I can spare my patient an extra operation. If the fine-needle aspiration's finding is inconclusive, I'll then do an excisional biopsy.

Ironically, to do a fine-needle biopsy, you need a good-sized lump. If there's something tiny that can be seen on a mammogram but not felt, the doctor won't be able to get a needle into it. We're working on a method of doing fine-needle aspirations under X-ray guidance. It would be a good way to detect cancer in tiny lumps, as well as cancers associated with microcalcifications; thus, it would be an alternative to wire localization biopsy. We've just completed a study of this technique on 100 patients and it looks very promising.

Biopsies and treatment can be done in one or two stages. The one-stage procedure was popular 10 to 20 years ago. You'd sign a form in advance, agreeing to an immediate mastectomy if cancer was found. This is still sometimes done today: it's what Nancy Reagan did in 1988. This one-stage approach was based on the old theory that when you operate on an area with cancer, you spread the cancer cells all around, and so you have to get them out before they get any further. However, there's absolutely no evidence that a one-stage procedure has any effect on survival or cure rates.[2]

A two-stage procedure is one in which the biopsy is performed, usually under local anesthetic, and then, later, you're given the diagnosis, after which you can take time to discuss the possible treatments and make your decision.

The advantage of a two-stage procedure is that it gives you time to think. Being told you have breast cancer is upsetting, even if you've suspected it. You need time to adjust to the idea, to decide, with full information, perhaps including a second opinion, what you want to do. I don't think you can really make that decision before you know if you've got cancer: the hypothetical is very different from the real; that is, what you think you'll decide *if* you have cancer may be very different from what you *will* decide *when* you learn you have cancer.

For many women, the thought of having cancer is so appalling that often their first thought is, "I don't want to deal with this, just get it out of me and let me go on with my life." But with a day or two to reflect on this new reality, your panic may subside and you may decide on a less drastic treatment than your original horror dictated. Whatever treatment you decide on, you'll have to live with it for the rest of your life—and that life won't be shortened by giving yourself a little time to think it over.

Obviously, if you've got cancer you want it taken care of as soon as possible, and you don't want to hang around for several months before your treatment. But the week or so you give yourself to decide won't kill you, and it will help you to make the clearest decision possible. No one should be put to sleep without knowing whether she'll have her breast when she wakes up.

How to Interpret a Biopsy Report

The pathologist looking at the tissue removed in an excisional biopsy can tell whether or not breast cancer is present, and if it is, what kind of breast cancer you have. The language of a pathologist's report, however, can be puzzling and intimidating.

Most breast cancers (86%) start in the ducts, 12 percent start in lobules, and the rest start in surrounding tissues. Thus, your cancer will probably be described as either *ductal carcinoma* or *lobular carcinoma*. Next, the report will state whether or not the cancer is invasive. Invasive cancers are also known as *infiltrating cancers*—a somewhat sinister-sounding description, which simply means the cancer has grown outside the duct or lobule where it started into the surrounding tissue. (See Figure 16-2.) In this case the report will read either *invasive ductal* (or *lobular*) *carcinoma* or *infiltrating ductal (lobular) carcinoma*.

Since lobules and ducts are kinds of glands, and the medical term meaning "related to a gland" is "adeno," sometimes these cancers are called *adenocarcinomas*.

An infiltrating ductal cancer forms a hard, firm lump, because it creates a lot of reaction caused by tough tissue (fibrosis) around the cells. Infiltrating lobular cancer tends to be a little more sneaky and will send out individual cells in little fingerlike projections into the

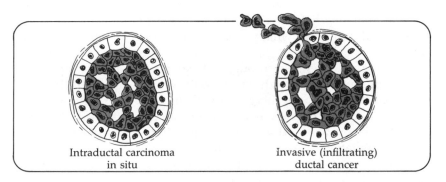

| Intraductal carcinoma in situ | Invasive (infiltrating) ductal cancer |

FIGURE 16-2

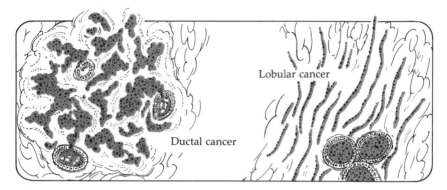

Lobular cancer

Ductal cancer

FIGURE 16-3

tissues without a lot of reaction around them, and you may feel it as a little thickening, rather than a hard lump. (See Figure 16-3.) For this reason, it's harder for surgeons to tell if they've got the lobular cancer all out, because the little projections can't be felt as easily as a hard lump. Aside from that, however, one form is no worse than the other: neither has a better or worse prognosis. There's a slightly higher tendency for lobular cancer to occur in both breasts. That is, although an infiltrating ductal cancer has about a 15 percent chance of occurring in the other breast, a lobular cancer has about a 20 percent chance—an increase in risk, but not an overwhelming one.[3]

If the cancer is *not* invasive, it will be called *intraductal carcinoma* or *ductal carcinoma in situ* or *lobular carcinoma in situ* or even *noninvasive carcinoma*. These are all names for what I call precancer and were discussed in Chapter 14. Sometimes both cancer and precancer are present in one lump, and the report might read *infiltrating ductal carcinoma with an intraductal component*.

There are other names for cancers that may appear on the pathologist's report. For the most part they're variations on invasive ductal cancer, named by the pathologist according to the visual appearance of the cells under the microscope. *Tubular cancer*, in which the cancer cells look like little tubes, is very unusual—1–2 percent of breast cancers—and usually less aggressive. *Medullary carcinoma* looks a little like brain tissue (the medulla) and can be aggressive or less aggressive. *Mucinous carcinoma* is a kind of infiltrating ductal cancer that makes mucus. *Papillary carcinoma* has cells that stick out in little papules, or fingerlike projections. (See Table 16-1.)

Once the pathologists have decided what kind of cancer you have, they try to determine by studying the cells further whether or not they're likely to be aggressive. This isn't 100 percent accurate, however; it's a little like looking at a lineup to pick out who the criminal is. If one of the people is seedy and scruffy-looking and one is

Table 16-1.   Types of Breast Cancer and Frequency[a, b]

Infiltrating ductal	70.0%
Invasive lobular	10.0
Medullary	6.0
Mucinous or colloid	3.0
Tubular	1.2
Adenocystic	0.4
Papillary	1.0
Carcinosarcoma	0.1
Paget's disease	3.0
Inflammatory	1.0
In situ breast cancer	5.0
ductal	2.5
lobular	2.5

[a] There can be combinations of any of these types.

[b] Henderson, C., J.R. Harris, D.W. Kinne, S. Helman, "Cancer of the Breast," in V.T. DeVita, Jr., Helman, S., Rosenberg, S.A. eds. *Cancer: Principles and Practice of Oncology*, Vol. I, 3rd edition. Philadelphia: J.B. Lippincott, 1989, pp. 1204–1206.

wearing a three-piece suit, you'll guess that the first one is the bad guy. But you could be wrong.

Similarly, the pathologist who sees wild-looking ("poorly differentiated") cells will know that such cells are usually more aggressive, while the cells that look closer to normal ("well differentiated") are usually less aggressive. (See Figure 16-4.) The cells in between are called "moderately differentiated." But poorly differentiated cells aren't a sign of doom—the fact that they look wild doesn't guarantee they'll act that way. It is important to realize that most breast cancers are poorly differentiated.

Another thing the pathologist will look for is how many cells are dividing, and how actively they're dividing. The most aggressive

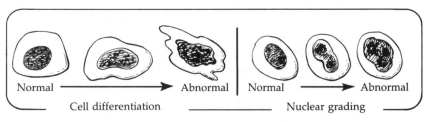

FIGURE 16-4

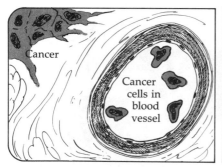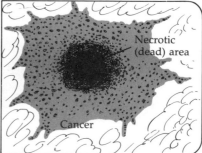

FIGURE 16-5

cancers tend to have a lot of cells dividing at the same time, because they're growing rapidly. Less aggressive cancers tend to have very few dividing cells. How many are dividing is indirectly measured by something called the *nuclear grade*. The nucleus of the cell is the part that goes through cell division, so the grade gives you an idea of the degree of cell division and how odd-looking the nuclei are. Pathologists usually grade on a scale of 1–3 or 1–4, with the higher number being the worst.

The pathologist will also look to see if there are any cancer cells in the middle of a blood vessel or a lymphatic vessel. This is called *vascular invasion*, or *lymphatic invasion*, and suggests that the cancer is potentially more dangerous than if it's not there. Another ominous sign can be "necrosis," or dead cancer cells. This usually means that the cancer has outgrown its blood supply, a sign that it is growing rapidly. (See Figure 16-5.)

All of these are methods of trying to get as much information as possible from looking at the cancer. None of them is 100 percent certain at predicting behavior.

In addition, the pathology report should be able to tell you if there's cancer at the margins of the tissue that's been removed. This is done by a fairly imprecise technique. Ink is put all around the outside of the sample, before it is cut up and fixed and slides are made. If on the slides there are cancer cells next to the ink, this means that there's cancer on the outer border, and if there are cancer cells only in the middle, not next to the ink, there is a clean margin. (See Figure 16-6.) So the report might say, "The margins are uninvolved with tumor," or "The margins are involved with tumor," or "The margins are indeterminate." If the lump has been taken out in more than one piece, we usually can't tell if the margins are clear or not. Also, we can only do representative sections of the margin; to get them all, we'd have to make thousands of slides. So when we

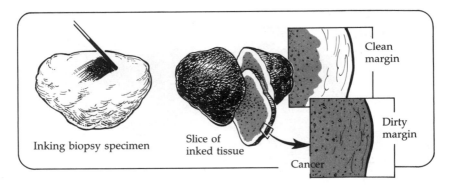

Inking biopsy specimen

Slice of
inked tissue

Cancer

Clean
margin

Dirty
margin

FIGURE 16-6

say the margins are clean, we're only making an educated guess—we can't be 100 percent sure.

How clearly any of these things are seen depends on the expertise of the pathologist looking at them, and how hard the pathologist looks. Someone who makes only a couple of slides and looks at them very hastily is obviously more likely to miss things than someone who makes a lot of slides and looks at them carefully. If you are at all concerned about the quality of the pathology evaluation, or even if you are not, you might want to have your slides sent to another pathologist in another institution (see Appendix E). Some of the things we've discussed aren't always easy to see on the slides. It can be somewhat subjective: are these cells bizarre-looking enough? Are they invading other structures? It's worth getting a second opinion. Often the pathologists themselves will ask other pathologists on the staff to look at the slides and give their opinions. If you live in a small town with a small hospital, you might want your slides sent to a big university center, where someone sees a lot of breast pathology. You can call the university hospital's pathology department and arrange to have them look at your slides, then call your hospital and have the slides sent. Make sure it *is* the slides they send, since that's what the second pathologist needs to see—not just the first pathologist's interpretation. You need to get the clearest information possible to decide what course of treatment to embark on.

Another important test to be performed on biopsied material is an *estrogen-receptor test*, done to find out whether or not the tumor is sensitive to hormones. A hormone is a chemical substance secreted into the bloodstream by a particular gland: its function is to stimulate a physiological process. It travels till it reaches a cell that's equipped with a matching receptor. The hormone functions a little like a key, and the receptor is the lock to a cell, which opens only to the right key. When, for example, an estrogen molecule finds a cell with an estrogen receptor, it attaches itself to the receptor, which then opens the door of the cell and lets it in. (See Figure 16-7.) Once inside, it can do its job in the cell. Not all cells have hormone receptors, and those that don't will never respond to a hormone—there's no lock for the key to open. Similarly, a specific hormone can't get into a receptor for another hormone—it's the wrong key for that door.

Like an apartment door in a big city, a cell can have a number of locks—or different hormone receptors. The number and types of receptors a cell has are variable, depending on the hormonal environment and on the type of cell itself. For example, a breast cancer cell may have receptors for both estrogen and progesterone, only estrogen, or only progesterone. We determine if a particular cancer is sensitive to estrogen (*estrogen-receptor-positive*) by doing a biochemical assay test. If it's *estrogen-receptor-negative*, it isn't sensitive to estrogen. Similar tests are also done for progesterone.

The implications of the hormone-receptor tests are twofold. In general, tumors that are sensitive to hormones—that have receptors—are slower growing and have a slightly better prognosis than tumors that aren't. Generally, postmenopausal women are more

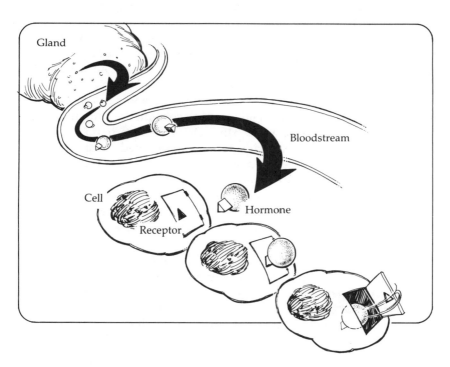

FIGURE 16-7

likely to be estrogen-receptor-positive and premenopausal women more likely to be estrogen-receptor-negative. Secondly, the test tells whether the tumor can be treated with some kind of hormonal therapy. If it's not sensitive to hormones, it rarely responds to hormone treatments (see page 323).

Flow cytometry[4] is a way of measuring the amount and type of DNA in a particular tumor. If the tumor cells have the correct amount of DNA, they're called *diploid;* if the amount of DNA is abnormal, they're called *aneuploid.* Tumors whose cells are aneuploid tend to behave more aggressively. In addition, these tests can measure the percentage of cells that are dividing at any one time. This is called the *S phase fraction.* If there are a lot of cells dividing (high S phase fraction), the tumor is behaving more aggressively than if there are a few cells dividing (low S phase fraction). These tests are not yet available everywhere, but they're being used in more and more places. They actually give the same information as nuclear grade but are more reliable. As in every test, however, there are drawbacks. They tend to confirm the information obtained by testing the lymph nodes and not to add any new information about the tumor's behavior.[5]

All of these tests are only tools which, added together, help to give us a picture of the cancer, and decide what to do. If you've got an infiltrating ductal carcinoma, poorly differentiated and with a high nuclear grade and vascular invasion, and estrogen-receptor-negative, and if flow cytometry shows that the tumor is aneuploid with a high S phase fraction—all of those are signs that it's fairly aggressive. Therefore, even if the lymph nodes are negative in a tumor like this, with all these signs we might still want to consider treating the tumor with chemotherapy (see page 315). On the other hand, if it's an infiltrating ductal cancer that's well differentiated, that's got low nuclear grade, no vascular invasion, is estrogen-receptor-positive, and is diploid on flow cytometry, with a low S phase fraction, it is more likely that it is a less aggressive tumor and we'd be less inclined to do a very aggressive systemic treatment—or any chemotherapy at all. Most cancers are actually combinations of these, and therefore treatment decisions are less clear.

It is important to remember that all any of these tests, and others that are being developed, can do is to give a picture of that particular tumor at one particular time—sort of like a snapshot. They cannot tell anything about how it actually acts in a particular woman. That is better determined by the staging tests we will discuss in the next chapter.

17

Staging

When cancer spreads, it travels through the lymph-carrying vessels—or the bloodstream. A few cells cluster together, move into the blood or lymph stream, and are carried until they find a body part where they settle in and begin to grow. Certain organs seem to attract certain kinds of cancer cells: breast cancer cells are most often drawn to the lung, liver, and bones. It is important to mention that a cancer that starts out as a breast cancer remains a breast cancer, wherever it travels, so that a breast cancer that has traveled to the liver will retain all the characteristics of breast cancer, which are very distinct from those of liver cancer. This is important because the treatments used for it are breast cancer treatments, not liver cancer treatments. (Very few other cancers travel to the breast, by the way.)

There are "gross" tests we can do to check the lungs, liver, and bones. They're called "gross" not because they are gross to have (although most medical tests are), but because they are looking for large chunks of cancer. We can do a chest X ray to find cancer in the lungs. We can do a blood test to see if it's spread to the liver. We also often do a blood test called a CEA. The CEA (*carcinoembryonic antigen*) is a nonspecific marker found in the blood. It can be followed over time and will often go up if metastases develop.

To learn if the cancer has spread to the bones, we do a bone scan. This is what we call a "nuclear medicine test." A technician injects a low level of radioactive particles into your vein. There they'll be selectively picked up by the bones, and will point out possible areas of cancer to the doctor. After the injection, you wait for a few hours while the particles are traveling through the bloodstream; then you go back to the examining room where you are put under a large machine that takes a picture of your skeleton. This big machine whirs above you, reading the number of radioactive particles in your body. (See Figure 17-1.) (The husband of one of my patients wears a Geiger counter, and the day of her bone scan it started clicking whenever she came near it.) In the areas where the bone is actively metaboliz-ing—that is, doing something—the radioactive particles will show up much more strongly than in the more inert areas.

This doesn't necessarily mean that what the bone is doing is dealing with cancer cells, however. It can mean there's arthritis (which most of us have in small amounts anyway), a fracture that's in the process of healing, or some kind of infection. All the scan will tell us is that something's happening. If there is, the next step is to X-ray the bone. This will help tell us what it is.

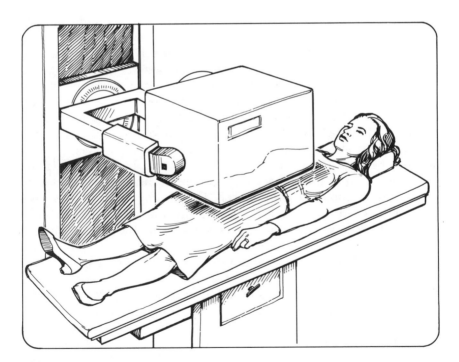

FIGURE 17-1

There's a similar test for the liver, which is used if the blood test is abnormal. A liver scan is similar to a bone scan—except that fewer radioactive particles show up in the liver when there's a metastasis. Sometimes we'll do an ultrasound test, in addition to the liver scan, to help confirm our findings.

If more information is needed, we can do a CAT scan (*computerized axial tomography*) on your liver, your lungs, an area of bone, or even your brain. The advantage of the CAT scan over X ray is that it doesn't just photograph you straight on, but divides your body into cross-sections that can be examined separately. For a CAT scan, you lie on a table inside a round machine, which rotates and takes pictures. It's a little more sensitive to lesions than a plain X ray, but it also exposes your body to much more radiation, so we do it only when the other tests have proved inconclusive. Finally, a new test called MRI (*magnetic resonance imager*) (see page 189) is sometimes used, especially on the brain, if more information is needed.

Some women ask why we don't do these other tests first if they are more sensitive? For some, the reason is that they use increasingly higher amounts of radiation. Other tests, such as the MRI, are more costly and less available.

In fact, since all these tests only pick up large chunks of cancer, they're likely to come out normal even if there's some metastatic cancer present. There's much disagreement among doctors about whether or not we should do any tests on someone with a very early breast cancer, since the chances are low that if cancer is present elsewhere it will have had time to grow to a size that these tests can detect.

I do think its worth doing the basic staging tests once, in the beginning, for two reasons. It gives us a baseline to see what those organs look like in you, and to make sure there's absolutely no sign of metastasis. Then we don't have to repeat them again later, unless there are new symptoms—if something shows up on the blood test or X ray, we can say, "Oh, yes, that's just her old arthritis," or "This is new, let's look into it more." However, the reasons for not doing the tests are often good ones. They're expensive, many involve radiation, and the chances of their finding anything is relatively low. Don't assume your doctor is being negligent or lazy for not wanting to do them. In any case, you have a say in it. If your doctor wants to do the test but you don't want the radiation to your body, you can say no; if your doctor doesn't want to do them and you feel more secure getting them, you can demand them.

It's important, however, to remember the limits of the tests. A negative finding doesn't give you a clean bill of health; it simply tells you that there are no *large* chunks of cancer in those organs.

Unfortunately, there's no foolproof method for determining the early (microscopic) stages of a cancer's spread. We do have a number of methods of finding the likelihood of early spread—sort of trying a case on circumstantial evidence. We do this by looking for other conditions that often occur when a cancer has spread: if these conditions exist, we can guess that the cancer has spread; if they don't we can guess that it hasn't.

Cushman Haagensen[1] has devised a method for trying to do this— the Columbia Classification of Breast Cancers. This is a staging classification used to determine which cancers are inoperable, and which are likely to be small enough that local treatment such as surgery and radiation is sufficient.

One sign that a cancer has probably spread is if the tumor is large—more than 5 centimeters (about 2 inches). If it's that big, there are probably microscopic cells elsewhere.

Another danger sign is swelling of the skin (edema) where the tumor is. As the skin swells, ligaments that hold the breast tissue to the skin get pulled in, and it looks like you've got little dimples on the area. Because this can create an appearance similar to that of an orange peel, it's known as *peau d'orange*. (See Figure 17-3.) If the tumor is ulcerating through the skin, it's ominous. If it's stuck to the muscles underneath so it doesn't move at all, that's also a bad sign. If there are lymph nodes you can feel above your collarbone (*supraclavicular nodes*), or walnut-sized lymph nodes in your armpit, that's also dangerous. And if the skin around the lump appears red and infected, it can be inflammatory breast cancer (see page 269), which is also likely to have spread.

Any one of these signs, which Haagensen calls "grave signs," (Figure 17-2) suggest a high probability that there are microscopic cancer cells elsewhere in the body. If they are present, we plan a systemic treatment (see Chapter 23) as well as a local treatment for the cancer.

If none of the grave signs are present, we investigate further. We begin with the axillary (armpit) lymph nodes. There are between 30 and 60 lymph nodes under the arm, and of these we remove about 10, and examine them under a microscope. (See page 287 for this surgery.) If they reveal cancer cells, we assume there's a high probability that there are cancer cells in other parts of the body. If the lymph nodes don't show cancer, it means that whatever cancer cells have got into the rest of the body have probably been taken care of by the immune system.

However, the lymph node evaluation doesn't give us a foolproof answer either. Even with negative lymph nodes, 20–30 percent of breast cancers will still have spread. So we look more carefully for

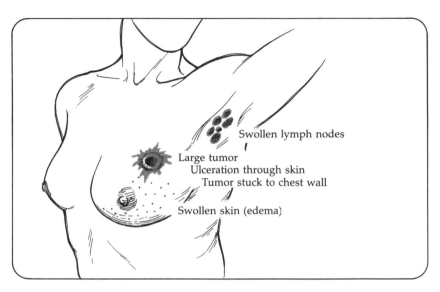

FIGURE 17-2

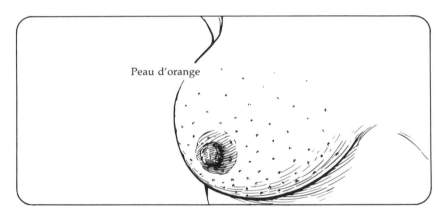

FIGURE 17-3

the other tumor characteristics mentioned in the last chapter, such as vascular invasion or necrosis, and the results of the hormone-receptor test and flow cytometry (also discussed on page 226).

When we've done all these tests, we put the information together to guess the probability that there are cancer cells present elsewhere in your body. This lets you know how serious we think your condition is, and it gives us the information necessary to determine the most effective course of treatment.

These tests have been combined into a fairly formal system called

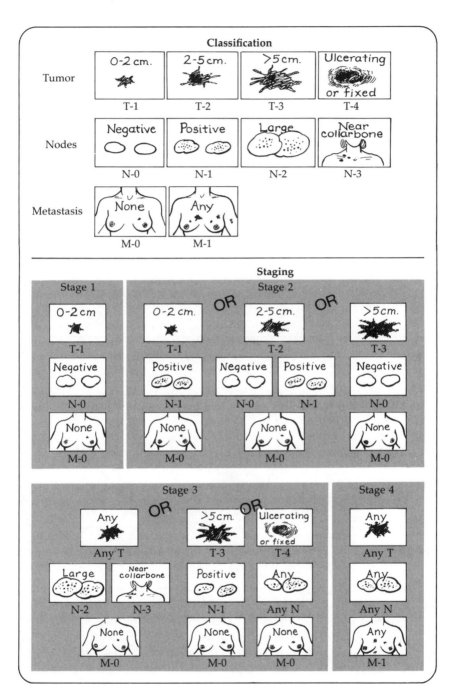

FIGURE 17-4

a staging system. With this system, we can group people according to what we believe to be the extent of their disease. The most widely used staging system is called the TNM system—short for tumor, nodes, and metastasis. (See Figure 17-4.)

We judge the tumor by how large it feels to the surgeon who initially diagnoses it. If it's between 0 and 2 centimeters, it's T-1; between 2 and 5 centimeters, T-2, above 5 centimeters is T-3 (1 centimeter is .39 inch). If it's ulcerating through the skin or stuck to the chest wall it's T-4.

Then we look at the lymph nodes. If there are no palpable nodes, it's N-0; if the surgeon feels nodes but thinks they're negative (with no cancer cells) it's N-1$_a$; if they're positive it's N-1$_b$. If they're large, and matted together, it's N-2; if they're near the collarbone it's N-3.

Finally, if there's obvious metastasis that's been discovered by any of the gross tests described earlier, it's M-l, and if not it's M-0.

Then all this information is combined into stage numbers. Stage 1 is a T-1 tumor with no lymph nodes. Stage 2 is a small tumor with positive lymph nodes; a tumor from 2 to 5 centimeters with positive or negative lymph nodes; or a tumor larger than 5 centimeters with negative lymph nodes. Stage 3 is a large tumor with positive lymph nodes or a tumor with "grave signs." Stage 4 is a tumor that has obvious metastasis. This staging system is continually being altered to reflect new information.

Most breast cancers today are found in either stage 1 or 2—which means they're usually responsive to treatment. Stage 3 cancers do sometimes respond well to treatment, but not as well as those caught earlier. Stage 4 cancers usually aren't curable, but they will often respond to treatment for a while and there is always a small percentage that do get cured. (See Table 17-1.)

We calculate the stages twice. First, the surgeon does it, making

Table 17-1. Breast Cancer: Clinical Stage and Prognosis[a]
(treated with local treatment only)

Stage	Approximate 5-year Survival
1	80%
2	65
3	40
4	10

[a] J.E. Henney and V.T. DeVita, "Breast Cancer," in *Harrison's Principles of Internal Medicine*, 11th ed. Ed E. Brainwald *et al.*, New York: McGraw-Hill, 1988.

a clinical estimate, and then later the pathologist confirms it micro-scopically, which gives a far more accurate finding. It has been shown that whether or not the surgeon who has felt the lymph nodes thinks they're positive, there's about a 30 percent chance that the surgical guess is wrong, and the study under the microscope afterward is essential for the highest possible accuracy.[2]

In addition to this staging system, we can break down the stages even further. The number of positive lymph nodes seems to make a difference: one positive lymph node is less ominous than 15. So we use another scale here to determine the likely extent of metastasis and thus the prognosis: 0 positive lymph nodes is the most hopeful; 1–3 is a little worse; 4–10 is more ominous; and above 10 suggests extensive micrometastasis. We also look to see how large the cancer in the nodes is: grossly positive means the cancer can be seen by the naked eye, and microscopically positive means it's small enough that only a microscope can pick them up.

None of this gives us absolute knowledge. All it means is that we look at large groups of patients and say, "the majority of women with these signs have this prognosis, and are likely to have this response to this treatment." But you, the individual patient, may or may not fall into the majority category. This has a number of impli-cations. If 80 percent of patients in your cancer category survive, you have reason for optimism—but not, unfortunately, for total rejoicing. You'll probably be in the 80 percent, but you might be in the 20 percent who don't survive. You need to be optimistic, but careful. Do everything possible to keep your advantage—careful follow-up and perhaps some of the adjunct, nonmedical techniques discussed in Chapter 24.

By the same token, if 80 percent of women in your category die, that doesn't mean you have to die. While it would make sense for you to think seriously about the possibility of your upcoming death and how you'd best want to prepare for it, it also makes sense to think in terms of being part of the 20 percent who survive. Again, it may be worth looking into additional nonmedical attitudinal and nutritional therapies.

It's also important to note that most of the survival statistics were compiled in prechemotherapy days, when the only treatment was local surgery. Since chemotherapy is aimed at the entire system, it's very likely that its use will have a positive impact on the stage 3 and 4 cancers. However, since we've only been using it widely in the past 5 to 10 years, we don't yet know.

Knowing what stage your cancer is in will help your doctor suggest the treatment that seems most medically useful. It will also help you decide the treatment you want—and those may or may not be the same thing. If, for example, you have stage 4 cancer, you might decide that painful chemotherapy treatments will ruin the time you have left to live, and so decide to risk a shorter but more comfortable lifespan. The writer Audre Lorde has explained her own reasons for making this choice in her recent book *A Burst of Light*: "I want as much good time as possible, and their treatments aren't going to make a hell of a lot of difference in terms of extended time. But they'll make a hell of a lot of difference in terms of my general condition and how I live my life."[3]

On the other hand, a year or two might feel like "a hell of a lot of difference" to *you*. You might decide that the possibility of living a little longer is worth the suffering chemotherapy entails. There are no right or wrong decisions here; there is only your need, and your right, to have the most accurate information possible, and to decide, based on who you are, what choices make the most sense for you.

18

Fears and Feelings

The first thing that anyone thinks of when diagnosed with breast cancer is: "Will I die?" This is quickly followed by "Will I have to lose my breast?" Obviously, breast cancer is a disease with a major psychological impact. In fact, whenever you think you have a lump, or get a mammogram, or have a biopsy, you rehearse the psychological work of having breast cancer. Although, as I have pointed out, most women *don't* die of breast cancer and most do *not* have to lose their breasts, these remain the major fears.

How does the average woman react to this terrifying diagnosis? In my experience, women go through several psychological steps in learning how to deal with breast cancer.

First there is shock. Particularly when you're relatively young and have never had a life-threatening illness before, it's difficult to believe you have something as serious as cancer. It's doubly hard to believe because, in most cases, your body hasn't given you any warning. Unlike, say, appendicitis or a heart attack, there's no pain or fever or nausea—no symptom that tells you something's going wrong inside. You or your doctor have found this painless little lump, or your routine mammogram shows something peculiar—and the next thing you know we're telling you you've got breast cancer.

Along with shock there's a feeling of anger at your body, which has betrayed you in such an underhanded fashion. In spite of the horror you feel at the thought of losing your breast, often your first reaction is to want to get rid of it: take the damn thing off and let me get on with my life!

While this is a perfectly understandable emotional response, it's not one you should act on. Getting your breast cut off will not make things go back to normal; your life has been changed, and it will never be the same again. You need time to let this sink in, to face the implications cancer has for you, and to make a rational, informed decision about what treatment will be best for you both physically and emotionally.

Unfortunately, not all doctors agree with this philosophy, and some may try to talk you into signing a consent form for a mastectomy right away. This kind of paternalism can have a certain appeal: you're scared and stunned and there's daddy to tell you what to do and make it all better. It doesn't matter how intelligent and rational and well-educated you are; sudden fear can turn anyone into a four-year-old. What you need to do is recognize your response for what it is, and, if you're tempted to sign the consent form right away, don't. As I've said earlier, a few days or even weeks won't make the difference between life and death, but they can make the difference between a decision you'll be comfortable with and one you'll regret.

Because patients are so vulnerable at the time they're told their diagnosis, I don't like to tell them about all their options at the same time I tell them they have cancer. I prefer to tell a woman she has cancer and that there are a number of treatment options that we'll discuss the next day at my office.

I begin this process early on. When a patient comes to me with what I think may be a malignancy, I start talking with her right away about the possibilities, from the most hopeful to the most grim, and ask her to consider what it would be like for her in the worst possible scenario. We discuss the general range of treatments we'd be likely to want to choose from. Then we talk about when I'm going to call her with the results of her biopsy, so she can decide where she'll be and who will be with her. I was taught in medical school that you should never tell a patient anything over the phone, but I've found that it works better if I do. If the patient doesn't have cancer, why keep her in suspense any longer? And if she does, I prefer that she find out in her own home, or in whatever environment she's chosen to be in beforehand.

Then if it's bad news, she doesn't have to worry about being polite because she's in my office and there are all these other people around. She can cry, scream, throw things, get drunk, deal with the blow in whatever way she needs to. And she won't have to lie awake all night hoping I'm not going to tell her something awful the next day but knowing the worst already. So I'll tell her on the phone, and then make an appointment to see her within 24 hours. By that time, the shock will have worn off a little bit, and she can absorb information about her options a little better.

Even then, it can be very difficult for a patient to take it all in. For this reason, I suggest that if you've been told you have breast cancer, you bring someone with you when the doctor explains your options—a spouse, a parent, a close friend. Sometimes the friend is the best idea: someone who cares a lot about you but who isn't close enough to be as devastated as you are by the news. The person is there partly to be a comfort and support, but also to be a reference later, so it's good if it's someone detached enough to remember everything we said at the meeting. It's also a good idea to bring along a tape recorder. Then you can go over the options your surgeon has discussed with you again later on and as many times as you need to.

These days, my approach isn't all that unusual. In the past, the surgeons were almost always very paternalistic: they told a woman she had cancer and she had to have a mastectomy but that when it was over she'd be cured and everything would be fine from then on. It was a lie, of course, but the patient usually believed it because she wanted to—who wouldn't?—and for the time being, at least, she was reassured.

Today there's much more emphasis on doctor and patient sharing the decision-making process, and there are more options to choose from. There's also a lot more knowledge available—there are articles about breast cancer and its survival rates in both the medical and the popular press; you *know* you have no guarantee that everything will be fine once "daddy doctor" makes you better. All this is good, of course, but it's also very stressful. In the long run, I'm convinced that you're better off when you've consciously chosen your treatment than when it's imposed on you as a matter of course. But in the short run, it's more difficult.

Of course, different patients have different needs. Some women still want an "omniscient" doctor to tell them what to do. I was involved in a pilot study on how patients decide their treatments, and what kinds of decision making had the best psychological results. I'd expected to find that women coped better when they got a lot of information from their doctors and learned all they could about their disease, its prognosis, and the range of available treatments. But we found that this wasn't always the case. What was far more important was whether the doctor's style matched the patient's. Some women preferred to deny their cancer as far as possible, and have their doctor

take care of it for them. They did better with old-fashioned paternalistic surgeons who told the women what was best for them, giving
them minimal information. Others liked to feel in control of their
lives, and to know all they could about their illness and its ramifications. They did better with surgeons like me, who wanted to
discuss everything with them.

I've begun to recognize this in my own practice. There's a well-
respected, excellent breast surgeon that I work closely with who's
very much in the old-fashioned mode, and he and I lose patients to
each other all the time—sometimes we refer patients to each other.
It works out very well, and we're both happy about it, since we're
both able to help people while remaining true to our own styles and
philosophies.

Sometimes I get a patient who clearly prefers not to know a lot,
and over the years I've come to recognize the signs and to respect
them. I'll give such a patient enough information, but not in as much
detail as I usually do, and then try to hear what she is choosing and
say something like, "It seems to me that you're leaning toward
mastectomy, and maybe that's the right decision for you." I still won't
tell her what to do, but I'll give a little more guidance than usual.

So if the first stage is shock, the second is investigating the options.
How extensive this is varies enormously among women. For some
patients, it consists simply of going over what I've told them and
discussing it with a friend. For others it involves research in medical
libraries and going for second and third and fourth opinions. You
can't take forever, but you don't want to hurry yourself, either. In
my experience, most patients can't handle prolonging this stage for
more than three or four weeks.

When you're exploring the options I think it is very important to
reflect seriously on what the possibility of the loss of a breast would
mean to you. Although many women will say "I don't care about
my breast," deep down this is probably not true for most of us. A
mastectomy may be the right choice for you, but it still will have a
powerful effect on how you feel about yourself. For many women,
the loss of a breast can mean feelings of inadequacy—she's "no longer
a real woman."

In her book, *First, You Cry*,[1] Betty Rollin talks about the first party
she went to after her mastectomy, where she felt that, although she
looked pretty with her clothes on, she was like a transvestite, only
playing at being a real woman.

The fear of feeling this way may start long before the mastectomy—indeed, it plays a part in how the woman copes with her
breast cancer from the first. Rose Kushner[2] surveyed 3,000 women
with breast cancer and concluded that most women "think first of

241

saving their breasts, as a rule, and their lives are but second thoughts." Often women feel robbed of their sexuality when they lose a breast. Betty Rollin[3] found that while her husband still desired her after her mastectomy, her own sexual feelings were gone. "If you feel deformed, it's hard to feel sexy," she writes. "I was dark and dry. I no longer felt lovely. Ergo, I no longer could love." Holly Peters-Golden, on the other hand, points out the importance of distinguishing between the distress caused by mutilating surgery and the distress that comes from having a life-threatening disease.[4] Certainly, my experience with patients has been that for them the latter far outweighs the former.

Ann Kaspar,[5] a sociologist whose Ph.D. dissertation involved studying 29 women between the ages of 29 and 72, 20 of whom had had mastectomies, and nine of whom had had lumpectomies, came up with somewhat different results. While, as she hastens to explain, she had no illusions that 29 women constituted a definitive study, her findings are interesting. She found that most of the women with mastectomies were deeply concerned before their surgery that the mastectomy would "violate their femininity." Yet, with one exception, they reported that after the surgery it was much less traumatic than they'd anticipated. "They said that they'd realized that being female didn't mean having two breasts," Kaspar says. "They got in touch with their identity as women, separate from social demands. Even the ones most determined to get reconstruction didn't feel that the plastic surgery would make them real women—they knew they already were real women." She did find that anxiety was higher among the single women in her study, especially the single heterosexual women, who worried that "No man will ever want me." The women already in relationships usually found their partners were still loving and sexual, and more concerned with the women's health than their appearance.

Although the experience of young, single, heterosexual women is consistent with my experience, I've also had many other patients with other reasons for wanting to keep their breasts. Often middle-aged women who are approaching or just over menopause will have very strong feelings about their breasts. They've experienced the loss of their reproductive capacity with menopause; often their children are leaving home to go to college and they are rediscovering their relationship with their spouse. This is no time to experience yet another loss around your womanhood. Also, elderly women will often want breast conservation. They're experiencing many losses and may well not want to add the loss of their breasts, which have been a part of them for such a long time. Nothing makes me more angry than hearing of an elderly woman who has been told by her surgeon, "You don't need your breasts anymore; you may as well have a mastectomy." Your choice should be based not only on the best medical information you can gather but also on what feels right to you. Don't let any generalizations about age, sexual orientation, or vanity get in your way.

Many studies[6] have been done recently comparing conservative surgery and mastectomy with or without immediate reconstruction, looking for differences in psychological adjustment. Interestingly, the important factor often appears to be the match between the woman and her treatment. That is, the way she feels about her body, about surgery, about radiation, about having a say in her treatment, and about a multitude of other factors will affect how she reacts to this new and enormous stress.

Having explored the options, most women move into a "get-on-with-it" stage. You know all you want to know, you've decided what you want to do, and now it's time to do it. This is the time to make your decision—you understand that you have cancer; you know the pros and cons of the different treatments; you're not happy about it but you're not still in shock.

How long this stage lasts depends on the treatment. If you're getting a mastectomy, with or without immediate reconstruction, it may just be four days at the hospital and a few recuperating weeks at home. If you're having wide excision and radiation, it will go on for six weeks, and if you're having chemotherapy in addition to your other treatments it can go on for another six to eight months. However long the treatment process lasts, it's important to have a lot of support around you, and it's important to allow yourself to feel lousy. You have a serious illness, and the treatments are all emotionally and physically stressful; you need to accept that and pamper yourself a bit. You don't have to be Superwoman. Get help from your friends and family—throughout the treatment. Sometimes, when you're having chemotherapy, the people who were supportive in the beginning start to dribble off. At that point, you may want to get into a breast cancer support group, where women who are going through what you're going through, or who have been through it, can be of enormous help to you.

As trying as the treatment period can be, it is an improvement on the earlier stages: you're *doing* something to combat your disease. (This feeling is often stronger when you're doing meditation, visualization, diet changes, or one of the other techniques we'll talk about in Chapter 24.) But when the treatment period is done, you're likely to find yourself in a peculiar sort of funk. This is what I see as the fourth stage. This posttreatment recovery stage often lasts as long as the treatment itself. You're depressed because the structure you've lived with so intensely is over, and where are you now? In fact, it's similar to postpartum depression, and it's just as real. The caregivers (nurses, doctors, and technicians) you've come to depend on are no longer a daily part of your life. Compounding it is a reasonable fear. There's no more radiation going into your body, no more chemotherapy; without them, is the cancer starting up again? It's a scary time. This depression is almost universal and can sneak up on you when you're least expecting it. You find yourself feeling sad and anxious; you can't sleep, or you want to sleep too much; you find you've lost interest and pleasure in people and activities that you used to enjoy. These symptoms are very normal and will often last a few weeks or months, but if they seem to drag on you may well want to see a counselor or therapist to help you get unstuck and enable you to go on with your life.

Many women find this period of intense feelings can be a time of emotional growth. They see it as a time to reevaluate their lives; they know their own mortality in a way they never have before. How are they living? Are they doing what they want to do for the rest of their lives? I've seen fascinating changes in some of my patients' lives during this period. One of my patients finally left a bad marriage she'd stuck with for years. Conversely, another decided it was time to make a commitment she'd avoided before—she married the man she'd been living with for years. A minister who lost her job because of her cancer left the ministry and got a job selling medical equipment. Another, a breast cancer nurse, left her job to work with a holistic health center. Another, whose husband had had Hodgkin's disease, had her first child: faced with life-threatening illnesses, the couple wanted to confirm their faith in life and bring a new life into the world. Several of my patients have begun psychotherapy, not only to deal with their fears around their cancer, but also to look into issues they'd been coasting by with for years. They want to make the best of the time they have left, whether it's five years or 50 years.

This period of depression and recovery lasts anywhere from two to six months. If you've been going through chemotherapy, it can last up to a year, since you're more tired and worn out, and a longer process tends to take a longer time to get over. It's not that you're always completely depressed and out of it; you're just tired, a bit listless. Your body and mind still haven't fully healed yet.

At the end of this period, you go back to your normal activities; you look fine and, physically, you feel fine. Everybody's relieved that things are back to normal again—everybody but you. You're still very nervous. Little things that wouldn't have bothered you before now seem ominous. That slight headache that two years ago you would have dismissed as tension—has the cancer metastasized to your brain? And what does the bruise on your arm mean—have you got leukemia now? You're now in the "I-can't-trust-my-body" stage. Well, why should you trust your body? It betrayed you once, and you know it can do it again. Every time you go for a checkup, every time you get a blood test, you're terrified. In my experience with patients, this stage usually lasts two or three years, until you've had enough innocent headaches and bruises, enough reassuring checkups and blood tests, to feel somewhat trusting of your body again.

And then, just when you are settling down and starting to forget about it, something pops up in the paper or on the news about a risk factor or new treatment, and it all comes back to you. You start wondering: was it the alcohol or birth control pills or whatever happens to be on today's "hit list" that caused your cancer? Or you start to regret the decision you made, thinking, "with this new information maybe I should have done things differently." Remember, what is past is past. You can't change the way you lived your life in the past based on new information just coming to light today. And you have to comfort yourself with the realization that you probably got the best treatment that was available at the time you were diagnosed. If there are improvements in treatments now, that's wonderful—but you can't waste your energy on what might have been. Read the newspapers and keep informed if you're interested, but don't use it to torture yourself. Gradually your perspective will return.

Though your life will never be completely the way it was before, you'll stop living in terms of your cancer. The fears and memories will come back occasionally—maybe on your yearly checkups, maybe on the anniversary of your diagnosis, maybe when you find out a friend had a recurrence. But they'll be part of your life, not the center of it.

If your cancer does recur, however, the process will start all over again; trusting your body may take longer when you've been doubly betrayed by it. All the feelings you experienced the first time around are back double because now you not only don't trust your body but you begin to wonder about your doctors and treatment in general. Although a recurrence is inevitable in a certain number of women, you didn't think it would be you. And now you're convinced that the chance of cure is slim. It is important to discuss these feelings with your caregivers or to get new ones if, after talking with them, you no longer feel you are part of a team that you have confidence in. In addition, it is important to get support and help from those around you—counselors, therapists, and support groups for women with recurrences. You can move through and out of the recovery stages if you give yourself half a chance. (See Appendix C for books about women with recurrences.)

What I've given is a general overview of the emotional recovery process. It's *not* a formula. You may not go through all these steps, and you may not experience the steps you go through in the way I've described them. Each person's recovery is individual, and there's no right or wrong way to cope with it. I've had patients tell me they're worried because they haven't started to cry yet! Some people cry a lot about their cancer and some don't cry at all. If you think you're holding back feelings that you're afraid to face, perhaps you'll want to see a therapist to help you face the feelings. But don't assume that you're not facing your feelings because you're not expressing them according to someone else's script.

Along with these fears and stages of recovery, there are also a number of related issues that come up for people with cancer.

One of these is the tendency to feel guilty for having cancer—a sense that you've somehow done something wrong. I found it sad and interesting that when Nancy Reagan was interviewed on TV by Barbara Walters about her breast cancer, the First Lady admitted that the first thing she said to her husband after her breast surgery was "I'm sorry." People have a tendency to blame themselves for being ill anyway, and, irrational though she knows it to be, a woman will often feel that she's betrayed her function as a woman by getting breast cancer.

In this connection, the "holistic" methods which we'll discuss in Chapter 24 can have their negative side. The mind–body connection is real, and its validation is very important, but it's not the only force at work in any disease. You didn't create your own cancer by eating too much sugar or thinking negative thoughts or allowing yourself to be too stressed out. I was appalled by a study that showed that 41 percent of women with breast cancer think they brought it on themselves because of the stress in their lives.[7]

In reality, most of the studies on the relation between stress and cancer have been done on rats, and are equivocal at that—some studies show that stress is a factor in cancer, others that it's a factor in preventing cancer. In any case, it's only one factor, not a significant cause. I wish there *were* some simple, clear cause of cancer so I could say, "Don't do this and you won't get breast cancer." Unfortunately, it doesn't work that way. We don't have total control over our own bodies; we don't always, to use the currently popular phrase, "create our own reality." You didn't give yourself breast cancer, and you won't help your healing by feeling guilty about something you didn't bring on yourself.

It's true that studies have shown that survival rates of someone who already has cancer can be affected by personality. People with a fighting spirit appear to have a somewhat better survival rate than passive victims. But the same studies also show that the people who try to pretend their cancer isn't there, who just get what treatments they have to and don't think about it, do just as well. It's the ones who admit they have cancer but assume they haven't got a chance against it, and just give up, who succumb sooner. I'm not sure how useful these studies are to someone who has cancer. It might be reassuring to a fighter, but not everyone has the goal of survival at any cost. Should anyone be expected to change personality over-night?

A particularly trying issue people face is the question of what to tell their children. Again, it's an individual decision, and there are no hard-and-fast rules. I do think, in general, it's wiser to be honest with your kids, and to use the scary word "cancer." If they don't hear it from you now, they're bound to find it out some other way— they'll overhear a conversation when you assume they're out of the room, or a friend or neighbor will inadvertently say something. And when they hear it that way, in the form of a terrible secret they were never supposed to know, it will be a lot more horrifying for them. By talking about it openly with them, you can demystify it.

How you tell them, of course, will depend on the ages of the children and their own emotional vulnerability. With a little child, you can say, "I have cancer, which is a dangerous disease, but we were lucky and caught it early, and the doctors are going to help me get better soon." What younger kids need to know is that you're going to be there to take care of them, that you're not suddenly going to be gone. They also need to know that the changes in your life aren't their fault. All kids get angry at their mothers, and they often say things like "I wish you were dead." When suddenly Mom has a serious illness, the child may well see it as a result of those hostile words or thoughts. They must be told very directly that they did not cause the cancer by any thoughts, words, anger, dreams, or wishes. Your children will also be affected in other ways. You're going to be gone for a few days in the hospital, and will need to rest when you come home. You may be getting radiation treatments, which consume a lot of your time and leave you tired and lethargic afterward. You may be having chemotherapy treatments that make you violently sick to your stomach. Your children need to know that the alteration in your behavior, and the decrease in your accessibility to them, aren't happening because you don't love them or because they've been bad and this is their punishment.

Some surgeons encourage their patients to bring young children to the examining room with them. I find it can be very helpful for a daughter to see me examining her mother. If you're being treated with radiation or chemotherapy in a center like Dana Farber or Beth Israel in Boston, where your children are permitted to see the treatment areas, it's a good idea to bring them along once or twice. The environments aren't intimidating, and a child who doesn't know what's happening to you can conjure up awful images of what those people are doing to mommy.

It is also important to be careful about changes in your older children's roles at home. You don't want to lean too heavily on them to perform the tasks you are unable to do, but rather to give kids things that they can do that will make them feel useful. You may well want to let the school know about what's going on at home.

Most important is addressing their two main fears: that they will not be abandoned and that they will be cared for. Hester Hill, a social worker I know who works closely with women with breast cancer, points out that it is also important not to make promises that you may not be able to keep. It is a mistake to promise, for example, that the cancer won't kill the mother—instead, if asked "Will you die?," a mother can answer, "I expect to live for a very long time and die as an old lady. The doctors are taking good care of me, and I am taking good care of myself, and I hope to live for years and years."

Frightening as it can be for kids to know their mother has a life-threatening illness, if you're honest and matter-of-fact with them, the chances are it won't be too traumatizing. One of my patients decided when she learned about her breast cancer that she would demystify the process for her seven- and ten-year-old daughters, by showing them a prosthesis (artificial breast) and explaining what it would be used for. The next day, she came into my office for her appointment. When I asked her how her experiment worked, she started to giggle. "Well, they certainly weren't intimidated by it. They listened very carefully to my explanation—and then started playing Frisbee with it!"

Breast cancer has particularly complex ramifications for a mother and her daughter. Aside from all the normal fears any child has to deal with, a daughter might well worry about whether this will happen to her, too. It's not a wholly unfounded fear. As we discussed in Chapter 11, there is a genetic component to breast cancer. You need to reassure your daughter, explain to her that it isn't inevitable but that as she gets older she should learn how to do breast self-exam and be very conscious of the need for surveillance.

Often teenage daughters of my patients come and talk with me about their mothers' breast cancer and their fears for themselves. It can be very useful to a girl to have her mother's surgeon help put the dangers she faces into perspective, and it might be worth asking your surgeon about the possibility of such a meeting with your daughter. This may also be useful years later, if your daughter *does* develop problems; she's already built a good relationship with a breast specialist, and she's more likely to seek treatment with confidence and a minimum of terror.

Often daughters will find themselves feeling angry at their mothers, as though the mother created her own breast cancer and in so doing made the daughter vulnerable to it. And mothers themselves often feel the same way; their feelings that they caused their own cancer expand into guilt over their daughters' increased risk. Often a patient will say to me, "What have I done to my daughter?" These feelings need to be faced, and dealt with. Without openness, the cancer can become a scapegoat for all the other unresolved issues between the mother and daughter, putting the relationship at risk.[8]

The husband or lover of a woman with breast cancer also has feelings that need to be acknowledged. They worry that she might die; they worry about how best to show their concern. Should they initiate sex, or will that be seen as callous and insensitive? Should they refrain, or will that be seen as an indication that she's now no longer sexually attractive?

It's important to realize that the cancer is affecting your whole family, not just you. While you're in treatment, you're usually focused chiefly on yourself, because you have to be. But as soon as you can you need to deal with how it's affecting those closest to you. If this is difficult, sometimes it can help to go into couples therapy with your spouse, or family therapy with your spouse and children. They too are feeling frightened, angry, depressed, maybe even rejected, if all your attention is going to your illness, and they may not have as much support for their feelings as you do for yours. It's crucial to communicate with each other at this time, to work through the complex feelings you're all facing.

At the same time, you might be feeling a little apart from the people you love. You're going through something they can't really understand—only somebody else who's been there can. Breast cancer support groups can be wonderful during this time. You'll meet other women who are at various stages of the disease—including some who had it 10 or 15 years ago and are living happy, healthy lives. Often the only people you've known with breast cancer were in an advanced stage—the ones who get better often don't talk about their disease with anyone. Knowing long-term survivors can help you to realize that you're not necessarily doomed. And knowing other women who are at your stage can give you a sense of shared problems, of comradeship with people who understand what's happening to you because it's also happening to them. (See Appendix D for a list of support groups and how to find them.)

Above all, you need to be patient with yourself. Healing, both emotional and physical, takes time. You're entitled to that time.

PART FIVE

TREATING BREAST CANCER

19

Treatment Options:
An Overview

Once you've been diagnosed with breast cancer, you'll be faced with a number of decisions about which treatment—or treatments—to undergo. All these treatments are described in more detail later, but we thought it useful to offer an overview first.

Treatments are divided into two categories: local (treatment of the breast itself) and systemic (treatment for the rest of the body). The latter is the most important in treating the disease: as I mentioned earlier, nobody dies from the cancer in the breast; people die from the cancer that's spread from the breast into other parts of the body.

Systemic Treatments

If microscopic cancer cells have been found in the lymph nodes, we know that cancer is likely to be in other parts of the body, and we go after it with one of the systemic treatments. It's a bit like fighting a guerrilla war: you're in the forest, and you know there may be enemy soldiers lurking behind a bush, though you can't see them there. So you shoot into the bush, to kill them while they're still hiding, so that they don't get the chance to ambush you.

Research studies concerning systemic therapy can be very confusing when they report their results. Some studies will talk about the *percentage reduction in mortality.* This refers to the number of patients who died as a percentage of the number of deaths that were expected. For example, if there were a study that showed that eight patients died in the control group and only six in the study group, there were two less deaths than expected. This is then reported out as a 25 percent reduction in mortality. A similar study with patients who are more likely to die, however, might show that 40 patients die in the control group compared to 30 in the study group. The reduction in mortality of 10 deaths over a possible 40 is still 25 percent; however, in the second study, 10 patients' lives were saved, while in the first it was only two. So these percentages are not always helpful for interpreting the value of a treatment. In breast cancer studies things are even more complicated. Since breast cancer is a slow disease, even the women who are going to die of it often don't do so for many years. Therefore, any study would have to follow patients for 10 or even 20 years to be able to say with confidence what the effect of a treatment is on the death rate (or, conversely, the cure rate). Many investigators and, indeed, many patients don't want to wait that long to look at the results of studies, so they look instead at the time to recurrence. This means the time between the diagnosis of the disease and the first recurrence.

Although time to recurrence isn't the same as cure, it is still very important. For example, if you were diagnosed with breast cancer and were destined to die in one year, and a new treatment would increase your disease-free survival by three years, so that you died instead at year four, your cure rate at five years would be zero either way, but you would have had three extra years of quality time. This is certainly a worthwhile goal.

Some studies, then, will average the difference in the time to recurrence in the two study groups and report out the median time to recurrence. Of course, since this is an average it means some women will have a longer time to recurrence and some shorter. And, of course, it doesn't mean that nobody is cured—just that this is a helpful way to look at early data in a study. (See Figure 19-1.) It also points out that cure may not be the only goal; extra years of disease-free survival may well be worthwhile even if the treatment doesn't totally eradicate the cancer.[1]

Studies have shown that when we give chemotherapy to premenopausal women with positive lymph nodes at the time of diagnosis, we can improve their survival rates at ten years by about 10 percent compared to women not given chemotherapy. Another way to state it is that about one fifth to one third of the women who would have died in the first five years after diagnosis will live beyond five years. It is too soon to tell how many women we are curing, but it is safe

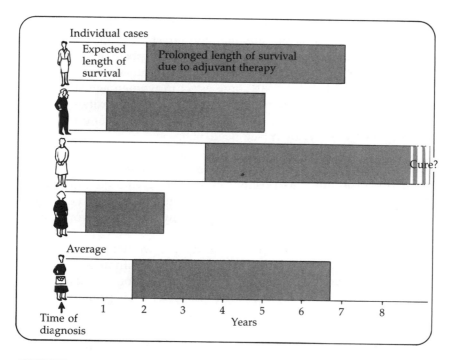

FIGURE 19-1

to say that even in those we don't cure we prolong their lifespan three to five years beyond what they would have had without chemotherapy.[2]

For reasons we don't yet understand, chemotherapy doesn't work as well with postmenopausal women, to whom it offers a smaller increase in survival.[3] In fact, in one study from Milan the postmenopausal women who received chemotherapy are doing worse than those who didn't.[4] Recent data, however, would indicate that this effect correlates with age. Women age 50–60 have a 4.5 improvement at ten years with the effect decreasing with advancing age. A better result for postmenopausal women is often brought about by another systemic treatment that has less drastic side effects, hormone therapy. Tamoxifen, an estrogen blocker, appears to be an effective agent in controlling cancer.[5] In the overview studies (studies that pool all the data from smaller studies to try and find an answer to a question), tamoxifen in postmenopausal women was shown to improve survival by about 10 percent, compared to those women not given tamoxifen; that is, about one fifth to one third of the women who would have died in the first five years lived beyond them, or all women added an average of two years to their lifespan.[6] Again, it is too soon to know if we are curing more women, but even those we don't cure will have an additional three to five years added to their lifespan. This effect, as well as its minimal side effects, makes tamoxifen a good choice for postmenopausal women with positive estrogen receptors. The effects of tamoxifen are also age related with the least effect in women less than 40, some effect in women age 40–50, and maximal benefit in women over 50. Currently, tamoxifen is being given for three to five years, but the optimal duration and long-term side effects are not known (see page 323).

Guidelines for treating women with positive lymph nodes have been drawn up by a nationwide group of specialists:[7] if a woman is premenopausal and has positive nodes, we give adjuvant chemotherapy for four to six months; if she's postmenopausal and estrogen-receptor-positive, we'll use hormone therapy (tamoxifen) for three to five years.

More controversial are treatments for the women with negative nodes. We know that 20 to 30 percent of women with negative lymph nodes will still get metastatic breast cancer and sooner or later die of it.[8] If we give these women chemotherapy for their primary cancer, some of them will have at least a delay in recurrence. But 70–80 percent of women with negative lymph nodes won't ever have a recurrence, and if we give them chemotherapy we subject them to an extremely unpleasant process which can have severe and permanent side effects, including, possibly, other cancers. The side effects, even the cancers, are worth it for women whose alternative is to die of breast cancer: it doesn't much matter that you'd get a second cancer at 60 if your breast cancer kills you at 40. But when there's a 70–80 percent chance that your cancer won't metastasize, should we expose you to the dangers of chemotherapy? Unfortunately, we do not yet know how to tell these two groups of women apart.

In 1988, the National Cancer Institute[9] issued a statement claiming that all women with breast cancer should have chemotherapy, whether their nodes show cancer cells or not. The statement got a lot of publicity and caused a lot of stir: women began frantically calling their doctors and demanding to be put on chemotherapy. Many breast cancer specialists thought that the pronouncement was premature.[10]

The study with the longest follow-up is that of Dr. Gianni Bonadonna in Milan, who studied node-negative, premenopausal women who were also hormone-receptor-negative.[11] He found that there's a significant difference between the survival rate of women who have had chemotherapy and that of women who haven't. But the study has a major problem: his control group—the women who didn't get chemotherapy—for some reason did a lot worse than similar control groups in other studies. So when you compare the survival rate of the women in his study who got chemotherapy with the women in his study who didn't, it looks great—but when you compare the survival rates of chemotherapy-treated women in his study with those of women in the control groups of other studies, it's a far less dramatic improvement. Three U.S. studies are just reporting preliminary data. In one,[12] hormone-receptor-negative patients were randomly assigned either to receive postoperative chemotherapy (methotrexate and fluorouracil) or to have no systemic treatment and be closely monitored. A total of 679 pre- and postmenopausal patients were randomized. After approximately four years, 80 percent of the chemotherapy patients had had no recurrence, while only 71 percent of the control group had had no recurrence. The second trial[13] studied 2,644 pre- and postmenopausal women with estrogen-receptor-positive tumors. Patients were randomized to receive either tamoxifen or a placebo. With a four-year median follow-up, the tamoxifen group had a significantly better disease-free survival—82 percent compared to 77 percent in the control group. Finally, a study reported on 406 randomized patients with a median follow-up of three years, showing an improvement in disease-free survival.[14] It is important to note than none of these studies showed a difference in survival, only in time to recurrence. Whether this will translate into a change in survival remains to be seen. Even Dr. Gianni Bonadonna himself has stated, "In node-negative tumors, available data do not yet clearly indicate that systemic adjuvant therapy can be recommended routinely."[15]

The 1990 National Cancer Institute consensus conference concluded that although the majority of women with node-negative breast cancer are cured by local treatment, there may be some benefit of systemic therapy in some women with tumors over 1 cm. "The decision to use adjuvant treatment should follow a thorough discussion with the patient regarding the likely risk of relapse without adjuvant therapy, the expected reduction in risk with adjuvant therapy, toxicities of therapy, and its impact on quality of life."

There are still many other unanswered questions about optimal treatments that are currently being studied. For instance, the best treatment for hormone-receptor-negative postmenopausal, node-positive women is still in question. And the answer as to whether to give chemotherapy to these women may well be age-related. Studies are also being done on the timing of chemotherapy. Dr. Gianni Bonadonna has found that three cycles of chemotherapy before surgery can shrink some medium-sized (greater than 3 cm) tumors and allow breast conservation for women who might otherwise need a mastectomy. Dr. Bernard Fisher and the NSABP are also looking at the effects of preoperative chemotherapy.

Studies are also being done to test whether the dose of chemotherapy is important. It is not clear whether higher doses of drugs will give better results or whether the problem is that the cancer cells become resistant to the drugs. The traditional limitation to high doses of chemotherapy, bone marrow toxicity, (see page 322) is being overcome with bone marrow transplants and biological response modifiers (see page 383). This will allow us to study whether higher doses are useful in women with more aggressive disease (greater than 10 positive lymph nodes.)

Additional studies are looking into the combination of tamoxifen and chemotherapy. Although it would seem that if one is good both would be better, this may not be true. Tamoxifen keeps cells from dividing and therefore may block the effect of chemotherapy and radiation. Also, some physicians have suggested that we give tamoxifen to all node-negative, hormone-receptor-positive women whether they are pre- or postmenopausal, on the theory that it is nontoxic and has no side effects. This may be fallacious on two counts. First, as my colleague Dr. Craig Henderson of the Dana Farber Cancer Institute is fond of saying, a nontoxic therapy is not justified just because it is nontoxic. Second, and probably more important, we don't actually know that it is nontoxic. It doesn't have many immediate side effects, but the potential for long-range problems such as increased heart disease or endometrial cancers is real. This may be especially significant in premenopausal women where tamoxifen is known to increase estrogen and progesterone levels in the body at the same time it is blocking them in the breast. The long-range consequences of this type of hormonal shift is not known.[16] Again, it behooves any woman contemplating any systemic treatment to get a second opinion and to consider becoming part of a clinical trial.

Finally, the question has come up regarding the need for axillary surgery. As we mentioned on page 210, there is no evidence that axillary surgery affects survival, and our main purpose in doing it is to decide about adjuvant therapy and prevent recurrence in the armpit. Some surgeons have argued that if we are going to give adjuvant therapy to all women (node-negative as well as node-positive), there is no reason to dissect the lymph nodes. They feel they can save women the potential complications of this operation (see page 289) by radiating the axilla instead. The fallacy in this argument—at least at the time of this writing—is that we are not at all sure that all women should be treated with systemic therapy. Until we know who to treat or have a better marker of prognosis than lymph nodes, I still feel it is an important operation. There are always the patients in whom the risks of general anesthesia outweigh the advantage of knowing the lymph node status, and in these women it may be reasonable to forego this operation in favor of axillary radiation.

Local Treatment

The secondary question is what to do about local treatment. Until recently, most surgeons have done mastectomies, assuming that this drastic procedure was the most effective way to save lives. But as we discussed on page 210, studies have proven them wrong.

A study done in Italy, begun in 1973, comparing mastectomy to quadrantectomy (the removal of one fourth of the breast) followed by radiation, found that there was no difference in the survival between the two methods of treatment.[17] Since then, the NSABP[18] has done a study in the United States comparing lumpectomy alone, lumpectomy and radiation, and mastectomy, and has had similar results: lumpectomy and radiation had almost the same survival and local control rate as mastectomy. After eight years, lumpectomy alone had a 39 percent local recurrence rate; lumpectomy and radiation had a 10 percent local recurrence rate; and mastectomy had an 8 percent rate. (These treatments are, of course, very different and are described at length in the next two chapters.) The study reported results at eight years, and it's possible that there will be more recurrence and death in the next five or ten years, but so far, it seems likely that the study will confirm the Italian study's findings. These two studies are important because they were randomized. Other, nonrandomized, studies have shown similar results. The Joint Center for Radiation Therapy,[19] where I send my patients, has one of the series with the longest follow-ups in this country, and their results for local control are similar to those of the randomized data.

The NSABP study conclusively demonstrated that in most kinds of breast cancer, radiation and lumpectomy are as good as mastectomy. And finally in June of 1990 the NCI Consensus Conference concluded "Breast conservation treatment is an appropriate method of primary therapy for the *majority* of women with Stage I and II breast cancer and is *preferable* because it provides survival equivalent to total mastectomy and axillary dissection while preserving the breast." (emphasis is mine)

In some special situations, lumpectomy and radiation might have an edge. If your cancer is right near the breastbone, even with a mastectomy we can't get a normal rim of tissue around the lump. However, radiation *will* treat the surrounding tissue. In fact, if your cancer is located there, even if you've had a mastectomy you might consider following it with radiation.

On the other hand, in some situations, you're better off with a mastectomy—for instance, if you have a large cancer in a small breast (although Dr. Bonadonna's studies with preoperative chemotherapy may help here), or two separate cancers in the same breast, or microcalcifications spread throughout your breast.

As with systemic treatment, there's a lot about local treatment that we've learned, and a lot we still don't know. For example, are there patients who do better with radiation and patients who do better with mastectomy? I've been working on a study with the Joint Center for Radiation, trying to learn more about this. We know that 4–8 percent of patients will have a recurrence after lumpectomy and radiation. In our study,[20] we've been looking at the patients who've had a recurrence, to try and figure out if there was something special in their cases that we could use to predict the likelihood of recurrence. When we restudied the tissue taken out at the time of the lumpectomy we found an important clue: most of these women had a lot of ductal carcinoma in situ—DCIS (see page 198)—in the area surrounding the tumor and in the tumor itself, along with the cancer cells. We call this extensive intraductal component (EIC). Strictly speaking, we define a biopsy as showing EIC if more than 25 percent of the lump is precancer and there's extensive precancer in the surrounding area.

In fact, we noted that women who had EIC in their original biopsy had a 25 percent risk of local recurrence, compared to 6 percent for those women without EIC. This observation has recently been confirmed by the Institute Curie,[21] and the surgical group at Westminster Hospital in London.[22]

When we first found this out, we thought that the presence of EIC might indicate a particularly bad cancer, making radiation inadequate. But if this were the case, these people should have been dying at a faster rate than those whose cancer didn't recur, and this wasn't happening.

Then we asked ourselves whether EIC indicated that all the cells in the breast were predisposed to become cancer cells. But if this were the case, the cancer would recur throughout both breasts, and the recurrences we were looking at were all in the same area of the breast the tumor had been taken from.

So it began to appear that it wasn't a question of whether or not this cancer responded to radiation—there was obviously another element involved. One of the things we discussed was the fact that precancer is usually not visible or palpable: it's in the ducts and it rarely forms lumps. So in taking out the lump and what appeared to be a rim of normal tissue, the surgeon was underestimating the amount of intraductal carcinoma and leaving some behind.

To test this hypothesis, we went back and did another study.[23] We looked at women who had had a reexcision after their first biopsy because of dirty or unknown margins. We found out that indeed the women who had EIC often had cancer left after the first biopsy, whereas the women who didn't have EIC rarely had any cancer left. (See Figure 19-2.)

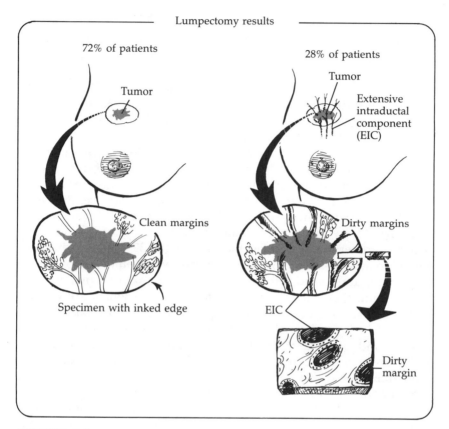

FIGURE 19-2

The reason that the people with EIC were having worse local control probably wasn't that radiation didn't work for them, but that we were leaving in too much cancer for the radiation to control. If we could get it all out and have clean margins, they should be okay. This hypothesis was supported by the work of Dr. Umberto Veronesi in the Milan study. When he looked back at the patients who'd had quadrantectomies and radiation, he found that the ones with EIC had no more recurrence than the patients without EIC. This makes sense, since the quadrantectomy by definition takes out more tissue than other forms of wide excision, so they were getting out the dangerous area of precancer. Similarly, the NSABP study backed us up: in their study, women without clean margins were all given mastectomies, and only those with clean margins were given lumpectomy and radiation. There was no greater recurrence among the patients who had EIC than among those who didn't.

We now feel that if a woman's lumpectomy reveals a lot of EIC (and this will be the case in about 30 percent of breast cancer patients), the surgeon needs to be sure the margins are clean. If there is any question, she or he should do a second operation and get more tissue out to make sure all the intraductal cancer is gone, before sending the patient for radiation. If the pathologist still finds cancer at the margins, the patient may need a mastectomy. We do know, from studies done by Dr. Peter Paul Rosen at Sloan Kettering,[24] that a mastectomy—which is really a *very wide* excision—does prevent the cancer from returning in EIC cases.

The NSABP also discovered that with lumpectomy *alone*, a woman has a 37 percent greater chance of a local recurrence of her cancer.[25] This brings up the question of whether all women with breast cancer need radiation. If 37 percent of women who have wide excision alone will have a recurrence, we're radiating 63 percent of women who *don't* need it—whose cancer wouldn't recur anyway. If we could find a way to determine which women are in the 37 percent who need radiation and which are in the 63 percent who don't, we could save those who don't need it the discomforts and risks of radiation.

We think there might be a way to determine which are the less aggressive cancers that may not require radiation for treatment. I'm involved in a protocol now, looking at women who fit very strict criteria and offering them the opportunity to be treated without radiation in a very controlled context. To qualify for this study, the woman must have a tumor less then 2 centimeters (¾ inch), negative lymph nodes, no EIC, no vascular or lymphatic invasion, and at least a centimeter of normal tissue around her tumor. We think that by selecting out these women with relatively less dangerous cancers, we can choose those patients who might not need radiation. We're following these women very carefully, and at the first sign of a recurrence we will add further treatment. We're not sure yet if this will work—it's a look at the future. Ideally, as more and more of these studies are done, we'll get to the point where we can say to a woman, "For your kind of cancer we don't need radiation," or "With your kind of cancer you should have radiation," or "In your case, you're really better off with a mastectomy."

Making the Choice

What are some of the factors that influence women's choices? Many doctors seem to feel that the older a woman is, the more likely she is to choose mastectomy. This isn't what I've experienced among my patients. Many of my older patients would just as soon live the rest of their lives with their breasts. Conversely, many doctors assume that young women, especially single young women, want to keep their breasts to help them catch a man. But some young women don't especially *want* to "catch a man," and others feel that a man worth catching is one who won't choose his mate on the basis of her breasts. Furthermore, some of my younger patients point out that we know the effects of radiation over a 20- or 30-year period, but not over a 40-year period: they don't want to risk a radiation-associated cancer in their old age. I've had patients of all ages make different decisions, and I think it's ludicrous to assume that older women should have mastectomies and younger women shouldn't. The real factors vary as much as women and their lifestyles vary. I'm sure there are many factors that I haven't come across, but I can discuss a few I'm familiar with.

Some women choose mastectomy for what I think of as a "biblical" reason—their breast has betrayed them, and they want to cut it off. Others simply don't want to go through the time-and-energy drain of radiation: one of my patients chose a mastectomy because she had planned to do extensive traveling, something she'd wanted to do all her life, and she didn't want to trade her travel time for radiation treatments.

Your work may also make a difference. Nancy Reagan explained in a television interview with Barbara Walters that her work as First Lady was too demanding to permit her to take off any more time than was absolutely necessary. A friend of mine who's a breast surgeon in rural Pennsylvania finds that her breast cancer patients almost always choose mastectomy: they're farmers who can't afford to take off six weeks for radiation treatments.

The availability of one kind of treatment or another is also a factor. In some areas there's no place nearby that offers radiation; in others, there's radiation available, but it's not especially good: a radiation therapist really has to know the technique to get good results. There's also the question of feeling safe with your choice. I've had patients who have lumpectomy and radiation and they wake up every morning afterward sure that the cancer's come back—they probably would have been better off with mastectomies in the first place.

The possibility of reconstruction, which we discuss at length in Chapter 25, may also play a role in a woman's decision. On the other hand, for some women breasts are an integral part of their sexuality and identity and they are willing (and able) to go to great inconvenience for the chance to preserve them: I have patients who move to Boston for six weeks to get radiation. I've had patients whose cancer has recurred after lumpectomy and radiation, and even though they've then had to have a mastectomy, they're grateful that they've had an extra few years with both breasts.

Remember above all that it's your body and no one else's. Don't decide on the basis of what anyone else thinks is best. By all means talk to your friends and your family and your husband or lover, and think about what they say. But make your own decision. Husbands and lovers come and go, but your body is with you all your life. A truly caring mate should support whatever course you think is best for you. In her book *Why Me?*, Rose Kushner tells a chilling story about then–First Lady Betty Ford's breast cancer surgery in 1974. Kushner had heard about Mrs. Ford's impending biopsy, and had been told by her friends in the Washington press corps that if the lump proved positive, they were going to do a Halsted radical mastectomy immediately. Alarmed that such a drastic operation would be done without Mrs. Ford having any time to consider, Kushner managed to get through to one of President Ford's speech writers. She told him of her misgivings, only to be told firmly that "The President has made his decision." Kushner's indignant observation that the decision belonged to Mrs. Ford and not her husband was met only with a reiteration that the president had made his decision. The next day, Mrs. Ford had both her biopsy and her mastectomy. As Kushner notes, "the president's decision had indeed been made."[26]

As far as systemic treatment is concerned, the choices are equally difficult. After you have received your local treatment, if you're found to be node-positive your doctor will probably bring up the question of chemotherapy or hormone therapy; if you're node-negative your doctor may or may not bring it up. If not, you should ask about it and even consider getting a second opinion from an oncologist who deals in chemotherapy. There's currently no "right" answer.

Some of my patients say, "If there's the slightest chance this will help, I want to do it." One of my patients, who, though node-negative, had chemotherapy back in 1984, before all the publicity about it, explained her reasons to me recently. "They told me at the time it was a small tumor and there was an 80 to 90 percent chance I'd be alive in 10 years. That wasn't very reassuring to me at 34. My mother had died of breast cancer years before. No one suggested chemotherapy to me, but I pursued it on my own. I know that cancer's a systemic disease, and it just made sense to me to pursue a systemic treatment. I'm glad that with this new focus on node-negative chemotherapy, women will at least be told about it as a possibility."

Other patients feel that unless they have proof that chemotherapy will make a difference, they don't want to risk it. "I decided against chemotherapy because there doesn't seem to be anything definite one way or another about it in my kind of case," says one of my node-negative patients. "They said it was 'just a precaution.' But that's six months of chemotherapy, with all the possible side effects. It seems sort of drastic, as a precaution, and there's no guarantee even with the chemo that the cancer won't spread. If I definitely needed it, okay, but not 'just in case.'"

Should you always choose chemotherapy if you're node-positive? If you're premenopausal, I think you should; if you're postmenopausal and hormone-receptor-negative, maybe. In this case, the evidence shows that it will only improve your survival rate by about 5 percent if you are less than 70, and there are other questions, like quality of life. If you're 80, for example, and have positive nodes, which means the cancer may come back in the next 10 years, you may decide it's worth the gamble not to do chemotherapy and live out your life in comfort—or you may decide that any chance of extra time to live is worth it. And if you're relatively young and have another life-threatening condition that could be exacerbated by the chemotherapy, such as a heart condition or severe kidney disease, maybe you won't feel the risk is worth it. On the other hand, you may be 50 and just postmenopausal and feel that even the chance of an extra 1 percent is worth it to you. Or you may have reasons of your own for wanting to risk or avoid risking chemotherapy. Your values and beliefs will play a large part in your decision.

Sometimes a patient asks me what I'd do if I had breast cancer. I never tell her. I couldn't, because what I think I'd do now might be very different from what I'd actually do if I were faced with the reality. But even if I did know, what difference would it make? My choice would be based on who I am—my values, my feelings about my body, my priorities, my neuroses. It would only be valid for me. My patient comes to me for my medical expertise, but *she* is the expert on herself.

Another option is participation in a clinical trial (see page 214). You should at least ask your doctor what protocols and trials are open to you.

We've talked about two components of treatment, systemic and local. There's a third component, which I'll touch on briefly here.

Breast cancer, like any cancer, is a fight between the cancer cells and your body's immune system (see page 212). The techniques we've just discussed are methods to decrease the total number of cancer cells. But other approaches take it from the opposite end— they try to boost your immune system and make it better able to fight the cancer off. Unfortunately, in science we haven't yet figured out a good method to do that. But the hope that we can boost the immune system through a mind–body connection is the basis of many of the so-called complementary treatments we discuss in Chapter 24. These range from visualization to diet to prayer, and it's worth your while to think about looking into these to complement whatever medical treatment you embark on. While we don't yet know if they can actually help you physically, they will often empower you psychologically by giving you something that you can do as part of your own treatment.

Second Opinions

Before you decide on which treatment, or treatments, you want, I think it's always wise to consider getting a second opinion, no matter how much you trust your surgeon's advice. The preference for a treatment is always somewhat subjective, and you're entitled to consult with more than one expert. Furthermore, special kinds of cancer might require a different approach than your doctor's, and different institutions may be involved in different research with new treatments that you might be interested in.

You may also want to consult with a radiation therapist—a doctor who specializes in giving radiation treatments—to see whether she or he thinks you're a good candidate for radiation treatment. And you will probably want to consult an oncologist. Oncologists are trained in giving chemotherapy and can help you sort out the options for systemic treatment.

Sometimes patients are shy about seeking second opinions—as though they're somehow insulting their doctor's professionalism. Never feel that way. You're not insulting us; you're simply seeking the most precise information possible in what may literally be a life-and-death situation. Most doctors won't be offended—and if you run into a doctor who *does* get miffed, don't be intimidated. Your life, and your peace of mind, are more important than your doctor's ego.

20

Special Cases

So far, I've been discussing the "typical" breast cancer—the small lump that forms inside a woman's breast, usually discovered by the woman herself or by her doctor, or detected on a screening mammogram. Sometimes, however, we find a cancer that manifests differently, or is unusual in its behavior.

Locally Advanced Breast Cancer

Once in a while, a breast cancer won't be discovered until it's fairly well advanced—a stage 3 cancer. It will be a large tumor—larger than 5 centimeters (2 inches), with positive lymph nodes. Or it will have one of the other features that we think give it a bad prognosis, like swelling (edema) of the skin, or a big, matted cluster of lymph nodes. It might be stuck to the chest muscle, or ulcerating through the skin.

These are all indications that the cancer has probably spread in your body, at least microscopically, and when we find them we often don't bother sampling your lymph nodes: we've already got the information we need. In these cases we use a treatment that will work on the rest of the body as well as on the local disease. With a large lump, a wide excision might not even be possible. If you've got very large breasts, it might be, but if your breasts are small, it may be impossible to get enough surrounding tissue out without a mastectomy. If the tumor is stuck to the muscle or ulcerating through the skin, an immediate local treatment might not be feasible at all: removing the muscle or all the skin that's ulcerated might not leave sufficient tissue to sew back together again.

These difficulties, combined with the fact that there's a strong chance the cancer has spread to other parts of your body, usually suggest that we should start with a systemic rather than a local treatment, usually chemotherapy (see page 315). This may not eradicate the whole tumor, but if it doesn't, it can still do two important things: it can work on the cells that have spread, and it can shrink the tumor to a size more easily managed with surgery or radiation.

Usually we'll continue with the chemotherapy for three to six cycles. Then if the tumor has completely disappeared, we might do only radiation. If it hasn't completely disappeared but is significantly smaller, we might do a wide excision plus radiation. If it hasn't disappeared at all, we might do a mastectomy. In the case of an ulceration, which doesn't leave enough skin to sew together, breast reconstruction has not only a cosmetic but also a medical advantage: it provides skin from another part of the body (see page 353).

Cancers of this sort usually fall into one of two categories, though both are generally treated the same way. Sometimes it's a very aggressive cancer that seems to have come up overnight as a large and evidently fast-growing tumor. At other times, the tumor has been there for several years and the woman has tried to pretend it wasn't there, until it's gotten huge or begun ulcerating through the skin and she finally gets to a doctor. This latter case we call a "neglected primary"—it's not an especially aggressive cancer, just an especially frightened woman. Patients with a neglected primary cancer often do better than you might expect: if you've had an untreated cancer for five years and it hasn't killed you or obviously spread anywhere, it's clearly a slow-growing cancer.

Few studies, however, have differentiated between aggressive cancers and neglected primaries. Studies of these types of cancer, taken together, show a five-year survival rate of around 35–40 percent— which isn't great, but it isn't absolute doom either. So if you've been putting off seeing your doctor about a lump that's been growing, or if you're suddenly faced with a new large or ulcerating tumor, don't ignore it and assume you're dying—get it diagnosed and start your treatment right away. Your prognosis won't be as good as it would be with a smaller tumor, but it's not hopeless, and the sooner you begin to take care of it, the better your chances are.

In many areas of the country there are protocols studying advanced cancers, trying to determine whether different combinations of chemicals, or different combinations of chemotherapy, radiation, and surgery, make a difference in survival rates. And, as I've said in earlier discussions about protocols, I think it's well worth it to consider participating in one if it's available to you.

Different hospitals have different preferences in treatment order and combination. In the centers where I work we usually do chemotherapy first and then radiation, and do mastectomy only when it seems absolutely necessary. We've had very good local control rates using what's called "radical radiation": we use more radiation to get rid of the big lump than we'd normally use after a wide excision.[1] There are, of course, more severe side effects as well—the skin gets noticeably thicker and more leathery, so the cosmetic results aren't quite as good, and there's a little more tendency to get a swollen arm. (See Chapter 22 for a discussion of radiation and its side effects.) But for most patients, it's preferable to losing a breast.

In other centers, they still usually do a mastectomy in these cases after chemotherapy, generally following it with radiation. [2]

Inflammatory Breast Cancer

"Inflammatory breast cancer" is a special kind of advanced breast cancer, and it's a serious one. Fortunately, it's also rare—it only accounts for 1 to 4 percent of all breast cancers. It's called inflammatory because its first symptoms are usually a redness and warmth in the skin of the breast, often without a distinct lump. Frequently the patient and even the doctor will mistake it for a simple infection and you'll be put on antibiotics. But it doesn't get better. It also doesn't get worse, and that's the tip-off: an infection will always get better or worse within a week or two—it won't ever stay the same. If there is no change, the doctor will perform a biopsy of the underlying tissue to see if it's cancer. Two of my patients who have had this cancer had similar stories. One had been breastfeeding and developed what her doctor thought was *lactational mastitis* (see page 97). It never cleared up and didn't hurt much—there was no fever or other sign of infection. It hadn't gone away or gotten worse in six months. The other patient, not breastfeeding, noticed that one breast had suddenly become larger than the other; there was also redness and swelling. In both cases, the doctors at first thought they had infections. It's important for the doctor to recognize the possibility of cancer, however, and if the symptoms continue after treatment, you should ask to have a biopsy done of the breast tissue and of the skin itself. With inflammatory breast cancer, you have cancer cells in the lymph vessels of your skin, which is what makes the skin red; the cancer is blocking the drainage of fluid from the skin.

Inflammatory breast cancer is the only form of breast cancer that virtually everyone agrees doesn't call for mastectomy as its only primary treatment. Because it involves the skin as well as the breast tissue, and the skin is sewn back together after a mastectomy, doing a mastectomy will still leave a great chance of a recurrence in the skin. So if we're going to do a mastectomy at all, we wait till after we've done other forms of treatment.

Statistics in the past suggested that most women with this aggressive cancer had a survival rate of about 18 months, with only 2 percent surviving five years. With the advent of systemic treatments, we're trying all kinds of different techniques and we're getting much better results. The five-year survival is now about 40 percent.

We usually treat it by administering some form of chemotherapy right away. Then, as with the advanced cancers, we'll do a local treatment—radiation or surgery, or both, depending on which center you're being treated at.[3, 4] So far, studies don't indicate that the order of local treatment affects survival.

Grim though it is, inflammatory breast cancer is still an extremely variable disease. Six or seven years ago, I diagnosed three cases of the disease. Two were unusually young—26 and 29. Both had chemotherapy first, followed by radiation, and both did fine for a couple of years. Then the 29-year-old had a recurrence in her breast: she had experimental chemotherapy but the cancer had spread and she died within the year. The other woman also had a recurrence in the breast; she had a mastectomy (with immediate reconstruction) and did well for a while. Then it recurred in her liver. She then had several recurrences which were treated with a variety of chemotherapies and hormone therapies. She finally died six years later, but after a longer life than statistics would have predicted. The third patient, an older woman, had inflammatory breast cancer seven years ago, was treated for it, and so far has had no recurrences.

The Unknown Primary

"The unknown primary" sounds a bit like the title of a murder mystery; actually, it's the name we give another kind of mystery—a breast cancer that we can't find in the breast. Someone shows up with an enlarged lymph node, usually in the armpit. It's biopsied and we find breast cancer cells, but there are no breast lumps. So we send the woman off for a mammogram, and it doesn't show any questionable areas. We know the cancer's there, but how do you treat a cancer you can't find?

In the old days, the doctors simply did a mastectomy on everyone in this situation, and discovered cancer in the breast in between 60 and 70 percent of the cases, depending on how finely they examined the breast tissue.[5] Now mammography is likely to show a density in the breasts of such patients, and there are fewer women with truly unknown (or undetected) primaries. In those that do occur, the treatment is controversial. There's no doubt that a mastectomy would get rid of the cancer, but we have to ask if a mastectomy is necessary, given that the primary cancer is so tiny we can't even detect it. Shouldn't radiation be sufficient? Many doctors think it should be,[6, 7] but this is very controversial right now. Some doctors still think that a mastectomy is called for, since there's no way to pinpoint the exact location of the cancer. And many radiation therapists don't like doing radiation in these cases, because they can't give the boost of radiation to the actual site of the tumor.

If a mastectomy is overkill and radiation is chancy, what can you do? Some doctors think you should have chemotherapy, then wait and see if something shows up, rather than do any primary therapy right away—but that's a little scary. Others have recommended an upper outer quadrantectomy.[8] Since most cancers are located in that area of the breast, there's a good chance that the mysterious tumor is there. Others favor doing multiple fine-needle aspirates—truly a needle-in-the-haystack approach, but sometimes an effective one.

Every case of unknown primary is different. I've had two recent cases. One was a woman with a strong family history of breast cancer. She was very thin and small-breasted, and her breasts weren't lumpy: it would seem that any lump, however small, would be easy to find. She had an enlarged node in her armpit, which was cancerous. I did nine fine-needle aspirates in different areas of her breast, and found cancer in four of them. I did fine-needle aspirates in the other breast as well, and one of these revealed cancer, so we decided to remove both breasts. It turned out that in the breast on the side with the enlarged node, she had a fairly widespread cancer that hadn't formed lumps but had snaked through the breast tissue.

In the other case, I did fine-needle aspirates again. This time they were negative, but she'd had a positive lymph node, so we had to do something. My patient emphatically didn't want a mastectomy. She was somewhat psychic, and was convinced that the cancer was in the upper outer quadrant. Since that's the site of most cancers anyway, a quadrantectomy seemed a good idea to both of us. After removing the tissue, I turned it upside down, and there, on the undersurface, was the lump. Both she and I were greatly relieved. Because we'd found the location of the cancer, she was able to have radiation, and to keep her breast.

It's unlikely that you'll have this kind of cancer, but if you do, it's important to think about what treatment you'll be most comfortable with. If your surgeon tells you there's one sure way to deal with it, be suspicious and insist on a second opinion.

It's interesting to note that, contrary to what you might expect, the survival rate in cancers that show up in the nodes but not in the breast is actually a bit better than it is for cancers that show up as both a breast lump and an enlarged node.

Paget's Disease of the Breast

Dr. Paget was an active gentleman, and he's gotten his name on any number of diseases: there's a Paget's disease of the bone and a Paget's disease of the eyelids, as well as a Paget's disease of the breast. The diseases have no relation to one another, except for their discoverer.

Paget's disease is a form of breast cancer that shows up in the nipple as an itchiness and scaling that doesn't get better. It's often mistaken for eczema of the nipple—a far more common occurrence. Paget's disease is almost never found in both breasts (bilateral), so if you've got itching and scaling on both nipples, you've probably got a fairly harmless skin condition. However, if it doesn't get better, you should get it checked out, whether it's on one or both nipples.

First you'll need to get a mammogram to make sure there's no cancer in the breast itself. Then you should get the skin on the nipple biopsied. This can be done in the doctor's office with local anesthetic; it's called a "punch biopsy," and involves removing only about a millimeter or two of tissue. If it's Paget's, the pathologist will see little cancer cells growing up into the skin of the nipple—that's what makes the skin flake and get itchy. Sometimes it's associated with a cancer inside the breasts; sometimes not. It's often associated with ductal carcinoma in situ (see page 198.)

There are probably two variants of Paget's disease: one associated with an invasive cancer in the breast and one which only involves the nipple. The former would be treated as any invasive cancer (see Chapter 19). If the invasive cancer lump is far from the nipple a mastectomy may be necessary to get both areas out; otherwise wide excision and radiation is a reasonable alternative.

Paget's disease, which only involves the nipple, has a better prognosis than regular breast cancer. It doesn't tend to be too aggressive, and usually the lymph nodes are found to be negative. Until recently most doctors assumed that you needed a mastectomy—they seemed to think that if you couldn't keep your nipple, your breast didn't matter.[9] Most women, of course, know better.

This has been a campaign of mine, and recently, some of us have managed to convince the rest of the medical establishment that all that's needed is to remove the nipple and areola, followed by radiation, and that many women prefer to keep the rest of the breast if they can.[10, 11]

True, your breast looks a bit funny after the nipple's been removed—somewhat like a football. An artificial nipple can be made by a plastic surgeon (see page 357). But many women don't mind the way the breast looks, as long as they look natural in a bra. Some of my patients with this kind of Paget's disease choose plastic surgery, and some don't bother with it.

Cystosarcoma Phylloides

The most dramatic thing about this kind of cancer is its name. It's fairly mild and takes the form of a malignant fibroadenoma (see page 118). It shows up as a large lump in the breast—it's usually lemon-sized by the time it's detected. It feels like a regular fibroadenoma—smooth and round—but under the microscope some of the fibrous cells that make up the fibroadenoma are bizarre-looking cancerous cells. It's usually not a very aggressive cancer. It rarely metastasizes; if it recurs at all, it tends to recur only in the breast. It can be treated with wide excision, removing the lump and a rim of normal tissue around it.[12] It doesn't require radiation, and we usually won't check the lymph nodes since it so rarely metastasizes. We'll watch you closely to see if it recurs, and if it does, another wide excision will usually take care of it. I had one patient who came to see me because her cystosarcoma phylloides had recurred three times, and her surgeon told her she'd have to have a mastectomy because it kept coming back. I told her I thought we should wait and see if it *did* come back, and in six years, it hasn't.

The medical literature will sometimes talk about a "benign" versus a "malignant" cystosarcoma phylloides, based on a subjective interpretation of how cancerous they think the cells are. The implication is that malignant cystosarcomas will behave more aggressively. Although there are rare cystosarcomas that do metastasize (5%) and ultimately kill the patient, it is hard to predict this accurately in advance. Most surgeons will suggest a more aggressive approach (mastectomy) if the pathologist feels that it's "malignant." These cancers are sufficiently rare that you may well want a second pathologist's opinion before embarking on any therapeutic approach.

Cancer of Both Breasts

Once in a great while, a woman will be diagnosed as having a cancer in each breast at the same time (synchronous breast cancer). Typically this will be discovered when, finding a lump in one breast, she gets a mammogram to find out what's going on there, and learns there's also a lump in the other breast. A biopsy shows them both to be cancer.

They're probably both primary cancers; one isn't a metastasis of the other. So they're both treated the same way: first we do staging tests and then a lumpectomy, or mastectomy, and lymph node dissection on one and then the other side. Usually the surgeon will first dissect the lymph nodes on the side that appears worse, so that, if the nodes are positive and will require chemotherapy, the other nodes won't have to be dissected. Unfortunately, the surgeon's guess isn't always right. I recently had a patient who had three cancers: she had a lump in the top of her right breast, and the mammogram showed two densities in the bottom of the left breast. They'd all been biopsied with needles. She really wanted to keep her breasts, so I did a wide excision of the right breast and sampled the lymph nodes, and they were fine. Then I did a wide excision of the two cancers in the left breast, and on the left side she had positive lymph nodes. Had I been able to guess better, I'd have started on the left side and wouldn't have had to do the extra surgery.

You can have radiation treatment on both breasts at the same time, but the radiation therapist has to be very careful that the treatment doesn't overlap and cause a worse burn in the middle area.

It isn't necessary to do the same treatment on both breasts. You might decide on a mastectomy on one side and wide excision plus radiation on the other, for example. It is important to note that your prognosis is only as bad as the worse of the two tumors—not doubly as bad as either one.

Cancer in the Other Breast

Sometimes a woman who has had cancer in one breast will turn up with cancer in her other breast (second primary). Usually this isn't a recurrence or a metastasis; it's a brand new cancer. It's possible for breast cancer to metastasize from one breast to the other, but it's rare. A new primary cancer has a different significance than a metastasis. What it suggests is that your breast tissue, for whatever reason, is prone to develop cancer, so you developed one on one side and then several years later the other side followed along. As with any new cancer, it's biopsied, you're given the staging tests again, your lymph nodes are dissected, and you're treated. Your prognosis isn't made any worse because you developed the second breast cancer; it's as bad as the worst of your two cancers. So if, for example, your original cancer was a stage 2, and your second was a stage 1, your prognosis is that of someone with a stage 2 cancer. If they were both stage 1, the prognosis is a stage 1 prognosis.

Cancer in Pregnancy

Sometimes a cancer is unusual, not in itself, but in the situation in which it occurs. Once in a very great while, a patient develops breast cancer while she's either pregnant or breastfeeding. We used to think that such a cancer was especially aggressive, and that the pregnancy-related hormones fired the cancer up and made it worse.

In fact, however, studies have shown that, stage by stage, it's no worse than any other breast cancer. The problem is that it usually isn't discovered right away. When you're pregnant, your breasts are going through a lot of normal changes, which can mask a more dangerous change. For one thing, they're much lumpier and thicker than usual. Similarly, when you're breastfeeding, as we discussed on page 41, you tend to have all kinds of benign lumps and blocked ducts, and you may not notice a change that ordinarily would alarm you. As I discussed earlier in this chapter, in the discussion of inflammatory breast cancer, the physician may also find diagnosis difficult.

Treatment is also a problem. What we can do about your cancer depends on what stage of pregnancy you're in. If you're in the first trimester, you might want to consider therapeutic abortion, depending on your beliefs about abortion and the importance this particular pregnancy holds for you. If you continue with the pregnancy, treatment options are somewhat limited. We wouldn't give you radiation in the first trimester because it can injure the fetus, and we're a little leery about chemotherapy, since the fetus's organs are being formed at this time. For the same reason, we don't want to give you general anesthetic, which rules out a mastectomy. We can do a biopsy or a wide excision under local anesthetic. But if further treatment is called for, we're very limited in what we can safely do.

In the second trimester, the fetus's organs are already formed, and it's safer to use general anesthetic, so we can do a mastectomy. We would rather not risk radiation or chemotherapy: we don't yet know what effects the chemicals can have on the fetus. There are some reports of women who have received chemotherapy while pregnant: it is possible but worrisome.

If you're in your third trimester, we could do a lumpectomy, or, if need be, a mastectomy, then wait for further treatment until the child is born.[13] If it seems necessary to do treatment right away, your obstetrician can keep testing and, as soon as the baby can be expected to survive outside the womb, do a cesarean section and then start you on chemotherapy and radiation.

Breast cancer during lactation isn't quite as complicated, since you can always stop breastfeeding and start your child on formula. Radiation will probably make breastfeeding impossible, and you won't want to breastfeed if you're on chemotherapy, since the baby will swallow the chemicals.

We're not sure yet if lactation affects the cancer itself. I've had two patients whose breast cancer showed up while they were lactating. Both were treated, both stopped breastfeeding, and both did well without a recurrence for several years. After much debate, both women decided to get pregnant again. One had a recurrence during the second pregnancy; the other had a second primary develop while lactating. This leads me to the question of whether, if a cancer shows up while a woman is pregnant or lactating, there is a higher risk of a recurrence in another pregnancy. Obviously we can't do a randomized study, and it's too unusual an occurrence to draw any conclusions. Our evidence is purely "anecdotal." For now, all I can suggest to someone who has developed breast cancer *while* pregnant or lactating is to seriously consider not having another pregnancy, in case it affects the chance of a recurrence.

See page 365 on the question of pregnancy after having breast cancer, and page 366 in regard to breast feeding after having breast cancer.

Breast Cancer in Men

This book addresses breast cancer in women, and there's a reason for that. It is the most common malignancy in women, and very rare among men, accounting for less than 1 percent of male malignancies. Many of the men who get it seem to have a family history on the father's side.[14] There's also a theory that it's connected to gynecomastia—femalelike breasts (see page 15), either in the present or during the man's puberty, but so far we have no proof of this. We do have proof that men with Klinefelter's syndrome, a chromosomal problem in which not enough testosterone is produced, are susceptible to breast cancer.[15]

For a time there was some concern that men who got estrogen treatments for prostate cancer would be more vulnerable to breast cancer, but this doesn't seem to be the case. What can happen is that the prostate cancer itself can metastasize to the breast.[16]

Breast cancer in men shows itself in all the ways it does in women—usually as a lump—but it tends to be discovered at a much later time because men don't tend to be as conscious of their breasts as women are of theirs. The treatments are the same as well, though men may have less problem with mastectomy, since the cosmetic implications are less charged for them. Usually, however, when a man has a breast lump, it isn't cancer, it's unilateral gynecomastia, which can happen anytime in a man's life, especially if he's been on some of the drugs used to treat heart conditions or hypertension or smokes marijuana. It's never a cyst or fibroadenoma—men don't get those.

Other Cancers

Although cancer in the breast is almost always breast cancer, there are rare occasions when another cancer shows up in the breast. Since the breast contains other kinds of tissue besides breast tissue, any of the cancers associated with that tissue can appear in the breast, such as a cancerous fat tumor (liposarcoma) or blood-vessel tumor (angiosarcoma). Connective tissue in the breast, as elsewhere, can become cancerous. Usually they're treated the same way they'd be treated in any other part of the body—the tissue is excised, and radiation and chemotherapy follow. (The chemicals are different from those used to treat breast cancer.)

You can also get a metastasis from a cancer that began somewhere else, though this too is extremely uncommon. I've had two patients with lymphoma that has metastasized to the breast. As I noted above, prostate cancer in men may metastasize to the breast. Other cancers almost never show up in the breast.

When another form of cancer shows up in the breast, we know it isn't breast cancer from the pathologist's report. As I've discussed earlier, each kind of cancer has its own distinct characteristics, and we rarely mistake one kind for another. We would treat it according to the primary cancer rather than as a breast cancer.

It's important to remember that having breast cancer doesn't immunize you from other forms of cancer. You have the same chances as anyone else of getting other cancers. I've had a couple of patients with breast cancer who were also heavy smokers: they were treated for their breast cancer, continued smoking, and ended up with lung cancer. A bout with any kind of cancer provides a useful time to consider altering your lifestyle in ways that promote overall health.

21

Surgery

Almost every form of breast cancer will involve some surgery—the initial biopsy, and probably a mastectomy or a partial mastectomy (lumpectomy) as well as axillary surgery. It's always a frightening thought, but demystifying the process can be helpful. For one thing, the old theory that surgery would "let the air get to the cancer" and thus cause it to spread all over is a myth. This misconception perhaps arose at a time when surgery was done only on very late cancers. The further spread of the cancer was then blamed on the surgery instead of the cancer. No one should be afraid to have an operation for cancer. As we mentioned in the previous chapter, it may not cure you by itself but it is an important part of the overall treatment.

We've already discussed some surgery in previous chapters (5 and 10). In this chapter we will go over what you can expect from your surgeon and your operation for breast cancer. I will be fairly explicit because I think the more information you have the less scared you will be. If you find surgical details not to your liking you may want to skip ahead.

In my own surgery practice, I talk with the patient a few days ahead of time and explain exactly what I'll do in the operation, and what risks and possible complications are involved. I draw them pictures and show them photographs, so they'll know what to expect. Before any operation, patients are asked to sign a consent form. This can be a little scary, especially if you read all the fine print, because it asks you to state that you're aware that you can die from the surgery or suffer permanent brain damage from the anesthetic. This doesn't mean that these things are likely to happen, or that by signing the form you're letting the doctors off the hook if something does happen. What it does is guarantee that you've been told about the procedure and its risk and that you still want to have the operation. (Obviously you have to balance for yourself the risk involved in the operation against the risks of not having the operation.)

It's very important that you do know the risks, and you should never permit yourself to be rushed through the signing of the consent form. You should be given the form well before you go in for surgery—it's hard to read small print when you're about to be wheeled into the operating room. You should have plenty of time to ask the surgeon any questions about risks and complications—and if anything at all is confusing, be sure to ask.

I usually send out a printed form to my patient's house in advance, explaining the risks, and then go over it again verbally before she signs the form. That gives her plenty of time to think about the procedure and its risks, and to formulate any questions she might have for me.

For the bigger operations (mastectomies) I often recommend that the patient donate some of her own blood a week or two prior to the operation. I don't often have to transfuse a patient, but it is a nice secure feeling for the patient to know that if she does need blood she can get the safest type possible, her own. If your surgeon doesn't offer this you should ask. The Red Cross is more than happy to assist in this procedure.

Finally, I tell all preoperative patients to stop taking any aspirin, aspirin containing products, and any nonsteroidal anti-inflammatory drugs at least two weeks prior to surgery. All of these will interfere with blood clotting and therefore cause more bleeding in surgery. If someone has taken a drug of this type we will do a "bleeding time" (a test that tells how fast your blood clots) prior to surgery to make sure it is safe to proceed. If not, I postpone the surgery for a week or two until the clotting returns to normal.

Anesthesia

In the old days, general anesthesia just meant ether, but in recent years it's become a very complex and sophisticated combination of drugs. The first element in any general anesthetic combination is something to induce sleep quickly—usually sodium pentothal. It's given intravenously, and it puts you out immediately. The effects of sodium pentothal last only about 15 minutes, so it's followed with a combination of other drugs. Sometimes the anesthesiologist will use a combination of narcotics to prevent pain, nitrous oxide ("laughing gas") to keep you unconscious, and a muscle paralyzer to keep you from coughing, or otherwise moving during the operation. Since the muscle paralyzer prevents you from breathing, it is necessary to put a tube down your throat and into your windpipe to keep your airway open, and hook you up to a breathing machine to assure that you get enough oxygen into your body during the operation. Sometimes, rather than use the narcotics, they'll just use gas: some kinds of gas can keep you asleep and get rid of pain.

Which of these various agents are used, and in what combination, will be chosen only after consultation with the individual patient. Your medical history will make a big difference here. If you have asthma, for example, a drug that opens up the airways is more suitable so that you don't get an attack under anesthesia. If you have a heart condition, a drug that doesn't aggravate the heart but has a calming effect on it will be chosen.

There are also drugs more suitable for different kinds of operations. If you're having your gallbladder removed, a drug that keeps your stomach muscles relaxed allows the surgeon to reach the gallbladder more easily. In a breast operation, that's not much of a problem, since the breast is on the surface of your body.

Since anesthesia and its administration are so sophisticated and precise, most hospitals will have you meet with the anesthesiologist before the operation. Anesthesiologists are well-trained doctors who've gone through at least three years of specialized training after their internships. Your anesthesiologist will take your medical history, looking for things in that history that might suggest using, or not using, various of the anesthetic agents. He or she will ask about chronic diseases you may have, past experiences with anesthetic, and so forth, and only after thoroughly exploring all this with you will decide what to use in your operation. This interview is very important. As much of the risk of any operation is in the anesthesia and its administration as is in the surgery. When you talk to the anesthesiologist, ask questions, and give her or him any information you think might be of importance. Many hospitals also have nurse anesthetists who help administer anesthesia under an M.D.'s supervision.

Before you're put to sleep, you're hooked up to a variety of monitoring devices. There's an automatic blood pressure cuff. There's an EKG monitoring your heart rate. Sometimes a little clip or piece of tape is put on your finger or other extremity to measure the amount of oxygen in your blood. If the operation is a lengthy one, a catheter is put in your bladder to measure the amount of urine output and make sure you're not dehydrated. So your bodily functions are all carefully monitored.

Once you're on the operating table, you're asleep very quickly. Many people who haven't had surgery for 20 or 30 years remember the old days of ether, and are nervous about unpleasant sensations they recall going under. But sodium pentothal works much differently, and most patients report it as a very pleasant experience. You may experience a garlic-like taste at the back of your mouth just before you go under, and you may yawn. Then you're asleep. Don't worry: in spite of all the television melodrama, you're not likely to reveal all your deep, dark secrets under sodium pentothal. You might mutter something just as you go under, but when you're asleep, you're quiet.

How you wake up from the operation will depend, again, on what drugs have been used. With some drugs an antidote can be given to end the drug's effects. So if, for example, you've been given a muscle paralyzer, a drug can restore your muscle mobility. But if you've been given gas to put you to sleep, you have to wait till the gas wears off. As soon as they think you're awake enough to breathe on your own, the tube is removed. Occasionally you'll be vaguely aware that this is happening, but usually you're still too out of it to notice. You stay a little fuzzy for a while. When the surgery is over, you're taken to the recovery room, where a nurse remains with you, monitoring your blood pressure and pulse every 10 or 15 minutes until you're fully awake and stable.

Patients often feel cold when they first wake up. Particularly in a big operation, when you haven't been covered up, you've lost body heat; in addition, the IV (intravenous) fluids going into you are cold. Some of the drugs can create nausea, and you may feel sick when you first wake up. This was succinctly described by a recovery room nurse I once saw on a TV show. She was asked what patients usually say when they first come out of anesthesia, and it was clear the host was expecting something profound or moving. Instead, she replied, "They say, 'I think I'm going to be sick'—and then they are."

You may find that you wake up crying, or shivering, but only rarely do patients wake up in great pain. You'll probably fade in and out for a while, and then you'll be fully awake. But expect to be groggy and out of it for a while. It's several hours before most of the drugs are out of your system, and a day or more till all of it's gone. If it's day surgery, you'll probably want to just go home and go to bed; if you're still in the hospital, you'll sleep it all off there.

Even apart from the surgery, anesthesia itself is a great strain on your body, and it will cause some degree of exhaustion for at least four or five days. People often don't realize this, especially if the surgery itself is very painful: they attribute all their exhaustion to the pain of the operation. But anything that puts great stress on your body—surgery, a heart attack, an acute asthma attack, or anesthetics that interfere with your body's functions—will have a lingering effect. It's as if your body takes all its energy to mobilize for the big stress, and doesn't have any left over for everyday life for a while. You need to respect that, and give your body time to recuperate from the stress of both the surgery and the anesthetic.

There are, of course, risks involved in using general anesthetic, but it's important to keep them in perspective. With the refinements in anesthesia in recent years, the risks are extremely low (about one death in 200,000 cases). It would be nice if we could always use local instead of general anesthesia, but we can't. Only a small area can be numbed by local anesthetic; too much becomes dangerous. It can't be used in a major operation. There are some anesthetics that are midway between local and general. A *nerve block* can sometimes be useful. The anesthesiologist finds the nerve that feeds into the area the surgeon will operate on, and anesthetizes the nerve itself, so that everything it feeds goes numb. But a nerve block works only in an area controlled by a single nerve and in which the controlling nerve is easily accessible. Since the breast area involves a number of nerves, we can't use it for major breast surgery.

There's also the *spinal*—more extensive than the nerve block, but less extensive than general anesthetic. Local anesthetic is put into the spinal fluid where it bathes the spinal column, making all the nerves below the area go numb. It's good for a number of operations—hemorrhoids, gynecological surgery, hernia—but only if they are below the waist. Unfortunately, it can't be used above the waist, since it would numb the nerves that control breathing and heartbeat. The *epidural* works similarly, and has similar limitations. So, for major breast surgery, general anesthesia is necessary and, as we said earlier, safer than it has ever been.

Preliminary Procedures

In the operating room, before you are anesthetized, the anesthesiologist will be setting up, and the nurses will put EKG leads and an automatic blood pressure cuff on you. Often we use something called "pneumatic boots"—plastic boots that pump up and down massaging your calves during the operation to prevent clots from forming. (See Figure 21-1.) A grounding plate is put on your skin to ground the electrocautery (a type of electric knife). The IV is put in, and then you're given pentothal. During this time, your surgeon may or may not be with you. Some surgeons prefer a more personal contact beforehand; others maintain a professional distance. I like to establish a connection with my patient beforehand, so I go into the operating

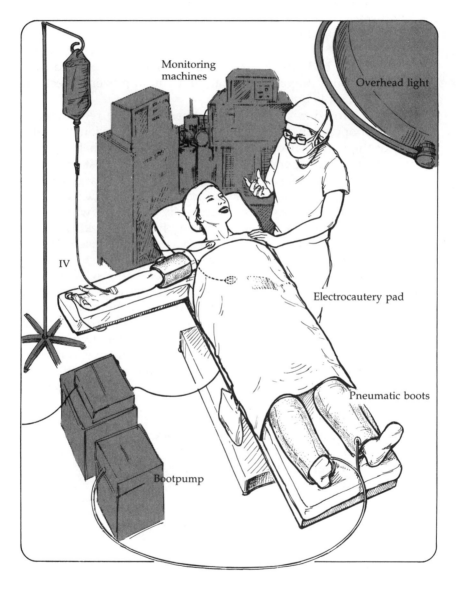

FIGURE 21-1

room and, while all these procedures are taking place, I'll stay there with my patient and hold her hand. My patient is scared, and usually I'm the only person there she knows. This contact also helps me confirm my commitment to the patient as an individual who has offered her trust to me.

Once my patient's asleep, I do what every other surgeon does: I go out to scrub (wash my hands). With personal contact established, I like to use this time to distance—I need to be an objective crafts-person to do the best job possible.

After scrubbing the surgeon goes back into the operating room. The area of your body that's going to be worked on is painted over with a disinfectant, drapes are put around you to prevent infection, and the operation is underway.

All of the procedures I've just described are done regardless of what kind of operation you're having. What varies, obviously, is the process of the particular operation. Now I'll describe what happens in each breast cancer operation, starting with the simplest and mov-ing on to the more complex. (See Figure 21-2.) (Biopsies have been de-scribed in Chapter 10 and plastic surgical operations in Chapter 5.)

Most surgical operations have traditionally been done with a scal-pel or scissors. More recently electrocautery has been used with less blood loss. The newest technique is the laser. Some people have the misconception that using the laser means you don't have to make an incision; you just vaporize the tissues. It is not that easy. The laser, however, is a new cutting tool for the surgeon and is being used more and more for breast operations. Although there have been claims of less postoperative pain, and less tumor recurrence, there are no good randomized studies as of yet and the data from animal experiments are mixed.[1, 2] I think the laser may well have a place in the future of breast surgery, but it is important for the patient to realize that it is just another tool to aid the surgeon in doing the operation.

In 1989 a retrospective study[3] of 44 patients suggested that the recurrence of breast cancer was less if women were operated on midcycle rather than perimenstrually. Although it is a provocative finding, it needs further study before we accept it as valid. We are trying to confirm this in a long-term prospective study.

Partial Mastectomy and Axillary Dissection

The alternative to mastectomy is an operation that removes the lump and part of the surrounding tissue, combined with postoperative radiation (see page 299). Partial mastectomy, lumpectomy, wide ex-

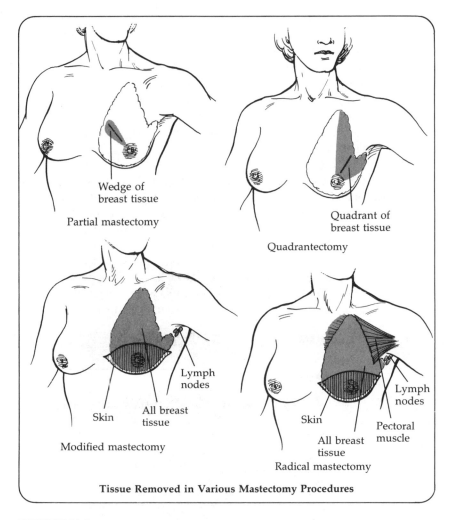

Wedge of
breast tissue

Partial mastectomy

Quadrant of
breast tissue

Quadrantectomy

Lymph
nodes

Skin   All breast
tissue

Modified mastectomy

Lymph
nodes

Skin

Pectoral
All breast muscle
tissue

Radical mastectomy

Tissue Removed in Various Mastectomy Procedures

FIGURE 21-2

excision, segmental mastectomy, and quadrantectomy are all names
for this type of operation and are used virtually synonymously. What
each term means depends on the surgeon who's using it. Except for
quadrantectomy, none of the terms suggests how much tissue will
be removed, and often surgeons use "quadrantectomy" when they
don't necessarily mean they'll remove a fourth of the breast. With a
partial mastectomy, the "part" removed can be 1 percent or 50 percent
of the breast tissue. "Lumpectomy" depends on the size of the lump.
"Wide excision" just says that you'll cut away tissue around the lump;
it doesn't say how *much* will be cut. "Segmental" sounds like the

breast comes in little segments, like an orange. But it doesn't, and the size of the segment removed can be tiny or huge or anything in-between. Your surgeon will use whatever term appeals most to her or him: I use "partial mastectomy" at the moment, because it's the term that insurance companies seem most comfortable with.

If you're opting for surgery that involves taking out part but not all of the breast tissue, you need to make sure your surgeon explains very precisely how much tissue will be removed, and what you're going to look like afterward.

Once again, different surgeons will have slightly different approaches. I prefer to do a partial mastectomy and lymph node surgery as day surgery. The operation begins with carefully monitored general anesthetic. I usually start with the breast, taking out the breast tissue in a wedge, like a piece of pie, all the way down to the level of the muscle. (See Figure 21-3.) That piece is given intact to the pathologist. Then the remaining breast tissue is rotated from either side, bringing it together so that you don't have a big dent in your breast, and it's sewn closed. Because of this, your breast may sit up a little higher than it did before. Some surgeons put drains into the

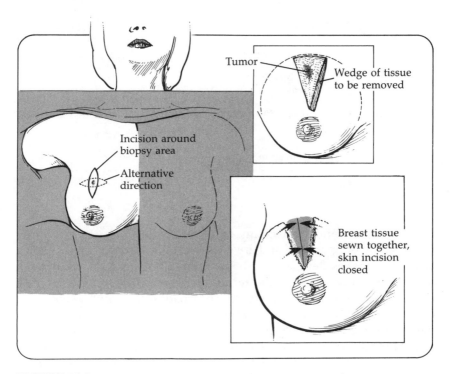

FIGURE 21-3

breast tissue to collect fluid afterward. I find this unnecessary, and rarely do it.

Because this is a relatively new procedure, standard techniques haven't been worked out. I'm currently working with a plastic surgeon to determine the best way to do a partial mastectomy which will give both good cancer results and good cosmetic results. One thing we've determined is that the direction of the incision should vary depending on which area of the breast contains the cancer. In addition, the way the tissue is removed and whether or not it is sewn back together will vary depending on the area of the breast involved. We are hoping to soon have an atlas published which will demonstrate for all surgeons the best technical approach to breast conservation.

When the breast surgery itself is finished, the surgeon will begin operating on the lymph nodes. (See Figure 21-4.) An incision is made about 2–3 inches across the armpit, and the surgeon removes the wad of fat in the hollow of your armpit that contains many of the lymph nodes. The lymph nodes, as I said earlier, are glands—sometimes they're swollen and big, but usually they're very small and embedded in fat. We take out a section of the fat, defined by certain anatomical boundaries, which usually contains at least 6 to 10 lymph nodes. The tissue is sent to the pathologist, who examines the fat and tries to find all the lymph nodes in it. Some women will have more nodes than others. Every now and then a patient will ask me, "How come you got 17 lymph nodes in me and only 7 in my friend?" We are all built differently. The most important thing is to sample the nodes in a certain area. There have been studies showing that the chance of missing a positive lymph node if you remove the tissue

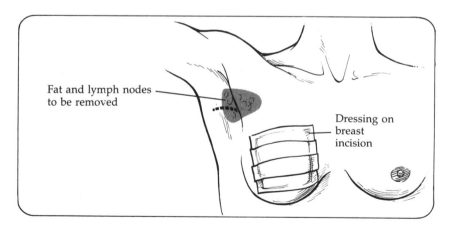

Fat and lymph nodes to be removed

Dressing on breast incision

FIGURE 21-4

in the lower two levels of the armpit is less than 5 percent.[4] Many surgeons put a drain in the axillary incision afterward, but again, I prefer not to—there's not enough fluid to worry about, in my experience.[5] I put a little long-acting local anesthetic into the wound, so my patient won't wake up in pain later, and then sew up the incision.

The operation takes from one to three hours altogether. You wake up in the recovery room and, according to your surgeon's preference, you can go home that night or in a day or two. As I said, I prefer to send you home that day, unless you have some medical condition that might be aggravated by anesthesia—severe asthma, or heart problems, for example.

You will be sent home with a small dressing. I use dissolvable sutures inside the skin and steristrips on the skin. This means you can take a shower or bath or go swimming without worry. There are no sutures to take out, but I do like to see my patients 10 days to two weeks after the surgery to trim the knots of the sutures as well as to monitor their progress.

AFTER THE OPERATION

Your surgeon may put your arm in a sling to prevent your moving your arm around and pulling the incision apart. I don't like to do this; I think the earlier you start moving your arm around normally the less chance there is that your arm will get stiff. Keeping the arm in a sling will cause it to stiffen, even if you haven't had an operation. If your arm is kept immobile for any length of time, you'll need physical therapy to help you start using it again. I have found that my patients are sufficiently sore that they don't tend to fling their arms about anyway.

Once you're sent home, the biggest problem, as we said, is that you're exhausted. Respect that tiredness: you've just been through major surgery, anesthesia, and an emotionally difficult operation. The exhaustion often comes and goes suddenly: you'll feel fine, and go out shopping; when you get home you'll suddenly feel completely wiped out and need to sleep. It will take several days before you feel fully recovered.

The pathology results will usually be available within a couple of days. I can then tell my patient what the margins around the cancer were like and what was actually in her breast tissue and, more importantly, whether there was any lymph node involvement. If the lymph nodes show cancer, or if there are any other ominous features of the tumor, I will refer her to an oncologist for a discussion of systemic therapy (see Chapter 23).

RISKS AND COMPLICATIONS

There may be some loss of sensation after a partial mastectomy, depending on the size of the lump removed. If it's a large lump, there may be a permanent numb spot, but there won't be the total loss of sensation that results from a mastectomy.

And, of course, there is always the possibility of a hematoma (see page 133) or infection (page 134).

Your breast will be different in size and shape than it was before, and consequently it will probably be somewhat different from your remaining breast. How great the difference is depends on how much tissue was removed and how skillfully the surgeon has sewn the breast back together. If your breasts are asymmetrical, you can't have a silicone implant put in the smaller breast to enlarge it, since that would interfere with our ability to follow the breast for a possible recurrence of the cancer. We are currently studying the advisability of using a small muscle flap, as we do with whole breast reconstruction, to fill in the defect. Depending on how large your breasts are to begin with, and how disturbed you are by the asymmetry, you can get the other breast reduced to create a more symmetrical appearance. Usually, however, that won't be necessary. If you have a small lump, and medium or large breasts, it's often hard to tell afterward which breast was operated on.

The possible complications resulting from lymph node surgery are more serious. There's a nerve—and sometimes two or three nerves—that goes through the middle of the fat that has been removed. This nerve gives you sensation in the back part of your armpit. It doesn't affect the way your arm works, but it does affect sensation. If that nerve is cut, you'll have a patch of numbness in the back part of your arm. (See Figure 21-5.) Most surgeons do cut the nerve, because it's difficult to save, and they don't think sensation in the armpit is very important anyway. Of course, most surgeons are men—and since most men don't shave their armpits, they don't know how awkward it can be when you can't feel the area you're shaving. I always try to save the nerve, though I'm more successful in some cases than in others. Even if the surgeon does save it, it may get stretched in the process and give you decreased sensation either temporarily or permanently. If the sensation is gone for more than a few months, it's probably permanent.

Another complication, one that's unusual, is fluid under the armpit. Most women get some swelling, but some will get so much that it feels like they've got a grapefruit under their armpits. When it gets to this point, it can be aspirated (drawn off) by the surgeon.

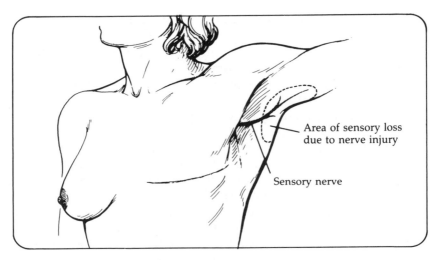

Area of sensory loss
due to nerve injury

Sensory nerve

FIGURE 21-5

Another early problem can be phlebitis in one of the arm veins. This usually shows up three or four days after surgery. The woman says, "I felt wonderful after the operation and now I have this tight feeling under my arm which goes down to the elbow and sometimes even to the wrist. The pain is worse and I can't move my arm nearly as well as I could before." This is an inflammation of the basilic vein. It is not serious but bothersome. The best treatment is ice and aspirin. It will go away within several days to a week.

The major complication, but fortunately an uncommon one (3%), is swelling of the arm, a condition called *lymphedema*. It can be so slight that you only notice it because your rings are suddenly feeling too tight on your fingers, or so severe that your arm is huge, even elephantine. It can be temporary or permanent. It can happen immediately, or years after your operation. Because it can be a long-term complication, it will be discussed at length on page 358.

Many doctors and nurses will send you home with extensive instructions regarding care of your arm after surgery. They are trying to prevent infections, since infection is thought to increase the chances of lymphedema. Since your lymph nodes have been removed you may be more susceptible to infections. They will insist that you never garden without gloves because you might get pricked by a thorn, or that you never reach into a hot oven, or cut your cuticles, or have injections in that arm. Be sensible: you want to reduce the risk of infection, but you're not going to die if you get a minor infection, and there's no need to live your life in terror of pinpricks. Be reasonably careful, and if you do get an infection, get to your doctor as soon as possible and have it taken care of. In

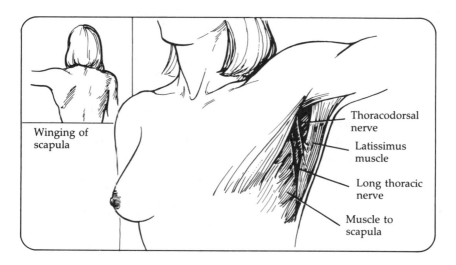

Winging of scapula

Thoracodorsal nerve

Latissimus muscle

Long thoracic nerve

Muscle to scapula

FIGURE 21-6

addition, be careful about lifting heavy things with your affected arm, especially with it lowered, as when you carry a heavy briefcase or suitcase. This may also increase chance of swelling.

Another rare complication of lymph node surgery involves the motor nerves. (See Figure 21-6.) These are different from the sensory nerves. Two motor nerves can be injured by lymph node surgery. One of them—the *long thoracic nerve*—goes to the muscle that holds your shoulder blade against your back when you hold your arm straight out. If that nerve is injured, your shoulder blade, instead of remaining flat, will stick out like a wing when you hold your arm out. Hence it's called a "winged scapula." (There are other causes of winged scapula as well; sometimes it's a congenital condition.) If you're not athletic, it probably won't affect you very much in your daily activities, but it affects activities like serving in tennis or pitching a baseball.

Permanent winged scapula cases are extremely rare; I've never had one among my patients, though I've had two women who've had it temporarily. If the condition is temporary, it should go away in a few weeks or months. In order to cause a permanent winged scapula, the surgeon would have to cut completely through the nerve. If that does happen and if it bothers you a lot, an orthopedic surgeon can perform an operation to remedy it.

The other nerve is called the *thoracodorsal nerve,* and it goes to the latissimus dorsal muscle. Damage to this nerve is rare and less noticeable than the winged scapula. It will probably give you some sensation of tiredness in the arm, which won't work quite as well as it did before, but it won't give you any glaring problem.

Total Mastectomy

The total mastectomy is an operation which removes only the breast tissue; muscles and lymph nodes are left alone. This is sometimes used for precancer (see page 198). The modified radical mastectomy includes some of the lymph nodes. This is sometimes termed a total mastectomy with axillary dissection. (Radical mastectomy which we will discuss on page 297 removes all the breast, all the lymph nodes, and the muscles of the chest wall.)

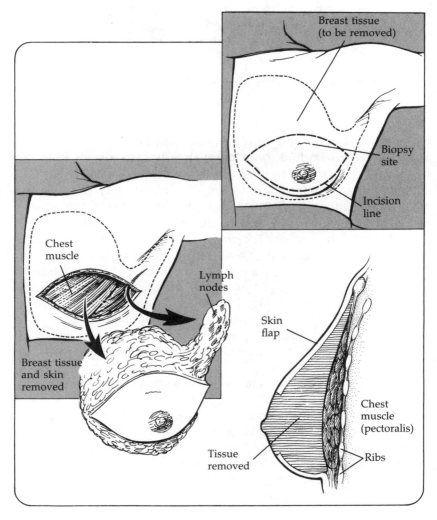

Breast tissue (to be removed)

Biopsy site

Incision line

Chest muscle

Lymph nodes

Skin flap

Breast tissue and skin removed

Tissue removed

Chest muscle (pectoralis)

Ribs

FIGURE 21-7

The breast tissue, as we discussed earlier, extends from the collarbone down to the edge of the ribs and from the breastbone out to the muscle in the back of the armpit. The surgeon wants to get all that breast tissue out. So we start with an elliptical incision that includes the nipple and whatever scar you have from the biopsy: exactly where it is depends on where your biopsy scar is. (See Figure 21-7.) We take that skin out. Then we tunnel underneath the skin all the way up to the collarbone, then down to the border of the ribs, from the middle of the sternum, and out to the muscle behind your armpit. Once the dissection is done, we peel the breast off, leaving the muscle behind. We send the breast tissue to the pathologist, who examines it and begins the process of fixing it to make slides. Meanwhile we sew together the flaps of skin around the incision. You end up completely flat (or, if you're very thin, slightly concave), with a scar going across the middle of that side of your chest. The skin doesn't completely stick down right away, and the body doesn't like empty spaces, so the area will fill up with fluid. To prevent this, we put some drains in—soft, plastic tubes with little holes in them, coming out of the skin below the scar. (See Figure 21-8.) They are attached to suction which holds the skin down against the muscle till it heals. Fluid will come out of these drains—it's just tissue fluid, the kind you get in a blister. Initially there'll be a little blood in the fluid, but after about 24 hours it will be clear. If we are doing a modified radical mastectomy (total mastectomy with axillary dissection) after the breast is fully removed we reach up under the skin to

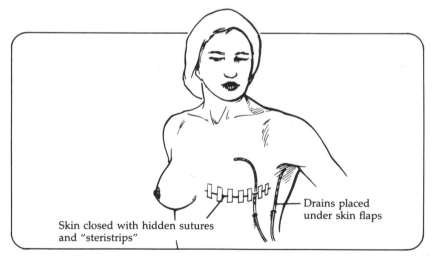

Skin closed with hidden sutures and "steristrips"

Drains placed under skin flaps

FIGURE 21-8

the armpit and remove some of the lymph nodes. We use the same anatomical boundaries described earlier for the axillary dissection.

If you've decided to have immediate breast reconstruction (see page 349), the plastic surgeon will come in after the mastectomy is finished but before the skin is sewn up, and do the reconstruction.

As in other operations the pathology results will be available in a couple of days. This will tell you what the breast tissue looked like and more importantly if there is node involvement. If there are any indications of systemic spread you will be referred to an oncologist for consideration of adjuvant systemic treatment (see page 315).

Different surgeons have different styles in postoperative treatment. I usually put a big, bulky wraparound dressing on my patients because it helps them feel protected from the world for a while. You'll probably stay in the hospital for several days. When there's no longer much fluid coming out of the drains—in about three or four days—we'll take the drains out and change the dressing. We used to keep people in the hospital till all the drains came out—nowadays patients sometimes go home and come back later to get the drains removed.

While you're in the hospital, someone from Reach to Recovery (see Appendix C) or a similar group may come to see you with what's called a "going-home prosthesis." Some insurance companies will pay for it if it's ordered from the hospital, but not if you wait till you're home. Insurance policies vary; make sure you check out what yours will cover. (See page 347 for a discussion of prostheses.)

Some women want to see the wound right away; some prefer to put off looking at it for a week or two. Either way is fine; you need to decide what will make you feel best. But it's important that you look at it at some point. It's amazing how, if you're determined to avoid looking at your body, you can do so when you shower, get dressed, even when you make love. That's okay for a while, but this is the body you're going to be living with, and you need to see it and accept it.

Many of my patients like me to be with them the first time they see their scar. This way I can offer emotional support and also answer any questions they have right away. If you feel comfortable with your surgeon and would like her or him with you when you first look at your chest, ask.

Others prefer to be alone when they first look at the scar. Some want to see it alone before showing it to their husband or lover. Again, there's no right or wrong way to face it, as long as you *do* face it. In my experience, most women are relieved that it doesn't look as bad as they feared it would.

Numbness around the chest wall is one of the more unfortunate results of the operation. The breast's nerve supply has been cut. So the area around the scar of the mastectomy will be permanently numb. Some sensitivity remains around the outer borders of the area on which your breast was located. Sometimes it's not entirely numb, however; you can tell if someone's touching you. Unfortunately, this isn't always a pleasant sensation. It can be very uncomfortable, like the sensation that you feel when your foot's asleep and starts coming back again, with a tingly feeling. This is known as *dysesthesia*, and, while it may lessen in severity, it will remain with you. Often people who've had mastectomies don't like their scars being touched because it brings about this slight unpleasant sensation.

Some women also experience phantom breast symptoms—like the amputee whose foot is removed but who still feels itchiness in the toes that are no longer there. Similarly, the mastectomy patient may feel her nipple itch, or her breast ache, as though it were still there. All this means is that the brain hasn't yet realized what's happened to the body. The nerve supply from the breast grows along a certain path in the spinal cord and goes to a certain area of the brain. The brain has been trained over the years that a signal from this path means, for example, that the nipple is itching. When the nipple's been removed, the signal may get generated in a different place further along the path, but the brain cells think it should be coming from the nipple, and that's the information they give you. This will gradually improve as your brain becomes reprogrammed.

Audre Lorde described some of the feelings wonderfully well in her book *The Cancer Journal*: "fixed pains and moveable pains, deep pains and surface pains, strong pains and weak pains. There were stabs and throbs and burns, gripes and tickles and itches." In addition, some women will feel a tightness around the chest as the healing starts. This will ease up over time, and all the weird sensations will start to settle down.

RISKS AND COMPLICATIONS OF
TOTAL MASTECTOMY

Like any operation, the mastectomy has a certain number of risks. The blood supply that goes to the flaps of skin that are left around the removed breast tissue comes entirely along the flaps. In the process of removing the breast tissue, we've severed a number of blood vessels. The only ones left are those that go the whole length of the flap: they can barely get to the ends. Sometimes this doesn't give us enough of a blood supply, and it doesn't heal right; a little area of skin dies and forms a scab. (See Figure 21-9.) Once the wound

Two possible complications . . .

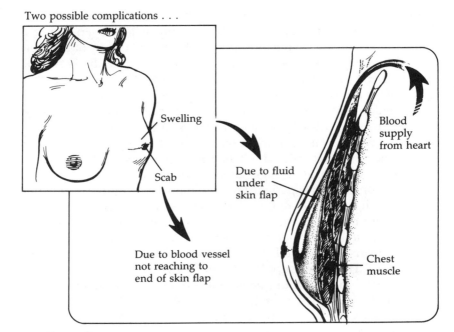

Swelling

Scab

Blood
supply
from heart

Due to fluid
under
skin flap

Due to blood vessel
not reaching to
end of skin flap

Chest
muscle

FIGURE 21-9

has healed, the scab falls off. It's usually not a very serious complication. If a big enough area of skin is involved, or there's an infection,
the surgeon may have to trim the dead tissue so the body can heal
the wound.

A second possible complication occurs when fluid continues to
collect under the scar after the drains are removed. (See Figure 21-
9.) You'll know this is happening because there's a swelling around
the incision; sometimes you'll hear a splash when you're walking, or
you'll simply feel the fluid on your chest. If it's a small amount of
fluid you can just leave it alone and it will eventually go away by
itself. If there's a lot of fluid, you can have it aspirated with a needle:
it won't hurt, since the area's numb, and it usually doesn't even
require local anesthesia. We try to avoid too many aspirations,
though, since there's always the slight risk of transmitting infection
through the needle. Again, this isn't a serious complication, but it
can be an annoying one.

The risks from the lymph node removal are exactly the same as
those in the partial mastectomy—loss of sensation, phlebitis, swelling, and winged scapula. It's important to move your arm around
and keep it from stiffening.

Radical Mastectomy

Radical mastectomies are rarely done anymore, for reasons I've discussed earlier. There are few situations when it may be a wiser choice than the modified radical. Sometimes the tumor is so large that a radical mastectomy is the only way to remove it. In other cases, the tumor is stuck to the muscle, so the muscle has to be removed in order to get the tumor out. (In very rare cases, the cancer will actually have spread into the muscle itself.)

The surgical procedure is basically the same as that for the modified radical, but, obviously, more extensive. In addition to removing the whole breast we remove the pectoralis major and pectoralis minor muscles. (See Figure 21-10.) All of the lymph nodes in the axillary area (up to the collarbone) are removed as well.

A radical mastectomy is far more deforming. With the chest wall muscle removed, the skin lies directly on the rib cage. Since the surgeon has access to the lymph nodes under the muscle, it's possible to remove those lymph nodes, which leaves more swelling and less arm mobility. Sometimes there's not enough skin left to sew it closed properly, so a graft is taken from another part of the body, usually the thigh, and put in the middle of the skin as a patch.

The risks and complications, however, are similar to those of the modified radical. The cosmetic results are worse, because there's no

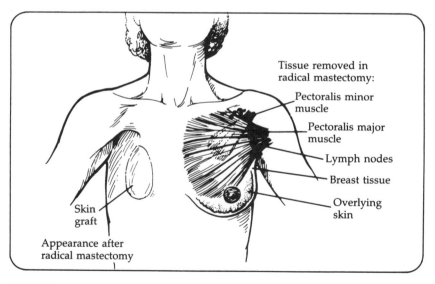

Tissue removed in radical mastectomy:

Pectoralis minor muscle

Pectoralis major muscle

Lymph nodes

Breast tissue

Overlying skin

Skin graft

Appearance after radical mastectomy

FIGURE 21-10

fold coming down from the arm. Functionally, your arm won't be as strong, because you're missing the pectoralis muscle. The risk of lymphedema will be higher because more nodes have been removed.

There's a variant of the radical mastectomy that's even more severe, called the extended radical, in which a section of the rib cage is removed in order to get to the lymph nodes behind it. It's rarely done nowadays. I can't think of any good reason to do this procedure, which simply adds further deformity and discomfort and, since it's more extensive surgery, increases all the normal surgical risks.

Surgery is never fun. But it's often necessary, and if you know what to expect ahead of time, you can reduce the stress and fear surrounding it.

22

Radiation Treatment

Radiation therapy is used to treat both early and metastatic cancer. The idea of getting radiation therapy may make you nervous. After all, radiation can *cause* cancer, and the last thing you want is to find yourself in danger of even more cancer: you've got quite enough now, thank you. But the doses given in radiation therapy rarely cause cancer, and often cure it. We've discussed this at length on page 161.

Radiation can be used in one of two ways. It can be used as a form of local control—that is, it can be used to help cure an original cancer. It's more effective in some forms of cancer than in others; it's been very effective with breast cancer.

It can also be used to help alleviate the pain and slow down the progress of metastatic cancer, by shrinking the tumor. We often use it when the cancer has spread to the bones or brain, but less often to the lung or liver, since it's harder to use radiation here without damaging other organs, and chemotherapy is a more effective treatment for these metastases.

Often radiation is used in conjunction with surgery, so that you might have had a lumpectomy, or even a mastectomy, before your radiation. Radiation works best when it has comparatively few cells to attack—it's least effective on large chunks of cancer. So we try, if

299

possible, to do the surgery first, getting rid of most of the tumor surgically and then cleaning up what's left with radiation. Sometimes that's not feasible: if you've got a large chunk of cancer in the middle of your backbone, for example, it can't be reached surgically, and so we'll use a higher dose of radiation to get rid of all the cancer. There's always a trade-off in these cases; the higher dose of radiation is more likely to affect other tissue. On the other hand, if we don't get rid of the cancer, it's almost certain to get bigger.

In the old days, we used a cobalt machine which was aimed at the general area instead of at a carefully plotted site, and the radiation scattered a lot. One of my patients had been treated with a cobalt machine for Hodgkin's disease in the 1960s, and, while it cured the Hodgkin's, it scattered a lot of low-dose radiation into her breasts, and she now has breast cancer. Though it's unfortunate that she has cancer again now, at the time the cobalt machine was the best form of radiation therapy we had, and if the Hodgkin's had gone un-treated, she probably would have long since died.

In the early days of radiation, women who were radiated post-mastectomy for breast cancer often developed other diseases because of the radiation. If the machine is aimed straight on at the breast, you also radiate the lungs and, if it's the left breast, the heart. Some studies[1] show that women whose left breasts were radiated 20 years ago, after they had mastectomies, had a higher incidence of heart disease than other women—including women whose right breasts were radiated.

We've come a long way since those days. We've refined the pro-cess of administering radiation, so that it's much more precise. We're much better able to hone into the specific site we want to radiate. We administer the radiation in tangents, as well as straight on, so that the radiation goes through a particular breast area and out into air, and less into your heart or lung. (See Figure 22-1.) At the same time we shield other body parts to prevent scatter radiation.

Radiation, like surgery, is a localized treatment. (Chemotherapy, given through an injection or a pill, goes through your bloodstream and affects your entire body.) It's aimed at a very specific area and affects only that area. It's usually administered by a machine called a "linear accelerator," which accelerates radioactive particles and shoots them directly at the body part they're intended for, like a gun.

Initial Consultation

Radiation therapists (who are always M.D.'s) like to see patients soon after the biopsy—ideally while they still have the lump, to get

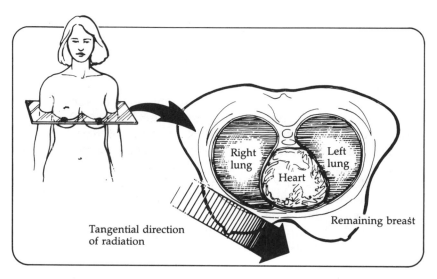

Right
lung

Left
lung

Heart

Remaining breast

Tangential direction
of radiation

FIGURE 22-1

a firsthand sense of the tumor. Sometimes the initial consultation will involve a team approach, including a specially trained radiation nurse, who will inquire into the patient's needs, taking into account her emotional response to her cancer. The consultation involves a physical exam as well as conversation with the patient.

This first visit to a radiation therapist doesn't mean you'll necessarily have radiation treatments. The therapist will talk with you and get your medical history, do an examination, review your X rays and slides from any surgery you may have had done, and talk with your primary doctor, your surgeon, and your oncologist if you have one. They will then come up with a recommendation. If radiation does seem appropriate, you'll be sent for a planning session and whatever X rays are needed after surgery, if any has been done.

The Planning Session

Usually you'll wait at least two weeks after surgery before the planning session, to make sure everything's healed and you can get your arm up over your head comfortably.

The session takes about an hour. You put on a johnny and lie on a table with your arm lifted and resting on a form above your head. Over you there's a machine, similar to the radiation machine. (See

Figure 22-2.) It's called a "simulator" because it doesn't actually give radiation, but it uses the same process that the radiation treatments will use. A lot of measurements and technical X rays are taken to map where your ribs are in relation to your nipple, where your heart is in relation to your ribs, and so on, figuring out precisely how that area of your body looks. Depending on what area of your body is going to be radiated, you may also be sent for X rays, a CAT scan, or ultrasound to get more information. In some centers a lympho-scintogram is used to help in the planning. This is a type of scan similar to the bone scan (see page 230) which is done to show the lymph nodes under your breastbone. It will help the radiation ther-apists to see where the nodes are in relation to other organs and therefore help them to direct the radiation more specifically. Then they'll put all the information into a computer, which calculates specifically the angles at which the area of your body should be radiated.

Before the treatments actually start, the radiation therapist will mark out the area of the breast that's going to be treated. You should be aware that the breast and the lymph node areas will be treated from different angles, which will mean covering a fairly large area of your chest. Some doctors use tattoos, which are permanent, to out-

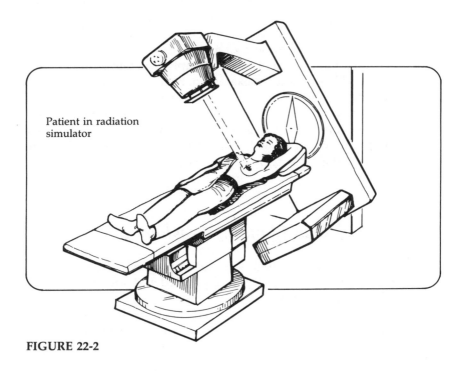

Patient in radiation simulator

FIGURE 22-2

line the area. (See Figure 22-3.) They're tiny and, depending on your skin coloring, can be invisible. One radiation nurse I know says, "I've had patients call me up and say, 'I've washed my tattoos off—I can't find them!'" Other doctors use Magic Markers; the problem with this is that the markings *can* be washed off and the patient has to be careful to avoid doing that.

The tattooing can be somewhat uncomfortable, like pinpricks, or bee stings at worst. The other discomfort patients sometimes feel is a stiff arm; especially after recent surgery, it can be awkward to lie with your arm above your head for an hour.

The Treatments

Radiation treatments are scheduled, paced out, once a day, for a given number of weeks. Time-consuming though this is, it's necessary, since you can't get too much radiation all at once or your skin will have a bad reaction. The treatment schedule varies from place to place. Usually it's given in two parts. First, the breast as a whole is radiated, from the collarbone to the ribs and the breastbone to the side, making sure all the area is treated, including, if necessary, lymph nodes. This is the major part of the treatment, and will last about five weeks, often using about 4,700 rads or centigrays of radiation (a chest X ray is a fraction of a rad). If there are any micro-

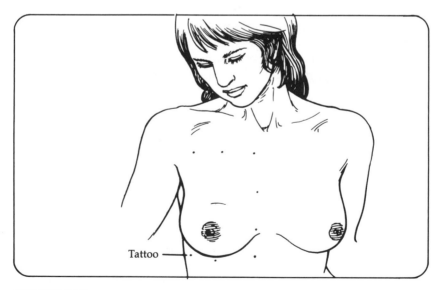

FIGURE 22-3

scopic cancer cells in the breast, this should get rid of them. After this, the boost (described later) is given.

How soon after the simulation the treatment begins varies from hospital to hospital, depending on how many radiation patients there are, how much room in the radiation department, and how large the staff is. Sometimes it will be between two weeks and a month, and often patients worry that the delay will cause the cancer to spread. Though the wait doesn't pose any real danger of the cancer worsening, it can be emotionally hard on the patient.

There may be delays for other reasons. Depending on the status of the lymph nodes, you may be getting chemotherapy first, and your doctors may not want you to get both treatments at the same time. (Sometimes they are given sequentially, sometimes they *are* given at the same time, and sometimes they're given in a sandwich-like sequence: chemotherapy, then radiation, then more chemotherapy.)

There are important skin-care guidelines to follow during your treatment. You should use a mild soap, such as Ivory, Pears, or Neutrogena. Avoid all soap that uses fragrance, deodorants, or any kind of metal during the course of your treatment. All of these can interact with the radiation, so it's important to avoid them. Don't use deodorant on the side that's being treated; deodorants have lots of aluminum. Through the course of the treatment, you can use a light dusting of cornstarch as a deodorant; it's usually pretty effective, though that will vary from patient to patient. But *don't* use talcum powder. You can check the health-food store for natural deodorants, some of which don't use aluminum—but read the label very, very carefully.

When you go for your first treatment, it's wise to bring someone with you for support. You're facing the unknown, and that's usually scary. Most patients don't feel the need to have someone with them after the first session.

For the treatment itself, you'll change into a johnny from the waist up. It's wise to wear something two-piece so you only have to remove your upper clothing. You can wear earrings or bracelets, but no neck jewelry. After you've changed, you'll be taken into a waiting room; the wait may be longish, and varies from place to place and day to day, so you may want to bring a good book or your Walkman. Then you're taken into the treatment room. You're only there for about 10 minutes, and most of that time is spent with the technologist setting up the machine and getting you ready. There's a table that looks like a regular examining table, and, above it, the radiation machine. (See Figure 22-4.) You lie down on the table, and a plastic or styrofoam form is placed under your head. This has an armrest above your

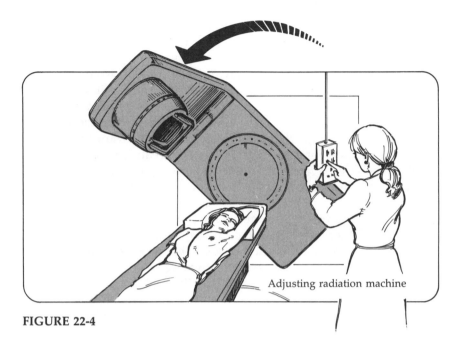

Adjusting radiation machine

FIGURE 22-4

head, where you keep your arm. When you're set up, the technologist leaves the room and turns on the machine. The radiation isn't given all at once; it's done a number of times from different angles—twice if only the breast is radiated, more if lymph nodes are also being treated. The technician will position you, leave, turn on the machine for a little less than a minute, come back in, reposition the machine, and go out again. If you're claustrophobic, you may find lying under the machine a little uncomfortable, but it doesn't last long, and the machine itself never moves down toward you.

Radiation therapy units have cameras, so they can see you while you're being treated, and an intercom system so that if you're anxious and need to talk with the technologist, you can. If a friend or family member has come with you, many hospitals will allow them in the room outside the treatment area, watching on the monitor and able to hear you through the intercom. The most important thing for you to do during the treatment is to keep still. You can breathe normally, but don't move otherwise.

Your blood will be drawn routinely during the course of the treatment—once at the beginning of the therapy process, once a few weeks later, to make sure there's no drop in your blood count. This usually isn't a problem with breast cancer, since there's not much bone marrow treated, but we do it to be safe.

What most people find hardest to deal with is the time that the treatments take. They last for six and a half weeks, five days a week. If your workplace and home are fairly near the hospital, you may be able to come right before or after work. Otherwise, you may have to cut into the middle of the workday, or take time off from your job. Some mothers use baby-sitters, others bring their children to the hospital, along with a friend who stays with them while the mother has her treatment. If your child is old enough to be curious, or is scared at not knowing what's going on, you might want to have the child wait in the room directly outside the treatment room, where you'll be visible on two monitors and can talk with your child through an intercom. This can demystify the process and alleviate the child's fear.

If you're being treated for metastatic cancer rather than the initial breast cancer, there are some slight differences. The treatment is the same, but it's for a different purpose—to alleviate pain or other symptoms. It usually takes a couple of weeks before the pain noticeably lessens. The timing is somewhat different as well. There are usually 10 to 15 treatments, spread over two and a half to four weeks. A smaller dose of radiation is used. While a primary radiation treatment might use 6,000 centigrays of radiation over six and a half weeks, with 180 centigrays per treatment, the treatment for someone with, for example, bone metastasis in the hip might use 3,000 centigrays over 10 treatments of 300 each.

The Boost

After a course of radiation to treat your breast, you'll be given a boost—an extra amount of radiation on the spot where the tumor was. The boost is done in one of two ways. The first is the implant, done either under general anesthetic or under local anesthetic and some kind of sedation. (See Figure 22-5.) Thin plastic tubing hooked like thread into a needle is drawn through the breast where the biopsy was done. Then the tubing is left in and the needle withdrawn. The number of tubes varies; sometimes they are inserted in two layers. Small radioactive pellets called iridium seeds, which give off high energy for a very short distance, are put into the tubes, "boosting" the immediate area of the biopsy. This implant is left in for about 36 hours. This can vary depending on how active the seeds are, how big your breast is, and how big the tumor was.

This radiation can be picked up by people around you, although not in large doses. If you were sitting across the table from someone for four hours, they'd get about the amount of radiation they'd get in a chest X ray. Normally, that's no problem, but for some people, like pregnant women, exposure to even that much radiation could be dangerous, so you can't be out in crowds during the time the tubing is in. Thus, you're usually kept in the hospital with a sign on the door saying "Caution: radioactive." (Your friends, unless they're at risk, can visit you; they can sit a distance across the room and chat with you.) At the end of about 36 hours, the tubes are removed, a process that requires no anesthesia, and, unless there's some other reason for you to stay hospitalized, you can go home.

A more recent, and more frequently used, boost is the electron beam. Electrons are a special kind of radioactive particle that gives off energy that doesn't penetrate very deeply, so it's good if the tumor wasn't very deep or there's not a lot of tumor left behind. The electron boost is given by a machine; it's aimed at the area where the tumor was. It doesn't require hospitalization but is given over several days. Whether the electron boost or the implant boost is used will depend on a variety of factors—the amount of surgery you had, the size of your tumor, the size of your breast, and the equipment available to your radiation therapist. Some therapists don't have an electron machine to use; others don't have training in the implant procedure; some therapists simply prefer one treatment to the other.

When both options are available, the doctor will often choose one based on the amount of surgery that's been done. When we first started doing lumpectomy and radiation, we tended just to take out the lump and then radiate the breast to clean up the margins, and

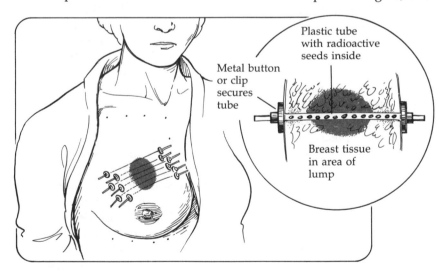

Plastic tube with radioactive seeds inside

Metal button or clip secures tube

Breast tissue in area of lump

FIGURE 22-5

then we used the implant. Now the trend is to do more surgery, taking out more tissue to obtain clean margins, and to use a smaller boost, the electron beam.

Side Effects

The side effects of radiation depend on the part of the body that's being treated. If it's the breast and you have soft bones you may have asymptomatic rib fractures, which you won't feel but will show up on X ray. Depending on how your chest is built, a little of the radiation may get to your lung and give you a cough. If you're being treated for metastatic cancer to the brain, your hair may fall out. If an area near the stomach is treated you may have nausea; if the area is lower, you may have diarrhea. Your radiation therapist will tell you about all the possible side effects before your treatment starts.

You'll usually have some kind of "sunburn" effect. The severity varies considerably from patient to patient—one person will get a severe skin rash, while another will barely be bothered at all. Unlike the case with sunburn, fairness of skin isn't relevant.

The other major symptom virtually every radiation therapy patient has is tiredness. I used to think that this was because of the amount of time involved in the treatment, but there's more and more evidence that, like anesthesia (see page 279), radiation in the body itself creates tiredness: the body seems to be using up all its resources to cope with the radiation, and doesn't leave much energy for anything else. The fatigue usually gets worse toward the end of the treatment, and its severity depends on what else is going on in your life. You'll probably want to cut back on your activities if it's at all possible. The fatigue may last several months after the treatment has finished, or may even begin after the course of treatment is over.

The extent of the fatigue varies greatly. One of my patients, a lawyer, had no problem working a full day, but says she "didn't feel like going out for dinner after work." For others, the fatigue is extremely unpleasant. One of my patients compares her fatigue to the effects of infectious hepatitis, which she'd had years before. "The symptoms sound very nondescript," she says, "but I felt really rotten. I was tired all the time—not the tiredness you feel after a hard day's work, which I've always found fairly pleasant. My body just felt wrong—like I was always coming down with the flu. Some days I couldn't function at all—I had to keep a cot at my job." She also experienced peculiar appetite changes. "My body kept craving lemon, spinach, and roast beef—I ate them constantly, and I couldn't make myself eat anything else; food just didn't interest me."

When the breast is being radiated, it may sometimes swell and get more sensitive; if you're used to sleeping on your stomach, you may find that uncomfortable. This, like the other side effects, can take months to disappear, and you may find that breast especially sore or sensitive when you're premenstrual.

Interestingly, few of my patients get depressed *during* radiation, but many get depressed afterward—possibly because, time-consuming as the treatments are, they have a sense of activity, of doing something to fight the cancer, and when it's done, there's a sense of letdown. This really shouldn't be too surprising. It happens in dozens of other intense situations, like the classical postpartum depression, or the feelings that occur when any time-consuming structure in your life is over—a job you've worked at, the end of a school term.

The skin will often feel a little bit thicker right after radiation, and it will sometimes be darker colored: that will gradually resolve itself over time. The nipple may get crusty, but that too will go away as the skin regenerates. This can take up to six months, and in the meantime you'll look like you've been out sunbathing with one breast exposed.

If there's been a lot of radiation to the armpit, it will compound whatever scarring the surgery caused, and the combination can also increase your risk of lymphedema (see page 358). Another, rare, side effect of radiation to the armpits is problems with the nerves that go from the arm to the hand, causing some numbness to the fingertips.

Aside from skin reaction and tiredness, there are some later side effects. Some women get costochondritis, which is a kind of arthritis that causes inflammation of the space between the breasts where the ribs and breastbone connect. The pain can be scary—you wonder if your cancer has spread. It's easy to reassure yourself, though. Push your fingers down right at that junction; if it hurts, it's costochondritis, and can be treated with aspirin and anti-arthritis medicines. (See Figure 22-6.)

There's a side effect that can occur between three and six months after you've finished your treatment. The muscle that goes above and behind your breast, the pectoralis major muscle (see Figure 22-6), will get extremely sore. That's because the radiation has caused some inflammation of the muscle, and as it begins to regenerate and get back to normal, it can get sore and stiff, just as it would if you threw it out using it in some strong athletic activity. Again, most women think that it's the cancer spreading—especially since the radiation's been over for months and they're not thinking in terms of new side effects from it. If you grab that muscle between your fingers, it will feel extremely sore.

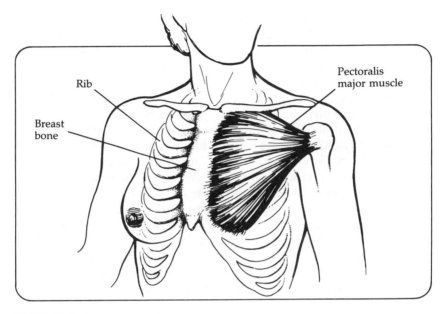

Pectoralis
major muscle

Rib

Breast
bone

FIGURE 22-6

When the treatments are over you'll continue to get some tenderness and soreness in your breast, which will gradually go away. But
it will never feel completely normal again: you'll continue to have
some sharp, shooting pains from time to time—how often varies
greatly from woman to woman.

Above a certain dosage, radiation given again will damage normal
tissue. So if you have breast cancer and it recurs in the same breast,
you can't have it radiated again. If you have the tattoos we mentioned
previously, they will make sure future doctors know you've had
radiation treatment in that area.

Finally, and, thank goodness, rarely, radiation can cause second
cancers. These are usually a different kind of cancer, a sarcoma, and
don't occur for at least five years after radiation therapy. They are
unusual but as best we can tell, for every 1,000 five-year survivors
of wide excision and radiation, about two will develop a radiation-
induced sarcoma over the next 10 years. As we mention in Chapter
25, sarcomas can also develop after a mastectomy if a woman develops a badly swollen arm. Both are rare but possible. I must say that
I've yet to see any cases myself.[2]

Often patients worry about being radioactive—that they'll harm
other people. They ask, "Can I hug my grandchild? Can I pick up
my kids?" Once the treatment is over, the radioactivity is gone and

you can be close to anyone (the implants described earlier are an exception). It's like lying in the sun—once you're out of it, the effects remain, but the sunlight isn't *inside* you, and can't be transmitted to anyone else.

The decision on how best to use radiation will depend on which procedure will have the best medical results, as well as the best cosmetic results. Sometimes a patient will have a tumor that's extremely large in comparison to her breast. In that case, removing the whole tumor surgically will cause extreme asymmetry, so we'll sometimes start with radiation to shrink it, and then do a lumpectomy; if the radiation eliminates the tumor completely, we'll skip the lumpectomy and just do a boost. The problem is that a lot of radiation will always be somewhat cosmetically displeasing, since it can cause permanent swelling in the breast as well as thickened skin. Usually lumpectomy followed by radiation creates the best results.

After your treatment is completed, your radiation therapist will continue to see you, as will your surgeon. In addition to making certain there are no new tumors, the radiation therapist is watching for signs of complications from the radiation, and the surgeon for signs of surgical complications. These complications are rare, and radiation remains one of our most valuable tools in the treatment of local or metastatic breast cancer.

23

Systemic Treatments: Chemotherapy and Hormone Therapy

As we have mentioned in previous chapters, treatment for breast cancer can be divided into local treatment (surgery and/or radiation) and systemic treatment. The hallmark of systemic therapies is their ability to affect the whole body and not just one local area. The systemic treatments used in the treatment of breast cancer include chemotherapy and hormonal therapy.

Chemotherapy has gotten a lot of bad press, and it's a pity, because it's one of the most powerful weapons against cancer that we have. The word means literally the use of chemicals to treat disease. As we use it, however, it usually refers only to the use of cytotoxic chemicals (those that kill cells).

How does chemotherapy work? Each cell goes through several steps in the process of cell division, or reproduction. Chemotherapy drugs interfere with this process so the cells can't divide. As a result, they die. Different drugs interfere in this process at different points, so often more than one kind of drug is used at a time. (See Figure 23-1.) Unfortunately this effect on cell division is not very selective. It acts on all cells that are rapidly dividing—including hair cells and, more importantly, bone marrow cells, as well as cancer cells. The bone marrow is a factory which produces red blood cells, white blood

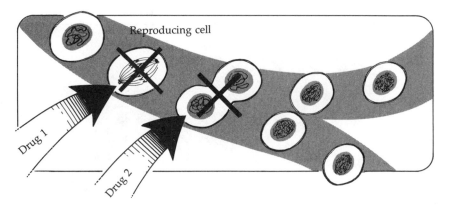

FIGURE 23-1

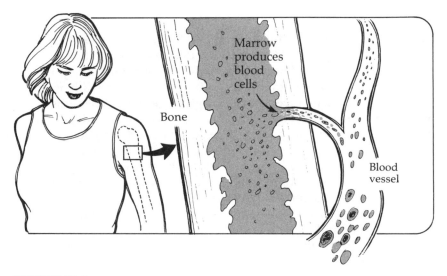

FIGURE 23-2

cells, and platelets on a continuous basis. (See Figure 23-2.) Chemotherapy slows this production down. When we give chemotherapy, then, we have to be careful not to stop the production altogether. This is one of the reasons that chemotherapy is given in cycles, with a time lapse between treatments to allow the bone marrow to recover.

Another reason the drugs are given in cycles is that not all the cancer cells are dividing at any one time. The first treatment will kill one group of cells; then three weeks later there will be a new set of

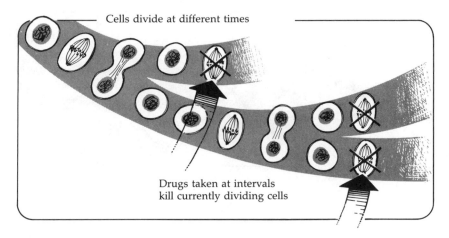

Cells divide at different times

Drugs taken at intervals
kill currently dividing cells

FIGURE 23-3

cancer cells starting to divide, and the drugs will knock them out, too. (See Figure 23-3.) The idea is to decrease the total number of cancer cells to a number small enough for your immune system to take care of, without wiping out the immune system while we're at it. Interestingly, when we first started giving adjuvant chemotherapy, we gave the treatments over a two-year period. Later studies showed that six months was as good as a year, which was as good as two.[1] The extra treatment may have actually harmed the immune system without having any additional effect on the cancer. There probably is a certain key dosage or duration beyond which any additional drug is useless, but it hasn't been determined yet.

The other kind of systemic therapy is the use of hormones or hormonal manipulations to change the body's own output of hormones in order to affect the growth of hormonally sensitive tumors. This can include surgical procedures such as oophorectomy (removing the ovaries), radiating the ovaries, using drugs that block hormones, or even using hormones themselves. We don't fully understand why these hormonal treatments work, but there is no question that they do work well in the right patient. Since hormone therapy affects only hormonally sensitive tissues, its side effects are more limited than those of chemotherapy. It doesn't have the same effect on other growing cells, such as hair and bone marrow. The goal, however, is the same: to kill cancer cells or prevent them from growing.

Systemic therapies are used at two different points in the natural history of breast cancer. First is at the time of diagnosis, when it's called adjuvant therapy. The second is at the time of recurrence elsewhere in the body, when the cancer has metastasized. We will discuss these two separately.

Adjuvant Chemotherapy

Chemotherapy was initially used to treat leukemia, a cancer which, by definition, is present throughout the bloodstream. Later it was used to treat any metastatic cancer. The idea was that drugs that circulated through the bloodstream could get to all the places that a cancer cell was likely to hide. Unfortunately, it didn't always work. On further study, the researchers came to understand that the failure stemmed from two problems: there were too many cancer cells for the drugs to handle, and some cancer cells became resistant to the drugs. They then began to consider giving chemotherapy earlier and earlier, and the concept of adjuvant chemotherapy was born. Perhaps the time to give chemotherapy was right after the primary local treatment—either surgery alone or surgery and radiation—when any spread would still be micrometastatic. And, indeed, this approach seemed to work. The first studies by Gianni Bonadonna[2] and by the NSABP[3] showed that, as we've mentioned in Chapter 15, premenopausal women with positive nodes had a significant increase in breast cancer survival when given adjuvant chemotherapy. This set the stage for the now-common practice of giving systemic treatments at the time of initial diagnosis.

As we have discussed in Chapter 19, adjuvant chemotherapy is now given to premenopausal women with positive nodes. There is still a lot of controversy, however, about the use of adjuvant chemotherapy in node-negative, premenopausal women. Many oncologists will recommend it to everyone, while others use it only as part of a protocol or in certain very high risk cases.

In postmenopausal women the effect of chemotherapy is less clear. We are still wondering why there is a difference between premenopausal and postmenopausal women. One thought has always been that chemotherapy causes a chemical menopause in the younger women and therefore acts much the same way tamoxifen or oophorectomy do. (These are discussed later in this chapter.) This wouldn't account for the total effect, however. The other possibility is that there is a small effect of cell kill (the same small percent seen in the postmenopausal woman) and an additional hormonal effect in the premenopausal women, but only the cell-kill effect in the postmenopausal women.

The fact remains that there is less effect from chemotherapy in the postmenopausal woman.[4] In the cases where the tumor is sensitive to hormones, tamoxifen has been shown to have a better response and is now used as an adjuvant treatment. In postmenopausal women who have positive nodes and tumors that are not sensitive to hormones, there may be some small effect of chemotherapy.

We have discussed the decision-making process and options for adjuvant therapy at length in Chapter 19. Now we will look at the actual experience of receiving chemotherapy or hormone therapy.

When there is a possibility that you'll need chemotherapy, you'll want an appointment with an oncologist, or cancer specialist, who specializes in systemic treatment. After talking with you at length, and reviewing your records, the doctor will decide what chemotherapy program you need and what your options are. These options may vary from place to place. There are guidelines for breast cancer treatment, drawn up by a group of nationwide breast cancer specialists, that are generally accepted as standard treatments. The alternative is to become involved in a protocol or clinical trial (see page 214).

There are many well-trained oncologists throughout the country now, and you can usually get very good treatment close to home. You may, however, want to get a second opinion about chemotherapy at a cancer center prior to starting. (See Appendix E for a list of comprehensive cancer centers.) The options for treatment are always changing, and you'll want the advantage of the most up to date information. Sometimes the cancer center and your local oncologist can work together in designing and supplementing your treatment, giving you the best of both worlds.

Your doctor or medical team will also discuss with you the role of systemic treatment in your overall treatment, the expected toxicity (side effects), and how the side effects will be managed. Before you make a decision together with the doctor and sign a consent form, all these things must be made very clear to you.

The time spent on this depends on the institution and the particular doctor or nurse you're dealing with. Ideally, you'll spend an hour or so, since the information is extremely detailed. Susan McKenney, a nurse practitioner with whom I work at the Dana Farber Cancer Institute, also gives the patient a written description of everything she needs to know. "I like to translate the information from a didactic, medical form to a written, easily understandable explanation that she can take home and look over at her own convenience; often this is the consent form for a protocol. It's hard to take that much in at one time, and the patient is often overwhelmed—she's dealing with the unknown. I've had patients sit with me for an hour and the next week when she comes in for her treatment, she can't tell me the names of the three drugs she's getting."

In addition, says McKenney, it's difficult for a patient to really feel that chemotherapy is going to help her, because she's being told about all the unpleasant things it may do to her in the process. She needs time to assimilate the information about the side effects she'll have to deal with, and written information helps her do this.

Once you've signed the consent form, you'll be scheduled to come in for your treatment. It may be in a hospital, a clinic, or your doctor's office. A blood sample is usually taken to check your blood count before your treatment, to help the doctor or nurse to know whether your body is capable of taking chemotherapy—and as a baseline for comparison later. Your initial dose is determined by your body surface area (height and weight). This is a good guess, but it's rarely perfect.

The bone marrow's recovery rate helps the doctor adjust the dosage of drugs—a process known as *titration*. We check to see if the marrow has recovered by doing a blood count. If the blood count is high that means that the dose of chemotherapy is probably too low for you and you will be given more. If your count is too low then the dose is probably too high and needs to be lower. Sometimes when the count is too low you will have to wait for a day or two before treatment to allow your bone marrow more time to recover.

Blood counts are taken throughout the course of your therapy, generally once a week, before and after therapy. When your white blood count is low you have an increased risk of infection, although interestingly enough this doesn't usually include colds; if your platelets are very low you are at an increased risk of bleeding (this is actually quite rare).

Sometimes the blood count will be taken the day before a treatment, but more often it's on the day of the treatment, in which case you'll have to wait for 15 to 45 minutes for the treatment to begin. In any event, you'll probably have to wait while the drugs are being mixed, though again this will depend on the practice in your institution. Though the wait may be annoying, it can also be an advantage: Susan McKenney finds that at the Dana Farber Cancer Institute, where the breast chemotherapy unit has its own area, women talk to each other and find support in being together.

Chemotherapy treatments are usually given either every three weeks, in 21-day cycles, or in 28-day cycles. If it's a 21-day cycle you may come in for an injection every 21 days. On a 28-day cycle, you come in for treatment on day 1 and day 8, and then go two weeks with no therapy. That's two weeks with therapy and two weeks off. During this time, your treatment may be all intravenous, or a combination of intravenous medicine and pills, taken orally at home. The treatments can last anywhere from 12 weeks to six months to a year of chemotherapy.

The treatment area will vary from hospital to hospital. Sometimes there's an entire floor for oncology patients, and sometimes just a separate area of a larger floor. Chemotherapy can also be given in a private doctor's office. Everyone is aware of the anxiety level of the patients and will try to make the area as comfortable as possible. Since the process doesn't involve any machines, it doesn't look as intimidating as the radiation area. The room will be comfortably lit, and often has TVs or stereos in it. You may have a room to yourself, or be sitting with several other patients who are getting their treatments. You'll sit on a comfortable lounge chair for the procedure. (See Figure 23-4.) Many patients bring a book or a Walkman. If your treatment is a long one, you might want to invest in one of those tiny, checkbook-sized TVs and watch your favorite game show or

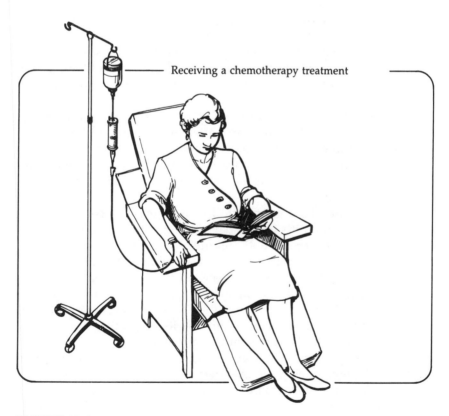

Receiving a chemotherapy treatment

FIGURE 23-4

soap opera during your treatments. Or if you have easily transportable paperwork for your job, you can bring that and work while the treatment is in progress. If you like to have a friend or family member with you, most hospitals and doctors will permit that.

The length of time a treatment takes, and the intervals at which treatments are given, will vary depending on the type of drugs being used, the institution giving you the treatment, and the protocol being used. Many different combinations of drugs may be used, each requiring a different time length for administration; in addition, you may be given extra fluid to control nausea and vomiting. All of this will affect how long a treatment takes. Sometimes a treatment will last 10 minutes; sometimes it will last three or four hours.

The treatments are given either by your oncologist or by a specially trained nurse. There's nothing especially painful about the treatment itself, which feels like any IV procedure. The chemicals come in different colors—in breast cancer, the drugs we use are usually clear, yellow, and red; there's a blue drug we also use sometimes.

You usually don't feel the medications going inside you, though some patients do feel cold, if the fluids are run very fast or if they're cold to begin with, and if the patient's body is especially sensitive to cold. The doctor or nurse will always be there with you, and they're both highly trained specialists in chemotherapy. Sometimes the drugs irritate veins and cause them to clot off and scar (sclerose) during the course of the treatment. This will make it very hard to get needles into the veins. If the patient has a lot of trouble with her veins, she may be given what we call a central access device, either a portacath or a Hickman line—a catheter-type device surgically placed under the skin into a major blood vessel, so that needles can go in and out of that device and spare the patient the discomfort of having peripheral veins (the ones close to the surface, which are normally used for needles) stuck. (See Figure 23-5.)

There are four drugs commonly given in adjuvant chemotherapy for breast cancer: Cytoxan(C), methotrexate(M), fluorouracil(F), and Adriamycin(A). These are usually given in combinations either as CMF or CAF (see Appendix A). Other drugs (hormones) may be added, such as tamoxifen or prednisone.

Side Effects of Chemotherapy

Side effects vary according to the drugs that are used. A detailed list of all the drugs used against breast cancer and their side effects will be found in Appendix A. The most immediate potential side effect concerns Adriamycin, which can leak out of the vein and cause a

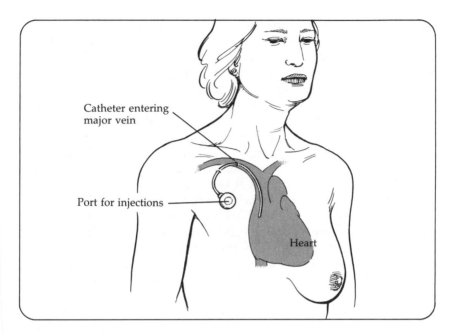

FIGURE 23-5

very severe skin burn that could require skin grafting. For this reason, it's generally given in a very specific way: avoiding weak veins, and running in the IV with lots of fluids, so that if it should leak out it won't cause as much harm.

A more common side effect is nausea and vomiting. Overall, about 20 percent of women who get CMF, and more of the women who receive CAF, will complain of nausea and vomiting. Usually the nausea doesn't start until four to six hours after the injection. It can last anywhere from a few hours to two days, and can come in waves at varying time intervals, or remain constant the whole time—again, this happens differently for each person, and we can't predict in advance how it will work for you. There are lots of different anti-nausea medications that can be given with the treatments, but again, which ones work for which patients varies greatly. If the first medication doesn't work for you, your nurse or therapist can change it to another. These range from tranquilizers to marijuana. Since each woman's reactions are different, you may have to experiment with several different drugs before you find the one that works for you.

The nausea can be so bad that the fear of it causes a conditioned reaction. A patient may get nauseated just at the sight of the therapist's face—a situation that can be difficult for both patient and therapist. One of my own patients who underwent chemotherapy over a year ago still gets waves of nausea when she runs into any of the doctors or nurses who worked with her, though she found them very helpful and supportive. To help lessen the nausea, some hospitals, like the Beth Israel in Boston, incorporate antistress mechanisms such as visualization, imagery, and relaxation techniques into their treatment program. They have found that these techniques are often very effective. If your hospital or doctor doesn't offer such techniques, you might want to think about taking a class in an adult education program, or reading one of the books discussed in Chapter 24 or listed in Appendix C. Many of the techniques are simple and easy to teach yourself.

Because you may start feeling nauseated right away, and because the thought of chemotherapy can be frightening, Susan McKenney recommends that you bring someone with you for your first treatment to see how well it goes and, if you've come by car, to do the driving if necessary. Then if the first treatment goes well and you feel all right afterward, you may not need anyone for the following ones. Usually, she says, if you start off feeling all right and your nausea is within a tolerable range, you'll probably get through the rest of the treatments with relative comfort.

Sometimes chemotherapy causes you to lose your appetite (*anorexia*, which is different from *anorexia nervosa*). In spite of this and the nausea, 21 percent of women will have some weight gain while on treatment—gains of between 5 and 15 pounds. Food may taste different to you, and some chemicals interact badly with certain foods, though both loss of appetite and chemical interaction are less common with breast cancer drugs than with others. The National Cancer Institute puts out a helpful recipe booklet for people whose eating is affected by their chemotherapy.

Fifty-seven percent of premenopausal women will have hot flashes while on treatment. The drugs can create a chemically-induced menopause, with hormonal changes, hot flashes, emotional mood swings, and no period. If you're under 40 your period will probably come back, but if you're close to menopause to begin with, it may not. If you do experience early menopause, you will, of course, be infertile. One study found that if your period comes back you can still conceive. Since it is difficult to tell which group you are in, it is wise to use mechanical birth control while on treatment.

Chemotherapy treatments used in breast cancer, as in many other cancers, often cause either partial or total hair loss. This is somewhat predictable according to the drugs used and the duration of treatment. Those women who get Adriamycin as part of their treatment will always lose their hair, usually fairly soon after the onset of

321

treatment. On the other hand, those women who are receiving CMF will only sometimes lose their hair; it will occur about three weeks after treatments have begun, and it won't fall out all at once. You'll wake up one morning and find a large amount of hair on your pillow or in the shower, or you'll be combing your hair, and notice a lot of hair in the comb. Susan McKenney finds that this is almost always traumatic for patients, and she recommends that you buy a wig before your treatment starts. "I suggest to people that they go to a hairdresser or wig salon at the start of the treatment, so that the hairdresser can know what their hair usually looks like and how they like to wear it—it makes for a better match." Often, she says, her patients don't end up having to use the wigs they've bought. But patients who haven't prepared in advance for the hair loss have a difficult time emotionally if their hair does fall out.

It may take a while after the treatments have ended for your hair to grow back. Usually a little down begins to form even before your treatments have ended, and within six weeks you should have some hair growing in, though the time depends on how fast your hair normally grows. Sometimes, though rarely, it will come back with a different texture—curly if it's been straight, or straight if it's been curly. It may come back in a different color, most commonly gray or black.

Some women experience sexual problems, often related to the frequently occurring vaginal dryness. Some of the chemicals can interact badly with your IUD, causing infection. And you may suddenly encounter problems with your diaphragm, if that's the birth control form you're using. In addition, there are the physical and psychological effects of the treatment. It's hard to feel sexy when you are throwing up and bald. This is an important time to communicate with your partner about each of your feelings and needs and to try and find a comforting compromise. (See page 263 for a discussion of sexual issues and breast cancer.)

Other common side effects include mouth sores, conjunctivitis, runny eyes and nose, diarrhea, and constipation.

You may have bleeding from your gums or nose, or in your stool or urine, though this is unusual. You may get headaches. Any of these can be mild or severe, or anything in between.

The long-term side effects include chronic bone marrow suppression and second cancers, especially leukemias. This risk is certainly small—0.5 percent in the NSABP series[5]—and probably worth the benefit of the treatment, but it's important to remember that no drug is without its long-term effect.

Though there's no way to know in advance for certain how you'll react to your treatments, your doctor or nurse *can* tell you how people who've been treated with the drugs you're on have done in the past.

While it's important to be prepared for the possible side effects, it's equally important not to assume you'll have all, or even any, of them. This assumption can intensify, and sometimes even create, the symptoms. Often people will see your side effects from the chemotherapy as signs that your illness is getting worse, and contribute to your own negative feelings. Dr. Bernie Siegel,[6] the doctor who has worked so intensively with mental techniques to reduce pain and help heal diseases, in his book *Love, Medicine and Miracles*, reports on a study done in England, in which a group of men were given a placebo and told it was a chemotherapy treatment. Thirty percent of the men had their hair fall out.

It is important to mention that the vast majority of these treatments are given on an outpatient basis. You will soon know whether you will feel sick on which day and how sick you will feel. Many women are able to continue their normal lives with minor adjustments while receiving treatments. You won't feel great, but you will be functional.

It may, however, be a good time to take up your friends' offers of help. A ride to your treatment can be wonderful: both for the company and the release from worry about traffic and parking. Childcare may well give you a breather in a stressful time, as can offers to cook dinner or clean the house. Most friends and family members really do want to help, and this may well be the best time to use all their support.

Don't expect to feel perfect the minute your last treatment is over. Your body has been under a great stress and needs time to recuperate. It often takes six months or even a year before you feel perfectly normal again. It will happen, however, so don't despair. (See Chapter 25 for a discussion of rehabilitation after breast cancer.)

Adjuvant Hormonal Therapy

Doctors have always been interested in the hormonal manipulation of breast cancers. In fact, the first adjuvant therapies were based on changing the body's hormonal milieu. If a premenopausal woman had a "bad" cancer, her ovaries were removed in an attempt to decrease the total amount of estrogen in her system. Although the idea was good, studies showed no difference in the recurrence rate or survival rate in the women who had had oophorectomy compared to the control group.[7]

Now we can predict who is likely to benefit from adjuvant hormonal therapy by using the estrogen-receptor test mentioned in Chapter 16. In those women whose tumors are sensitive to hormones we can use a hormonal treatment as adjuvant therapy.

We remove the ovaries, or we use tamoxifen, which is an estrogen blocker. Since it's not a male hormone, it doesn't have any of the side effects often suggested by the words "hormone therapy"—you won't grow a beard, or develop a baritone voice.

Tamoxifen blocks the estrogen receptor on the breast cancer cell interfering with protein synthesis. The result, we hope, will be to stop the growth of malignant cells dependent on estrogen for growth.

Tamoxifen is given as a pill, usually twice a day. Side effects are usually minimal but may include hot flashes, nausea which usually abates after a month or two, and vaginal spotting. Other less common side effects include depression, vaginal itching, bleeding or discharge, loss of appetite, and headache. In essence, it will put you into menopause—not entirely, however. In premenopausal women it has the effect of increasing both estrogen and progesterone, probably by stimulating the ovary while also stopping your periods. It thus can have such contradictory effects as increasing ovarian cysts and even causing ovulation while blocking estrogen in the breast. This means you will need to consider using some type of barrier contraceptive while taking the drug. In postmenopausal women it increases FSH and LH (see page 16) but not estrogen and progesterone.

Most of the studies of adjuvant tamoxifen have used it for three to five years in postmenopausal women. Although there is some data on its use in premenopausal women,[8] it is limited. We do not as yet know the optimal duration in either group. Laboratory studies would indicate that tamoxifen acts by preventing cell growth (cytostatic) rather than by killing cells. This would suggest that a longer duration of use would be better. In other words, would the cancer cells start growing again as soon as you stopped taking it? The recent overview suggests a second mechanism. Even women who took tamoxifen for only two years had a continued and increasing good effect. This suggests we don't really understand how tamoxifen works. But what about the possible long-term side effects of this drug? Because it induces early menopause in premenopausal women and blocks estrogen in postmenopausal women we have worried that it could increase heart disease or osteoporosis. But it turns out that this is an estrogen blocker to the breast, but acts as an estrogen to the bones, uterus, and liver; thus, it may actually *decrease* osteoporosis. In rats at high doses it has been found to increase liver cancers and ovarian cancers, and one study from Sweden has shown it to cause endometrial cancer in women.[9] Therefore, tamoxifen should not be considered lightly. Researchers continue to look for other hormonal drugs with fewer side effects as they monitor the long-range effects of tamoxifen.

Systemic Therapies for Metastatic Cancer

Although both surgery and radiation therapy are used for metastatic breast cancer, the mainstay of treatment is systemic. Like adjuvant therapy, this includes both chemotherapy and hormonal therapy. With metastatic cancer, we can't cure you. Our goal is twofold: first, to control your symptoms and make you feel better; and second, to prolong your survival. Although most people don't think of chemotherapy as improving their quality of life, that is just what it can do. A woman with metastatic breast cancer is often not feeling well. She may have pain in her bones or shortness of breath or just generally feel weak and lethargic. By shrinking the tumor, systemic therapy can make her feel dramatically better.

Which type of systemic treatment should be used? This depends on the site of recurrence and whether the tumor is sensitive to hormones. If a tumor is sensitive to hormones, a hormone treatment may be tried, while a tumor that is not sensitive to hormones will call for chemotherapy. Chemotherapy usually has about a 60 percent response rate, and the mean time to response is usually about three months. This means that 60 percent of women with metastatic disease will have some symptomatic improvement within three months. Hormone therapy usually has about a 50-percent response rate in hormone-receptor-positive tumors, and also has an average three-month time to response. The advantage of hormone therapy, when it works, is that it creates far fewer side effects.

During and after your treatment you will be followed with the staging tests: bone scan, chest X ray and blood tests. Other tests will be used as well. These will help to determine if you are indeed responding to treatment.

CHEMOTHERAPY FOR METASTATIC CANCER

The actual chemotherapy for metastatic disease may be similar to that given adjuvantly, *but* you might experience it differently. You may be feeling unwell already, and the drugs may compound that at first; they may also bring back old memories of the side effects you experienced in your first treatments. On the other hand, you may well feel dramatically improved. This is in contrast to adjuvant chemotherapy, where you start out with no symptoms and so can only feel worse.

Often similar drugs are used in treating a first recurrence and in adjuvant therapy—that is, CMF or CAF. These will usually have a good response and their toxicity is predictable. Some oncologists will give them for six to nine months and then stop, on the theory that the maximum effect is usually obtained by that time. Others will continue the chemotherapy until there is some sign of toxicity or new disease. Many drugs can be taken indefinitely, but some can't: they have cumulative side effects that, after you've been given a certain amount, can kill you. Adriamycin is the best example of this; after a certain dose (which depends on your body size), it can be toxic to your heart. In order to avoid that infamous "the-operation-was-a-success-but-the-patient-died" syndrome, when you've reached the danger point, you'll be taken off that drug and given another.

Furthermore, like bacteria, if cancer is subjected to the same drug over a long period of time, it builds up a resistance to that drug. If you have a recurrence or progression of disease while on one drug, your doctor will assume your cancer is becoming resistant and will switch you to another drug.

The original drugs are known as first-level drugs. When we've used up the appropriate first-level drugs, we go onto the others. There's a large variety of chemotherapy drugs available now, and more being developed every day. (See Appendix A for a list of common drugs used against breast cancer and their side effects.)

The way the chemotherapy is given may well differ from the adjuvant setting. Some drugs are given in a continuous infusion, or weekly, while others may require hospitalization. Often a portocath or central access catheter will be placed surgically so that you don't have to be stuck so often.

There are also a lot of experimental drugs and techniques that hold a lot of promise. Again, these are not just last-resort treatments; you may want to explore them before you've used up all the standard chemotherapy regimens. It is always worth considering the possibility of a protocol, clinical trial, or new experimental therapy.

As we have said, at the time of this writing, we do not have a chemotherapy regimen that can cure metastatic breast cancer. We can, however, dramatically relieve your symptoms and prolong your survival. How long depends on the cancer and the patient. Although most women will show some improvement, some will not, and the duration of remission will vary considerably from patient to patient. In spite of the side effects of the drugs and their effect on your immediate day-to-day life, it has been clearly shown that your quality of life will be improved, with an increased symptom-free survival.[10]

For most women, chemotherapy for metastatic breast cancer is worth it. Each woman, however, must decide for herself.

HORMONAL THERAPY FOR METASTATIC CANCER

Before the development of modern chemotherapy, hormone therapy was the only available treatment for metastatic breast cancer. Premenopausal women were treated with oophorectomy. Postmenopausal women were also given estrogens to try and control their cancers. These treatments worked for about 30 percent of women. If the cancer then recurred we would take out their adrenal glands and sometimes even their pituitary glands in an attempt to control the disease. In each case about a third of women would respond.

As we said before, we now have a test for predicting which women will have a response to hormonal manipulation: the estrogen-receptor test (see page 226). If the test is positive, the tumor is sensitive to hormones, and if it's negative, it's not sensitive. In hormone-receptor-positive tumors 50–70 percent will respond to a hormonal treatment, and it can often bring on a relatively long remission. On average, the response lasts for 12 to 14 months, but there have been reports of responses lasting up to 40 months.[11]

For premenopausal women with hormone-receptor-positive tumors and metastatic disease, oophorectomy has been the mainstay of treatment. Now we often use the estrogen blocker tamoxifen instead because of its limited side effects. They can also be used sequentially. If a woman responds to oophorectomy and then her cancer recurs several years later, she can be given tamoxifen at that point and get another response.

In fact, once a woman has responded to hormone therapy there is a whole list of potential treatments that can be used. They are usually used sequentially in order of toxicity, so that the drugs with the least toxicity are used first. The second most common after tamoxifen is a progestin (Megace) which is also given in pill form. Next in line is aminoglutethimide, which chemically blocks the adrenal hormones. Other hormones that have been used include estrogen (DES) and androgens (Halotestin). As the cancer becomes resistant to one the next one is tried. Women with hormonally sensitive tumors are lucky because these treatments are less toxic than chemotherapy and there are a vast variety. Eventually, however, the tumor will become resistant to hormones altogether, and chemotherapy will be needed.

Hormonal therapies sometimes will produce a flare. That is, the areas of metastatic disease will produce more symptoms before they go away. This is usually brief and, if anticipated, should not be alarming. If, for example, you have metastatic cancer in your bone, it may first cause your bones to hurt more, and then will relieve the pain.

Newer hormones which will block even more precisely the hormones necessary for breast cancer growth are being developed all the time, and so it is always a good idea to look into new research protocols.

24

Complementary and Alternative Treatments

Twenty years ago, if you told people you were doing daily meditation to help cure your cancer, or closing your eyes and pretending your cancer cells were dirt stains and your immune system was a scrub brush washing them away, they'd have assumed your disease had driven you completely crazy. Some people still would. But thanks to the pioneer work of physicians like Herbert Benson, Carl Simonton, and Bernie Siegel, psychologists like Stephanie Matthews-Simonton and Lawrence LeShan, and informed laypeople like Norman Cousins, there is increasing evidence that these mind–body techniques can help the body cope with the side effects of medical treatment, and in some cases, may help prolong life and even cure cancer. Many cancer patients are now combining these techniques with their regular treatments, often with their doctors' blessing, and sometimes with their doctors' participation.

Therapies involving particular diets, vitamins, or the use of herbs are also becoming increasingly popular. Almost all of these therapies are based on theories about the role of the immune system in fighting off disease, and the need to strengthen that system (see page 213). Unfortunately up to now, none of these therapies have been conclusively shown to have an effect on the immune system, but they do bear examining.

In one chapter, I can't do much more than give you a brief description of some of the most commonly used techniques, and I have drawn on the expertise of some of my colleagues to do this. If you're interested in further pursuing any of these techniques, you'll find a list of useful books in Appendix C.

Mental Techniques

There are a number of techniques that seem to work because of the so-called placebo effect. The placebo effect is what takes place when your mind, in effect, tells your body that it's getting a certain healing substance, and your body responds as though it were true.

For years, placebos have been used to test the effectiveness of new drugs. If, for example, we're looking to see if substance X relieves symptom Y, we take 100 randomly chosen subjects, and give 50 pills containing substance X and 50 apparently identical pills without substance X. None of the subjects knows who is really getting substance X. When we look at the results, we discover that 49 of the 50 subjects who took the substance X pills no longer suffer from symptom Y, while only 10 of the other 50 are relieved of their symptom. We now have good reason to believe that substance X indeed does cure symptom Y. But what accounts for the 10 subjects who didn't really take substance X and yet were cured? They thought they were taking it, and it had the same effect on their symptom as if they were actually taking it. In other words, your belief that a particular substance, or withdrawal from a particular substance, will relieve your condition may, in itself, cause it to do so.

This doesn't mean you're gullible or stupid or imagining things; it means that the mind affects the body in ways we don't yet fully understand, and that you're fortunate enough that the body–mind interaction is working in your favor. Norman Cousins, the *Saturday Review* editor whose *Anatomy of an Illness* recounts his recovery from a degenerative and supposedly terminal bone disease, devoted much of the book to the placebo effect. "The history of medication," he wrote, "is far more the history of the placebo effect than of intrinsically valuable relevant drugs," pointing to the success doctors in ancient times had with such "treatments" as bloodletting with leaches and giving their patients powdered unicorn horns.[1] He calls the placebo "the doctor who resides within,"[2] who "translates the will to live into a physical reality."[3] But if a sugar pill can reduce swelling and eliminate pain in substantial numbers of people, perhaps that ability can be used directly and consciously by the mind. This is the theory behind most mental-healing techniques.

PRAYER

The most obvious mental technique is one that's probably very familiar to you—prayer. For centuries, people of all religions have believed in the power of prayer—and for some of them, it seems to have worked. In spite of the fraudulence of some charismatic healers, many are sincere; more to the point, the deep faith people bring to these services may have an effect on their actual ability to heal. Estelle Disch, a therapist who has worked with many cancer patients, is not herself a believer in Christian theology, but she has seen the belief work for others. "A deeply religious Catholic woman I know has bad colon cancer," she says, "and she goes to every charismatic healing service she can find. I firmly believe her faith has kept her alive. If you're praying for health, on some level you're seeing yourself as healthy, and I believe that makes a difference." One of my patients went to Yugoslavia, where there are alleged appearances of the Virgin Mary, in an attempt to help her with her breast cancer. Although it is too soon to know if she was cured, the peace of mind and well-being she experienced were more than worth the trip. Believing that there is a power that can make you well—whether that's God, or your surgeon, or your own will—can help you to *get* well. History is full of accounts of miracles, and while we have no laboratory proof that these accounts are accurate, there are simply too many of them to dismiss. No doubt some "miracles" are fraud, and some self-delusion, but I'm convinced that some are indeed exactly what they claim to be, and that faith, of whatever sort, has played a part in their occurrence.

MEDITATION AND VISUALIZATION

To many people, the word "meditation" conjures up images from sitcoms: the dippy heroine sitting cross-legged on the floor, with her eyes closed, chanting "om" while her bemused friends stare at her. But meditation has been a very serious part of almost every major religion in history—Buddhism, Catholicism, Native American religions. And while there are many forms of meditation, the ones most commonly used in conjunction with healing work are variants of that very simple one in which the person sits in a comfortable position, eyes closed, focusing on the inhaling and exhaling of breath, and chanting a "mantra," a particular word or phrase. The Eastern "om" is fine if you like it, but it usually doesn't have much meaning for Americans, and you might do better to use a phrase consistent with your own beliefs—"peace," for example, or a brief phrase from a prayer used in your religion.

Herbert Benson, an M.D. who has extensively studied various forms of nonmedical healing, describes this particular form of meditation as "the Relaxation Response." He uses it as the basis of his work as Director of Behavioral Medicine at Boston's Deaconess Hospital. He and his colleagues run a number of groups for people with a variety of diseases. Their cancer group is co-led by oncologist Leo Stolbach. "What the relaxation response can do," says Dr. Stolbach, "is to slow down or even stop the continuous chatter the mind is constantly putting us through. It gives the mind a rest from those thoughts and then a chance to deal with the issues they raise. Physiological responses occur when you elicit the relaxation response. These include a decrease in pulse, blood pressure, respiration rate, oxygen consumption and overall metabolism. These physiological responses contribute to stress reduction."

Most programs that use meditation combine it with visualization, or imagery. This too is an ancient technique, recently discovered by "New Age" devotees. It's used for a variety of purposes, from finding a parking space to curing cancer. Its basis is the belief that if you create strong mental pictures of what you want, while affirming to yourself that you can and will get it, you can make virtually anything happen.

The pioneers of visualization in disease treatment were the then-husband-and-wife team of Carl and Stephanie Simonton (an oncologist and a psychologist). Their 1978 book, *Getting Well Again*, has influenced many cancer patients as well as doctors and psychologists. In it, they recount their experiences with "exceptional cancer patients"—those who recover in spite of a negative prognosis—and maintain that their visualization techniques have significantly extended patients' lives. Equally popular has been the work of Dr. Bernie Siegel, a surgeon who has also used visualization and meditation techniques as part of his cancer treatment approach.

Though Siegel, the Simontons, and others claim their techniques have cured cancer, the evidence is chiefly what we call "anecdotal"—that is, stories of individuals or groups of individuals, rather than studies set up in controlled situations. This doesn't mean visualization can't cure cancer or prolong cancer patients' lives; it simply means that so far we have no firm proof that it does.

What studies have proved, however, is that visualization and meditation combined can reduce pain and the uncomfortable side effects of cancer treatments—we've already discussed this a bit in page 321. This in itself is impressive, and combined with the possibility that it might affect the outcome of the disease itself, makes a meditation-visualization program well worth trying.

How does visualization work? Typically, you would do a meditation/relaxation exercise first, to become fully relaxed and receptive to the imagery that came to you. Then you would begin to visualize your cancer in terms of some concrete image—gray blobs inside your breast (or whatever area you're dealing with). Then you would picture your white blood cells, or your radiation or chemotherapy treatments, as forces countering the cells. (See Figure 24-1.)

The Simontons have favored violent images—soldiers attacking the cells, or sharks destroying them. These images, however, aren't always right for everyone. Therapist Estelle Disch, who works with cancer patients individually and in groups, says that "many people I work with don't like violent imagery. They do better with beams of light drying up the cells, or water flowing through the area and washing the cells away." Leo Stolbach also emphasizes the importance of patients' finding the imagery that works best for them.

In order to help her clients find the best images for themselves, Disch works with each client separately, helping them create the imagery that feels best for them, and then makes a tape based on that discussion. This is especially helpful when people have problems with certain relaxation images. Some people relax deeply while paying attention to their breathing; others find climbing slowly down a staircase effective, and others prefer to drift or float gently on air or

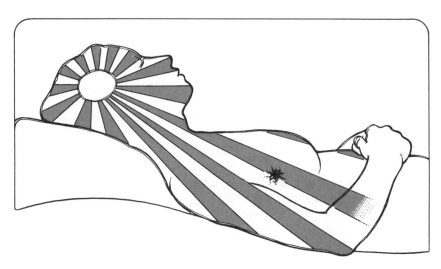

FIGURE 24-1

water. "Obviously if someone has a fear of water, or heights, or something else, then I'd avoid using those images on the tape," she says.

Most people do relaxation and visualization images as part of a group, working on a regular basis with the group, and doing the exercises daily between group meetings. Such groups exist in different parts of the country, and in Appendix C you'll find a list of places to call to locate a group. If there is no such group near you—and even if there is—you can learn the techniques on your own. I've had patients who've used the techniques in groups and on their own. One of my patients started off in Dr. Stolbach's group, and found it helpful in the beginning. "But what I got out of it mostly was the techniques, which I use at home on my own. I'm not much of a joiner, I guess." She is convinced that the techniques have been a "useful part of my healing," and have helped her deal with the anxieties her cancer caused. "Cancer is no longer the first thing I think of in the morning, and the last thing I think of when I go to bed."

If you want to try working with the techniques on your own, there are a number of relaxation and imagery tapes you might want to try out. "I'd recommend Bernie Siegel's tapes," says Disch. "But with so many available, you might want to buy three or four, check them out, and see which feels most comfortable to you." If none of these tapes is exactly right for you, you can try creating your own. In his *The Road Back to Health*, psychologist Neil Fiore suggests a model for creating your own visualization tape.[4]

Similar to visualization, and often used in conjunction with it, are affirmations. These are statements affirming one's value and one's intentions, recited aloud if possible, mentally if necessary. Like visualization, they can be used for any goal, from wealth to spiritual growth, and they're often used for health. One of my patients has a list of her favorites, which include "I am now willing to become free of all pain and illness," "I am now renewing my body's ability to heal itself," and "I now let the light from above heal me with love." Others prefer to frame their affirmations in terms of choice: "I choose health."

I'm told by people who work with affirmations that it's important to frame them positively rather than negatively—not "I am not staying ill," but "I am growing more and more healthy each day."

They also suggest that affirmations should be repeated regularly, and frequently. You can say them while you're taking your shower, walking to your car, or unloading your groceries. Unlike many of the other mental practices, they needn't take time from a busy schedule.

LAUGHTER

Reader's Digest has for many years had a section of humor called "Laughter, the Best Medicine." They meant it metaphorically, but when Norman Cousins set about to cure himself of his degenerative illness, he took it literally. "I discovered that ten minutes of genuine belly laughter had an anesthetic effect and would give me at least two hours of pain-free sleep," he wrote.[5] There appears to be some medical basis for this: laughter can stimulate endorphins—chemicals that act like narcotics in the brain.

Some of my patients have found that laughter is an important part of their healing process. One woman has had breast cancer twice, and, along with her medical treatments and her meditation, she has worked laughter into her regime. "I told people I wanted to laugh. Friends send me funny books, cut out cartoons, call me and say funny things," she says.

Certainly giving yourself time *not* to think about your cancer, just to escape into zany humor, can be emotionally very healing. Be sure to pick the things that make you laugh. Cousins enjoyed Marx Brothers movies and "Candid Camera" TV shows. You might prefer stand-up comedians such as Robert Kline, or P.G. Wodehouse novels, or "I Love Lucy" reruns—whatever makes you laugh out loud and hold your sides, totally absorbing you into its delightful nonsense.

PSYCHIC HEALING

Before you scoff at the idea of psychic healing, remember that it's been respected by some intelligent people. In his work in Africa, Albert Schweitzer, in his hospital in the African jungle, often consulted with a witch doctor whose work he respected.[6] Much of charismatic Christian healing involves laying-on-of-hands, a classical psychic healing technique. And the relatively new "therapeutic touch," designed by nurses in the United States, uses a similar approach.

I haven't had much experience with psychic healers, in terms of my own patients, but there is a fair amount of anecdotal evidence about cures through psychic healing, and a friend of mine, severely asthmatic, had a brief but dramatic improvement after a few sessions with a healer. She's not certain whether this is the result of the healer's power or of her own mind, and she doesn't care: "What I care about is breathing, and he helped me do it," she says.

Certainly if the placebo effect has any validity, there's no reason why psychic healing can't trigger it off. As long as you're not paying exorbitant sums to a psychic who guarantees a cure, a few sessions with a psychic healer won't do you any harm—and it might do some good.

Sometimes psychic healing isn't even done in person—healers and even ordinary people "send healing energy." And again, according to anecdotal evidence, it sometimes seems to help. One of my Jewish patients had a Catholic nun as a fellow patient at the time of her mastectomy. "Sister Cecile got all the nuns in her convent praying for me," recounts my patient. "I know that helped. Every time I've had surgery I've gotten people from every religion, every belief system, working for me—prayer, positive vibrations, whatever. I'd say, 'I'm going into surgery at 8 o'clock this Thursday, and I need your positive thoughts.'"

Whatever else such healing thoughts can do, they can achieve a twofold benefit. For the patient, it is a reminder of all the love and support that's out there for her—from friends, from loved ones, even from strangers. And for those who love her, it can alleviate some of the terrible sense of helplessness they feel in the face of a loved one's suffering. For the most part, your friends can't operate on you or administer your chemotherapy, but they can pray or send healing thoughts.

Unfortunately psychic healing has barely been studied at all by scientists, but Herbert Benson, in his *Beyond the Relaxation Response,* cites studies done in Canada by Dr. Bernard Grad that suggest the possibility that such healing, even when the subject isn't aware it's being done, may actually have an effect on illness.[7] Hopefully, when doctors become less territorial about their healing abilities, more and more research will be done in this area.

Something else in the psychic realm to which people attribute healing powers are crystals and other stones. Many believe that these can affect different parts of your physical and emotional health, and that using them to meditate, wearing them as jewelry, or simply keeping them around can help you remain healthy, or restore health if you're ill.[8] As far as I know, no scientific studies have been done on the healing power of stones, but that doesn't mean they can't work. Some of my patients have great faith in them, and I like to keep a small collection of amethysts in my office.

A writer who has done some research on the popularity of healing stones speaks of them this way: "In an age when many people don't believe in a personal God, but *do* believe in some kind of higher power, crystals can function like the Catholic rosary or the Jewish *mezuzah*. They provide a concrete symbol of the person's own belief in her/his ability to heal, but they don't tie that belief into a particular theology. And the fact that different stones are connected to different healing functions links them with the Catholic saints." According to this writer's research, amethyst is seen as an all-purpose healer, while sugalite and tiger's eye are considered particularly effective with cancer, and moonstone is seen as helpful in the healing of women's cancers. "But almost everyone who works with stones will tell you that the most important thing is that you feel strongly drawn to a particular stone, and that its power comes as much from your connection to it as from any outside definition of its particular function," she says.

Some patients bring their healing stones to radiation, chemotherapy, or other frightening or unpleasant treatments; they can be very soothing. One of my patients had her favorite crystal taped to her hand during surgery. Another carried her sugalite with her to her chemotherapy treatments, and held it to the parts of her body that the chemicals most negatively affected.

My writer friend recommends a touch of common sense in regard to healing stones. "If a salesperson tells you that a $100 crystal is more powerful than a $10 one, you might want to take your business elsewhere. Stones aren't capitalists; if they really can heal, I don't think their ability will be limited by their price-tag or their karat count."

Herbs, Vitamins, and Special Diets

All the treatments I've discussed so far use purely mental or spiritual techniques—they don't involve putting any physical substance into the body. Other forms of nontraditional treatments use herbs, vitamins, or other substances, as well as particular diets believed to heal cancer.

I've already discussed the theories about the connection between diet and cancer prevention on page 152. But are there diets and/or vitamin supplements that can help you cure cancer? Some doctors believe there are. Once again, however, research to date is at best inconclusive. There are currently efforts underway to study the effect of a low-fat diet in postmenopausal women with breast cancer.[9] It will be some time until we know if it has any effect. There are many diets recommended for cancer in general, and some for breast cancer in particular: most of which are low in fat. If you decide to attempt a nutrition approach to healing your cancer, you should work very closely with your nutritionist and your physician both to create your particular diet and to coordinate it with your other treatments.

One physician who combines dietary treatment with conventional treatment is my friend Dr. Jeanne Hubbuch, who has treated many cancer patients, a number of whom have breast cancer. Some of her dietary suggestions are basic ones that most nutritionists agree are helpful in preventing a number of diseases. "I try to get people to cut down on fats, especially fried food and margarine, and decrease dairy foods, sugar, and white flour. For patients with breast cancer, it's especially important to eliminate meat or chicken that's been fed hormones, because breast cancer can be estrogen dependent. Also, I try to get them to eliminate caffeine, alcohol, soda, anything with additives or chemicals. And I put in their diet vegetables, fruits, whole grains, fish, chemical-free sources of chicken." If a patient with breast cancer is overweight, she includes a reducing component to the diet, "because of the estrogen effect of stored fat. In addition, people who are lean have much more resistance to chemical toxins, probably because pesticides and other pollutants are stored in the fat, so the more fat you've got the more places you have to store them and the more burden there is on your body to detoxify them."

Hubbuch also uses a variety of vitamin supplements with her patients. She favors "antioxidants" like vitamin C, vitamin E, selenium, vitamin A, and carotene, particularly for patients undergoing radiation or chemotherapy. She does not advise abandoning standard treatments in favor of diet and vitamin treatment, although if patients are adamant about doing only nutritional or other nonmedical treatments, she is supportive. "If a patient wants to go that route, I explain the data from different studies, and tell her that she must understand the risk she's taking by working only with nutrition—that there's a real possibility that it won't work. If a woman wants to avoid all treatments and toxic effects—chemotherapy and radiation—and only use nutritional and immune-enhancing methods, I try to help her evaluate the risks of standard treatment versus the risks of relying solely on natural methods. I think the decision about which treatments to use is intensely personal, and can only be made by the woman facing her own situation with cancer. I try to support each woman in her choice of treatments, and encourage her to include immune-enhancing methods." Hubbuch recommends that anyone interested in exploring a dietary component for her breast cancer treatment read Carlton Frederick's *Winning the Fight against Breast Cancer: The Nutritional Approach*.[10]

Macrobiotic diets have also been extremely popular with many who believe that cancer can be cured or prevented through nutrition. Based on a Zen philosophy too complex to begin to describe here, *macrobiotics* emphasizes whole grains, miso soup, fresh vegetables, and beans, with little fruit (only the fruit grown in your own region), and no sugar. Michio Kushi's *The Cancer Prevention Diet*[11] explains the diet in detail, and has specific suggestions for breast cancer patients, including 50–60 percent whole-grain cereals, 5–10 percent tamari or miso soup, 20–30 percent cooked vegetables, 5 percent small beans, and 5 percent "sea vegetables." He rules out any fats, iced foods and drinks, and a number of fruits. Unfortunately, unlike Jeanne Hubbuch, Kushi recommends that patients refrain from chemotherapy, radiation, and surgery. This, especially in cancer that is not yet metastatic, can be dangerous, even tragic.

The diet itself, while generally a healthful one, can, if too strictly followed, cause some problems for a patient undergoing chemotherapy or radiation, or recovering from surgery. It's low in calories and in protein, and when your body is depleted from these processes, that can be dangerous. If you're on a macrobiotic diet while undergoing medical treatments, make certain that it's not causing medical problems—and perhaps, at least while you're being treated, you might want to modify the diet somewhat.

For many western palates, a macrobiotic diet can be odd and unappetizing. If it's unpalatable to you, it probably won't do you any good. If a state of well-being is an essential part of getting well, as the concepts I discussed earlier in this chapter suggest, regularly eating foods you loathe can be counterproductive.

Changing one's diet, however, can be an active way to participate in one's own recovery. A patient of mine who started her macrobiotic diet when she was diagnosed with cancer is certain it played some part in her healing, and continues on a modified macrobiotic diet. "It's part of how I changed my life around in the wake of learning about my cancer, part of taking control of my body again," she says. She finds the diet comfortable and helpful.

Some branches of complementary healing involve taking substances not usually defined as medicine. One of these is *homeopathy*, which practitioners describe as a method of self-healing stimulated by very small doses of those drugs that would produce in a healthy individual symptoms like those of the disease being treated. The drugs are chosen by the patient with the assistance of a homeopathic practitioner, who may or may not also be an M.D. The substances are all legal, and over-the-counter; you can take them on your own, but it's wiser to consult with someone who's trained and can suggest remedies suited to your problem and your overall health history. Common homeopathic substances include belladonna and bryony. Ted Chapman, a homeopathic M.D. who works at Turning Point, a holistic healing center in the Boston area, has worked with patients who are being medically treated for breast cancer. "I have a number of patients with breast cancer, and homeopathy is part of their healing," he says. He emphasizes that it doesn't cure cancer, and he doesn't recommend it in place of medical treatment. "Doctors work on the end product of the disease, and they come in from the outside. We're working from the inside, on what makes you vulnerable to your disease in the first place." Like many other adjunctive therapies, homeopathy is thought to work on the immune system, working to strengthen the patient's mind and body. It's helpful in alleviating some of the side effects of radiation or chemotherapy. The only negative side effect of homeopathy, says Dr. Chapman, is a brief aggravation of your symptoms—pain, fever, et cetera—before they begin to regress.

A treatment related to homeopathy—and perhaps better known— is the ancient Chinese science of *acupuncture*. Dolores Heeb, Dr. Chapman's colleague at Turning Point, has written a booklet in which she describes acupuncture as a treatment method "based on Chinese ideas about the order and harmony of the universe as a whole. All pain and disease, whether physical, mental or emotional, are the result of an imbalance of energy. . . . Traditional acupuncture does not treat the disease or pain itself, but it does treat the whole person and the energy balance that led to the disease or pain."[12] It does this by inserting needles into areas of the body known as "meridians." Heeb says the needles can cause a brief sensation that is "sometimes painful, sometimes just strange." Dr. Chapman says that his colleague treats breast cancer patients at Turning Point, just as he does, and that she has had some positive results. As with homeopathy, however, acupuncture isn't a substitute for medical treatment, but an adjunct to it.

Alternative Treatments

Some treatments have been proposed to take the place of medical treatments. Most of them have not been studied in any scientifically rigorous way and their risks and complications are largely unknown. We mention them to be complete, but I don't endorse their use.

The best known of these is *laetrile*, a substance made from apricot pits. It hasn't been shown to work in any randomized, controlled studies, but it has a fair amount of nonscientific support. It's illegal in the United States, and is currently being used in clinics in Mexico. Unfortunately, its method of action has been misrepresented. Those who advocate its use claim that the cyanide it contains will be broken down by normal cells and not by cancer cells, thus causing the latter to die. This is not true, since neither type of cell can break down the cyanide. There have been reports of deaths from cyanide poisoning in patients taking laetrile.[13]

Another treatment is *immuno-augmentative therapy* (IAT), invented by Lawrence Burton who practices it in the Bahamas since it is illegal in'the United States. It is an individualized treatment that is considered by its advocates to restore natural immune defenses against all forms of cancer. One of my patients who believes strongly in IAT has described her treatment, and her reasons for choosing it over chemotherapy or radiation, after I had surgically removed her tumor. She says, "I have an extremely sensitive body, and if there's going to be a side effect, I'm going to have it. I'd been exhausted constantly for four years before the cancer showed up. . . . It seemed to me that the direction I should move in was toward greater health, and that everything I did should make my body stronger and healthier. Putting chemicals into my body or undergoing radiation seemed like the wrong direction." She learned of Burton's clinic, and spoke to people who were being treated there. She was impressed with what she heard. "One woman had breast cancer that had gone into her bones and now seemed symptom-free." She has gone to the Bahamas for the treatment twice, and believes it's been the best course for her. "You go there, stay a couple of months or longer, and he takes blood every day and gives various amounts of what he calls 'blood protein fractions,' which block the cancer and strengthen the immune system. He keeps watch on your immune system to see how much cancer you're killing off. Once he's able to forecast what your body will do given further amounts of the stuff, he gives you what you need to take at home, and you go home and give yourself injections every day, and go back down for a week or two every four to six months."

A word of warning: If you're considering immuno-augmentative therapy, you need to take into consideration the fact that it uses injections of blood proteins—some of which have been shown to carry hepatitis and AIDS.

If you are interested in researching any unproven cancer therapy, I suggest that, in addition to the material you get from the therapy's advocates, you go to your local American Cancer Society's division office (see Appendix F). They keep statements on these treatments which are fair and will describe for you exactly what is involved, as well as the known risks, side effects, opinion of the medical establishment, and any lawsuits that have been filed. Make sure you are really informed.

While I don't recommend that patients take on a treatment that excludes the use of traditional treatments, I do feel that this is a highly personal decision. My patient who chose IAT read literature on chemotherapy and radiation, as well as on IAT; she made her own decision. (She has since had a local recurrence and is at present taking radiation and hormones.) What risks any of us will take, and for what reasons, depends very much on who we are and what our values are.

To be honest, there are situations when refusing traditional treatment isn't really much of a risk. There are some cancers, and some stages in the development of other cancers, when the treatments we have simply aren't very helpful. If your prognosis isn't good, and chemotherapy isn't likely to extend your life for any length of time, you may well consider that the discomforts of the treatment aren't worth the slight chance that it will cure you, and that an alternative treatment offers both better survival hope and more comfort during the remainder of your life. Audre Lorde, the poet and political activist whose book *The Cancer Journals* describes her experiences with breast cancer, published a new book of essays, *A Burst of Light*, in 1988.[14] In the title essay, she describes how, when she learned her cancer had metastasized to her liver, she decided to forego chemotherapy and use "homeopathic" methods instead. When the tumor in her liver was first discovered, in February 1984, she refused even to have it biopsied, fearing the surgery would spread the cancer cells—a common, although not very realistic, fear. Instead, while in Berlin teaching classes, she went to a homeopathic doctor who treated her with injections of Iscador, a substance made from mistletoe that is believed to strengthen the immune system. Later, she continued this treatment at a homeopathic clinic in Switzerland. When a sonogram later demonstrated that she did indeed have metastatic cancer, her doctor told her, accurately, that chemotherapy could add only about a year to her life. She decided to stick with her homeopathic healing, adding visualization and meditation to the process, and determinedly living her life to the fullest. As of this writing, she is still alive—an impressive achievement with liver metastasis; and who's to say that it isn't because she chose a treatment that she believed in, and that allowed her to remain as active as possible, doing the work to which she is so passionately committed?

As much as I wish it were otherwise, traditional medical treatments are imperfect. They are often successful, and should not be lightly discarded. But they *can* be supplemented, in ways we have good reason to believe may increase some patients' survival rates. Whether any of these ways is right for you, I can't say. But I recommend that you look into them, and take from them what seems helpful to you. I like the attitude of one of my patients, a 46-year-old woman whose cancer has metastasized to her bone marrow, and who is doing remarkably well. A devout Catholic, she cherishes the advice of a nun who told her to "work as though everything depended on you, and pray as though everything depended on God."

She has had surgery, and is currently on a course of tamoxifen therapy. She is also on a macrobiotic diet, which she has recently reinforced with a diet of linseed oil and cottage cheese recommended by a holistic doctor in Germany. She took Dr. Stolbach's course at Deaconess Hospital, and one of Bernie Siegel's workshops, and continues a regular meditation and visualization program. Whenever a church has a healing service, she goes to it—"Catholic or Protestant, I go wherever I'll get healed." She went to Lourdes, France, with her aunt, who also had cancer. ("I stayed for three days," she says. "It was a very emotional, very draining, experience—my aunt's tumor disappeared.") She carries an amethyst with her, and is interested in crystals. "Because I'm Catholic, my friends gave me a rosary made of crystal, which I carry with me all the time, so I've got the healing power of the rosary and of the crystal combined. I'm not settling for just one thing."

Though she still has her cancer, her health improved during the year she began integrating these methods into her healing. "Because it was in my bones, I was weak—I couldn't climb a flight of stairs. Now I go mountain climbing and cross-country skiing. I can dance now, too."

I don't know which component of this patient's healing work is doing the most good, and I don't know whether or not her good health will last indefinitely. But I do know that her commitment to taking control of her healing process has turned a terrifying experience into a triumphant challenge. She is giving herself every chance to survive, and to live a fine, intense life. Not everyone, of course, will have the time or energy to follow all the routes she has, but everyone can learn from her example, and use whatever techniques best suit them to make a wholehearted commitment to life.

PART SIX

LIVING WITH
BREAST CANCER

25

$$\equiv$$

Rehabilitation

You've had breast cancer, you've been treated for it, and now it's time to get on with your life. But your life has changed now, and you have to adjust to your new situation on a number of levels.

Prosthesis?

If you've had a mastectomy, the first decision you'll probably want to deal with is whether, and how, to create the appearance of a breast. Most women take it for granted that they have to appear to the outside world as though they had both breasts. Until recently, there was only one way to do that—through a prosthesis, a sort of elaborate falsie designed for women with mastectomies. (See Figure 25-1.) Nowadays, there is also another option, the "reconstruction" of an artificial breast that will, to a greater or lesser extent, have the appearance of a real breast.

Before you decide on one of these options, you might want to consider a third possibility—not disguising your mastectomy at all. It's not a choice many women make, but there are a few women who do choose it, and are happy with the choice. One of my patients thought about her options, then decided that "a prosthesis sounded

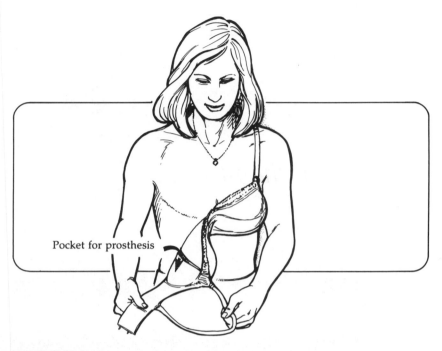

Pocket for prosthesis

FIGURE 25-1

too uncomfortable, and reconstruction hasn't been around long enough to see what long-term effects it can have. And then I decided I was comfortable with the way I look." She goes to work, jogs in a loose T-shirt, and feels that "it's other people's problem if they're uncomfortable with it." Once in a while, she feels a need to look more "normal"—especially when she has important meetings with new business associates. Her solution is to stuff shoulder pads from other dresses into her bra. "I never liked shoulder pads anyway," she laughs, "and all the new clothing has them—so I get to put them to good use!" For other women, refusing to create the illusion of a breast is part of their feminist beliefs. The poet Audre Lorde writes in *The Cancer Journals* about her rejection of "cosmetic sham": "I believe that socially sanctioned prosthesis is merely another way of keeping women with breast cancer silent and separate from each other."[1]

It's wonderful to have the self-confidence to feel comfortable without the appearance of a breast, but most of us are products of our culture and need to feel that we are cosmetically acceptable to the outside world. Also, in some cases there are penalties for failing to appear "normal." If your nonconformity will cost you your job, for example, you're likely to want to wear a prosthesis at least part of the time.

The option of wearing a prosthesis will probably be offered to you right away. In most areas of the country the hospital will arrange for someone to visit you while you're still in the hospital to talk to you about prostheses—your visitor will be either from Reach to Recovery (see Appendix C) or from a firm that sells prostheses. You can get a temporary prosthesis and then shop around for your permanent one. Usually you can buy them in medical supply houses or in fancy lingerie stores. Each environment has its advantages and disadvantages—in the former, you may be put off by the implications of mutilation, the wheelchairs and artificial limbs; in the latter you might feel painfully reminded of the breast you no longer have. Your doctor or the American Cancer Society can help you find places to buy your prosthesis, or you can ask friends who've had mastectomies.

There are stores that will custom-make a prosthesis for you; it's expensive, and your insurance company may not pay for it, but it might be worth it to you to get a totally precise match. (In general, it's a good idea to check with your insurance company before buying your prosthesis anyway; different companies have different quirks, and you want to be sure of what your own expenses will and won't be. If you're on Medicare, they'll pay for a prosthesis every year or two years—with a prescription. Why you need a prescription for a prosthesis, I don't know—I've never met a woman who bought one for the fun of it—but the ways of bureaucracies are mysterious.)

Prostheses, of course, are made in different sizes, and they're also made for different operations. If you've had a radical mastectomy, you can get a fuller prosthesis than if you've had a simple mastectomy. If you've had a wide excision that's left you noticeably asymmetrical, you can get a small "filler" that will fit comfortably in your bra. In the past, prostheses didn't have nipples, and this caused some problems for women whose remaining breast had a prominent nipple. (Betty Rollin, in her book *First, You Cry,* has a very funny description of her efforts to make her own "nipple" out of cloth buttons.)[2] Fortunately, that's changed: any prosthesis you buy will have a nipple, and you can get a separate nipple to attach to it if your own nipple is more prominent than the one on the prosthesis.

Reconstruction

Another option is reconstruction—the creation, by a plastic surgeon, of an artificial and natural-appearing breast. Breast reconstruction has made a big difference both physically and emotionally for many women who have had mastectomies. But it's important to understand its limits before you decide to have it done.

What's constructed is *not* a real breast. When it's well done, it will *look* real, but it will never have full sensation, as a breast does. It's more like a prosthesis attached to your chest. Any surgeon who tells you, "We're going to take off your breast and give you a new one, and it'll be as good as new" is either stupid or dishonest. Sometimes they'll tell you that the new breast "feels normal"—at best, a half-truth. It will feel normal to the hand that's touching it, but it will have little feeling itself. It will never feel completely normal to you.

Is it worth doing, then? For most women, yes. It can make you feel more normal, to yourself and to other people, since it looks like a breast. And it can make your life a little easier—you can wear a T-shirt or a housedress and not worry about putting on a bra. If the doorbell rings while you're still in your bathrobe, you don't have to deal with whether or not you want the mail carrier to see your unevenness. It makes it easier to buy bathing suits and other "revealing" clothes. In *Why Me?*, Rose Kushner explains why she decided to have reconstruction done. She was alone in a hotel room one night, when she was awakened by the sound of the fire alarm and the smell of smoke. She jumped out of bed, threw on her clothing, grabbed her glasses, and ran. Downstairs in the lobby with the other guests, she realized that only she had gotten dressed; the others were all in their robes. Then she realized why: "This 'well-adjusted' mastectomee wasn't going anywhere publicly with one breast."[3]

A reconstruction can help some women put their cancer experiences behind them. As one of my patients said, "When I was wearing my prosthesis every day, when I looked at my body and it was concave where there had been a breast, I felt that I was a cancer patient, that I was living with that every single day. With the reconstruction I feel that I'm healthy again, that I can go on with my life." Another patient says that after her mastectomy, "I always felt the hollows under my arm. After my reconstruction, I put my arms down, and something was there. That's when the tears came; it was splendid to have that back."

On the other hand, it isn't necessarily right for everybody. One of my patients regrets her decision to have reconstruction. Displeased with the appearance of her reconstructed breast, she also feels that getting the reconstruction functioned as a form of denial. "It caused me to postpone the mourning I had to do over losing a breast," she says. "Instead of mourning the loss of a breast, I was thinking in terms of getting a breast. So it wasn't until the process was over, and I saw my new breast, which wasn't like my other breast, that it hit me that I'd lost a breast. If I had the decision to make now, I don't think I'd have reconstruction."

The best reconstructions look like real breasts—but not all operations are the best, and some look real only through bras or clothing.

Reconstruction surgery is done in a number of ways. There are two basic kinds—those using artificial substances and those using your own body. Within these categories, there are also variations.

In the first category is the silicone implant, much like the implant described on page 66. The implant is placed behind the pectoralis muscle and the skin is sewn together, which will give you a bulge. (See Figure 25-2.) The silicone has some weight and bounce to it, which will help it feel real. The problem is that it can't give you a very large breast because it's behind the muscle pushing everything forward and everything has to close over the top of it, so you're limited in size. It works best in smaller-breasted women, or on women who have had bilateral mastectomies and are happy with small breasts. It's easier to do than any of the other operations. With

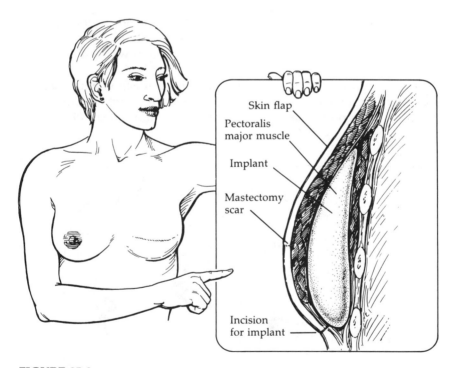

Skin flap

Pectoralis
major muscle

Implant

Mastectomy
scar

Incision
for implant

FIGURE 25-2

the implant, your hospital stay won't be longer than usual. If you're having it done some time after your mastectomy, the hospital stay will be about two to three days.

A variation on this is the expander. A hollow, empty sack is placed behind the muscle and everything is sewn closed. There's a little tube and a little valve on the sack under the skin, and gradually, over the course of six months, the doctor injects more and more saline (salt water) into it, which stretches the skin out. (See Figure 25-3.) When it's become the size you want, the sack is removed and replaced with a permanent silicone sack. (The saline won't work long-term, since the fluid can leak out more easily. Scientists are in the process of developing a permanent, leakproof saline implant, but we don't know yet when it will be ready.) The disadvantage is that the process drags out over several months, and while the skin and muscle are stretching it can be uncomfortable. Since the reconstructed breast doesn't sag much, it may be higher than you want it to be. One of my patients who has been very unhappy with her operation found this particularly displeasing. "The reconstructed breast didn't look like my real breast, and it was much higher," she says. "I had to start wearing a bra, which I don't like at all." More typical, however, is the gratifying experience of another patient, who says, "I forget it's there—it's a part of me now. It's a little harder than my other breast, but otherwise great: I don't have to worry about what I wear."

There's always the danger of postoperative infection with surgery, but with the expander or an implant it can be more serious. Since they are foreign to your body any infection will not heal. One of my

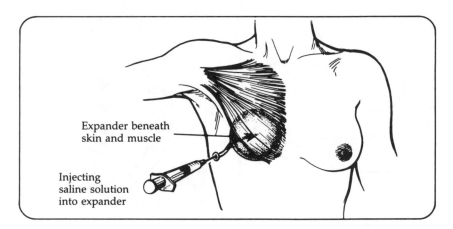

Expander beneath
skin and muscle

Injecting
saline solution
into expander

FIGURE 25-3

patients had a very bad infection and had to have the expander removed.

The expander will probably add no additional days to your hospital stay or, if done separately, will keep you in the hospital about two to three days. There has been concern lately over the safety of silicone implants. Although there have been two million implants used over the last 20 years, there is still very little information about its long-term effects. (See page 66 for a discussion of problems with implants.) In the situation of breast reconstruction there is no fear of interfering with mammography, and no evidence that implants interfere with the detection of recurrences.[4] The other potential problems with silicone will need more study.

There are also several procedures using your own tissue. In the *myocutaneous flap,* a flap of skin, muscle, and fat is taken from either your back (latissimus) or your abdomen (rectus). (See Figure 25-4.) The tissue is removed except for its feeding artery and vein, which remain attached, almost like a leash. The site from which the tissue was removed is sewn closed. The new little island of skin and muscle is then tunneled under the skin into the mastectomy wound. Since the blood vessels aren't cut, the blood supply remains. It's better than the silicone implant in the sense that it's your own tissue; and because you've got extra skin it can make a bigger breast and a more natural droop. You may feel more normal externally, since it's real tissue, skin, and fat, though it will still have little sensation.

At the same time, you're robbing Peter to pay Paul—you're taking muscle, skin, and fat from someplace else. If you take it from the abdomen, your abdominal muscle will no longer be as strong and you won't be able to do things like sit-ups. One of my patients now has to wear a panty girdle all the time, to help support her weakened abdominal muscle. Another has found that since the operation the area around her upper abdomen is so sensitive that she can't wear anything with a waistband. I should add, however, that these problems are relatively rare, and most of my patients who have had the procedure have had few problems, and much satisfaction. If the tissue is taken from your back there will be fewer problems, although you may weaken your back somewhat.

Sometimes if the patient wants a bigger breast, a combination operation is done, using the latissimus flap and a silicone implant behind it. In any case, you'll have a scar on the area from which the flap has been taken. There is usually less available tissue there and so only a smaller mound can be made.

With the flap, you'll probably be in the hospital for four or five days; the stitches will be out in two to three weeks, and by five or six weeks, you'll be ready for a fully active lifestyle again.

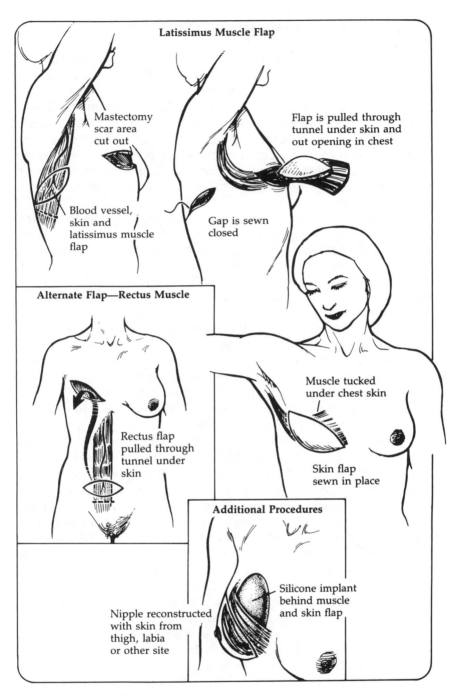

Latissimus Muscle Flap

Mastectomy scar area cut out

Flap is pulled through tunnel under skin and out opening in chest

Blood vessel, skin and latissimus muscle flap

Gap is sewn closed

Alternate Flap—Rectus Muscle

Muscle tucked under chest skin

Rectus flap pulled through tunnel under skin

Skin flap sewn in place

Additional Procedures

Nipple reconstructed with skin from thigh, labia or other site

Silicone implant behind muscle and skin flap

FIGURE 25-4

There's a last kind of reconstructive surgery that's very complex, difficult surgery, and I'd only recommend it if there were no other alternative. This is the free-gluteus flap, taken from the buttocks. The blood vessels can't reach in this operation, since it's too far from the chest, so they are cut off, and resewn together to blood vessels in the chest. (See Figure 25-5.) It's about eight to ten hours of surgery, and you'll probably be in the hospital for seven days. If the blood supply gets messed up, part of the flap can die off, and further surgery will be necessary. The patient I mentioned earlier, who had gotten an infection from her silicone expanders, was unable to have either the latissimus or rectus procedure, because of medical problems she had had in her back and abdomen. The free-gluteus flap was the only alternative she had left, and, though it was difficult surgery that involved a long healing period, she feels it was well worth the pain and inconvenience it involved.

In order to decide what's best for you, you should discuss it with your surgeon, and, separately, with a plastic surgeon. They will look at you and your body, see how your body hangs together and how your breasts look before your surgery, and tell you what kind of procedure they think would be best for you.

Any of these procedures can be done immediately, or at some later time. The advantage of having it done immediately is that you don't have to face another operation later: your regular surgeon performs your mastectomy and then, while you're still under anesthesia, the plastic surgeon comes in and does the reconstruction. In my experience, many women don't have reconstruction because they don't want to go through more surgery. The disadvantages are that it's a longer time in the operating room, and that it's harder to schedule, since you have to get the surgeon and the plastic surgeon at the same time. Occasionally, immediate reconstruction can't be done because your skin or muscles are too tight, and there's not enough room for the new breast.

It's also possible that you won't be sure at first whether you want reconstruction. My colleague Dr. Robert Goldwyn, a plastic surgeon who has done many reconstructions, says that many premastectomy patients he sees are too upset by the cancer and the prospect of a mastectomy to make yet another major decision at the time. When he comes across this kind of ambivalence, he suggests that the patient have her mastectomy, take whatever time she needs to deal with it, and then, when she feels ready, come back to him if she still wants reconstruction.

He also points out something crucial: your plastic surgeon should show you pictures of the best and the worst results he or she has had. Some doctors will show women only the best results—an act

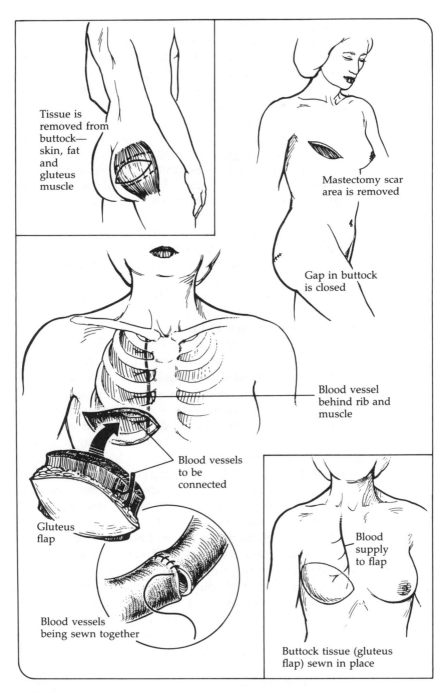

Tissue is removed from buttock—skin, fat and gluteus muscle

Mastectomy scar area is removed

Gap in buttock is closed

Blood vessel behind rib and muscle

Blood vessels to be connected

Gluteus flap

Blood vessels being sewn together

Blood supply to flap

Buttock tissue (gluteus flap) sewn in place

FIGURE 25-5

he compares to false advertising. It's important for you to know the limits of what the procedure can do for you, and the risks you run of having far-from-ideal results.

Many general surgeons don't like to offer immediate reconstruction because it's a new procedure and they're leery of it. If you want it done and the surgeon tries to argue you out of it, don't give up—just look for a surgeon who's had experience and is comfortable with it.

There is no time limit for reconstruction. In fact, current techniques have made it a better option than it used to be. If you had a mastectomy in the past and are now thinking about reconstruction, you should feel encouraged. Even with a radical mastectomy, reconstruction is still possible. Or if you'd decided against reconstruction, and now want to reconsider, that's also fine. (I've had patients who've had their mastectomies in the winter and didn't want reconstruction, and then decided in the summer, when they want to wear bathing suits and sundresses, that maybe it's a good idea after all.) Women with bilateral mastectomies can have both sides reconstructed—and to any reasonable size they'd like. If you were an A cup and always wanted to be a C, now you can do it!

Once the new breast is on, you can also get a nipple made. It will look "real," and match the color of your original nipple. Usually the skin from your thigh is used, and interestingly, it will darken in color once it's transplanted. Whether or not you want to bother with the nipple depends on why you want the reconstruction. If it's just for convenience, you may decide against it. If you want the new breast to look as real as possible, you'll probably want the nipple. Again, it's *your* decision—you're the one who'll go through the surgery, and you're the one who'll live with the results.

What kind of reconstruction you want depends on your goal. Some women are very concerned about achieving precise symmetry; many others aren't. Are you chiefly concerned about looking good in clothes, or is it important that a new lover won't even know you've had surgery? Do you want to have your remaining breast altered to achieve a more perfect match? None of these are foolish concerns, and you should never hesitate to look for what you want out of guilt over "vanity." You've been through an unpleasant and life-changing experience; you're entitled to do what you can to make its aftermath as comfortable as possible for yourself. Talk with your plastic surgeon about all the possibilities, and decide what's best for you.

Whatever you decide, check with your insurance company. Some companies will pay for either a prosthesis or a reconstruction but not one and then the other, and that might affect your decision.

Lymphedema

Aside from the cosmetic implications of breast surgery, there are other problems you may have to deal with. Unfortunately, not all of the complications from your treatment are over when the treatment is. Some of them can occur years later or last for years, even permanently. We have already mentioned the most significant of these, lymphedema, or swelling of the arm, which can happen as a result of the removal of lymph nodes (see page 290). As we said, it can be so slight that you only notice it because your rings suddenly feel too tight on your fingers, or so severe that your arm is huge. (See Figure 25-6.) It can be temporary or permanent. It can happen immediately, or years after your operation.

What causes it to happen? Basically, lymphedema—sometimes called "milk arm"—is a plumbing problem. Normally, the lymph fluid is carried through the lymph vessels, passes through the lymph nodes, and gets dumped back into the bloodstream, near the heart. The lymph nodes act like a strainer, removing foreign material and

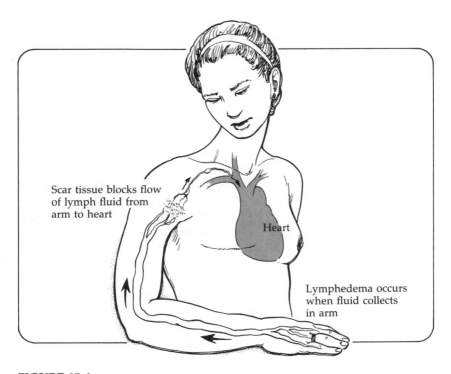

Scar tissue blocks flow of lymph fluid from arm to heart

Heart

Lymphedema occurs when fluid collects in arm

FIGURE 25-6

bacteria. So if you have surgery in the area and it scars over, some of the holes are blocked and the drainage can't work as effectively. The fluid doesn't drain out as well as it needs to, and everything backs up and swells. This used to be much more common—we'd see it in about 20 percent of cases—because more extensive surgery was done. Nowadays, since we remove less tissue, it only happens in about 5 percent of mastectomies.

If it happens, there's not much you can do about it. Therefore it is important to try and prevent it. Although it is important to avoid significant trauma to the involved arm (having blood drawn, blood pressure cuffs, etc.), this is not as vital as it was in the days of a radical mastectomy. As we said, probably the most important prevention is avoiding heavy lifting with your arm hanging down, for example, carrying a suitcase or briefcase. Try to get your groceries delivered instead of carrying them yourself; if that's not feasible, get one of those little grocery carts and wheel them home. Get suitcases with wheels if you do any traveling.

Once lymphedema develops, treatment is difficult. You can elevate your arm to help reduce some of the swelling. Physical therapy and exercise can help in early cases. There are long support gloves similar to the stockings they make for varicose veins, which are unaesthetic but can reduce the swelling. For extreme cases, you can pump out the fluid daily with an electric pump, which will keep the swelling down to a manageable level—you can rent or buy them from a medical supply store.

There have been a number of operations that have been used on lymphedema, but none of them have been very effective. Until a better treatment is discovered, lymphedema is an uncomfortable and aesthetically displeasing complication.

You should never take lymphedema lightly. Not only is it uncomfortable and aesthetically displeasing, in about 10 percent of cases it can develop into a rare form of cancer called *lymphangiosarcoma*, which shows up as red nodules on the arm. This occurs 8 to 10 years following the development of lymphedema and can be fatal. (See Appendix C for further help and information.)

Exercise

Exercise is important after your treatment, and not only in terms of lymphedema. Again, doctors can often be over-restrictive. After you've had a mastectomy or a lymph node sampling, your surgeon may tell you not to move your arm at all. There's a lot of controversy about how protective of the area you should be.

If you do keep your arm very still at first, you'll probably find your shoulder extremely stiff when you do start moving around. That's to be expected—if you take someone who's in perfect health and put her arm in a sling for a week, she'll end up with a stiff shoulder.

Certain exercises, however, can help your shoulder. (See Figure 25-7.) One is called "climbing the walls." It involves walking your fingers up the wall, stretching a little bit farther each time. You can do it while you're watching TV or talking on the phone. The other one involves leaning over and making bigger and bigger circles with your arm. Swimming is also an excellent exercise.

If your arm remains very stiff, after two or three weeks, ask your doctor to refer you to a physical therapist. I find only about 10 to 15 percent of my patients need physical therapy. But it's *very* important to get your shoulder flexible again, and soon; otherwise you can end up with a condition called "frozen shoulder," which is difficult to treat successfully.

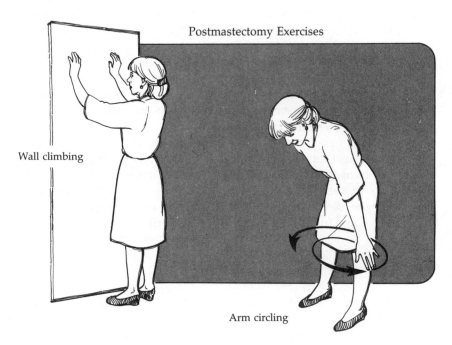

Postmastectomy Exercises

Wall climbing

Arm circling

FIGURE 25-7

Any sport or exercise you did before your cancer, you can do now—and you should, if you want to. If you've been a fairly sedentary person, you might want to change that. You might also want to examine your eating habits, and health habits in general. Often people who have suffered life-threatening illnesses are more aware of the importance of health than they were before, and want to invest energy into maintaining their health as much as they can.

Emotional Exercise

Obviously, not all the aftereffects of breast cancer are physical. You've had a life-threatening illness, and one that affects your sense of yourself as a woman. Emotional healing techniques are more varied and individual than physical ones, but there are many that have proven helpful to my patients and other women with breast cancer.

Many women find it helpful to keep a journal of their experiences to refer to later and to help them cope with their feelings. Some take their healing out beyond themselves—reaching out to other women who are going through what they've been through. Writers like Audre Lorde, Betty Rollin, and Rose Kushner have written about the experience. Actress Ann Jillian wrote and starred in a TV movie about her battle with breast cancer, in the hope of helping other women. Years ago, when breast cancer was still considered somehow shameful, public figures like Shirley Temple Black, Happy Rockefeller, and Betty Ford spoke out about their experiences, hoping to encourage women to examine their breasts and have any suspicious lump checked out immediately.

It's not only famous women, or women in glamorous occupations, who can turn their work toward helping other women with breast cancer. Two of my patients are psychotherapists who now specialize in breast cancer therapy. Another has begun doing breast cancer workshops at her corporation. A salesclerk might want to work in a store selling prostheses, since she now has a special understanding which might help her customers.

If your profession isn't one that can be adapted to some form of working with breast cancer, or if you don't feel drawn toward spending your work life dealing with the disease, you can still help other women—and thus yourself—on a volunteer basis. You can become involved with Reach to Recovery (see Appendix C), or similar groups that work with breast cancer patients. You know how frightened you were when you were first diagnosed: and the presence of someone who's survived the disease can be enormously reassuring to a newly diagnosed woman who's known only of people who died from it.

Finally, make sure you don't feel ashamed of what you've been through. Cancer still carries a stigma in our culture, and breast cancer can have especially difficult associations. You need to demystify it to yourself, and to others. You don't have to dwell on it, but it's not a good idea to repress it either. You need to have friends you can talk freely to about your disease and your feelings about it; you need to know you can include it in casual conversation, that you don't have to avoid saying, "Oh, yes, that was around the time I was in the hospital for my mastectomy."

Insurance and Getting a Job

Unfortunately, maintaining a healthy attitude isn't always easy, in the face of what often amounts to discrimination against people with cancer. There are some precautions everyone with cancer needs to take.

In the first place, be sure you don't let your insurance lapse. Your company can't drop your policy because of your illness, so you're safe on that score. But many insurance companies won't take on someone who's had a life-threatening illness, and others will take you on but exclude coverage in the area of your illness. If you change jobs and go from one company's coverage to another, you'll probably be all right (but make certain of this before you accept the new job). If you quit for a while, make sure you keep up your insurance on your own. It's costly, but not nearly as costly as not being covered if you have a recurrence.

Life insurance and disability insurance are also harder to get if you've had breast cancer. More and more cancer survivors are fighting to get this changed, and it should get better in the future. But for now, be very alert.

One of the hardest questions is whether or not to tell employers and co-workers about your cancer. There are pros and cons either way. Federal law prohibits discrimination against the handicapped or anyone mistakenly thought to be handicapped by federal employers, employers who get a federal grant or who get federal financial assistance. But state laws vary, and the federal legislation doesn't cover other parts of the private sector.[5] Besides the risk of overt discrimination, there are many forms of more subtle discrimination. This has persuaded many women to keep quiet about their illness at work. The risk of missing a promotion or being passed over for an opportunity increases if your employers know that you have cancer.

On the other hand, there is the increased support that may be forth-coming if you are open. It is a dilemma that is probably best solved on an individual basis. There is more and more attention being given to cancer survivors in the workplace, and you may well be able to find a career counseling center that can give you good advice.

If you are looking for a new job there is even more difficulty. Some companies are reluctant to hire someone with cancer; you might be frank in the interview because you don't want to work for someone with that attitude. On the other hand, you might need the job too much to risk being turned down. But if you don't tell them and then end up missing a lot of time for medical appointments or sickness, you might run into problems that could have been avoided if you'd been frank in the beginning. It's a tough problem, and there are no easy answers. We have included some references and reading about cancer and the workplace in Appendix C.

Sex

One of the least discussed subjects about life after breast cancer is sexuality. Your surgeon won't bring it up if you don't, and in fact most surgeons assume that if you are not complaining then every-thing must be all right. I remember a surgeon who had referred a patient to me. He said that she had surprised everyone after her mastectomy with her rapid recovery and how well she had "dealt with it." I took over the case, and in my first conversation with the patient found out that, however well adjusted she seemed on the surface, she had not yet looked at her scar five years after the oper-ation. She had never resumed sex with her husband and even dressed and undressed in the closet so he couldn't see her.

Many women have difficulties with sex and intimacy following a breast cancer diagnosis. Aside from the feeling that your body has betrayed you, there is a feeling of invasion from all the treatments. All these strangers have been poking and prodding you for weeks: you can feel almost as though you've been raped. It takes a while to feel good and in control of your body again. You need to commu-nicate these feelings to your partner so he or she can help you in your healing.

Some women find after surgery, whether mastectomy or lumpec-tomy, that a sexual relationship becomes even more important in helping them to regain their sense of worth and wholeness. There may, however, be subtle changes. One patient of mine who had had bilateral mastectomies felt that all the erotic sensations she had for-merly had in her breasts had "moved south," and that her orgasms

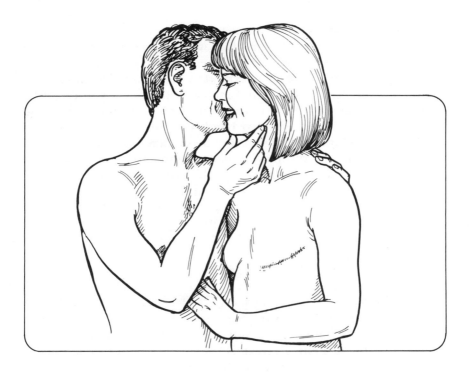

were doubly good. Other women miss the stimulation from a lost breast so much that they will prefer no breast attention whatsoever. Your arm or shoulder may not be as strong on the side of your surgery. This may make certain positions more difficult during intercourse, such as kneeling above your partner. For many months you may feel uncomfortable lying on the side of the surgery. It is important that you communicate with your partner so that together you can explore new ways of lovemaking that you both enjoy.

It is also important to note that there are no aspects of sexual intimacy that will cause cancer or increase the chance of recurrence. Nor can cancer be "caught" by sucking on a nipple.

Sheila Kitzinger,[6] in her book *Woman's Experience of Sex*, says that some women have told her that an important part of their healing process was having a brief affair. They said it was all well and good for a husband of 35 years to still love them without a breast, but they needed the confirmation that they were still sexually attractive to feel whole again.

This brings up another issue. If you are single and dating, should you tell or not? Again, this is an individual issue. Some women will tell a prospective lover way in advance, preferring to have it out in the open before the moment of passion. Other women will wait until the last instance when there is no turning back to disclose their secret. For the woman who has had only a small lumpectomy, or who has had mastectomy and a very effective reconstruction, the need to tell a casual lover about her situation may or may not arise.

Working out these issues and feeling comfortable with yourself are all part of the healing process. If you find it difficult, or if you get stuck on some issue, you may well want to try some counseling. A diagnosis of breast cancer reminds you that life can be short and you certainly want to live it as fully as you can.

Pregnancy

One question that comes up frequently with my younger cancer patients is whether or not they should get pregnant once they've had breast cancer. There are two areas to consider—the ethical implications and the health-related implications.

In the not-too-distant past, doctors (usually male) tended to impose their own value judgments on patients, telling them not to get pregnant until at least five years after having breast cancer. If you'd survived five years, they reasoned, there was a good chance you'd won your bout with breast cancer; otherwise, they didn't want you bringing a child you couldn't raise into the world.

Clearly, this is a moral decision for the patient, not the doctor, to make, and there are two equally valid ways to look at it. Some women do indeed feel that they don't want to have a child if they can't be reasonably sure they'll be around to raise it. Others feel that even if they do die in a few years, they'll be able to give a child the love and care she or he needs to grow up well, and that they want to pass on their genes before they die.

Having a child is never a decision to make lightly, and having a life-threatening illness complicates it further. Think it through carefully and get the thoughts of people whose opinions you respect— and then make *your* decision.

Can getting pregnant decrease your chances of surviving breast cancer? I wish I knew. Although there are no randomized studies, cancer centers that have reported on the outcome of women who have had pregnancies following breast cancer have shown no difference in survival.[7, 8]

We do know that getting pregnant won't cause the cancer to spread: it has either spread or not—before you got pregnant. But if you had a hormone-sensitive tumor that left microscopic cancer cells in your body, it's possible that pregnancy, with its attendant hormones, can make them grow faster than they would have if you weren't pregnant. This could decrease the time you have left, so that, for example, if you would have died of breast cancer four years from now, you'll die in three years instead.

So the question is, do you want to take that risk? If you've had a lot of positive nodes, or a very aggressive tumor, or some other factor that increases the likelihood of micrometastases, you'll want to take that into consideration. It might be worth the risk to you, or it might not. Again, it's a highly individual decision.

If you get pregnant, how will your breasts react? If you've had a mastectomy, obviously nothing will happen on the chest area where your breast was, but your other breast will go through all the usual pregnancy changes we discussed in Chapter 3. If you've had lumpectomy and radiation, the nonradiated breast will probably go through the normal changes. Radiation damages some of the milk-producing parts of the breast, so the radiated breast, while it will grow somewhat larger, won't keep pace with the other breast, and will have little or no milk production. You can nurse on one side only, if you want. The only problem with that is increased asymmetry; the milk-producing breast will grow, and will stay larger even after you've finished breastfeeding. If this disturbs you a great deal, you can have the larger breast reduced later through plastic surgery (see Chapter 5). One of my patients got pregnant shortly after she finished her radiation treatments, and successfully breastfed the baby. But one breast is now twice as large as the other. Knowing she wanted another child, she waited till after her next pregnancy. She's pregnant now, and planning to have reduction surgery after she's nursed her new baby.

Chemotherapy presents another set of problems. As we discussed on page 321, it depresses your ovaries and stops your period. If you're close to menopause, your period will probably never come back; if you're young, it probably will. Unlike the man's sperm, which is constantly being produced, the woman's eggs are all there at the time of her birth; since the eggs aren't made up of dividing cells, the chemotherapy can't affect them. It's probably a good idea to wait till a year or so after your treatment to get pregnant, because it's a stressful process and you won't want to add morning sickness to the leftover nausea from chemotherapy.

On the other hand, I had a patient who inadvertently got pregnant right after she'd finished her chemotherapy and, after talking it over with her husband and her caregivers, decided to have the baby—who's now a perfectly healthy little girl.

So the decision is up to you. If the stress of dealing with cancer and its uncertainties is too great, you may not want to have a child. On the other hand, if you *do* want to have a child, perhaps creating a new life can help you to cope with the knowledge of mortality that a life-threatening illness carries with it—a reminder that even death isn't the end.

26

Recurrence

You've had breast cancer, you've finished all your primary treatments, and it's time to go on with your life. How can you be sure the cancer's all gone, or that it won't come back?

Unfortunately, that's a difficult question to answer. Just as we don't know for sure that there are microscopic cancer cells when we start treatment, we can't know for sure that there aren't any left when we're done. It would be wonderful if we had some method like a blood test that would tell us if there were still cancer cells anywhere in your body, but we don't. We gauge the likelihood of micrometastasis with as much accuracy as possible, treat you with a systemic treatment if we think there might be spread, and then hope we've succeeded. We also monitor you very carefully so that if there *is* a recurrence we catch it early.

The Follow-Up

Usually the surgeon and/or other specialists who did your primary treatment—your mastectomy or wide excision—will follow you at regular intervals for a period of time. I see patients every three to four months for the first two years, and every six months after that.

When I see them, I ask how they're feeling, and then I do a thorough examination. I examine both breasts, or the chest wall where the breast was if the patient has had a mastectomy. I check the lymph node area. I want to be sure that, in the case of a mastectomy, no cancer has come back in the scar or the chest wall, and, in the case of wide excision and radiation, that no cancer is in the breast itself.

Part of the reason I like to check so often is that after treatment, the radiated breast undergoes a lot of changes. There will be a lumpy area under the scar and perhaps some skin firmness and/or puckering from the radiation. By keeping track regularly, I can assure my patient and myself that the changes she's experiencing are related to the treatment—and if there's a different, more ominous change, I can distinguish it from the others.

For the same reasons, your surgeon will probably want you to have mammograms every six months for a year or two, and then once a year. In addition to monitoring the treated breast, we watch your other breast for the possible development of a new cancer. Women with cancer in one breast have an increased risk of getting it in the other breast. This is *not* an inevitability: your risk is about 1 percent per year, or an average of 15 percent.[1] (See page 274 for a discussion of the second primary cancer.) There are some types of cancer that indicate a greater propensity for a second cancer to develop. Cancers with a lot of lobular carcinoma in situ (see page 194) have been thought to fit into this category.[2] Even in this situation, however, the increased risk to the second breast is about double, or 2 percent per year, with a cumulative risk of 30 percent. Obviously, the younger you are and the longer you live the more chance you will have to develop a second cancer. If this is too scary for you, you may want to consider a preventive mastectomy on the other side (total, not subcutaneous: see page 150), but I find that most women prefer close follow-up to such a drastic step.

Sometimes it won't be just one doctor who follows you. You may be followed by your whole team—your radiation therapist and/or your chemotherapist (oncologist) might also want to check on you regularly. Some patients find this a little overwhelming, and don't want to spend all that time trekking back and forth to doctors. I don't think it's all that necessary, as long as one person is following you regularly—and as long as that person is some kind of cancer specialist. You don't want to be followed only by your local family doctor, who may not have much experience with breast cancer. I had one patient who'd had wide excision and radiation, and her first mammogram after that showed skin thickening and edema: her family doctor told her the cancer had come back. She called me in a panic and came to see me, convinced she was dying—when in fact both findings were perfectly normal in the wake of radiation and surgery.

In the past, we did the staging tests described on page 229 every year. Today we're more aware of what these tests can and can't do, so we tend to hold off on them until we're convinced there's a reason to do them. Since they only find large cancers, doing them once a year when the patient has shown no symptoms is rarely helpful. We're unlikely to detect a cancer even if it has recurred; in the meantime, you're being subjected to the possible side effects of the tests themselves, and to a false sense of security if they come out negative. And the early diagnosis of recurrent systemic cancer does not improve the prognosis.[3] So unless you're taking part in a protocol that requires regular staging tests, you may not want to have them.

With some cancers we can be reasonably sure that if they haven't recurred within a few years, they won't. Breast cancer, however, isn't one of them. It's usually a slow-growing cancer, and there are people who have had recurrences 10 or even 20 years after the original diagnosis. So you really have to see it as a chronic disease: don't expect a recurrence, but be prepared for it.

Time does, however, affect the likelihood of recurrence—the longer you go without a recurrence, the less likely you are to have one. So going 10 years without the cancer coming back should give you reason for optimism, if not certainty.

Types of Recurrence

How will you know if a recurrence appears? The cancer can come back locally, in the breast area, or in another part of the body, like the bones or liver.

There are three ways it can come back in the breast area, and they mean different things. Most commonly, it can come back in the area of the original cancer. If you've had a wide excision and radiation, it can come back in the breast itself. (See Figure 26-1.) In this case, we see it not as a spread but as leftover cancer inadequately treated in the first place. (See page 259 for a discussion of why and how this happens.) Studies of women who've had this kind of reappearance of cancer in the breast itself show that their likelihood of dying of the disease is not much greater than that of women who haven't had this sort of recurrence.[4] The first step to take if a local recurrence is detected is to repeat the staging tests (see page 229) to make sure that there is no sign of cancer anywhere else in the body. If the tests are normal (and they usually are), then we have to figure out what is best to do to eradicate the tumor from the breast. Usually in these

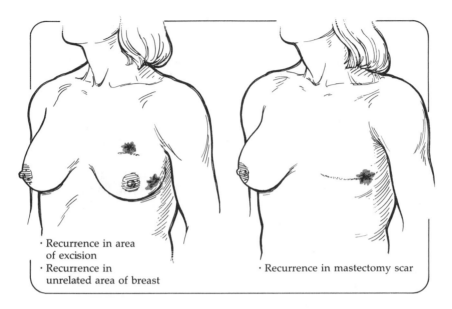

· Recurrence in area
  of excision
· Recurrence in
  unrelated area of breast

· Recurrence in mastectomy scar

FIGURE 26-1

cases we do a mastectomy, since the less drastic surgery and radiation didn't take care of it before. (In France they're experimenting with just doing another wide excision; so far we don't know how effective that will turn out to be.) When we do a mastectomy in this setting, we often include immediate reconstruction with a muscle flap (see page 353). The skin has been irradiated and may not heal as well, so the added tissue from the back or abdomen, with its own blood supply, will not only give a good cosmetic result but also help healing. This type of local recurrence is *not* considered a metastasis and does not imply spread anywhere else in the body. In this way it is very different from the type of recurrence that occurs following a mastectomy.

Another type of local recurrence is one in the lymph nodes under the arm. Now that we are taking out fewer lymph nodes (see page 287), a cancerous node may be left behind. This is rare, about 2 percent.[5] Further treatment to this area with either surgery or radiation will often take care of the problem. Recurrence in lymph nodes elsewhere, such as in the neck or above the collarbone, has a more serious implication, since these are probably metastases. They are more akin to local recurrence following mastectomy and usually warrant a more aggressive approach.

If the local recurrence is in the scar or chest wall after a mastectomy, it's also very serious. (See Figure 26-1.) Since you don't have any breast tissue left, the cancer can't be residual; it can only have gotten there from the bloodstream or lymphatic system. And it's probably in other areas of your body as well. Studies confirm this: most women who have this kind of recurrence will usually have cancer show up elsewhere within two years.[6]

Finally, cancer can metastasize in the area of the second breast. This can be in the breast itself or in the fat right under the skin— just as you can get a recurrence in the scar or in the chest wall after a mastectomy. This is fairly rare.

Such recurrence is, of course, metastasis, and with metastatic cancer, we can't cure you. But we *can* do a lot for you. We can relieve your discomfort, and we can put you into a remission that in some cases will last for many years. For example, if the cancer appears in the vertebrae or in other bones, and is painful, we can radiate the area and shrink the cancer, thus eliminating the pain for a time. You'll probably be fine for several months or even several years, and then it will come back in, say, your lungs, and since we can't radiate the lungs we'll give you something systemic—either chemotherapy or hormone therapy—and again, you'll be fine for a time. Eventually it will come back in enough places, or with enough severity, that it starts to tip the balance and the cancer cells will win. But usually that takes a significant period of time, and for most of that time, you'll feel all right. I had one patient, a teacher in an elementary school, whose cancer was fairly aggressive: in fact, the metastasis showed up while she was in the midst of her original chemotherapy treatment. It appeared in her lungs, so she was given hormone treatment—in this case, they altered her hormones by removing her ovaries—and the lung lesions disappeared. Two years later they resurfaced, and she was given a hormone blocker, tamoxifen. Again the lesions disappeared. A year and a half later they returned and she was treated with a different hormone; they returned again in nine months and she was given chemotherapy. She lived for another year. Although she did finally die from her cancer, systemic treatment gave her six years, during which time she raised her son and taught school.

The time your metastasized cancer is under control is called a "remission." Unlike a cure, a remission implies that the cancer will come back at some point, so it's a somewhat tentative state. It's also, in the long run, an undefinable state. We can't really know how long you'll be in remission: it can be for a few months or 20 years, or anything in between.

Even with the cancers we define as "incurable," there are always the miracles—the person who shouldn't have been cured, whose condition strongly suggested she'd only live a few more months and who lived on for years. In any study, there are always 1 or 2 or 3 percent of people who don't fit into the overall pattern. I had one patient who had breast cancer when she was quite young, and her doctors told her she had "galloping breast cancer." I don't know exactly what that means—I've never seen it in a medical dictionary—but it sounds pretty ominous, and they obviously thought she wasn't going to last too long. She had a radical mastectomy and was fine for 17 years. Then she found a lump in her armpit on the side where her cancer had been—that's when she came to me. The lump was a recurrence of her cancer. We treated it with hormone therapy, and she went into remission two years ago. How long that remission will last, I don't know, and probably she'll eventually die from her cancer. But that's an awfully slow gallop.

I've said that we can't cure a metastatic cancer, and that's true—today, as I write this. But we're doing a lot of research, and learning new things every day. If you've got a slow-growing cancer, and you're in remission, it's possible that by the time your cancer returns, we will have advanced still farther—far enough to keep you alive for many more years, and perhaps even to cure your cancer. We're not there yet, but we do have reason to be hopeful (see Chapter 27).

The Symptoms of Recurrence

Once you've had cancer, you're naturally nervous about your body. How can you trust it after it's betrayed you? Normal aches and pains suddenly seem abnormal: is this a tension headache, or has the cancer spread to your brain? You've got a stomachache—or is that the cancer in your liver? All of a sudden an ache that you might have had a hundred times before and never noticed is terrifying, and you know you're dying. And the breast or the scar has all kinds of weird sensations from tingling to shooting pains to aches and pulls. All this constantly reminds you of your recent experience.

There's nothing neurotic or hypochondriacal about this. You had assumed you were all right once before, and then found out a tumor had been growing in your body for years. You're watching your body in a way you never did before, and you're confused about how to interpret what's going on in it. It usually takes two or three years for a cancer survivor to learn to trust her own body again, and to trust her own sense of what's normal and what's dangerous. (This was discussed further on page 244.)

Meanwhile, don't hesitate to call your doctor if anything scares you. I get calls all the time from patients who have symptoms that scare them, and it only takes me a minute or so to say, "No, breast cancer almost never recurs in that way." Eventually, you'll recapture your sense of what's normal and what's not, but until then, any medical care provider should be willing and glad to help relieve your very reasonable anxieties.

What are the real danger signs? When I do follow-up examinations, there are a few things I'm looking for. In the breast or mastectomy scar I look for lumps. I check the neck and above the collarbone for lumps which might indicate a lymph node, and I feel under both arms. Once a year or once every six months we do a mammogram.

In addition, I question the woman very carefully about how she is feeling. When breast cancer spreads to the bones, it's almost always to the big bones—hips, thighs, backbones—not to knees or elbows or ankles. So I check to see if the patient has had any persistent pain in those bones. (Most of the time, however, it won't mean anything: lower-back pain is very common in America, and having breast cancer doesn't make you immune to it.) When the cancer has spread to the lungs, it may just show up on an X ray or it could cause a persistent dry cough that doesn't go away. Once again, most coughs are going to be fairly innocent. Much less frequently, it shows up as shortness of breath. In the liver, breast cancer rarely shows symptoms until it's very far advanced—then it will probably appear as jaundice, or as a pain in the right upper quadrant of the abdomen. Occasionally there's a recurrence in the brain, which may show as an unchanging headache that lasts for weeks, or a blocking of part of your visual field, or numbness or tingling in your fingers or toes, caused by the pressure on the brain. In general, if you have any symptom that doesn't go away in a week or two, check it out.

Usually, that's what my patients do anyway—it's unusual that I'll find something on a follow-up that the patient hasn't already noticed. Patients are often surprised that I haven't found anything: they've been waiting for the cancer to pop up again, and tend to be very anxious about examinations and sure I'll find something. Often they're especially anxious on the anniversary of their original diagnosis—and my examination serves a psychological purpose as well as a medical one.

If a recurrence occurs it is often more devastating than the original diagnosis. Your body has betrayed you again and this time it is even more serious. It becomes hard to trust your doctors, and hard to believe that anything will work. It is important to take time to acknowledge these feelings and to get counseling or other support if necessary. Talking to women who have been through it is probably the most helpful.

Treatment

If your cancer *has* spread, the first step is to repeat the initial staging tests in order to figure out the extent of the problem. The treatments are basically the same as for the first occurrence. There are more limitations, however. You can only radiate a certain area once, so we won't use radiation if we've already done so. Surgery can only be performed in limited conditions: a cancerous tissue that is easy to cut out without damaging other structures. Even chemotherapy has its restrictions. Some drugs have severe side effects if more than a certain dosage is given. Overdoses of Adriamycin, for example, can cause serious heart problems. So the treatment must be tailored to the problem. The goal is also different: in adjuvant therapy, we're trying to cure you; with metastatic cancer, we're trying to prolong your life and alleviate your symptoms. (Chemotherapy and radiation for metastatic cancer are discussed on pages 306, 325, and 327.)

Often people ask their doctor, "How long have I got to live?" I never answer that—not because I want to withhold information from my patient, but because I simply don't know. There are statistical likelihoods, but they never cover everyone. There are patients who, according to the statistics, should die in three months and they live three years; there are others who should last three years and die in three months. I'm always amazed at the variations. One of my patients had a small cancer and negative nodes, with what should have been a good prognosis, but when she finished her radiation we discovered the cancer had metastasized to her lungs, and she died in three months. It often works the other way, as in the case of my patient with the so-called galloping cancer. Another patient, a Chinese woman who spoke no English, had a cancer that was very bad and I privately thought she wouldn't live very long. I had to talk to her through her sons, who kept trying to get me to say how long she had. I wouldn't tell them. It's a good thing, because seven years later, she's still alive. Sometimes I think she's lived so long because she didn't know she was supposed to die!

At the same time, it's important for your doctor to be honest with you. I think it's sensible to say to a patient who has asked, "This is serious, but we don't know how long you'll live until we see how you respond to treatment. You'll probably eventually die of breast cancer, and you probably won't live another 40 years, so you may want to plan your life with that in mind." If you insist on more specific predictions, a doctor may quote statistics—but you should always be reminded that there are exceptions to statistics. Even if 99 out of a hundred patients in your condition die within a year, one out of a hundred doesn't—and there's no reason to assume you won't be that one.

Eventually, however, there comes the hardest part for a doctor. We've tried all the available treatments, and we know that you don't have much longer. Even then, we don't know if it's days or weeks, and even then, there is still the possibility of a miracle. But there's a point at which you're clearly dying, and you have a right to know that. It used to be the prevailing belief that it was better not to tell patients they were dying. But this sets up an unhealthy climate of denial. Often the patient senses it herself, but since no one else wants to talk about it she pretends it's okay in order to spare them, and they pretend it's okay in order to spare her. Such denial can keep you from finishing up your business—clearing up relationships, saying good-bye, saying the things you won't get another chance to say to the people you love, giving them the chance to say those things to you. I think doctors make a great error in denying death: we tend to look at it too much as a defeat, and to get caught up in our own denial, at the patient's expense.

None of us is immortal, and death can come for anyone at any time. While you're still feeling fairly well, you might want to talk with your doctor, and with your family members or friends, about how you want to die when the time comes. Do you want extraordinary measures taken, or not? Do you want to die at home, or in the hospital? Do you want to be heavily medicated or as alert as possible? No way is universally better, but one way might be better for you. If your wishes are clearly known—especially if they can be documented in a living will—you might be able to prevent one of those tragic situations where doctors and family members fight over whether to keep a patient on a life-support system.

These questions are important for every one of us to consider, since none of us will live forever. Of course, you may live another 10 or 20 years anyway—but you haven't lost anything by having those discussions, and you might even have gained a little peace of mind.

27

The Future

We've made a lot of progress in treating breast cancer in recent years. But the discoveries being made now by cancer researchers are so vast, and their potential to virtually eliminate the disease is so great, that the real excitement is in the future, not the present.

Surgery, radiation, and chemotherapy are all gross ways to deal with disease. The real answer is on the molecular level. If you look at the history of how we've dealt with any disease, you'll see that, when we don't yet understand it, we do things like surgery. As we begin to get a real understanding of the disease and its causes, instead of counting on surgery, we start acting to prevent it or to cure it at a much earlier stage. For example, in the area of heart disease, when it gets severe enough to be atherosclerosis, the "gross" way to deal with it is through bypass surgery: you've got a plugged-up artery and the surgeon makes a detour around it. This helps, and it's worth doing. But it would be far more effective if we could find a way to unplug the artery—and that's what some of the new laser treatments, angioplasties, and drug therapies are working on now. What would be even better would be to prevent atherosclerosis in the first place—keeping cholesterol levels and blood pressure down early on, so that you'd never get to the point where you needed surgery. Today in some medical circles, coronary artery disease is considered a pediatric concern: it's pediatricians who are working on it, developing new diets, checking cholesterol levels, and devising exercise schedules so that the seeds of later heart disease won't get planted in children.

Cancer, too, is still discovered and treated at a relatively late stage: as we noted on page 210, even such "early detection" methods as mammography can detect a tumor only when it's been around for about six years. If we had a way of detecting the abnormal cells at a very early stage, or of figuring out what makes them malignant in the first place, we'd be much better able to cure the cancer—and without the rugged and sometimes disfiguring treatments we must use today.

Researchers have already found that among the viruses that cause cancers in animals, each has a specific gene that is responsible for starting and maintaining the cancer. These genes appear to be derived from normal genes called *proto-oncogenes*. (Readers may find the glossary of particular help in this chapter.) Proto-oncogenes control the cell's growth or turnover. Because of how they function, certain parts of your body grow at different rates. Your hair grows at a relatively speedy rate, so you have to get it cut every couple of months. Different parts of your skin turn over at different rates. Your permanent teeth don't turn over at all. Your liver and heart make a few new cells now and again, but not many—so if they're irreparably damaged you need a transplant; you can't remove them and expect your body to make new ones. All these types of cells grow for a period and, more importantly, stop growing after a certain period.

If there's a mutation on a proto-oncogene, or if more than the usual number of proto-oncogenes are directing things, the message may change. Instead of saying, "Turn over and grow every six weeks and then stop," it may say, "Turn over and grow every six days," or even "every six minutes"; and the message to stop may be left out entirely. (See Figure 27-1.) Suddenly the tissue is getting a new message, and certain restrictions and limitations on growth are no longer there. So when we say that cancer cells are out of control, what we mean is that the oncogenes are giving them the wrong messages, making the cells grow without control and allowing them to take over normal structures.[1] Probably there are other factors as well—the organ that the newly programmed cell finds itself in, the availability of a sufficient blood supply, the right nutrients for the cancerous cell to thrive on, and the growth factors (see below). But the oncogenes do seem to have a very significant role in starting cancer.

The question then arises, is it that these genes are just sitting around and then all of a sudden they mutate, triggering the cancer

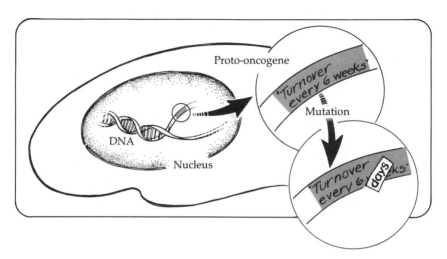

Proto-oncogene

"Turnover every 6 weeks"

Mutation

"Turnover every 6 days"

DNA

Nucleus

FIGURE 27-1

process? Or are you born with a gene that has something wrong with it already, and in a certain environment or milieu it is activated? In the latter case, perhaps people with a family history of a particular cancer might be born with the mutated gene, and then another factor—diet, perhaps, or environmental pollutants—interacts with it and it becomes a new oncogene. If this is what happens, perhaps we could devise a test on the DNA of people with a particular family history, a test that would pick up the mutant gene.

An example of this situation has actually been shown for *retino-blastoma* (a rare eye cancer that sometimes runs in families and other times is sporadic). Researchers have found that for each gene there is an anti-oncogene which keeps the oncogene turned off. When two anti-oncogenes are deleted the cells grow without control and the patient has retinoblastoma. In the patient with a family history there is already one anti-oncogene gone and it only takes one further deletion to get to cancer. In those without a family history there needs to be two deletions to get to cancer. There is now a screening test for this anti-oncogene which can tell if you are at high risk or not. This work is important not because retinoblastoma is such a common disease, but because it is a model from which we can learn how to understand the process of malignancy. Breast cancer probably isn't as simple. However, the work with retinoblastoma gives us hope that we will one day be able to apply its accomplishments to more complex cancers.

It would be great if we could identify an oncogene for genetic breast cancer. With this gene identified, maybe we could do genetic engineering, with a virus or something like it, to alter the nature of the DNA and normalize it, so the person would never get that cancer. If this could work, it would probably work only on the small percentage of the people who would eventually get the particular cancer—those with a family history, whom we could screen in childhood.

Women without a family history of breast cancer, while not born with that oncogene, can develop it sometime later in life. Could we screen every woman for the breast cancer oncogene when she's 20? Or when she's 35? Or 50?

One problem with research on breast cancer is that unlike retinoblastoma it is a heterogeneous disease. That means there are many different types of cells involved in one cancer and probably many different oncogenes. And the oncogenes involved in one woman's cancer are probably different from those in another's. All oncogenes aren't necessarily the same, and we might have to do a different test for each one. This makes breast cancer a much harder puzzle to unravel.

Finally, we are finding that the number of oncogenes or proto-oncogenes may well be a predictor of the severity of the cancer. If you compare two stage 2 breast cancers (i.e., those in which the lymph nodes have shown up positive), you may well be able to predict which one will be more virulent by looking at the number of oncogenes each contains. Some early data seem to indicate that oncogenes may even be helpful in differentiating ductal carcinomas in situ.[2] This type of information will be helpful in determining who should get the more aggressive treatments in the future.

Another area of study is *growth factors*. Cancer cells create these substances and release them into their environment to make it more suitable for them. These factors stimulate the development of blood vessels to supply nutrients, allowing cells to stick together and even helping them invade the bloodstream and travel to other parts of the body. (See Figure 27-2.) Eventually, the cancer cells are able to take over the vital parts of the body, and the patient dies. Researchers are trying to develop a blocker for the receptor that directs the production of a particular growth factor. That way we could prevent the tumor from growing by blocking only its particular growth factors and leaving the rest of the cells alone, unlike chemotherapy, which blocks the growth of any cell that happens to be dividing. In short, we could poison the cancer without poisoning the person. This may be what happens in hormone therapy. It appears that the hormone blocker tamoxifen may also block the production of growth factors (see page 324).

Other research concentrates not on ways to prevent the cancer cell

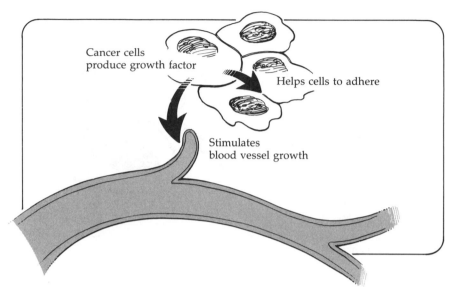

FIGURE 27-2

from existing in the first place, but on ways to detect and stop it at a very early stage of its growth—perhaps when there are only one or two cells in the body.

Another area of exploration is in *monoclonal antibodies*[3]—antibodies made in the lab—that would work against cancer cells the way your own body's antibodies work against bacteria. Monoclonal antibodies are proteins matched to a cancer cell, somewhat the way a key is matched up to a lock. A little tag could be put on the antibody, something that could be picked up by a scanner. Then the antibody could be injected into the bloodstream where it would search for a cancer cell and, if it found one, attach itself to it. (See Figure 27-3.) A scan could then identify the presence of cancer cells.

This could be helpful in two ways. Women could have scans for breast cancer yearly, along with a mammogram, as a routine form of early detection; any cells found could potentially be destroyed. If cancer had already been found, the test could determine if there were microscopic cancer cells elsewhere in your body. So far, however, the antibodies that have been developed are not sensitive or specific enough to track down only breast cancer cells, or even only cancer cells.

For example, some investigators have tried using a monoclonal antibody to determine whether the lymph nodes of patients were positive or not. They injected it in the hand, under the skin, scanned the armpit a couple of hours later, and tried to predict, on the basis

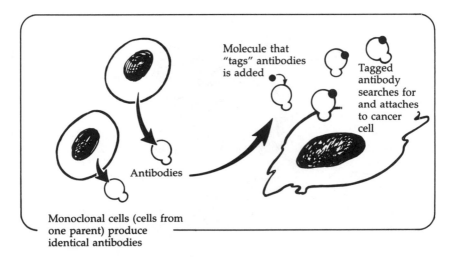

Molecule that "tags" antibodies is added

Tagged antibody searches for and attaches to cancer cell

Antibodies

Monoclonal cells (cells from one parent) produce identical antibodies

FIGURE 27-3

of the test, who had positive lymph nodes. After the usual operation had removed the patient's lymph nodes, it turned out that they were right in only 50 percent of the cases. The antibody wasn't sensitive or specific enough; it attached not only to breast cells but to other cells as well.

Despite our current failures, however, I would predict that within 10 or 20 years, we won't need to remove lymph nodes to determine whether the cancer has actively spread. The kind of chemotherapy we do now will not be necessary. Instead, we may attach the molecule of a powerful drug to the antibody so that it becomes a kind of delivery system, a little kamikaze pilot that attaches to the cancer cell and blows it up on contact. Only the cancer cell will be harmed, and the painful side effects of chemotherapy will become a thing of the past.

Another area of research I've been involved in at Beth Israel Hospital and now at the Faulkner Hospital in Boston is a blood test for cancer, based on lipoproteins.[4] *Lipoproteins* are the proteins that carry fat around in the bloodstream. We've discovered that in people with cancer the lipoproteins change a little bit, and that, if a nuclear magnetic resonance (NMR) test is done on the blood of people with cancer, that difference can be detected.

The problem so far is that we don't know how specific the test is. The first experiments were done on people who had extensive cancer and on people with no cancer at all—not on people with early cancers. They found that the people with extensive cancer had abnormal tests compared to those with no cancer. This has left several questions unanswered. Would it show on people with a little bit of cancer? If it did show and we took the cancer out, would the next test show normal, or would it stay abnormal because the person had once had cancer? If it shows normal, will repeated tests show if the cancer has come back again? And how many cancer cells must be in the person's body to make the test positive? All these questions are being looked at now—many of my own patients are involved in the protocols. We draw their blood before their operations, then follow them 6 and 12 months later with more blood tests to see what happens; then we see how our information fits with how well they do.

There are other questions to deal with before we do this as a screening test. Suppose we do a blood test and it comes back positive, but nothing shows up as a lump or a calcification on a mammogram? We can do all kinds of screening tests to see if the patient has cancer, but what if they all come out negative? It won't tell us what kind of a cancer, so we can't use chemotherapy, which varies from cancer to cancer, or surgery or radiation, both of which require knowledge of the cancer's site. So at least for now, it's not a feasible screening test for cancer. We have reason to be hopeful, however, that continued research will uncover ways to make it more useful.

Perhaps our best hope for treating cancer lies in mobilizing the body's own immune forces, which fight off cancers once they've appeared in the body (see Chapters 15 and 24). With all the research being done on AIDS, which destroys the immune system, we're learning much more than we ever knew about how that system works. The research is likely not only to help cure AIDS, but also cancers and other diseases. One of these new areas of investigation is *biological response modifiers*.[5] These include natural factors that can be used to help increase the body's normal immune response. For example, *lymphokines* are the messengers of the immune system that activate the armies of killer cells mobilized to fight foreign invaders. These lymphokines, such as *interleukin-2*, trigger killer cells; while *tumor necrosis factor* kills cancer cells itself, as well as directing other cells to kill them. The interferons (alpha, beta, and gamma) both activate white blood cells and kill cancer cells.

In one technique, lymphocytes (a type of white blood cell) are removed from a patient with cancer and activated by interleukin-2 to their "killer state," then given back to the patient in the hope that they'll attack and kill the cancer cells. The preliminary studies have shown some promise, but so far, the side effects are high and some patients have even died from the treatment.[6] Further research will probably help us refine the techniques. Another kind of biological response modifier is being used to modify the side effects of chemotherapy. *Colony stimulating factor* is a growth factor that can be used to stimulate the bone marrow into making more blood cells. This won't itself kill cancer cells but it will allow us to give higher doses of chemotherapy without wiping out the bone marrow. These various "biologicals" are being used in various clinical trials now in an effort to find their best application in cancer treatment.

Some of the "alternative healing" methods we discussed in Chapter 24 may also help us in this area. As they, too, become more sophisticated and well-honed, we may find better and better ways to teach the body how to fight off the invading cancer cells. For instance, there's a lot of experimentation on the effects of stress on the immune system in cancer patients.[7]

The work on arresting cancer at an early stage is moving forward on many fronts. Meanwhile, our techniques of radiation and chemotherapy are also being refined every day. As these treatments are currently used, they aim at the rapidly dividing cancer cells, but in the process they harm normal rapidly dividing cells as well. In both cases, however, techniques are being developed that will enable us to treat only the specific cancer cells and leave the healthy cells alone. For instance, radiation sensitizers are being developed.[8] Particular tissues may be sensitized in such a way that they'll respond more to radiation than other tissues. Interestingly, chemotherapy is one sensitizer. Chemotherapy also sensitizes to hyperthermia (heating tissues to super-high temperatures).[9] In some cases this alone kills cancer cells; in others using chemotherapy to sensitize the tissue may make a difference.[10]

In chemotherapy itself, there's a vast array of new drugs under study all the time, as well as inquiries into ways of administering the drugs. And different ways of combining surgery, radiation, and chemotherapy are being worked on. For example, one protocol I'm working with is looking at whether it's more helpful to do radiation before chemotherapy or vice versa.

The more we come to understand cancer at a basic level, the more we'll learn about how to treat and even prevent it. There's no question in my mind that we're going to accomplish this within my lifetime. I think it will be like tuberculosis. In my parents' youth, if you had TB, you went to a sanitarium. No one knew how to treat it, so there were all these textbooks arguing about whether or not your lung should be collapsed, whether or not you should be treated with radiation, and which of the many operations for it was best. It was known as "the great masquerader" because it was so hard to diagnose. There were specialists who worked with nothing but TB. Once the germ (the tubercle bacillus) was identified and an antibiotic was found to kill it, all these treatments were dropped. Today, all we do is a skin test; if it's positive we put you on an antibiotic or two for a year, and that's that. Within a generation, the sanitariums have closed down, all the textbooks ended up in antique shops, and all the specialists had to turn to something else. A good friend of mine, a chest surgeon in his 60s who's now doing lung cancer surgery, was trained on doing lung surgery for TB.

Polio, too, has virtually vanished, though many of us are old enough to remember how terrifying it once was, and how hopeless it once seemed. When we finally figured out the cause, a vaccine was found, and all those iron lungs and polio wards are gone.

Though cancer is a complex set of diseases that manifest themselves differently in different organs, we now know that the same basic defect causes all cancers. And we're well on our way to figuring out what that defect is and how to stop it.

Even for people with cancer today, this is a hopeful sign. No matter how "incurable" your cancer is now, the ability of radiation and chemotherapy to help put you into remission may keep you alive until we've discovered more effective treatments, and your remission may become a cure. The women who are now participating in clinical trials are in the vanguard, paving the way to this ultimate cure.

And for the next generation, the outlook is even brighter. It pleases me to think that my daughter won't be able to follow in my footsteps, because there won't be enough breast cancer for her to treat.

And it's nice to think that, in my old age, my expertise won't be that of a practitioner but of an historian, recounting, to a disbelieving audience, what it was like back in the days when breast cancer killed people.

APPENDICES

A

Drugs Used for Systemic Treatment of Breast Cancer

This chart lists drugs, their method(s) of administration, and only common and some less common side effects and toxicities and is not meant to be exhaustive. You should check with your oncologist about your specific drugs. Any unusual signs or symptoms should be reported to your doctor immediately.

I. Chemotherapy

cyclophosphamide (Cytoxan)	oral, IV	**common:** nausea, vomiting, loss of appetite, menstrual irregularities, low blood counts, hair loss
		rare: urinary bladder problems, liver problems, infertility
methotrexate	IV	**common:** nausea, vomiting, mouth sores, low blood counts, conjunctivitis, ulcers, rash
		rare: hair loss, headache, liver problems, blurred vision, lung injury

5 fluorouracil (5-FU)	IV	**common:** mouth sores, nausea, vomiting, diarrhea, low blood counts, loss of appetite, hair loss, sore throat
		rare: rash, nail changes, skin darkening
doxorubicin (Adriamycin)	IV	**common:** hair loss, mouth sores, nausea, vomiting, low blood counts
		rare: heart problems, nail and skin darkening, liver problems
chlorambucil (Leukeran)	oral	**common:** low blood counts, tiredness
		rare: hair loss, nausea, vomiting, menstrual irregularities
melphalan (L–PAM)	oral	**common:** low blood counts, nausea, vomiting
		rare: rash, loss of appetite, mouth sores, lung problems
thiotepa	IV	**common:** low blood count, nausea, vomiting, pain at IV site
		rare: stomach pain, rash, loss of appetite, menstrual irregularities, hair loss, headache, dizziness
vincristine	IV	**common:** hair loss, tingling and numbness in fingers and toes, pain at IV site, constipation, headache
		rare: muscle and jaw pain, loss of reflexes, depression, insomnia
vinblastine (Velban)	IV	**common:** nausea, vomiting, low blood count, hair loss
		rare: numbness and tingling and weakness in hands and feet, jaw pain, constipation
mitomycin	IV	**common:** low blood count, nausea, vomiting
		rare: blood in urine, loss of appetite, mouth sores, hair loss, rash, lung or kidney damage
mitoxanthrone	IV	**common:** low blood count, mild nausea, vomiting, bluish discoloration along vein, blue-green urine
		rare: hair loss

II. Hormonal Therapy

tamoxifen (Nolvadex)	oral	**common:** hot flashes, temporary nausea, vaginal discharge or itching **rare:** headache, flare of bone pain, depression
progestins (Megace)	oral	**common:** weight gain, edema, breast tenderness **rare:** carpal tunnel syndrome, hair loss
aminoglutethimide	oral	**common:** sleepiness, fatigue, rash **rare:** low thyroid, headache, liver toxicity, may need cortisone replacement
diethylstilbestrol (DES)	oral	**common:** weight gain due to fluid retention, nausea, increase in blood pressure, breast swelling and tenderness **rare:** blood clots, increased body hair
fluoxymesterone (Halotestin)	oral	**common:** fluid retention, lowering of voice, skin changes, increased libido, changes in period **rare:** nausea, vomiting, liver damage
prednisone	oral	**common:** mood changes, increased appetite, fluid retention **rare:** after prolonged use: acne, muscle weakness, diabetes, high blood pressure

Common combinations of chemotherapy used in breast cancer:

CMF   (Cytoxan, methotrexate, 5-FU)
CAF   (Cytoxan, Adriamycin, 5-FU)
CMFVP (Cytoxan, methotrexate, 5-FU, vincristine, prednisone)
CFP   (Cytoxan, 5-FU, prednisone)
FAC   (5-FU, Adriamycin, Cytoxan)

B

How to Lower the Fat
in Your Diet

Purpose: To reduce the percentage of calories coming from fat to 20 percent

1. Figure out how much fat you are currently eating.
   a. Keep a food diary for several days. Religiously write down everything you eat and estimate the amount.
   b. Get a booklet (U.S. Dept. of Agriculture's "Nutritive Value of American Foods." Agriculture handbook #456) that lists the fat and caloric content of most common foods and calculate the total number of grams of fat and total number of calories you have eaten. One gram of fat equals 9 calories. For each day's totals make this calculation:

$$\frac{\text{total number of grams of fat} \times 9}{\text{total number of calories}} \times 100 = \% \text{ of calories coming from fat}$$

   This will give you an idea of where you are starting from.

2. Start a low-fat diet, being especially careful to decrease animal fats.
   a. Foods high in fat: beef, pork, lamb, and luncheon meats, most dairy products, most desserts, oils, margarines, butter
   b. Foods low in fat: fruits, vegetables, simple grains, soups (except creamed), beans, legumes
   c. Diet principles:
      • Visible fat (butter, cream, margarine, salad dressing) is restricted to 1 teaspoon per meal
      • Only lean meats (cut the fat off and use only lean cuts) and only 2–3 servings per week; emphasize fish and chicken

- No fried foods, gravies, cream sauces, whipped cream, cheese sauces
- Prepare foods without added fat: broil, bake, or stew
- Increase your consumption of fruits, vegetables, rice, pasta, whole-grain breads, cereals, beans

3. Repeat the food diary and recalculate your percentage of fat to see how you are doing.

Sample meal plan:

calories	1600–1800
protein	70–75 grams
fat	up to 27 grams
carbohydrates	260–280 grams

Breakfast		*Luncheon and Dinner*	
fruit juice	½ cup	broth or juice	½ cup
cereal	½ cup	lean meat or beans	2 oz
toast	1 slice	potato or rice or grain	½ cup
margarine	1 tsp	vegetable	½ cup
jelly	1 tsp	salad	½ cup
skim milk	1 cup	bread	1 slice
coffee or tea		margarine	1 tsp
		fruit or dessert	½–1 cup
		skim milk	1 cup
		coffee or tea	

C

Resources, References, and Additional Reading*

This listing has been culled from my own experience as well as from many other sources. Individuals are listed only if I think they provide a unique service. Although I believe each listing is helpful, I am not personally familiar with every one, and I welcome any comments, feedback, and additions that readers may have. These can be sent to the Faulkner Breast Centre, 1153 Centre Street, Jamaica Plain, MA 02130.

Many of the cancer-related pamphlets listed below are from one of the following three major organizations.

American Cancer Society. For materials listed contact your local American Cancer Society unit or state chartered division. If the material is not available locally, contact the ACS National Office, 15999 Clifton Road NE, Atlanta, GA 30329. (404) 320-3333.

National Cancer Institute. Order all materials from Public Inquiry Section, Office of Cancer Communications, National Cancer Institute, Building 31, Room 10 A 24, Bethesda, MD 20892. 1-800-4CANCER

NABCO. Order all NABCO Fact Sheets and *NABCO News* articles from The National Alliance of Breast Cancer Organizations, 1180 Avenue of the Americas, Second Floor, New York, NY 10036. (212) 719-0154.

*Parts of this list have been adapted from the December 1990 NABCO Resource List and are used here with their kind permission. This list is revised annually and can be obtained by writing to NABCO.

Part I.
The Healthy Breast

NORMAL FEMALE ANATOMY AND DEVELOPMENT

National Women's Health Network, 1325 G Street NW, Washington, DC 20005. *Written packets and booklets on many aspects of women's health, including menopause and benign and malignant breast diseases.*

Daphna Ayalah and Isaac J. Weinstock, *Breasts: Women Speak about Their Breasts and Their Lives* (New York: Summit Books, 1979). *Wonderful book of photographs and interviews about women and their breasts. Out of print but may still be available in some libraries.*

The Boston Women's Health Book Collective (a source of information on all issues of women's health), 47 Nichols Ave., Watertown, MA 02172, (617) 924-0271, the authors of *The New Our Bodies Ourselves* (New York: Simon and Schuster, 1984). *Still the feminist's bible for women's health issues.*

Penny Wise Budoff, M.D., *No More Menstrual Cramps and Other Good News* (New York: Penguin Books, 1980) $6.95.

Paula Brown Doress and Diana Laskin Siegel and the Midlife and Older Women Book Project, *Ourselves, Growing Older* (New York: Simon and Schuster, 1987). *Good overview of midlife and beyond, written in cooperation with the Boston Women's Health Book Collective.*

Sadja Greenwood, M.D., *Menopause Naturally: Preparing for the Second Half of Life* (Volcano, California: Volcano Press, P.O. Box 270, Volcano, CA 95689, 1984, revised 1989). $11.95. *Good discussions of menopause without hormone replacement therapy and the risks of hormonal replacement.*

Rosetta Reitz, *Menopause: A Positive Approach* (New York: Penguin Books, 1977).

"A Step by Step Guide to BSE." Primary Care and Cancer, P.O. Box 86, Williston Park, NY 11596. *A good detailed instruction.*

"Special Touch: A Personal Plan of Action for Breast Health" (2095-LE/87). American Cancer Society. BSE instructions. (Also available in Spanish.)

BREASTFEEDING

La Leche League International, P.O. Box 1209, Franklin Park, IL 60131-8209. *Best source of support and information about breastfeeding. Send a stamped self-addressed envelope to LLLI and request a copy of the LLLI directory (No. 504). This publication lists two key representatives of every area of the United States and 43 other countries. Contact the particular representative for names and addresses of groups near you. The League is very zealous about the virtues of breastfeeding. If you're ambivalent, they may not be the best resource for you. In addition, the La Leche League has over 200 information sheets, reprints, and booklets covering many aspects of breastfeeding, including such topics as sore nipples, prevention of plugged ducts and breast infections, nursing twins, nursing an adopted child, and nursing and working. A catalogue (No. 501) will be sent if you send a stamped, self-addressed business-size envelope. For information in languages other than English, ask for the Translation List (No. 508).*

Marsha Walker and Jeanne Watson Driscoll, "Expressing, Storing and Transporting Breastmilk." Pamphlet available from Lactation Associates, Educators and Consultants to Health Care Professionals, 254 Conant Road, Weston, MA 02193.

Margot Edwards, "A Working Mother Can Breastfeed When . . ." Pennypress, Inc. Available through ICEA, P.O. Box 20048, Minneapolis, MN 55420.

La Leche League International, *The Womanly Art of Breastfeeding,* 3d edition (New York: New American Library, 1981, 4th edition, 1987). *A very supportive book.*

Ruth Lawrence, *Breastfeeding: A Guide for the Medical Profession,* 3d edition (St. Louis: Mosby, 1989). *Written by a professor of pediatrics, this is a good source of scientific information as well as practical advice about breastfeeding.*

VARIATIONS AND PLASTIC SURGERY

American Society of Plastic and Reconstructive Surgeons, 444 East Algonquin Road, Arlington Heights, IL 60005. (312) 228-9900; (800) 635-0635 (referral message tape). *Will provide written information and mail a list of certified reconstructive surgeons by geographical area after caller provides details on above (800) message tape.*

Command-Trust Network, Cosmetic Surgery Division, P.O. Box 17082, Covington, KY 41017. *For women who wish to contact other women in regard to breast implant concerns.*

A draft of a pamphlet, and eventually the pamphlet, containing basic information about silicone implants, can be obtained from the Dockets Management Branch (HFA-305), Room 4-62, Food and Drug Administration, 5600 Fishers Lane, Rockville, MD 20857.

The Maryland informed consent statement regarding silicone implants can be obtained by writing the Maryland Dept. of Health and Mental Hygiene, Family Health Administration, Division of Cancer Control and High Blood Pressure, 201 West Preston Street, Room 320, Baltimore, MD 21201.

Robert Goldwyn, *The Patient and the Plastic Surgeon* (Boston: Little, Brown, 1981). *An easy-to-read book written for doctors but very informative for patients as well. Concerns the various procedures and their pitfalls.*

Robert Goldwyn, *Plastic and Reconstructive Surgery of the Breast* (Boston: Little, Brown, 1976). *Medical textbook covering all aspects of breast plastic surgery.*

Part II.
Common Problems of the Breast

American College of Surgeons, 55 East Erie Street, Chicago IL 60611. (312) 664-4050. *Will provide names by geographical area of certified surgeons specializing in breast surgery.*

"Questions and Answers about Breast Lumps" (85-2401, revised 9/83). National Cancer Institute. *This pamphlet describes some of the most common noncancerous breast lumps and what can be done about them.*

Is Fibrocystic Disease of the Breast Precancerous? (May 1986). Questions and answers from the College of American Pathologists. 6 pages. Request from: *CAP*, 325 Waukegan Road, Northfield, IL 60093-2750. (708) 446-8800.

"Breast Biopsy: What You Should Know" (87-657, 7/87). National Cancer Institute. *This pamphlet describes the one- and two-step procedures and what to expect.*

Kerry A. McGinn, R.N., *Keeping Abreast: Breast Changes That Are Not Cancer* (Palo Alto, Calif.: Bull, 1987). $7.95.

Cushman Haagensen, ed., *Diseases of the Breast*, 3d edition (Philadelphia: Saunders, 1986). *This textbook is the ultimate reference for benign breast tumors. His approach to breast cancer is dated.*

Part III.
Risks, Prevention,
and Detection of Breast Cancer

RISKS AND PREVENTION

"Cancer Risk Analysis and DNA Banking." Patricia Kelly, Ph.D. The Breast Health Center, Children's Hospital of San Francisco, 3700 California Street, San Francisco, CA 94118. (415) 750-6420. *Dr. Kelly, a geneticist, will review your family history and other risk factors and help you realistically assess your breast cancer risk.*

Nancy C. Baker, *Relative Risk: living with a family history of breast cancer.* (Viking 1991). *Will be available in the Spring of 1991. Discusses risk factors as well as women's reactions to being at "increased risk."*

I. Craig Henderson, "What Can a Woman Do About Her Risk of Dying of Breast Cancer?" *Current Problems in Cancer,* Vol. 24, No. 4 (July/August 1990). Mosby Year Book. *This is an excellent summary of the literature on risk factors and prevention. Unfortunately it has no magic answers. It will probably have to be obtained in a hospital or medical library.*

"Good News, Better News, Best News . . . Cancer Prevention" (84-2671). *National Cancer Institute. Cancer risks in general and ways to reduce them.*

"Diet Nutrition and Cancer Prevention: A Guide to Food Choices" (87-2878). National Cancer Institute. *This booklet describes what is known about diet, nutrition, and cancer prevention.*

"The Diet Your Doctor Won't Give You" (1987). $1.00. National Women's Health Network, 1325 G Street NW, Washington, DC 20005. *Explains a low-fat diet.*

"Nutrition and Cancer, Cause and Prevention" (3389, /84). American Cancer Society.

Alice Holyoke Bakemeier, "The Potential Role of Vitamins A, C, and E and Selenium in Cancer Prevention," *Oncology Nursing Forum*, Vol. 15, No. 6 (1988): 785–791. *You will probably have to get this from a hospital or medical library. This is a good review of the field in a readable format.*

"DES Exposure: Questions and Answers for Mothers, Daughters and Sons." $2.00. DES Action, 1615 Broadway, Suite 510, Oakland, CA 94612. (415) 465-4011.

"Taking Hormones and Women's Health: Costs, Risks, and Benefits" (1989). National Women's Health Network, 1325 G Street NW, Washington, DC 20005. *An excellent review of the current state of knowledge about postmenopausal hormone therapy.*

DETECTION

"Breast Exams: What You Should Know" (86-2000, 8/86). National Cancer Institute. 14 pages. *This booklet discusses breast cancer screening methods.*

"Other Breast Cancer Diagnostic Techniques: Diaphanography, Thermography and Ultrasound." NABCO Fact Sheet.

National Consortium of Breast Centers, c/o Barbara Rabinowitz, R.N., M.S.W., A.C.S.W., Comprehensive Breast Center, Robert Wood Johnson Medical School, One Robert Wood Johnson Place, CN19, New Brunswick, NJ 08903-0019. *Will send you a list of the breast centers throughout the country that are registered with them. Many are diagnostic only and others are involved in both diagnosis and treatment.*

American College of Radiology, 1891 Preston White Drive, Reston, VA 22091. *Will provide a list of accredited mammography programs.*

Part IV.
Making the Diagnosis of Breast Cancer

BREAST CANCER IN GENERAL

Cancer Information Service, National Cancer Institute. This information service can be reached toll-free at (800) 4-CANCER. *They give information and direction through their national and regional network on all aspects of cancer. Spanish-speaking staff members are available on request.*

Cancer Information Service (Canada). Ontario region only. (800) 263-6750. In other provinces contact the local branch of the Canadian Cancer Society.

National Alliance of Breast Cancer Organizations (NABCO), 1180 Avenue of the Americas, Second Floor, New York, NY 10036. (212) 719-0154. *Central source of information about breast cancer and a lobby for breast cancer patients' legislative concerns. Provides up-to-date information packets and resource list on written request.*

AMC Cancer Research Center's Cancer Information Line. 1-800-525-3777. *Professional cancer counselors provide answers to questions about cancer, support, and advice, and will mail instructive free publications on request. Equipped for deaf and hearing-impaired callers.*

The Komen Alliance. *A comprehensive program for the research, education and treatment of breast disease. Information on screening, BSE, treatment and support, including the booklet "Caring for Your Breasts" in English, Spanish and Braille, is available by calling (800) I'M AWARE or The Susan G. Komen Foundation at (214) 980-8841.*

"What You Need to Know about Breast Cancer" (88-1556). National Cancer Institute. 33 pages. *A newly updated pamphlet on breast cancer. Includes symptoms, diagnosis, treatment, emotional issues, and questions to ask your doctor.*

Nadine Shannon, et al., *Canadian Breast Cancer Series*, YM–YWCA of Winnipeg, Canada, 1988. $20. (To obtain write to the YM–YWCA, 100–290 Vaughan Street, Winnipeg, Manitoba R3B 2N8, Canada. Tel.: (204) 943-0381). *A series of four books covering breast cancer in general, diagnosis and treatment, emotional aspects and a glossary and resources. An excellent overview.*

Nancy Brinker, *The Race is Run, One Step At a Time*, (Simon and Schuster, 1990). *Nancy Brinker's and her sister's stories with good overall information. Excellent photographs of women who have had reconstruction.*

"If You've Thought about Breast Cancer" (1990). Edited by Rose Kushner. Order from Y-Me or the Komen Foundation. For multiple copies order from the Women's Breast Cancer Advisory Center, P.O. Box 224, Kensington, MD 20895.

J.R. Harris, S. Hellman, I.C. Henderson, and D.W. Kinne, *Breast Diseases* (Philadelphia: J.B. Lippincott, 1987). *Medical textbook with a very comprehensive treatment of breast cancer.* New edition expected 1991.

PSYCHOLOGICAL ASPECTS

Y–ME National Association for Breast Cancer Information and Support, Inc., 18220 Harwood Avenue, Homewood, IL 60430. *Provides support and counseling through their national toll-free hot line (800) 221-2141 (9 a.m.–5 p.m. CST), or 24 hours at (708) 799-8228. Trained volunteers, most of whom have had breast cancer, are matched by background and experience to callers whenever possible.*

Cancer Care, Inc. and the National Cancer Care Foundation, 1180 Avenue of the Americas, New York, NY 10036. (212) 211-3300. *A social service agency which helps patients and their families cope with the impact of cancer. Direct services are limited to the greater New York area, but callers will be referred to similar assistance available in their areas.*

Mimi Greenberg, Ph.D., *Invisible Scars: A Guide to Coping with the Emotional Impact of Breast Cancer* (New York: Walker, 1988). 204 pages. $17.95. *A useful guide which helps you to be in charge of your treatment.*

Judi Johnson and Linda Klein, *I Can Cope* (Minnetonka, MN: DCI Publishing, 1988, $8.95). *A co-founder of ACS' 8-week "I Can Cope" program has published a guide to staying healthy with cancer using the experiences of several cancer patients.*

Danette G. Kauffman, *Surviving Cancer* (Washington, D.C.: Acropolis Books, 1989, $8.95). *A practical guide to experiencing cancer and its treatment, with an emphasis on lists of resources for managing the medical, emotional and financial aspects of the disease.*

"Victories: Three Women Triumph over Breast Disease," (MBM Communications, San Francisco, CA, 1989). *A video tape of three personal stories (mastectomy/reconstruction, benign disease, lumpectomy/chemo/RT/recurrence) told with frankness and optimism. Includes segments showing group discussions, husband/wife counseling, and mammography. To order call (415) 642-0460. 23 minutes, $195.00 sale/$45.00 rental. Quantity discounts available.*

Amy Gross and Dee Ito, *Women Talk About Breast Surgery, from diagnosis to recovery.* (Clarkson Potter, New York, 1990). *A cross-section of women's stories describing the range of situations and treatments. Better for its support aspects than the accuracy of the medical information.*

"Taking Time: Support for the People with Cancer and the People Who Care about Them" (87-2059, 11/86). 31 pages. National Cancer Institute. *Addresses the feelings of other people in similar situations and how they coped.*

"Sexuality and Cancer" (1988 edition). 90 pages. American Cancer Society. *A booklet giving information about cancer and sexuality in areas that might concern the patient and her partner.*

Linda Dackman, *Up Front: Sex and the Post-Mastectomy Woman* (New York: Viking, 1990, $17.95). *A personal account, with frank details about the intimate challenges faced by a single woman in her 30's.*

We Can Weekends, c/o Judi Johnson, R.N., Ph.D., North Cancer Center, 3300 Oakdale North, Robbinsdale, MN 55422. (612) 520-5155. *Weekend retreats for families dealing with cancer. Provides an opportunity to focus on the problems and concerns that are encountered in living with cancer. Designed for families with children. Scholarships and baby-sitters available.* Contact North Cancer Center to learn if there is a local group.

Pat Brack and Ben Brack, *Moms Don't Get Sick,* (Melius Publishing Corp., Aberdeen, SD, 1990). *One woman's story as told through her eyes and those of her ten-year-old son. Excellent for women with children.*

"Helping Children Cope When A Parent Has Cancer." 12 pages, American Cancer Society. *A booklet to help you help your children.*

Judylaine Fine, *Afraid to Ask, A Book For Families To Share About Cancer,* (Lothrop, Lee and Shepard Books, New York, 1986).

Deborah Kahane, MSW. *No Less A Woman, Ten Women Shatter The Myths About Breast Cancer.* (Prentice Hall Press, 1990). *A cross-section of women with breast cancer tell their own stories.*

"Not Alone—Women Coping with Breast Cancer." (Adelphi Oncology Support Program, Garden City, NY, Fall 1988). *Filmed during actual sessions, a group of breast cancer patients accompanied by a social worker discuss their concerns and offer mutual support.* 22 minute video, $150.00. Order from *Adelphi*, (516) 877-4444.

Roz Perry, *Rose Penski*. (Naiad Press Inc., Tallahasse, FL). A novel about a lesbian and her lover through the diagnosis and initial treatment of breast cancer.

Part V.
Treating Breast Cancer

TREATMENT OPTIONS

"Breast Cancer: Understanding Treatment Options" (87-2675, 9/87). 19 pages. National Cancer Institute. *This booklet summarizes treatment options for local treatment.*

"Some Questions and Answers Re: The Clinical Alert (Adjuvant Chemotherapy for Node-Negative Breast Cancer)." *NABCO News* article.

"What Are Clinical Trials All About?" (85-2706). 23 pages. National Cancer Institute. *This booklet helps explain what clinical trials (protocols) are all about and helps you decide if you want to participate.*

Community Clinical Oncology Program (CCOP). (October 1989). National Cancer Institute. (800) 4-CANCER. *This is a list of the 52 community programs in 31 states that have been selected by the National Cancer Institute to participate in the introduction of the newest clinical protocols and to enlist patients to clinical trials.*

National Surgical Breast Adjuvant and Bowel Project (NSABP), 3550 Terrace Street, Room 914, Pittsburgh, PA 15261. (412) 648-9720. *Will let you know of physicians who are participating in their trials in your area.*

Physician Data Query (PDQ). National Cancer Institute. *This cancer treatment data base provides prognostic stage and treatment information and more than 1,000 protocol summaries which are open for patients. Access by computer equipped with a modem. For more information call the NCI (301) 496-7403.*

SURGERY

Reach to Recovery. American Cancer Society. *A national program sponsored by the American Cancer Society in which women who have had breast surgery visit and directly counsel women after surgery, providing practical information and support. Includes women who have had mastectomies with and without reconstruction as well as women who have had lumpectomies.* Contact your local branch.

"Mastectomy: A Treatment for Breast Cancer" (87-658, 8/87). 24 pages. National Cancer Institute. *Information about different types of breast surgery.*

Betty Rollin, *First, You Cry* (New York: New American Library, 1986).

Audre Lorde, *The Cancer Journals* (San Francisco: Spinsters Inc., Aunt Lute Book Co., 1980) P.O. Box 410687, San Francisco, CA 94141. *A wonderful Black lesbian feminist poet relates her experience with breast cancer and mastectomy.*

RADIATION

"Radiation Therapy: A Treatment for Early Stage Breast Cancer" (87-659, 9/87). 20 pages. National Cancer Institute. *This booklet discusses the treatment and side effects of primary radiation therapy.*

"Radiation Therapy and You: A Guide to Self-Help during Treatment (88-2227, 11/87). 39 pages. National Cancer Institute. *Written for the patient receiving radiation.*

Larry and Valerie Althouse, *You Can Save Your Breast: One Woman's Experience with Radiation Therapy* (New York: W.W. Norton, 1982). This book is out of print but may still be available in some libraries.

SYSTEMIC THERAPY

American Society of Clinical Oncology (ASCO), 435 North Michigan Avenue, Suite 1717, Chicago, IL 60611. (312) 644-0828. *Will mail to medical professionals a list of member oncologists by geographical area.*

"Chemotherapy and You: A Guide to Self Help during Treatment" (88-1136, 11/87). 65 pages. National Cancer Institute. *This booklet addresses problems and concerns of patients receiving chemotherapy.*

"Chemotherapy: *Your* Weapon Against Cancer" (1990 edition). *The Chemotherapy Foundation's explanation of the benefits and side effects of chemotherapy. Includes glossary of terms.* 36 pages. *The Chemotherapy Foundation, 183 Madison Avenue, Suite 403, New York, NY 10016. (212) 213-9292.*

Nancy Bruning, *Coping with Chemotherapy* (New York: Ballantine Books, 1986). 329 pages. $11.95. *A good practical and comprehensive guide to the medical and emotional aspects of chemotherapy treatment. If unavailable from bookstores it can be ordered in hardcover from* Coping *magazine, Book Order Dept., P.O. Box 1700, Franklin, TN 37065-1700. (615) 790-7553.*

"Eating Hints: Recipes and Tips for Better Nutrition during Cancer Treatment" (87-2079). 86 pages. National Cancer Institute. *This cookbook-style booklet includes recipes and suggestions for maintaining optimum realistic nutrition during treatment.*

"Tamoxifen." *NABCO News* article.

"Endocrine Manipulation and Breast Cancer." *NABCO News* article.

Helene Davis, *Chemo-poet and other poems.* (Alice James Books, Cambridge, MA, 1989).

COMPLEMENTARY THERAPIES

The Institute for the Advancement of Health, 16 East 53d Street, New York, NY 10022. (212) 832-8282. *A national organization devoted to promoting awareness of mind–body health interactions. Supplies information on behavioral techniques to promote comfort and health.*

The Planetree Health Resource Center. *A non-profit, consumer-oriented resource for health information, including materials on relaxation and visualization techniques. Write or call for a catalogue and price list: 2040 Webster Street, San Francisco, CA 94115. (415) 923-3680.*

Bernie Siegel, M.D., *Love, Medicine and Miracles* (New York: Perennial Library, 1987). $8.95. *Promotes visualization, meditation, discussion, and positive thinking.*

Herbert Benson, *The Relaxation Response* (New York: Avon Books, 1985).

Neil Fiore, *The Road Back to Health* (New York: Bantam Books, 1984). *Good explanation on how to make your own visualization tapes, by a psychologist and former cancer patient. This book is out of print but may still be found in some libraries.*

ALTERNATIVE THERAPIES

"Unproven Methods of Cancer Management" (3028 /88). American Cancer Society. *The local division offices have statements providing details on each of 27 treatment methods listed in this brochure.*

The National Council Against Health Fraud. (Call the Council's Resource Center at (800) 821-6671, or write to Dr. John Renner, Consumer Health Information Research Institute, 3521 Broadway, Kansas City, MO 64111).

FINANCIAL AID

United Cancer Council, Inc., Park Place Office Centre, 4010 W 86th Street, Suite H, Indianapolis, IN 46268-1704. (317) 879-9900. *A federation of independent voluntary cancer agencies whose mission is to promote and assist in programs of service for cancer patients. Offers a Cancer Patient Assistance Fund to provide direct financial assistance to qualified cancer patients for medical expenses.*

Adria Laboratories, Patient Assistance Program, P.O. Box 16529, Columbus, OH 43216-6529. (614) 764-8100. *Provides chemotherapy drugs (Adriamycin, vincristine, vinblastine) free of charge to patients with financial need. Request must be made by the patient's doctor to Adria Laboratories or a local Adria representative.*

Bristol-Myers Indigent Patient Assistance Program, Bristol-Myers Oncology Division, 2400 Lloyd Expressway, Evansville, IN 47721. (812) 429-5000. *Provides chemotherapy (Cytoxan) free of charge to patients with financial need. Request must be made by patient's physician.*

ICI Pharmaceutical Nolvadex (tamoxifen) Patient Assistance Program, Manager, Professional Services, ICI Pharmaceuticals, Division of ICI Americas, Inc., Wilmington, DE 19897. (800) 456-5678. *Provides tamoxifen to patients with financial need. Write for an application.*

American Association of Retired People (AARP) Pharmacy Service, Catalog Dept., P.O. Box 19229, Alexandria, VA 22320. *Members can use their non-profit service to save on prescriptions delivered by mail. Good for tamoxifen (Novaldex). Write for a free catalog.*

Corporate Angel Network, Inc. (CAN), Westchester County Airport, Building 1, White Plains, NY 10604. (914) 328-1313. *A nationwide program designed to give patients with cancer the use of available seats on corporate aircraft to get to and from recognized treatment centers. There is no cost or any financial need requirement.*

Mission Air Transportation Network (Canada), 77 Bloor Street West, Suite 1711, Toronto, ONT M5S 3A1. (416) 924-9333. *Same as above.*

National Cancer Institute, Bethesda, MD 20892-4200. (800) 638-6694. *Patients who are treated here as part of a clinical study receive their treatment free and may be housed free of charge at the hospital facilities of the NCI.*

Part VI.
Living with Breast Cancer

The National Coalition for Cancer Survivorship, 323 Eighth Street SW, Albuquerque, NM 87102. (505) 764-9956. *A national network of independent groups and individuals concerned with survivorship and sources of support for cancer patients and their families.*

Marion Morra and Eva Potts, *Triumph, Getting Back To Normal When You Have Cancer.* (Avon Books, New York, 1990).

"Look Good . . . Feel Better" is a public service program from the Cosmetic, Toilet and Fragrance Association Foundation in partnership with ACS, and the National Cosmetology Association. *It is designed to help women recovering from cancer deal with changes in their appearance resulting from cancer treatment. The program's print and videotape materials are designed for both patients and health professionals.* Call (800) 395-LOOK or your local ACS office.

"Look Good . . . Feel Better: Caring for Yourself Inside and Out." (CTFA Foundation, 1988). *The LGFB Program's video for cancer patients undergoing chemotherapy and radiation therapy. Women discuss their experiences, and beauty professionals review ways to look and feel better during treatment, including makeup, nail care and wigs.* 16 minutes. Order from CTFA, (800) 345-LOOK.

RECONSTRUCTION

"Breast Reconstruction following Mastectomy." American Society of Plastic and Reconstructive Surgeons, 444 East Algonquin Road, Arlington Heights, IL 60005. (312) 228-9900. *For referrals call the Society's message tape at (800) 635-0635.*

Breast Implant Information Network, 256 South Linden Drive, Beverly Hills, CA 90212. (213) 556-1738. *A breast implant support network. Regarding reconstruction call Sybil Goldrich.* See the section above (Part I) on plastic surgery for further references on silicone implants.

RENU Breast Reconstruction Counseling. Einstein Medical Center, Philadelphia. (215) 456-7383. *A support program staffed by trained volunteers who have had postmastectomy reconstruction. Hot-line counseling and written materials are available.*

"Breast Reconstruction after Mastectomy" (4630-PS /85). 20 pages. American Cancer Society. *Describes types of surgery with photographs and drawings.*

Marilyn Snyder, *An Informed Decision: Understanding Breast Reconstruction* (New York: M. Evans, 1989). Paperback. $12.95. *An informative mixture of one woman's account and clearly presented illustrated information about breast reconstruction after mastectomy.*

"A Sense of Balance: Breast Reconstruction." $29.95. To order call (617) 732-3379. *An interactive video developed by the staff at the Breast Evaluation Center of the Dana Farber Cancer Institute to give information about the pros and cons of various types of reconstruction.*

LYMPHEDEMA

The National Lymphedema Network, 2211 Post Street, Suite 404, San Francisco, CA 94115. (800) 541-3259. *Nonprofit organization providing patients and professionals with information about prevention and treatment of this complication of lymph node surgery.*

"Lymphedema after Treatment for Breast Cancer." NABCO Fact Sheet.

EXERCISE

The YWCA ENCORE Program, National Headquarters, 726 Broadway, 5th Floor, New York, NY 10003. (212) 614-2827. *A program to provide supportive discussion and rehabilitative exercise for women who have had surgery for breast cancer. Contact the National Headquarters for the location nearest you.*

"Get Up and Go: After Breast Surgery." (ACS/University of Michigan, Oak Park, MI, 1989). Order from *Health Tapes Inc.*, (313) 662-5100. *Total body exercises demonstrated by five women who have had a mastectomy, lumpectomy or reconstructive surgery. Increasingly challenging levels.* 60 minutes, $39.95.

EMOTIONAL EXERCISE

The Wellness Community, 1235 Fifth Street, Santa Monica, CA 90401. (213) 393-1415. *Extensive support and education programs which encourage emotional recovery and a feeling of wellness.*

The National Self-Help Clearinghouse, c/o Graduate School and University Center of City University of New York, 33 West 42nd Street, Rm. 620N, New York, NY 10036. *Will refer written inquiries to regional self-help services.*

INSURANCE AND EMPLOYMENT

Information and Counseling about Cancer and the Workplace. Phyllis Stein, Radcliffe Career Services, Radcliffe College, 10 Garden Street, Cambridge, MA 02138; and Barbara Lazarus, Associate Provost for Academic Programs, Carnegie-Mellon University, Pittsburgh, PA 15213.

"What You Should Know about Health Insurance" (731, 7/87). "What You Should Know about Disability Insurance" (733, 10/87). Health Insurance Association of America, 1025 Connecticut Avenue NW, Washington, DC 20004-3998. (202) 223-7780.

"Cancer: Your Job, Insurance and the Law" (4585-ps, /87). 6 pages. American Cancer Society. *Summarizes cancer patients' legal rights regarding insurance and employment.*

"Job and Credit Discrimination, Insurance." NABCO Fact Sheet.

Karen M. Hassey, "Pregnancy and Parenthood after Treatment for Breast Cancer," *Oncology Nursing Forum*, Vol. 15, No. 4 (1988): 439–444. *You will probably have to get this from a hospital or medical library. A very good review of all that has been published on the subject.*

HOW DO YOU KNOW IF YOU HAVE A RECURRENCE?

"After Breast Cancer: A Guide to Follow-Up Care" (87-2400). National Cancer Institute. 11 pages. *Considers the importance of follow-up, signs of recurrence, and the physical and emotional effects of having had breast cancer.*

"When Cancer Recurs: Meeting the Challenge Again" (87-2709, 1/87). National Cancer Institute. *This booklet details the different types of recurrence, types of treatment, and coping with cancer's return.*

Lucy Shapero and Anthony Goodman, M.D., *Never Say Die* (New York: Prentice-Hall, 1980). *A woman and her doctor discuss her care through metastatic breast cancer. This book is out of print but may still be found in some libraries.*

"Advanced Cancer: Living Each Day" (85-856). National Cancer Institute. 30 pages. *A booklet providing practical information to make living with advanced cancer easier.*

"Questions and Answers about Pain Control: A Guide for People with Cancer and Their Families" (4518-PS, 1986 edition). 44 pages. American Cancer Society. *This booklet discusses pain control using both medical and nonmedical methods. The emphasis is on explanation and self-help.*

"Caring for the Patient with Cancer at Home: A Guide for Patients and Families" (4656-PS, 1988 edition). 40 pages. American Cancer Society. *A guidebook providing detailed helpful information on how to care for the patient at home.*

National Hospice Organization, 1901 North Moore Street, Suite 901, Arlington, VA 22209. (703) 243-5900. *Will provide a directory of hospice programs by state.*

Royal Victoria Hospital Palliative Care Service, 687 Pine Avenue West, Montreal, QC H3A 1A1. (514) 843-1542. *An independent national organization of groups providing palliative care and hospice in Canada.*

Concern for Dying, 250 West 57th Street, Room 831, New York, NY 10107. (212) 246-6962. *A nonprofit educational organization which distributes the living will, a document that records a patient's wishes during treatment and in regard to terminal care.*

THE FUTURE

NABCO News. *A quarterly newsletter addressing the latest in breast cancer treatments and research.* Can be obtained by membership in the National Alliance of Breast Cancer Organizations, 1180 Avenue of the Americas, Second Floor, New York, NY 10036.

"Interferon, Interleukin II and Other Biological Response Modifiers for the Treatment of Breast Cancer." NABCO Fact Sheets and *NABCO News* articles.

D

Regional Support Organizations for Cancer and Breast Cancer Patients

AR–Ft. Smith	Breast Cancer Support Group	(501) 782-9929
AZ–Phoenix	Bosom Buddies	(800) 826-9475
CA–Anaheim	Breast Care For Life Program	(714) 999-6035
CA–Beverly Hills	Beverly Hills Breast Cancer Support Group	(213) 859-1273
CA–Beverly Hills	Spalding Support Group	(213) 276-1420
CA–Burbank	Valley Support Group	(818) 846-0453
CA–Covina	Queen of the Valley/Breast Cancer Support Group	(818) 814-2401
CA–Davis	Davis Breast Cancer Support Group	(916) 756-8181
CA–Encinitas	Scripps Breast Cancer Support Group	(619) 942-7763
CA–Escondito	"The Health Concern"	(619) 746-0700
CA–Fremont	Tri-City Breast Cancer Support Group	(415) 357-1961
CA–Long Beach	Long Beach Memorial Breast Center	(213) 595-3838

CA–Napa	Bosom Buddies/Queen of the Valley Hospital	(707) 257-4047
CA–Oakland	Women's Cancer Resource Center	(415) 548-WCRC
CA–Rancho Mirage	Eisenhower/After Breast Cancer	(619) 773-1295
CA–San Francisco	Cancer Support Community	(415) 929-7400
CA–Santa Barbara	Y-Me of Santa Barbara	(805) 687-3360
CA–Stockton	Bosom Buddies	(209) 474-3694
CA–Studio City	Vital Options (young adults)	(818) 508-5657
CA–Van Nuys	The Breast Center Support Group	(818) 787-9911
CT–Madison	Y-Me of New England	(203) 245-0054
DC–Washington	Lombardi Breast Cancer Support Group	(202) 784-3750
DC–Washington	Mary-Helen Mautner Project for Lesbians With Cancer	(202) 332-5536
DC–Washington	My Image After Breast Cancer	(703) 237-1797
FL–Boca Raton	Y-Me of Florida	(407) 338-2101
FL–Jacksonville	FCC/Bosom Buddies	(904) 396-5973
FL–Tampa	FACTors	(813) 935-7594
IA–Mason City	The Mastectomy Support Group	(800) 327-0122
ID–Coeur d'Aline	North Idaho Cancer Care/ Support	(208) 765-0565
ID–Meridian	Breast Cancer Support Group	(208) 888-0985
IL–Chicago	Lesbian Community Cancer Project	(312) 549-4729
IL–Palatine	A Time To Heal	(708) 381-9600, x5330
IL–Peoria	Susan G. Komen Breast Center	(309) 655-2585
IN–Warsaw	Women Winning Against Cancer	(219) 269-9911
KY–Lexington	Y-Me of Central Kentucky	(606) 277-7159

LA–New Orleans	Tulane/Friedler Cancer Counseling	(504) 587-2120
MA–Boston	Faulkner Breast Centre Support Group	(617) 522-8484
MA–Boston	Dana Farber Cancer Institute: Breast Reconstruction Group	(617) 732-3666
	Crossroads (post-primary treatment transitions)	(617) 732-3669
	Living with Breast Cancer (Information/Education)	(617) 732-3669
MA–Boston	New England Deaconess Hospital: Mind/Body Cancer Group	(617) 732-9530
MA–Cambridge	Women's Community Cancer Project	(617) 354-9888
MA–Peabody	J.B. Thomas Hospital Breast Cancer Support Group	(508) 531-2900, x312
MD–Baltimore	Arm-In-Arm	(301) 828-3301
MD–Hagerstown	Y-Me of the Cumberland Valley	(301) 791-5843
MI–Flint	McLaren Mastectomy Support Group	(313) 230-0520
MI–Grand Rapids	Woman to Woman/Program for Husbands	(616) 774-6756
MI–Midland	The Center for Women's Health	(517) 839-0020
MI–St. Joseph	Center for Women's Health Mastectomy Support Group	(616) 429-0810
MO–Kansas City	Cancer Hotline	(816) 932-8453
NJ–Atlantic City	Atlantic City Medical Center "B.E.S.T. Care"	(609) 652-3500
NJ–Livingston	Concern	(201) 533-5633
NJ–Pompton Plains	Woman to Woman	(201) 278-4124
NJ–Somerville	Post Breast Surgery Support Group	(201) 725-4664
NM–Albuquerque	Living Through Cancer	(505) 242-3263
NY–Binghamton	Breast Cancer Support Group	(607) 748-1333
NY–Buffalo	Support for Women with Breast Cancer	(716) 836-6460

NY–Garden City	Adelphi Breast Center Information HOTLINE	(516) 248-8866
NY–Johnson City	Women's Health Connection	(607) 770-6546
NY–New York	Post-Treatment Resource Program (MSKCC)	(212) 639-3292
NY–New York	SHARE (Self-Help for Women with Breast Cancer)	(212) 260-0580
NY–New York	NYU/Rusk Institute CRS	(212) 340-6847
NY–Rochester	Breast Cancer Support Group/Cancer Action	(716) 423-9700
NY–Rye Brook	Cancer Support Team (lumpectomies)	(914) 253-5334
OH–Springfield	HERS Post-Mastectomy Support Group	(513) 390-5030
OR–Portland	Breast Cancer Outreach/ Support Group	(503) 291-2081
PA–Camp Hill	Breast Cancer Support Group	(717) 731-4035
PA–Lancaster	After Breast Cancer	(805) 945-7585
PA–Norristown	Montgomery Breast Cancer Support Program	(215) 270-2700
PA–Philadelphia	Linda Creed Foundation	(215) 242-3633
PA–Pittsburgh	Magee-Women's Hospital Breast Cancer Support Group	(412) 647-4253
PA–Pittsburgh	Support Center for Cancer	(412) 622-1212
TX–Dallas	Someone to Talk To/SG Komen	(214) 521-5225
TX–Dallas	W.I.N. (Women's Information Network)	(214) 387-2504
TX–Houston	Spring Shadows/ACS	(713) 895-7722
TX–Houston	The Rose Garden	(713) 484-4708
TX–Richardson	Support of Self/Bosom Buddies	(214) 414-8690
UT–Salt Lake	Holy Cross Hospital Breast Care Services Outreach Program	(801) 350-4000
UT–Vernal	Ashley Valley Breast Care Center	(801) 789-3342
WA–Port Angeles	Operation Uplift	(206) 457-5141

WA–Pot Ludlow	CANHELP (treatment decisions)	(206) 437-2291
WA–Seattle	Cancer Lifeline	(206) 461-4542
VA–Arlington	My Image	(703) 237-1797

E

Cancer Centers

The National Cancer Institute supports a number of cancer centers throughout the country that develop and investigate new methods of cancer diagnosis and treatment. Information about referral procedures, treatment costs,
and services available to patients can be obtained from the individual cancer
centers listed below.

ALABAMA

*University of Alabama Comprehensive
Cancer Center*
1918 University Boulevard
Basic Health Sciences Building,
Room 108
Birmingham, AL 35294
(205) 934-6612

ARIZONA

University of Arizona Cancer Center
1501 North Campbell Avenue
Tucson, AZ 85724
(602) 626-6372

CALIFORNIA

*University of Southern California
Comprehensive Cancer Center*
Kenneth Norris Jr. Cancer Hospital
and Research Institute
1441 Eastlake Avenue
Los Angeles, CA 90033-0804
(213) 226-2370

*Jonsson Comprehensive Cancer Center
(UCLA)*
10-247 Factor Building
10833 Le Conte Avenue
Los Angeles, CA 90024-1781
(213) 825-8727

City of Hope National Medical Center
Beckman Research Institute
1500 East Duarte Road
Duarte, CA 91010
(818) 359-8111, ext. 2292

University of California at San Diego
Cancer Center
225 Dickinson Street
San Diego, CA 92103
(619) 543-6178

Charles R. Drew University of
Medicine and Science (consortium)
12714 South Avalon Boulevard,
Suite 301
Los Angeles, CA 90061
(213) 603-3120

Northern California Cancer Center
(consortium)
1301 Shoreway Road
Belmont, CA 94002
(415) 591-4484

COLORADO

University of Colorado Cancer Center
4200 East 9th Avenue, Box B190
Denver, CO 80262
(303) 270-3019

CONNECTICUT

Yale University Comprehensive Cancer
Center
333 Cedar Street
New Haven, CT 06510
(203) 785-6338

DISTRICT OF COLUMBIA

Howard University Cancer Research
Center
2041 Georgia Avenue, NW
Washington, DC 20060
(202) 636-7610 or 636-5665

Vincent T. Lombardi Cancer Research
Center
Georgetown University Medical
Center
3800 Reservoir Road, NW
Washington, DC 20007
(202) 687-2110

FLORIDA

Sylvester Comprehensive Cancer
Center
University of Miami Medical School
1475 Northwest 12th Avenue
Miami, FL 33136
(305) 548-4850

ILLINOIS

Illinois Cancer Council (includes
institutions listed and several
other organizations)

Illinois Cancer Council
36 South Wabash Avenue
Chicago, IL 60603
(312) 226-2371

University of Chicago Cancer Research
Center
5841 South Maryland Avenue
Chicago, IL 60637
(312) 702-6180

KENTUCKY

Lucille Parker Markey Cancer Center
University of Kentucky Medical
Center
800 Rose Street
Lexington, KY 40536-0093
(606) 257-4447

MARYLAND

The Johns Hopkins Oncology Center
600 North Wolfe Street
Baltimore, MD 21205
(301) 955-8638

MASSACHUSETTS

Dana-Farber Cancer Institute
44 Binney Street
Boston, MA 02115
(617) 732-3214

MICHIGAN

Meyer L. Prentis Comprehensive
Cancer Center of Metropolitan
Detroit
110 East Warren Avenue
Detroit, MI 48201
(313) 833-0710, ext. 429

University of Michigan Cancer Center
101 Simpson Drive
Ann Arbor, MI 48109-0752
(313) 936-2516

MINNESOTA

Mayo Comprehensive Cancer Center
200 First Street Southwest
Rochester, MN 55905
(507) 284-3413

NEW HAMPSHIRE

Norris Cotton Cancer Center
Dartmouth-Hitchcock Medical
  Center
2 Maynard Street
Hanover, NH 03756
(603) 646-5485

NEW YORK

Memorial Sloan-Kettering Cancer
  Center
1275 York Avenue
New York, NY 10021
1-800-525-2225

Columbia University Cancer Center
College of Physicians and Surgeons
630 West 168th Street
New York, NY 10032
(212) 305-6730

Roswell Park Memorial Institute
666 Elm Street
Buffalo, NY 14263
(716) 845-4400

Mt. Sinai School of Medicine
One Gustave L. Levy Place
New York, NY 10029
(212) 241-8617

Albert Einstein College of Medicine
1300 Morris Park Avenue
Bronx, NY 10461
(212) 920-4826

New York University Cancer Center
462 First Avenue
New York, NY 10016-9103
(212) 340-6485

University of Rochester Cancer Center
601 Elmwood Avenue, Box 704
Rochester, NY 14642
(716) 275-4911

NORTH CAROLINA

Duke University Comprehensive Cancer
  Center
P.O. Box 3843
Durham, NC 27710
(919) 684-6342 or (919) 286-5515

Lineberger Cancer Research Center
University of North Carolina School
  of Medicine
Chapel Hill, NC 27599
(919) 966-4431

Bowman Gray School of Medicine
Wake Forest University
300 South Hawthorne Road
Winston-Salem, NC 27103
(919) 748-4354

OHIO

Ohio State University Comprehensive
  Cancer Center
410 West 12th Avenue
Columbus, OH 43210
(614) 293-8619

Case Western Reserve University
University Hospitals of Cleveland
Ireland Cancer Center
2074 Abington Road
Cleveland, OH 44106
(216) 844-8453

PENNSYLVANIA

Fox Chase Cancer Center
7701 Burholme Avenue
Philadelphia, PA 19111
(215) 728-2570

University of Pennsylvania Cancer
  Center
3400 Spruce Street
Philadelphia, PA 19104
(215) 662-6364

Pittsburgh Cancer Institute
230 Lothrop Street
Pittsburgh, PA 15213-2592
1-800-537-4063

RHODE ISLAND

Roger Williams General Hospital
825 Chalkstone Avenue
Providence, RI 02908
(401) 456-2070

TENNESSEE

St. Jude Children's Research Hospital
332 North Lauderdale Street
Memphis, TN 38101
(901) 522-0694

TEXAS

The University of Texas M.D.
Anderson Cancer Center
1515 Holcombe Boulevard
Houston, TX 77030
(713) 792-6161

UTAH

Utah Regional Cancer Center
University of Utah Medical Center
50 North Medical Drive, Room 2C10
Salt Lake City, UT 84132
(801) 581-4048

VERMONT

Vermont Regional Cancer Center
University of Vermont
1 South Prospect Street
Burlington, VT 05401
(802) 656-4580

VIRGINIA

Massey Cancer Center
Medical College of Virginia
Virginia Commonwealth University
1200 East Broad Street
Richmond, VA 23298
(804) 786-9641

University of Virginia Medical Center
Box 334
Primary Care Center, Room 4520
Lee Street
Charlottesville, VA 22908
(804) 924-2562

WASHINGTON

Fred Hutchinson Cancer Research
Center
1124 Columbia Street
Seattle, WA 98104
(206) 467-4675

WISCONSIN

Wisconsin Clinical Cancer Center
University of Wisconsin
600 Highland Avenue
Madison, WI 53792
(608) 263-6872

For additional information about cancer, write to the Office of Cancer Communications, National Cancer Institute, Bethesda, MD 20892, or call the toll-free telephone number of the Cancer Information Service (800) 4-CAN-CER.

In Hawaii, on Oahu call 524-1234 (neighbor islands call collect). Spanish-speaking staff members are available to callers from the following areas (daytime hours only): California, Florida, Georgia, Illinois, New Jersey (area code 201), New York, and Texas.

Notes

INTRODUCTION

1. N. Turnbull, "Women Go Topless," *Sojourner* (August 1985):13.
2. C.E. Welch, "Cancer of the Breast," *Journal of Clinical Surgery* 1(1982):425.

CHAPTER 1. THE BREAST AND ITS DEVELOPMENT

1. D. Ayalah and I.J. Weinstock, *Breasts* (New York: Summit Books, 1979).
2. J.E. Robinson and R.V. Short, "Changes in Breast Sensitivity at Puberty, during the Menstrual Cycle, and at Parturition," *British Medical Journal* 1(1977):1188.
3. *Breasts*, p.33.
4. A. Stanway and P. Stanway, *The Breast* (London: Granada Publishing Ltd., 1982), p.23.

CHAPTER 3. BREASTFEEDING

1. W.L. Donegan, "Mammary Carcinoma and Pregnancy," *Major Problems in Clinical Surgery* 5(1979):448–463.
2. J. Yuan and M.C. Yu, "Risk Factors for Breast Cancer in Chinese Women in Shanghai," *Cancer Research* 48(1988):1949–1953.

3. R.E. Little, K.W. Anderson, C.H. Irvin, et al., "Maternal Alcohol Use during Breast Feeding and Infant Mental and Motor Development at One Year," *New England Journal of Medicine* 321(1989):425–430.

CHAPTER 4. VARIATIONS IN DEVELOPMENT

1. A. Stanway and P. Stanway, *The Breast* (London: Granada Publishing Ltd., 1982), p.206.

CHAPTER 5. PLASTIC SURGERY

1. G. Letterman and M.A. Schurter, "A History of Mammoplasty with Emphasis on Correction of Ptosis and Macromastia," in R. Goldwyn, ed., *Plastic and Reconstructive Surgery of the Breast* (Boston: Little, Brown, 1976), p.361.
2. J.T. Heuston, "Unilateral Agenesis and Hypoplasia: Difficulties and Suggestions," in R. Goldwyn, ed., *Plastic and Reconstructive Surgery of the Breast* (Boston: Little, Brown, 1976), p.361.
3. S. Gifford, "Emotional Attitudes toward Cosmetic Breast Surgery: Loss and Restitution of the 'Ideal' Self," in R. Goldwyn, ed., *Plastic and Reconstructive Surgery of the Breast* (Boston: Little, Brown, 1976), p.117.
4. "Safety of Silicone Breast Prostheses," *FDA Drug Bulletin* (February 1989):2.
5. M.D. Deapen, M.C. Pike, J.T. Casagrande, et al., "The Relationship between Breast Cancer and Augmentation Mammoplasty: An Epidemiologic Study," *Plastic and Reconstructive Surgery* 77(1986):361.
6. H. Spiera, "Scleroderma after Silicone Augmentation Mammoplasty," *Journal of the American Medical Society* 260(1988):236.
7. M.J. Silverstein, N. Handel, P. Gamagami, et al., "Breast Cancer in Women after Augmentation Mammoplasty," *Archives of Surgery* 123(1988):681.
8. G.W. Eklund, R.C. Busby, S.H. Miller, et al., "Improved Imaging of the Augmented Breast," *American Journal of Radiology* 151(1988):469.

CHAPTER 6. THE MYTH OF FIBROCYSTIC DISEASE

1. S.M. Love, R.S. Gelman, and W.S. Silen, "Fibrocystic 'Disease' of the Breast: A Nondisease," *New England Journal of Medicine* 307(1982):1010.
2. D.L. Page, R. Vanderzwagg, L.W. Rogers, et al., "Relationship between the Component Parts of Fibrocystic Disease Complex and Breast Cancer," *Journal of the National Cancer Institute* 61(1978):1055.
3. W.D. Dupont and D.L. Page, "Risk Factors for Breast Cancer in Women with Proliferative Disease," *New England Journal of Medicine* 312(1985):146.
4. The Cancer Committee of the College of American Pathologists, "Is 'Fibrocystic Disease' of the Breast Precancerous?," *Archives of Pathology and Laboratory Medicine* 110(1986):173.
5. J.P. Minton, M.K. Foecking, D.J.T. Webster, et al., "Response of Fibrocystic Disease to Caffeine Withdrawal and Correlation of Cyclic Nucleotides with Breast Disease," *American Journal of Obstetrics and Gynecology* 135(1979):157.

6. V.L. Ernster, L. Mason, W.H. Goodson, et al., "Effects of Caffeine-Free Diet on Benign Breast Disease: A Randomized Trial," *Surgery* 91(1982):263.

7. S.S. Allen and D.C. Froberg, "The Effect of Decreased Caffeine Consumption on Benign Proliferative Breast Disease: A Randomized Clinical Trial," *Surgery* 101(1986):720.

8. J.A. Petrek, W.A. Sandberg, M.N. Cole, et al., "The Inhibitory Effect of Caffeine on Hormone-Induced Rat Breast Cancer," *Cancer* 56(1985):1977.

9. F. Lubin, E. Ron, Y. Wax, et al., "A Case Control Study of Caffeine and Methylxanthine in Benign Breast Disease," *Journal of the American Medical Association* 253(1985):2388.

10. F. Lubin, E. Ron, Y. Wax, et al., "Coffee and Methylxanthines and Breast Cancer: A Case-Control Study," *Journal of the National Cancer Institute* 74(1985):569.

11. A.A. Abrams, "Use of Vitamin E in Chronic Cystic Mastitis," *New England Journal of Medicine* 272(1965):1080.

12. R.S. London, E.D. Solomon, et al., "Mammary Dysplasia: Clinical Response and Urinary Excretion of 11-deoxy-17-ketosteroids and Prenanediol following Alpha Tocopherol Therapy," *Breast* 4(1978):19.

13. R.S. London, G.S. Sundaram, L. Murphy, et al., "The Effect of Vitamin E on Mammary Dysplasia: A Double-Blind Study," *Obstetrics and Gynecology* 65(1985):104.

CHAPTER 7. BREAST PAIN

1. P.E. Preece, R.E. Mansel, and L.E. Hughes, "Mastalgia: Psychoneurosis or Organic Disease?," *British Medical Journal* 1(1978):29.

2. J. Birkett, *The Diseases of the Breast* (London: Longman & Co., 1850).

3. D.H. Patey, "Two Common Non-Malignant Conditions of the Breast," *British Medical Journal* 1(1949):96.

4. W.H. Goodson, R. Mailman, M. Jacobson, et al., "What Do Breast Symptoms Mean?," *American Journal of Surgery* 150(1985):271.

5. F. Kuttenin, S. Fournier, R. Sitruk-Ware, et al., "Progesterone Insufficiency in Benign Breast Disease," in A. Angeli, H.L. Bradlow, Dogliotti, eds., *Endocrinology of Cystic Breast Disease* (New York: Raven Press, 1983).

6. J.W. Ayres and G.P. Gidwani, "The 'Luteal Breast': Hormonal and Sonographic Investigations of Benign Breast Disease in Patients with Cyclic Mastalgia," *Fertility and Sterility* 40(1983):779.

7. P.E. Preece, L.E. Hughes, R.E. Mansel, et al., "Clinical Syndromes of Mastalgia," *Lancet* 2(1976):670.

8. R. Sitruk-Ware, N. Sterkers, and P. Mauvais-Jarvis, "Benign Breast Disease I: Hormonal Investigation," *Obstetrics and Gynecology* 53(1979):457.

9. S. Watt-Boolsen, P.C. Eskildsen, and H. Blaehr, "Release of Prolactin, Thyrotropin, and Growth Hormone in Women with Cyclical Mastalgia and Fibrocystic Disease of the Breast," *Cancer* 56(1985):500.

10. S. Kumar, R.E. Mansel, L.E. Hughes, et al., "Prolactin Response to Thyrotropin-Releasing Hormone Stimulation and Dopaminergic Inhibition in Benign Breast Disease," *Cancer* 53(1984):1311.

11. J.K. Page, R.E. Mansel, and S.E. Hughes, "Clinical Experience of Drug Treatments for Mastalgia," *Lancet* 2(1985):373.

12. D.R. Miller, L. Rosenberg, D.W Kaufman, et al., "Breast Cancer before Age 45 and Oral Contraceptive Use: New Findings," *American Journal of Epidemiology* 129(1989):269.

13. M. Blichert-Toft, A.N. Anderson, O.B. Henriksen, et al., "Treatment of Mas-

talgia with Bromocriptine: A Double-Blind Crossover Study," *British Medical Journal* 1(1979):237.

14. R.B. Greenblatt, W.P. Dmowsky, V.B. Mahesh, et al., "Clinical Studies with an Antigonadotropin-Danazol," *Fertility and Sterility* 22(1971):102.

15. N.C. Estes, "Mastodynia Due to Fibrocystic Disease of the Breast Controlled with Thyroid Hormone," *American Journal of Surgery* 142(1981):764.

16. I.S. Fentiman, M. Caleffi, K. Brame, et al., "Double-Blind Controlled Trial of Tamoxifen Therapy for Mastalgia," *Lancet* 1(1986):287.

17. C. Lafaye and B. Aubert, "Action de la Progesterone Locale dans les Mastopathies Benignes," *Journal of Gynecology, Obstetrics, Biology and Reproduction* 7(1978): 1123.

18. D.P. Rose, L.A. Cohen, and A.P. Boyar, "Effect of a Low-Fat Diet on Hormone Levels in Women with Cystic Breast Disease: I. Serum Steroids and Gonadotropins," *Journal of the National Cancer Institute* 78(1987):623.

19. D.P. Rose, L.A. Cohen, and A.P. Boyar, "Effect of a Low-Fat Diet on Hormone Levels in Women with Cystic Breast Disease: II. Serum Radioimmunoassayable Prolactin and Growth Hormone and Bioactive Lactogenic Hormones," *Journal of the National Cancer Institute* 78(1987):627.

20. J.K. Page, R.E. Mansel, and S.E. Hughes, "Clinical Experience of Drug Treatments for Mastalgia," *Lancet* 2(1985):373.

21. P.E. Preece, L.E. Hughes, R.E. Mansel, et al., "Clinical Syndromes of Mastalgia," *Lancet* 2(1976):670.

22. M.M. LeBan, J.R. Meerscharet, and R.S. Taylor, "Breast Pain: A Symptom of Cervical Radiculopathy," *Archives of Physical Medicine and Rehabilitation* 60(1979):315.

CHAPTER 8. BREAST INFECTIONS AND NIPPLE PROBLEMS

1. A.C. Thomsen, M.D. Espersen, and S. Maigaard, "Course and Treatment of Milk Stasis, Noninfectious Inflammation of the Breast and Infectious Mastitis in Nursing Women," *American Journal of Obstetrics and Gynecology* 149(1984):492.

2. W.P. Maier, A. Berger, and B.M. Derrick, "Periareolar Abscess in the Nonlactating Breast," *American Journal of Surgery* 144(1982):359.

3. O. Sartorius, personal communication.

4. S. Watt-Boolsen, R. Ryegaard, and M. Blichert-Toft, "Primary Periareolar Abscess in the Nonlactating Breast: Risk of Recurrence," *American Journal of Surgery* 153(1987):571.

5. S.M. Love, S.J. Schnitt, J.L. Connolly, and R.L. Shirley, "Benign Breast Diseases," in J.R. Harris, S. Hellman, I.C. Henderson, and D.W Kinne, eds., *Breast Diseases* (Philadelphia: J.B. Lippincott, 1987), p.22.

CHAPTER 9. LUMPS AND LUMPINESS

1. L. Tabar, Z. Pentek, and P.B. Dean, "The Diagnostic and Therapeutic Value of Breast Cyst Puncture and Pneumocystography," *Radiology* 14 (1981):1659.

2. J.B. Herrman, "Mammary Cancer Subsequent to Aspiration of Cysts in the Breast," *Annals of Surgery* 173(1971):40.

3. C.D. Haagensen, "The Relationship of Gross Cystic Disease of the Breast and Carcinoma," *Annals of Surgery* 185(1977):375.

4. W.D. Dupone and D.L. Page, "Risk Factors for Breast Cancer in Women with Proliferative Breast Disease," *New England Journal of Medicine* 312(1985):146.

CHAPTER 11. RISK FACTORS: HORMONAL AND GENETIC

1. H. Seidman, M.H. Mushinski, S.K. Gelb, E. Silverberg, et al., "Probabilities of Eventually Developing or Dying of Cancer," *CA: A Cancer Journal for Clinicians* 35(1985):36–56.

2. S.M. Love, "Use of Risk Factors in Counseling Patients," Hematology/Oncology Clinics of North America, 3(1989):599–610.

3. G.R. Newell and V.G. Vogel, "Personal Risk Factors: What Do They Mean?," *Cancer* 62(1988):1695–1701.

4. J. Cuzick, "Women at High Risk of Breast Cancer," *Reviews on Endocrine-Related Cancer* 25(1987):5.

5. A.B. Miller, "Epidemiology and Prevention," in J.R. Harris, S. Hellman, I.C. Henderson, and D.W. Kinne, eds., *Breast Diseases* (Philadelphia: J.B. Lippincott, 1987).

6. H. Seidman, S.D. Stellman, and M.H. Mushinski, "A Different Perspective on Breast Cancer Risk Factors: Some Implications of the Nonattributable Risk," *CA: A Cancer Journal for Clinicians* 32(1982):301.

7. B. MacMahon, P. Cole, and J. Brown, "Etiology of Human Breast Cancer: A Review," *Journal of the National Cancer Institute* 50(1973):21–42.

8. L. Rosenberg, J.R. Palmer, D.W. Kaufman, B.L. Strom, D. Schottenfeld, and S. Shapiro, "Breast Cancer in Relation to the Occurrence and Time of Induced and Spontaneous Abortion," *American Journal of Epidemiology* 127(1988):981–989.

9. S.G. Korenman, "The Endocrinology of Breast Cancer," *Cancer* 46(1980):874–878.

10. B.E. Henderson, R.K. Ross, H.L. Judd, M.D. Krailo, and M.C. Pike, "Do Regular Ovulatory Cycles Increase Breast Cancer Risk?," *Cancer* 56(1985):1206–1208.

11. E. Ron, B. Lunenfeld, J. Menczer, T. Blumstein, L. Katz, G. Oelsner, and D. Serr, "Cancer Incidence in a Cohort of Infertile Women," *American Journal of Epidemiology* 125(1987):780–790.

12. H. Olsson, J. Ranstam, and M. Landin Olsson, "The Number of Menstrual Cycles Prior to the First Full-Term Pregnancy an Important Risk Factor of Breast Cancer?," *Acta Oncologica* 26(1987):387–389.

13. R.E. Firsch, G. Wyshak, N. Albright, et al., "Lower Lifetime Occurrence of Breast Cancer and Cancer of the Reproductive System among Former College Athletes," *American Journal of Clinical Nutrition* 45(1987):328.

14. Henderson et al., op. cit. Note 10.

15. H.T. Lynch, W.A. Albano, J.J. Heieck, et al., "Genetics, Biomarkers, and Control of Breast Cancer: A Review," *Cancer, Genetics, and Cytogenetics* 13(1984):43–92.

16. S.H. Moolgavkar and A.G. Knudson, Jr., "Mutation and Cancer: A Model for Human Carcinogenesis," *Journal of the National Cancer Institute* 66(1981):1037–1052.

17. F.P. Li and J.F. Fraumeni, Jr., "Soft Tissue Sarcomas, Breast Cancer, and Other Neoplasms: A Familial Syndrome?," *Annals of Internal Medicine* (1969): 747–751.

18. M.H. Brownstein, "Cowden's Disease: A Possible New Symptom Complex with Multiple System Involvement," *Annals of Internal Medicine* 48(1978):136–142.

19. H.T. Lynch, R.E. Harris, H.A. Guirgis, et al., "Familial Association of Breast/ Ovarian Carcinoma," *Cancer* 41(1978):1543–1549.

20. D.E. Anderson, "Some Characteristics of Familial Breast Cancer," *Cancer* 28(1971):1500–1504.

21. H.O. Adami, J. Hansen, B. Jung, et al., "Characteristics of Familial Breast Cancer in Sweden: Absence of Relation of Age and Unilateral versus Bilateral Disease," *Cancer* 48(1981):1688–1695.

22. S.M. Love, "Use of Risk Factors in Counseling Patients," in I.C. Henderson, ed., *Clinics in Oncology: Breast Cancer* Philadelphia: Saunders, 3(1989):599–610.

23. L.D. Goldman and R.M. Goldwyn, "Some Anatomical Considerations of Subcutaneous Mastectomy," *Plastic and Reconstruction Surgery* 51(1973):501–505.

24. C.F. Jackson, M. Palmquist, J. Swanson, et al., "The Effectiveness of Prophylactic Subcutaneous Mastectomy in Sprague-Dawley Rats Induced with 7,12 Dimethylbenzanthracene," *Plastic Reconstruction Surgery* 73(1984):249.

25. L.J. Humphrey, "Subcutaneous Mastectomy Is Not a Prophylaxis against Carcinoma of the Breast: Opinion or Knowledge?," *American Journal of Surgery* 145(1983):311–312.

CHAPTER 12. RISK FACTORS: EXTERNAL

1. A.B. Miller, "Epidemiology and Prevention," in J.R. Harris, S. Hellman, I.C. Henderson, and D.W. Kinne, eds., *Breast Diseases* (Philadelphia: J.B. Lippincott, 1987).

2. E.L. Wydner, "Reflections on Diet, Nutrition and Cancer," *Cancer Research* 43(1983):3024.

3. B. Armstrong and R. Doll, "Environmental Factors and Cancer Incidence and Mortality with Special Reference to Dietary Practices," *International Journal of Cancer* 15(1975):617–631.

4. B. MacMahon, "Incidence Trends in North America, Japan and Hawaii," in K. Magnus, ed., *Trends in Cancer Incidence* (New York: McGraw-Hill, 1982).

5. O. Bjarnson, M. Day, G. Snaedal, et al., "The Effect of Year of Birth on the Breast Cancer Age Incidence Curve in Iceland," *Journal of Cancer* 13(1974):689.

6. P. Buell, "Changing Incidence of Breast Cancer in Japanese-American Women," *Journal of the National Cancer Institute* 51(1973):1479–1483.

7. R.L. Phillips, L. Garfinkel, J.W. Kuzma, et al., "Mortality among California Seventh Day Adventists for Selected Cancer Sites," *Journal of the National Cancer Institute* 65(1980):1097–1107.

8. L.J. Kinlen, "Meat and Fat Consumption and Cancer Mortality: A Study of Religious Orders in Britain," *Lancet* (1982):946–949.

9. J. Chen, T.C. Campbell, L. Junyao, and R. Peto, "The Dietary, Lifestyles and Mortality Characteristics of 65 Rural Populations in the People's Republic of China" (Division of Nutritional Sciences, Cornell University, Ithaca, N.Y., 1987).

10. W.C. Willet, M.J. Stampfer, G.A. Colditz, B.A. Rosner, C.H. Hennekens, and F.E. Speizer, "Dietary Fat and the Risk of Breast Cancer," *New England Journal of Medicine* 316(1987):22–28.

11. F. de Waard, E.A. Baanders-van Haliwijn, and J. Huizinga, "The Bimodal Age Distribution of Patients with Mammary Cancer," *Cancer* 17(1964):141.

12. F. de Waard and E.A. Baanders-van Haliwijn, "A Prospective Study in General Practice on Breast Cancer Risk in Postmenopausal Women," *International Journal of Cancer* 14(1974):153.

13. D. Medina, "Selenium and Murine Mammary Tumorgenesis," *Cancer Bulletin* 34(1983):162–165.

14. G.N. Schrauzer, D.A. White, and C.J. Schneider, "Cancer Mortality Correlation Studies: III. Statistical Associations with Dietary Selenium Intakes," *Bioinorganic Chemistry* 7(1977):23–24.

15. W.C. Willet, B.F. Polk, J.S. Morris, M.J. Stampfer, et al., "Prediagnostic Serum Selenium Levels and Risk of Cancer," *Lancet* 2(1983):130–134.

16. P.A.H. VanNoord, H.J.A. Collette, M.J. Mass, and F. deWaard, "Selenium Levels in Nails of Premenopausal Breast Cancer Patients Assessed Prediagnostically in a Cohort-Nested Case-Referent Study among Women Screened in the DOM Project," *International Journal of Epidemiology* 16(Suppl.)(1987):318–322.

17. F. Meyer and R. Verreault, "Erythrocyte Selenium and Breast Cancer Risk," *American Journal of Epidemiology* 125(1987):917–919.

18. B.R. Goldin, H. Adelercreutz, S.L. Gorbach, J.H. Warram, J.I. Dwyer, L. Swenson, and M.N. Woods, "Estrogen Excretion Patterns and Plasma Levels in Vegetarian and Omnivorous Women," *New England Journal of Medicine* 307(1982):1542–1547.

19. W.C. Willet, M.J. Stampfer, G.A. Colditz, B.A. Rosner, C.H. Hennekens, and F.E. Speizer, "Moderate Alcohol Consumption and the Risk of Breast Cancer," *New England Journal of Medicine* 316(1980):1174–1180.

20. A. Schatzkin, D.Y. Jones, R.N. Hoover, P.R. Taylor, L.A. Brinton, R.G. Ziegler, E.B. Harvey, C.L. Carter, L.M. Licitra, M.C. Dufour, and D.B. Larson, "Alcohol Consumption and Breast Cancer in the Epidemiologic Follow-Up Study of the First National Health and Nutrition Examination Survey," *New England Journal of Medicine* 316(1987):1169–1173.

21. E.B. Harvey, C. Schairer, L.A. Brinton, R.N. Hoover, and J.F. Fraumeni, Jr., "Alcohol Consumption and Breast Cancer," *Journal of the National Cancer Institute* 78(1987):657–661.

22. M. Tokunaga, C.E. Land, T. Yamamoto, et al., "Breast Cancer among Atomic Bomb Survivors," in J.D. Boice, Jr. and J.F. Fraumeni, Jr., eds., *Radiation Carcinogenesis Epidemiology and Biological Significance* (New York: Raven Press, 1984), pp.45–46.

23. A.B. Miller, G.R. Howe, G.J. Sherman, et al., "The Canadian Study of Cancer following Multiple Fluoroscopies," in *Mortality from Breast Cancer in Women, 1950–1980*, in press.

24. F.A. Mettler, L.H. Hempelmann, A.M. Dutton, J.W. Pifer, E.T. Toyooka, and W.R. Ames, "Breast Neoplasma in Women Treated with X Rays for Acute Postpartum Mastitis. A Pilot Study," *Journal of the National Cancer Institute* 43(1969):803–811.

25. J.D. Boice, N.E. Day, A. Anderson, et al., "Second Cancer following Radiation Treatment for Cervical Cancer. An International Collaboration among Cancer Registries," *Journal of the National Cancer Institute* 74(1985):955.

26. N.G. Hildreth, R.E. Shore, and P.M. Dvoretsky, "The Risk of Breast Cancer after Irradiation of the Thymus in Infancy," *New England Journal of Medicine* 321 (1989):1281.

27. D.A. Hoffman, J.E. Lonstein, M.M. Morin, et. al., "Breast Cancer in Women with Scoliosis Exposed to Multiple Diagnostic X Rays," *Journal of the National Cancer Institute* 81(1989):1307.

28. M.A. Tucker, C.N. Coleman, R.S. Cox, et al., "Risk of Second Cancers after Treatment for Hodgkin's Disease," *New England Journal of Medicine* 318(1988):76.

29. F.P. Li, J. Corkery, G. Vawter, et al., "Breast Carcinoma after Cancer Therapy in Childhood," *Cancer* 51(1983):521.

30. L. Rosenberg, D.R. Miller, D.W. Kaufman, et al., "Breast Cancer and Oral Contraceptive Use," *American Journal of Epidemiology* 119(1984):167.

31. J.L. Kelsey, D.B. Fischer, T.R. Holford, et al., "Exogenous Estrogens and Other Factors in the Epidemiology of Breast Cancer," *Journal of the National Cancer Institute* 55(1981):327.

32. D.R. Miller, L. Rosenberg, D.W. Kaufman, et al., "Breast Cancer before Age 45 and Oral Contraceptive Use: New Findings," *American Journal of Epidemiology* 129(1989):269.

33. E.R. Greenberg, A.B. Barnes, L. Resseguie, J.A. Barrett, S. Bernside, L.L. Langer, R.K. Neff, M. Stevens, R.H. Young, and T. Colton, "Breast Cancer in Mothers Given Diethylstilbestrol in Pregnancy," *New England Journal of Medicine* 311(1984):1393–1398.

34. J.L. Kelsey and G.S. Berkowitz, "Breast Cancer Epidemiology," *Cancer Reasearch* 48(1988):5615–5623.

35. Ibid.

36. R.D. Gambrell, "Role of Progestins in the Prevention of Breast Cancer," *Mauritas* 8(1986):169–176.

37. L. Bergkvist, A.O. Adami, I. Persson, et al., "The Risk of Breast Cancer after Estrogen and Estrogen-Progestin Replacement," *New England Journal of Medicine* 321(1989):293.

38. E. Barrett-Connor, "Postmenopausal Estrogen Replacement and Breast Cancer," *New England Journal of Medicine* 321(1989):319.

39. E. Seeman, J.L. Hopper, L.A. Bach, et al., "Reduced Bone Mass in Daughters of Women with Osteoporosis," *New England Journal of Medicine* 320(1989):554.

40. E.M. Brown and M.S. LeBoff, "Osteoporosis: Recent Advances in Diagnosis and Management," *Brigham and Women's Hospital Medical Update* 1(1989):1.

41. V.L. Ernster, T.L. Bush, G.R. Huggins, et al., "Clinical Perspectives: Benefits and Risks of Menopausal Estrogen and/or Progestin Hormone Use," *Preventative Medicine* 17(1989):201.

42. W.D. Dupont, D.L. Page, L.W. Rogers, et al., "Influence of Exogenous Estrogens, Proliferative Breast Disease, and Other Variables on Breast Cancer Risk," *Cancer* 63(1989):948.

43. J. Waterhouse, C. Muir, P. Correa, et al., eds., *Cancer Incidence in Five Continents*, Vol. 3. IARC Scientific Publications No. 42. International Agency for Research on Cancer, Lyons, France, 1982.

44. A.B. Miller, "Epidemiology and Prevention," in J.R. Harris, S. Hellman, I.C. Henderson, and D.W. Kinne, eds., *Breast Diseases* (Philadelphia: J.B. Lippincott, 1987).

45. A.B. Miller, "Approaches to the Control of Breast Cancer," in M.A. Rich, J.C. Hager, and P. Furmanski, eds., *Understanding Cancer. Clinical and Laboratory Concepts* (New York: Marcel Dekker, 1983), pp.3–25.

CHAPTER 13. DETECTION: MAMMOGRAPHY AND OTHER TECHNIQUES

1. S. Shapiro, W. Venet, P. Strax, et al., "Ten- to Fourteen-Year Effects of Screening on Breast Cancer Mortality," *Journal of the National Cancer Institute* 69(1982):349.

2. K.C. Chu, C.R. Smart, and R.E. Tarone, "Analysis of Breast Cancer Mortality and Stage Distribution by Age for the Health Insurance Plan Clinical Trial," *Journal of the National Cancer Institute* 80, 14(1988):1195.

3. L.H. Baker, "Breast Cancer Detection Demonstration Project: Five-Year Summary Report," *Cancer* 32(1982):194.

4. H. Seidman, S.K. Gelb, E. Silverberg, et al., "Survival Experience in the Breast Cancer Detection Demonstration Project," *CA-A Cancer Journal for Clinicians* 37(1987):258.

5. L. Tabar, C.J.G. Fagerberg, A. Grad, et al., "Reduction in Mortality from Breast Cancer after Mass Screening with Mammography Randomized Trial from the Breast Cancer Screening Working Group of the Swedish National Board of Health and Welfare," *Lancet* 1(1985):829.

6. A.L.M. Verbeek, J.H.C.L. Hendricks, R. Holland, et al., "Reduction in Breast Cancer Mortality through Mass Screening with Modern Mammography: First Result of the Nijmegen Project 1975–1981," *Lancet* 1(1984):1222.

7. D.M. Eddy, B. Hasselbad, W. McGivney, and W. Hendee, "The Value of Mammography Screening in Women under Age 50 Years," *Journal of the American Medical Association* 259(1988):1512–1519.

8. J.C. Bailar, "Mammography: A Contrary View," *Annals of Internal Medicine* 84(1976):77.

9. N. Sadowski, M.D., Director of the Sagoff Center for Breast Health, Faulkner Hospital, Jamaica Plain, Mass., personal communication.

10. J.N. Wolfe, "Risk for Breast Cancer Development Determined by Mammographic Parenchymal Pattern," *Cancer* 37(1976):2486.

11. S. Kumar, "ACR Program Accredits Nearly 800 Mammography Units," *Journal of the National Cancer Institute* 81(1989):1211–1212.

12. "Mammography Coverage on the Rise in the States," *Journal of the National Cancer Institute* 81(1989):1276.

13. P.C. Stomper, D.B. Kopans, N.L. Sadowski, et al., "Is Mammography Painful? A Multicenter Patient Survey." Unpublished paper.

CHAPTER 14. PRECANCEROUS CONDITIONS

1. H.H. Davis, M. Simons, and J.B. Davis, "Cystic Disease of the Breast Relationship to Cancer," *Cancer* 17(1974):957.

2. W.D. Dupont and D.L. Page, "Risk Factors for Breast Cancer in Women with Proliferative Breast Disease," *New England Journal of Medicine* 312(1985):146.

3. C.D. Haagensen, N. Lane, R. Lattes, et al., "Lobular Neoplasia (So-called Lobular Carcinoma in Situ) of the Breast," *Cancer* 42(1978):737–769.

4. J.E.W. Wheeler, H.T. Enterline, J.M. Roseman, et al., "Lobular Carcinoma in Situ of the Breast: Long-Term Follow-Up," *Cancer* 34(1974):554–560.

5. J.A. Anderson, "Lobular Carcinoma in Situ: A Long-Term Follow-Up in 52 Cases," *Acta Pathology and Microbiology of Scandinavia (A)* 82(1974):519–525.

6. P.P. Rosen, P.H. Lieberman, and D.W. Braun, "Lobular Carcinoma of the Breast," *American Journal of Surgical Pathology* 2(1987):225–251.

7. P.P. Rosen, D.W. Braun, and D.E. Kinne, "The Clinical Significance of Preinvasive Breast Carcinoma," *Cancer* 46(1980):919–925.

8. C.E. Alpers and S.R. Wellings, "The Prevalence of Carcinoma in Situ in Normal and Cancer-Associated Breasts," *Human Pathology* 16(1985):796–807.

9. M. Nielsen, J. Jensen, and J. Andersen, "Precancerous and Cancerous Breast Lesions during Lifetime and at Autopsy," *Cancer* 54(1984):612–615.

10. W.L. Betsill, P.P. Rosen, P.H. Lieberman, et al., Intraductal Carcinoma: Long-Term Follow-Up after Treatment by Biopsy Alone," *Journal of the American Medical Association* 239(1978):1863–1867.

11. D.L. Page and W.D. Dupont, "Intraductal Carcinoma of the Breast," *Cancer* 49(1982):751–758.

12. M.D. Lagios, P.R. Westdahl, F.R. Margolin, et al., "Duct Carcinoma in Situ," *Cancer* 50(1982):1309–1314.

13. M.D. Lagios, F.R. Margolin, P.R. Westdahl, and M.R. Rose, "Mammographically Detected Duct Carcinoma in Situ: Frequency of Local Recurrence following Ty-

pectomy and Prognostic Effect of Nuclear Grade on Local Recurrence," *Cancer* 63(1989):618.

14. A. Recht, B.S. Danoff, L.J. Solin, et al., "Intraductal Carcinoma of the Breast: Results of Treatment with Excisional Biopsy and Irradiation," *Journal of Clinical Oncology* 6(1983):281–285.

15. P. Findlay and R. Goodman, "Radiation Therapy for Treatment of Intraductal Carcinoma of the Breast," *American Journal of Clinical Oncology* 6(1983):281–285.

16. E.D. Montague, "Conservative Surgery and Radiation Therapy in the Treatment of Operable Breast Cancer," *Cancer* 53(1984):700–704.

17. E.R. Fisher, R. Sass, B. Fisher, et al., "Pathological Findings from the National Surgical, Breast and Bowel Project (Protocol 6). 1. Intraductal Carcinoma (DCIS)," *Cancer* 57(1986):197–208.

CHAPTER 15. BREAST CANCER: AN OVERVIEW

1. G. Robbins, ed., *Silvergirl's Surgery: The Breast*. Silvergirl, Inc., Austin, Texas, 1984.

2. B. Fisher, "Laboratory and Clinical Research in Breast Cancer—A Personal Adventure. The David Karnofsky Memorial Lecture," *Cancer Research* 40(1980):3863–3874.

3. J. Gershon-Cohen, S.M. Berger, and H.S. Klickstein, "Roentgenography of Breast Cancer Moderating Concept of 'Biological Predeterminism'," *Cancer* 16(1963):961.

4. B. Fisher, C.B. Redmond, E. Fisher, et al., "Ten-Year Results of Randomized Clinical Trial Comparing Radical Mastectomy and Total Mastectomy with or without Radiation," *New England Journal of Medicine* 312(1985):674–681.

5. J.R. Harris and R.T. Osteen, "Patients with Early Breast Cancer Benefit from Effective Axillary Treatment," *Breast Cancer Research and Treatment* 5(1985):17.

CHAPTER 16. DIAGNOSIS AND TYPES OF CANCER

1. L. Palombini, F. Fulciniti, A. Vetrani, et al., "Fine-Needle Aspiration Biopsies of Breast Masses: A Critical Analysis of 1956 Cases in 8 Years (1976–1984)," *Cancer* 61(1988):2273.

2. E.R. Fisher, R. Sass, and B. Fisher, "Biological Considerations Regarding the One- and Two-Step Procedures in the Management of Patients with Invasive Carcinoma of the Breast," *Surgery, Gynecology, and Obstetrics* 161(1985):245.

3. J.M. Dixon, T.J. Anderson, D.L. Page, et al., "Infiltrating Lobular Carcinoma of the Breast: An Evaluation of the Incidence and Consequence of Bilateral Disease," *British Journal of Surgery* 70(1983):513.

4. J.L. Flowers, G.V. Burton, E.R. Cox, et al., "Use of Monoclonal Antiestrogen Receptor Antibody to Evaluate Estrogen Receptor Content in Fine-Needle Aspiration Breast Biopsies," *Annals of Surgery* 203(1985):250.

5. C.J. Cornelisse, C.J.H. van de Velde, R.J.C. Caspers, et al., "DNA Ploidy and Survival in Breast Cancer Patients," *Cytometry* 8(1987):225.

CHAPTER 17. STAGING

1. C. Haagensen, *Diseases of the Breast*, 2d edition (Philadelphia: Saunders, 1971), chapter 33.
2. D. Schottenfield, A.G. Nash, G.F. Robbins, et al., "Ten-Year Results of the Treatment of Primary Operable Breast Carcinoma," *Cancer* 38(1976):1001–1007.
3. A. Lorde, *A Burst of Light* (Ithaca, N.Y.: Firebrand Books, 1988), p.550.

CHAPTER 18. FEARS AND FEELINGS

1. B. Rollin, *First, You Cry* (New York: New American Library, 1976), p.111.
2. R. Kushner, *Alternatives* (Cambridge, Mass.: Kensington Press, 1984), p.192.
3. Rollin, p.114.
4. H. Peters-Golden,"Breast Cancer: Varied Perceptions of Social Support in the Illness Experience," *Social Science Medicine* 16(1982):483–492.
5. Telephone interview with Anne Kaspar.
6. W. Schain, "Update on the Psychological Issues of Breast Cancer Treatments," in J.K. Harness, H.A. Oberman, A.S. Lichter, S.S. Adler, and R.L. Cody, eds., *Breast Cancer: Collaborative Management* (Chelsea, Mich.: Lewis, 1988).
7. S.E. Taylor, R.R. Lichtman, and J.V. Wood, "Attributions, Beliefs about Control and Adjustment to Breast Cancer," *Journal of Perspectives on Sociology and Psychology* 46(1984):489.
8. R.R. Lichtman, S.E. Taylor, et al., "Relations with Children after Breast Cancer: The Mother–Daughter Relationship at Risk," *Journal of Psychosociology and Oncology* 2(1984):1–19.

CHAPTER 19. TREATMENT OPTIONS: AN OVERVIEW

1. I.C. Henderson, D.F. Hayes, L.M., Parker, S. Love et al., "Adjuvant Systemic Therapy for Node-Negative Patients," *Cancer* (*in press*).
2. Early Breast Cancer Trialist Collaborative Group, "Effects of Adjuvant Tamoxifen and of Cytotoxic Therapy on Mortality in Early Breast Cancer: An Overview of 61 Randomized Trials among 28,896 Women," *New England Journal of Medicine* 319(1988):1681.
3. Ibid.
4. C. Brambilla, A. Rossi, P. Valagussa, et al., "Adjuvant Chemotherapy in Post-menopausal Women: Results of Sequential Non-cross-resistant Regimens," *World Journal of Surgery* 9(1985):728.
5. Breast Cancer Trials Committee, Scottish Cancer, Trials Office, "Adjuvant Tamoxifen in the Management of Operable Breast Cancer: The Scottish Trial," *Lancet* (1987):171.
6. Early Breast Cancer Trialist Collaborative Group.
7. Consensus Development Conference Report, "Adjuvant Chemotherapy for Breast Cancer," *Journal of the American Medical Association* 254(1985):3461.
8. B. Fisher, M. Bauer, R. Margolese, et al., "Five-Year Results of a Randomized Clinical Trial Comparing Total Mastectomy and Segmental Mastectomy with or with-

out Radiation in the Treatment of Breast Cancer," *New England Journal of Medicine* 312(1985):665.

9. Clinical Alert from the National Cancer Institute (May 18, 1988).

10. W.L. McGuire, "Adjuvant Therapy of Node-Negative Breast Cancer: Another Point of View," *Journal of the National Cancer Institute* 80(1988):1075.

11. G. Bonadonna, P. Valagussa, G. Tacini, et al., "Current Status of Milan Adjuvant Chemotherapy Trials for Node-Positive and Node-Negative Breast Cancer," *National Cancer Institute Monograph* 1(1986):65–69.

12. B. Fisher, C. Redmond, N.V. Dimitrov, et al., "A Randomized Clinical Trial Evaluating Sequential Methotrexate and Fluorouracil in the Treatment of Patients with Node-negative Breast Cancer Who Have Estrogen Receptor-negative Tumors," *New England Journal of Medicine* 320(1989):473.

13. B. Fisher, J. Costantin, C. Redmond, et al., "A Randomized Clinical Trial Evaluating Tamoxifen in the Treatment of Patients with Node-Negative Breast Cancer Who Have Estrogen-Receptor-Positive Tumors," *New England Journal of Medicine* 320(1989):479.

14. E.G. Mansour, R. Gray, A.H. Shatila, et al., "Efficacy of Adjuvant Chemotherapy in High-Risk Node-Negative Breast Cancer: An Intergroup Study," *New England Journal of Medicine* 320(1989):485.

15. G. Bonadonna, "Conceptual and Practical Advances in the Management of Breast Cancer," *Journal of Clinical Oncology* 7(1989):1380.

16. R.L. Love, "Tamoxifen Therapy in Primary Breast Cancer: Biology, Efficacy, and Side Effects," *Journal of Clinical Oncology* 7(1989):803.

17. U. Veronesi, "Randomized Trials Comparing Conservative Techniques with Conventional Surgery: An Overview," in J.S. Tobias and M.J. Peckham, eds., *Primary Management of Breast Cancer: Alternatives to Mastectomy Management of Malignant Disease Series* (London: E. Arnold, 1985).

18. B. Fisher, C. Redmond, R. Poisson, R. Margolese, et al., "Eight-Year Results of a Randomized Clinical Trial Comparing Total Mastectomy and Segmental Mastectomy with or without Radiation in the Treatment of Breast Cancer," *New England Journal of Medicine* 320(1989):822.

19. A. Rech, J.L. Connolly, S.J. Schnitt, et al., "Conservative Surgery and Primary Radiation Therapy for Early Breast Cancer: Results, Controversies and Unresolved Problems," *Seminars in Oncology* 13 (1986):434–450.

20. J.R. Harris, J.L. Connolly, S.J. Schnitt, et al., "The Use of Pathological Features in Selecting the Extent of Surgical Resection Necessary for Breast Cancer Patients Treated by Primary Radiation Therapy," *Annals of Surgery* 201(1985):164.

21. R. Calle, J.R. Viloq, B. Zafrani, et al., "Local Control and Survival of Breast Cancer Treated by Limited Surgery Followed by Irradiation," *International Journal of Radiology, Oncology and Biophysics* 12(1986):873.

22. R. Lindley, A. Bulman, P. Parsons, et al., "Histological Features Predictive of an Increased Risk of Early Local Recurrence after Treatment of Breast Cancer by Local Tumor Excision and Radical Radiotherapy," *Surgery* 105(1989):13.

23. M. Brenner, S.J. Schnitt, J.L. Connolly, et al., "The Use of Reexcision in Primary Radiation Therapy for Stage I and II Breast Carcinoma," Proceedings of the American Society of Therapeutic Radiology and Oncology, *International Journal of Radiology, Oncology and Biophysics* 11(Suppl. 1)(1985):186.

24. P.P. Rosen, D.W. Kinne, M. Lesser, et al., "Are Prognostic Factors for Local Control of Breast Cancer Treated by Primary Radiotherapy Significant for Patients Treated by Mastectomy?," *Cancer* 57(1986):1415.

25. B. Fisher, M. Bauer, R. Margolese, et al.

26. R. Kushner, *Why Me?* (Cambridge, Mass.: Kensington Press, 1982), p.372.

CHAPTER 20. SPECIAL CASES

1. T.A. Sheldon, L.M. Parker, and B. Cady, "Management of Locally Advanced Breast Cancer," in Chapter 15, "Special Therapeutic Problems," in J.R. Harris, S. Hellman, I.C. Henderson, and D.W. Kinne, eds., *Breast Diseases* (Philadelphia: J.B. Lippincott, 1987).

2. G.N. Hortobagyi, G.R. Blumenschein, W. Spanos, et al., "Multimodal Treatment of Locally Advanced Breast Cancer," *Cancer* 51(1983):763.

3. A.M. Chu, W.C. Wood, and J.A. Doucette, "Inflammatory Breast Carcinoma Treated by Radical Radiotherapy," *Cancer* 45(1980):2730.

4. M.M. Sherry, D.H. Johnson, D.L. Page, et al., "Inflammatory Carcinoma of the Breast: Clinical Review and Summary of the Vanderbilt Experience with Multimodality Therapy," *American Journal of Medicine* 79(1985):355.

5. R. Ashikari, P.P. Rosen, J.A. Urban, et al., "Breast Cancer Presenting as an Axillary Mass," *Annals of Surgery* 183(1976):415–417.

6. J.R. Viloq, R. Calle, F. Ferme, et al., Conservative Treatment of Axillary Adenopathy Due to Probable Subclinical Breast Cancer," *Archives of Surgery* 117(1982):1136–1138.

7. E.D. Montague, "Axillary Metastases from Unknown Primary Sites," in G. Fletcher, ed., *Textbook of Radiotherapy* (Philadelphia: Lea and Febiger, 1980).

8. Z. Feigenberg, M. Zer, and M. Dintsman, "Axillary Metastases from an Unknown Primary Source: A Diagnostic and Therapeutic Approach," *Israeli Journal of Medical Science* 12(1976):1153–1158.

9. S.J. Kister and C.D. Haagensen, "Paget's Disease of the Breast," *American Journal of Surgery* 119(1970):606–609.

10. G. Malak and L. Tapolcsanyi, "Characteristics of Paget's Carcinoma of the Nipple and Problems of Its Negligence," *Oncology* 30(1974):278–293.

11. M.D. Lagios, P.R. Westdahl, M.R. Rose, et al., "Paget's Disease of the Nipple," *Cancer* 54(1984):545–551.

12. C.D. Haagensen, *Diseases of the Breast*, 2d edition (Philadelphia: W.B. Saunders, 1975), pp.227–249

13. M.L. Bunker and M.V. Peters, "Breast Cancer Associated with Pregnancy and Lactation," *American Journal of Obstetrics and Gynecology* 85(1963):312–321.

14. R.M. Schwartz, R.B. Newell, J.F. Hauch, et al., "A Study of Familial Male Breast Carcinoma and a Second Report," *Cancer* 46(1980):2629–2701.

15. A.W. Jackson et al., "Carcinoma of the Male Breast in Association with the Klinefelter Syndrome," *British Medical Journal* 1(1965):223–225.

16. J.H. Campbell and S.D. Cummins, "Metastases Simulating Mammary Cancer in Prostatic Carcinoma under Estrogenic Therapy," *Cancer* 4(1951):303.

CHAPTER 21. SURGERY

1. R.J. Lanzafame, C.J. McCormick, D.W. Rogers, et al., "Mechanisms of the Reduction of Tumor Recurrence with the Carbon Dioxide Laser in Experimental Mammary Tumors," *Surgery, Gynecology and Obstetrics* 67(1988):493.

2. S.M. Murthy, R.A. Goldshmidt, L.N. Rao, et al., "The Influence of Surgical Trauma on Experimental Metastasis," *Cancer* 64(1989):2035.

3. W.J.M. Hrushesky, A.Z. Bluming, S.A. Gruber, R.B. Sothern, "Menstrual Influence on Surgical Cure of Breast Cancer," *Lancet* 2(1989):949.

4. P.P. Rosen, M.T. Lesser, D.W. Kinne, et al., "Discontinuous or 'Skip' Metastases in Breast Carcinoma. Analysis of 1228 Axillary Dissections," *Annals of Surgery* 197(1983):276.

5. B.M. Siegel, K.A. Mayzel, S.M. Love, "Level I and II Axillary Dissection in the Treatment of Early-Stage Breast Cancer: An Analysis of 259 Consecutive Patients," *Archives of Surgery*, 1990, in press.

CHAPTER 22. RADIATION TREATMENT

1. J. Cuzuik, H. Stewart, R. Peto, et al., "Overview of Randomized Trials of Postoperative Adjuvant Radiotherapy in Breast Cancer," *Cancer Treatment Report* 71(1987):15–29.

2. J.M. Kurtz, R. Amalric, H. Brandone, et al., "Contralateral Breast Cancer and Other Second Malignancies in Patients Treated by Breast-Conserving Therapy with Radiation," *International Journal of Radiation, Oncology, Biology and Physics* 15(1987):277.

CHAPTER 23. SYSTEMIC TREATMENTS: CHEMOTHERAPY AND HORMONE THERAPY

1. G. Bonadonna, V.E. Valagussa, A. Rossi, et al., "Ten-Year Experience with CMF-Based Adjuvant Chemotherapy in Resectable Breast Cancer," *Breast Cancer Research and Treatment* 5(1985):95.

2. Ibid.

3. B. Fisher, E.R. Fisher, and C. Redmond, "Ten-Year Results from the NSABP Clinical Trial Evaluating the Use of L-phenylalanine Mustard (L-PAM) in the Management of Primary Breast Cancer," *Journal of Clinical Oncology* 4(1986):929.

4. Early Breast Cancer Trialist Collaborative Group, "Effects of Adjuvant Tamoxifen and of Cytotoxic Therapy on Mortality in Early Breast Cancer: An Overview of 61 Randomized Trials among 28,896 Women," *New England Journal of Medicine* 319 (1988):1681.

5. B. Fisher, H. Rockette, E.R. Fisher, et al., "Leukemia in Breast Cancer Patients following Adjuvant Chemotherapy or Postoperative Radiation: The NSABP Experience," *Journal of Clinical Oncology* 3(1985):1640.

6. B.S. Siegel, *Love, Medicine and Miracles* (New York: Harper & Row, 1986), p.133.

7. R.G. Ravdin, E.F. Lewison, N.H. Slack, et al., "Results of a Clinical Trial Concerning the Worth of Prophylactic Oophorectomy for Breast Carcinoma," *Surgery, Gynecology, and Obstetrics* 31(1970):1055.

8. Early Breast Cancer Trialist Collaborative Group.

9. R.L. Love, "Tamoxifen Therapy in Primary Breast Cancer: Biology, Efficacy, and Side Effects," *Journal of Clinical Oncology* 7(1989):803.

10. A. Coates, V.G.M. Stat, J.F. Bishop, et al., "Improving the Quality of Life during Chemotherapy for Advanced Breast Cancer: A Comparison of Intermittent and Continuous Treatment Strategies," *New England Journal of Medicine* 317(1987):1490.

11. L.R. Morgan, Jr., P.S. Schein, P.V. Wooley, et al., "Therapeutic Use of Tamoxifen in Advanced Breast Cancer: Correlation with Biochemical Parameters," *Cancer Treatment Report* 60(1976):1437.

CHAPTER 24. COMPLEMENTARY AND ALTERNATIVE TREATMENTS

1. N. Cousins, *Anatomy of an Illness* (New York: Bantam Books, 1979), p.45.
2. Ibid., p.69.
3. Ibid., p.56.
4. N. Fiore, *The Road Back to Health* (New York: Bantam Books, 1984), p.149.
5. Cousins, p.39.
6. Cousins, p.68–69.
7. H. Benson, *Beyond the Relaxation Response* (New York: Berkley Books, 1985).
8. D.L. Mella, *The Legendary and Practical Use of Gems and Stones* (Albuquerque, N.M.: Domel, 1979).
9. A.P. Boyar, D.P. Rose, J.R. Loughride, et al., "Response to a Diet Low in Total Fat in Women with Postmenopausal Breast Cancer: A Pilot Study," *Nutrition and Cancer* 11(1988):93.
10. C. Frederick, *Winning the Fight against Breast Cancer: The Nutritional Approach* (New York: Grosset & Dunlap, 1977).
11. M. Kushi, *The Cancer Prevention Diet* (New York: St. Martin's Press, 1983), pp.157–160.
12. D. Heeb, "*Traditional Acupuncture: What Can It Do for You?*" Self-published pamphlet.
13. D. Kennedy, Food and Drug Administration's warning on laetrile.
14. A. Lorde, *A Burst of Light* (Ithaca, N.Y.: Firebrand Books, 1988), pp.89–134.

CHAPTER 25. REHABILITATION

1. A. Lorde, *The Cancer Journals* (New York: Spinsters Ink, 1980), p.16.
2. B. Rollin, *First, You Cry* (New American Library, 1976), pp.173–175.
3. R. Kushner, *Why Me?* (Cambridge, Mass.: Kensington Press, 1982), p.277.
4. C.H. Johnson, J.A. van Heerden, J.H. Donohue, et al., "Oncological Aspects of Immediate Breast Reconstruction following Mastectomy for Malignancy," *Archives of Surgery* 124(1989):819.
5. P. Stein, B. Lazarus, N. Stearns, C. Secor, and B. Hoffman, "Cancer and the Workplace," a panel discussion sponsored by Radcliffe Career Services, The Cronkhite Graduate Center, Radcliffe College, Cambridge, Mass., November 4, 1988, p.34.
6. S. Kitzinger, *Woman's Experience of Sex* (New York: G.P. Putnam's Sons, 1983), pp.308–309.
7. L. Mignot et al., "Breast Cancer and Subsequent Pregnancy," *American Society of Clinical Oncology Proceedings* 5(1986):57.
8. M. Peters, "The Effect of Pregnancy in Breast Cancer," *Prognostic Factors in Breast Cancer* 65(1968).

CHAPTER 26. RECURRENCE

1. G.F. Robbins and J.W. Berg, "Bilateral Primary Breast Cancers: A Prospective Clinical Pathological Study," *Cancer* 17(1964):1501.
2. C.D. Haagensen, N. Lane, and C. Bodian, "Coexisting Lobular Neoplasia and Carcinoma of the Breast," *Cancer* 51(1983):1468.

3. M. Stierer and H.R. Rosen, "Influence of Early Diagnosis on Prognosis of Recurrent Breast Cancer," *Cancer* 64(1989):1128.

4. A. Recht, S.J. Schnitt, J. Connolly, et al., "Prognosis following Local or Regional Recurrence after Conservative Surgery and Radiotherapy for Early Stage Breast Carcinoma," *International Journal of Radiation, Oncology, and Biophysics* 16(1989):3.

5. B. Fisher, N. Wolmark, et al., "The Accuracy of Clinical Nodal Staging and of Limited Axillary Dissection as a Determinant of Histological Nodal Status in Carcinoma of the Breast," *Surgery, Gynecology, and Obstetrics* 152(1981):765.

6. M.D. Gilliland, R.M. Barton, and E.M. Copeland, "The Implication of Local Recurrence of Breast Cancer," *Annals of Surgery* 197(1983):284.

CHAPTER 27. THE FUTURE

1. A.H. Friend, T.P. Dryja, and R.A. Weinberg, "Oncogenes and Tumor-Suppressing Genes," *New England Journal of Medicine* 318(1988):618.

2. M.J. van de Vijver, J.L. Peterse, W.J. Mooi, et al., "Neu-Protein Overexpression in Breast Cancer: Association with Comedo-Type Ductal Carcinoma in Situ and Limited Prognostic Value in Stage II Breast Cancer," *New England Journal of Medicine* 319(1988):1239.

3. A. Thor, M.O. Weeks, and J. Schlom, "Monoclonal Antibodies and Breast Cancer," *Seminars in Oncology* 13(1986):393.

4. E.T. Fossel, J.M. Carr, and J. McDonagh, "Detection of Malignant Tumors: Water-Suppressed Proton Nuclear Magnetic Resonance Spectroscopy of Plasma," *New England Journal of Medicine* 315(1986):1369.

5. M.S. Mitchell, "Combining Chemotherapy with Biological Response Modifiers in Treatment of Cancer," *Journal of the National Cancer Institute* 80(1988):1445.

6. S.A. Rosenberg, "The Development of New Immunotherapies for the Treatment of Cancer Using Interleukin-2. A Review," *Annals of Surgery* 208(1988):121.

7. L.R. Heberman, M. Lippman, and T. d'Angelo, "Correlation of Stress Factors with Sustained Depression of Natural Killer Cell Activity and Predicted Prognosis in Patients with Breast Cancer," *Journal of Clinical Oncology* 5(1987):348.

8. C.N. Coleman, E.A. Bump, and R.A. Kramer, "Chemical Modifiers of Cancer Treatment," *Journal of Clinical Oncology* 6(1988):709.

9. J.R. Stewart and F.A. Gibbs, "Hyperthermia in the Treatment of Cancer: Perspectives on Its Promise and Its Problems," *Cancer* 54(1984):2823.

10. Ibid.

Glossary

abscess: Infection that has formed a pocket of pus.

adenocarcinoma: Cancer arising in gland-forming tissue. Breast cancer is a type of adenocarcinoma.

adjuvant chemotherapy: Anticancer drugs used in combination with surgery and/or radiation as an initial treatment before there is detectable spread, to prevent or delay recurrence.

adrenal gland: Small gland found above each kidney. Secretes cortisone, adrenalin, aldosterone, and many other important hormones.

alopecia: Hair loss; a common side effect of chemotherapy.

amenorrhea: Absence or stoppage of menstrual period.

androgen: Hormone that produces male characteristics.

anorexia: Loss of appetite.

areola: Area of pigment around the nipple.

aspiration: Putting a hypodermic needle into a tissue and drawing back on the syringe to obtain fluid or cells.

atypical cell: Mild to moderately abnormal cell.

atypical hyperplasia: Cells that are not only abnormal but increased in number.

autologous: From the same person. An autologous blood transfusion is blood removed and then transfused back to the same person at a later date.

axilla: Armpit.

axillary lymph node dissection: Surgical removal of lymph nodes found in the armpit region.

axillary lymph nodes: Lymph nodes found in the armpit area.

benign: Not cancerous.

bilateral: Involving both sides, such as both breasts.

biological response modifier: Usually natural substances which alter the body's natural response, such as colony-stimulating factor, which stimulates the bone marrow to make blood cells.

biopsy: Removal of tissue. This term does not indicate how much tissue will be removed.

bone marrow: Soft inner part of large bones that makes blood cells.

bone scan: Test to determine if there is any sign of cancer in the bones.

breast reconstruction: Creation of artificial breast after mastectomy by a plastic surgeon.

bromocriptine: Drug used to block the hormone prolactin.

calcifications: Small calcium deposits in the breast tissue which can be seen by mammography.

carcinoembryonic antigen (CEA): Nonspecific (not specific to cancer) blood test used to follow women with metastatic breast cancer to help determine if the treatment is working.

carcinogen: Substance that can cause cancer.

carcinoma: Cancer arising in the epithelial tissue (skin, glands, and lining of internal organs). Most cancers are carcinomas.

cellulitis: Infection of the soft tissues.

centigray: Measurement of radiation-absorbed dose; same as a rad.

chemotherapy: Treatment of disease with certain chemicals. The term usually refers to cytotoxic drugs given for cancer treatment.

choriogonadotropin: Hormone produced by the corpus luteum.

colostrum: Secretion from the breast during pregnancy or after birth before the milk comes in.

corpus luteum: Ovarian follicle after ovulation.

costochondritis: Inflammation of the connection between ribs and breastbone; a type of arthritis.

cyclical: According to a cycle, such as the menstrual cycle.

cyst: Fluid-filled sac.

cystosarcoma phylloides: Unusual type of breast tumor.

cytology: Study of cells.

cytotoxic: Causing the death of cells. The term usually refers to drugs used in chemotherapy.

danazol: Drug used to block hormones from the pituitary gland; used in endometriosis and, rarely, breast pain.

diethylstilbestrol (DES): Synthetic estrogen once used to prevent miscarriages, now shown to cause vaginal cancer in daughters of women who took it. Sometimes used for metastatic breast cancer.

differentiated: Clearly defined. Differentiated tumor cells are similar in appearance to normal cells.

doubling time: Time it takes the cell population to double in number.

ductal carcinoma in situ: Ductal cancer cells that have not grown outside of their site of origin; sometimes referred to as precancer.

eczema: Skin irritation characterized by redness and open weeping.

edema: Swelling caused by a collection of fluid in the soft tissues.

electrocautery: Instrument used in surgery to cut, coagulate, or destroy tissue by heating it with an electric current.

embolus: Plug of tumor cells or clot within a blood vessel.

estrogen: Female sex hormones produced by the ovaries, adrenal glands, placenta, and fat.

estrogen receptor: Protein found on some cells to which estrogen molecules will attach. If a tumor is positive for estrogen receptors it is sensitive to hormones.

fat necrosis: Area of dead fat, usually following some form of trauma or surgery; a cause of lumps.

fibroadenoma: Benign fibrous tumor of the breast; most common in young women.

fibrocystic disease: Much-misused term for any benign condition of the breast.

fibroid: Benign fibrous tumor of the uterus (not in the breast).

flow cytometry: Test that measures DNA content in tumors.

fluoroscopy: Use of X-ray machine to examine parts of body directly rather than taking a picture and developing it, as in conventional X rays. Fluoroscopy uses more radiation than a single X ray.

frozen section: Freezing and slicing tissue to make a slide immediately for diagnosis.

galactocele: Milk cyst sometimes found in a nursing mother's breast.

genetic: Relating to genes or inherited characteristics.

hematoma: Collection of blood in the tissues. Hematomas may occur in the breast after trauma or after surgery.

heterogeneous: Composed of many different elements. In relation to breast cancer, heterogeneous refers to the fact that there are many different types of breast cancer cells within one tumor.

homeopathy: System of therapy using very small doses of drugs which can produce in healthy people symptoms similar to those of the disease being treated. These are believed to stimulate the immune system.

hormone: Chemical substance produced by glands in the body which enters the bloodstream and causes effects in other tissues.

hot flashes: Sudden sensations of heat and flushing associated with the menopause.

hyperplasia: Excessive growth of cells.

hypothalamus: Area at the base of the brain that controls various functions, including hormone production in the pituitary.

hysterectomy: Removal of the uterus. Hysterectomy does not necessarily mean the removal of ovaries (oophorectomy).

immune system: Complex system by which the body is able to protect itself from foreign invaders.

immunocytochemistry: Study of the chemistry of cells using techniques that employ immune mechanisms.

infiltrating cancer: Cancer that can grow beyond its site of origin into neighboring tissue. Infiltrating does not imply that the cancer has already spread outside the breast. Infiltrating has the same meaning as invasive.

informed consent: Process by which the patient is fully informed of all risks and complications of a planned procedure before agreeing to proceed.

in situ: In the site of. In regard to cancer, refers to tumors that haven't grown beyond the site of origin, into neighboring tissue.

intraductal: Within the duct. Intraductal can describe a benign or malignant process.

intraductal papilloma: Benign tumor that projects like a finger from the lining of the duct.

invasive cancers: Cancers that are capable of growing beyond their site of origin and invading neighboring tissue. Invasive does not imply that the cancer is aggressive or has already spread.

lactation: Production of milk from the breast.

lidocaine: Drug most commonly used for local anesthesia.

lobular: Having to do with the lobules of the breast.

lobular carcinoma in situ: Abnormal cells within the lobule that don't form lumps. Can serve as a marker of future cancer risk.

lobules: Parts of the breast capable of making milk.

local treatment of cancer: Treatment only of the tumor in the breast.

lumpectomy: Surgery to remove lump with small rim of normal tissue around it.

luteinizing hormone: Hormone produced by the pituitary that helps control the menstrual cycle.

lymphatic vessels: Vessels that carry lymph (tissue fluid) to and from lymph nodes.

lymphedema: Milk arm. This swelling of the arm can follow surgery to the lymph nodes under the arm. It can be temporary or permanent and occur immediately or any time later.

lymph nodes: Glands found throughout the body that help defend against foreign invaders such as bacteria. Lymph nodes can be a location of cancer spread.

magnetic resonance imaging (MRI): Imaging technique using a magnet and electrical coil to transmit radio waves through the body.

malignant: Cancerous.

mastalgia: Pain in the breast.

mastitis: Infection of the breast. Mastitis is sometimes used loosely to refer to any benign process in the breast.

mastodynia: Pain in the breast.

mastopexy: Uplift of the breast through plastic surgery.

menarche: First menstrual period.

metastasis: Spread of cancer to another organ, usually through the bloodstream.

metastasize: To spread to a distant site.

methylxanthine: Chemical group to which caffeine belongs.

microcalcification: Tiny calcifications in the breast tissue usually seen only on a mammogram. When clustered can be a sign of ductal carcinoma in situ.

micrometastasis: Microscopic and as yet undetectable but presumed spread of tumor cells to other organs.

necrosis: Dead tissue.

nodular: Forming little nodules.

nuclear magnetic resonance (NMR): Another name for magnetic resonance imaging (MRI).

oncogenes: Tumor genes that are present in the body. These can be activated by carcinogens and cause cells to grow uncontrollably.

oncology: Study of cancer.

oophorectomy: Removal of the ovaries.

osteoporosis: Softening of the bones that can occur with age.

oxytocin: Hormone produced by the pituitary gland, involved in lactation.

palliation: Act of relieving a symptom without curing the cause.

pathologist: Doctor who specializes in examining tissue and diagnosing disease.

phlebitis: Irritation of a vein.

polymastia: Literally, many breasts. Existence of an extra breast or breasts.

progesterone: Hormone produced by the ovary. Involved in the normal menstrual cycle.

prognosis: Expected or probable outcome.

prolactin: Hormone produced by the pituitary that stimulates progesterone production by the ovaries and lactation.

prophylactic subcutaneous mastectomy: Removal of all breast tissue beneath the skin and nipple, to prevent future breast cancer.

prosthesis: Artificial substitute for an absent part of the body, as in breast prosthesis.

protocol: Research designed to answer a hypothesis. Protocols often involve testing a specific new treatment under controlled conditions.

proto-oncogene: Normal gene-controlling cell growth or turnover.

pseudolump: Breast tissue that feels like a lump but when removed proves to be normal.

quadrantectomy: Removal of a quarter of the breast.

rad: Radiation-absorbed dose; same as centigray. One chest X ray equals one tenth of a rad.

randomized: Chosen at random. In a randomized research study, subjects are chosen to be given a particular treatment by means of a computer programmed to choose names at random.

recurrence: Return of cancer after its apparently complete disappearance.

remission: Disappearance of detectable disease.

sarcoma: Cancer arising in the connective tissue.

sebaceous: Oily, cheesy material secreted by glands in the skin.

selenium: Metallic element found in food.

seroma: Collection of tissue fluid.

side effect: Unintentional or undesirable secondary effect of treatment.

silicone: Synthetic material used in breast implants because of its flexibility, resilience, and durability.

systemic treatment: Treatment involving the whole body, usually using drugs.

tamoxifen: Estrogen blocker used in treating breast cancer.

thoracic: Concerning the chest (thorax).

thoracoepigastric vein: Vein that starts under the arm and passes along the side of the breast and then down into the abdomen.

titration: Systems of balancing. In chemotherapy titration means using the largest amount of a drug possible while keeping the side effects from becoming intolerable.

trauma: Wound or injury.

triglyceride: Form in which fat is stored in the body, consisting of glycerol and three fatty acids.

tumor: Abnormal mass of tissue. Strictly speaking, a tumor can be benign or malignant.

xeroradiography: Type of mammogram taken on a Xerox plate rather than X-ray film.

Index

Note: Page numbers in italics refer to illustrations in the text.

Reach to Recovery, 362, 400
Reagan, Nancy, 262
Reconstruction, 349–357
  benefits of, 350
  expander, 352–353
  free-gluteus flap, 355, *356*
  immediate reconstruction, 355, 357
  information sources on, 402
  insurance coverage, 357–358
  myocutaneous flap, 353, *354*, 355
  nipple and, 357
  silicone implant, *351–352*
Recurrence of breast cancer
  early detection and, 370
  emotional factors, 245–246
  information sources on, 404
  and lumpectomy, 261
  meaning of, 211–212
  positive approach to, 372
  symptoms of, 373–374
  time to recurrence, 254
  treatment and, 375–376
  types of, 370–373
Regional support organizations, listing of, 405–408
Relative risk, *138*, 139–141
Relaxation response, 332
Remission, 372
  meaning of, 212
RENU Breast Reconstruction Counseling, 402
Research
  control group, 212
  information sources on, 404
  programs for participation, 215
  protocols, 212–213
  randomized group, 212
  rationale for participation in, 213–214, 215
Research areas, future directions
  biological response modifiers, 383
  growth factors, 380–*381*
  immune system, 383–384
  lipoproteins, 382–383
  monoclonal antibodies, 381–*382*
  proto-oncogenes, 378–380
Retinoblastoma, 379
Retreats, dealing with cancer, 399
Rollin, Betty, 241, 242, 349, 361
Rosen, Peter Paul, 261
Royal Victoria Hospital Palliative Care Service, address, 404

Sagging breasts, surgical lift for, 61–62
Sarcoma, radiation-induced, 310
Sartorius, Otto, 101
SBLA syndrome, 147–148
Screening
  age and, 175, 176
  lead-time bias of, *171–172*
  length bias of, *171*, 172
  overdiagnosis bias of, *171*, 172–173
  selection bias of, *171*, 172
  See also Detection methods.
Sebaceous glands, 5, *8*
Second opinions, 266
Second primary, 273–274
  prognosis for, 274
Segmental mastectomy. *See* Partial mastectomy
Selection bias, of screening, *171*, 172
Selenium, breast cancer prevention, 157–158
Self-examination. *See* Breast self-examination
Sensory loss, post-surgical, 289, *290*, 294–295
Seventh Day Adventists, breast cancer rate, 155
Sex
  breastfeeding and, 44
  post-surgical, 363–365
Sex differentiation, embryo, 12
Sexual problems, chemotherapy and, 322
Sexual stimulation, breasts and, 10–11
Siegel, Bernie, 323, 329, 332, 334
Silicone implants, 55
  mammograms and, 66–67
  in reconstruction, *351–352*
  safety factors, 66–67, 353
  See also Breast augmentation.
Silicone injections, lumps from, 28, 119–120
Simonton, Carl, 329, 332, 333
Simonton, Stephanie, 332, 333
Single patients
  mastectomy and, 242, 261–262
  sex after mastectomy, 364–365
Small breasts, 54–55
Sodium pentothal, 280, 281
S phase fraction, 228

About the Authors

SUSAN M. LOVE, M.D., a breast surgeon, is Director of the Faulkner Breast Centre in Boston, Massachusetts. She is Clinical Assistant Professor in Surgery at the Harvard Medical School and a surgical oncologist at the Breast Evaluation Center of the Dana Farber Cancer Institute. Dr. Love has pursued extensive research in the diagnosis and treatment of breast cancer and has been a leader in innovative approaches to treatment. The author of many scientific papers, she is collaborating on a breast surgery atlas and is dedicated to improving public education about the breast and breast disease.

KAREN LINDSEY, writer and teacher, is the author of *Friends as Family* (Beacon Press) and *Falling Off the Roof* (Alice James Books). Her articles have appeared in *Ms.*, *The Women's Review of Books*, *Viva*, *Sojourner* and many other publications and anthologies. She has taught at the University of Massachusetts and currently teaches writing at Emerson College in Boston.